IELTS®
PREMIER
with 8 Practice Tests
Third Edition

Special thanks to the team who made this book possible: Kim Bowers, Louise Cook, Scarlet Edmonds, Joanna Graham, Brian Holmes, Bharat Krishna, Richard Patterson, Alison Ramage, Teresa Rupp, Nimesh Shah, Noel Smaragdakis, Paul Stafford.

*IELTS® is a registered trademark of University of Cambridge ESOL Examinations, British Council and IDP Education Australia, which neither sponsor nor endorse this product.

This publication is designed to provide accurate information in regard to the subject matter covered as of its publication date, with the understanding that knowledge and best practice constantly evolve. The publisher is not engaged in rendering medical, legal, accounting, or other professional service. If medical or legal advice or other expert assistance is required, the services of a competent professional should be sought. This publication is not intended for use in clinical practice or the delivery of medical care. To the fullest extent of the law, neither the Publisher nor the Editors assume any liability for any injury and/or damage to persons or property arising out of or related to any use of the material contained in this book.

Published by Kaplan Publishing, a division of Kaplan, Inc.
750 Third Avenue
New York, NY 10017

10 9 8 7 6 5 4 3 2 1

ISBN: 978-1-5062-0867-1

Kaplan Publishing print books are available at special quantity discounts to use for sales promotions, employee premiums, or educational purposes. For more information or to purchase books, please call the Simon & Schuster special sales department at 866-506-1949.

TABLE OF CONTENTS

PART ONE: INTRODUCTION TO IELTS

PART TWO: LISTENING

PART THREE: READING

PART FOUR: WRITING

PART FIVE: SPEAKING

PART SIX: IELTS PRACTICE TESTS

PART SEVEN: LISTENING SCRIPTS

PART EIGHT: IELTS PRACTICE TEST ANSWER KEYS

How to Use This Book

WELCOME TO KAPLAN IELTS PREMIER, THIRD EDITION

Congratulations on your decision to improve your English proficiency, and thank you for choosing Kaplan for your IELTS preparation. You've made the right choice in acquiring this book—you're now armed with a comprehensive IELTS program that is the result of decades of researching the IELTS and similar tests and teaching many thousands of students the skills they need to succeed. You have everything you need to score higher—let's start by walking through what you need to know to take advantage of this book and the Online Study Plan.

Your Book

There are two main components to your *Kaplan IELTS Premier* study package: your book and your Online Study Plan. This book contains the following:

- Detailed instruction covering the essential Listening, Reading, Writing and Speaking concepts and skills
- Time-tested and effective Kaplan Methods and strategies for every question type
- Eight full-length practice tests (including two for IELTS General Training) and four chapters full of practice questions for each IELTS subtest

Your Online Study Plan

Your Online Study Plan lets you access additional instruction and practice materials to reinforce key concepts and sharpen your IELTS skills. Resources include the following:

- Printable answer sheets to use when taking the practice tests in this book
- Online answer grids for the practice tests in this book
- Detailed answers and model Writing responses
- Online answer grid for the practice test found in this book
- Mock Speaking interviews with expert feedback
- Self-assessment rubrics for Writing and Speaking
- Listening tracks that accompany the chapters and practice tests in this book (also available on CD-ROM)

GETTING STARTED

1. Register your Online Study Plan.
2. Take a IELTS practice test to identify your strengths and weaknesses.
3. Create a study plan.
4. Learn and practice using this book and your Online Study Plan.

Step 1: Register Your Online Study Plan

Register your Online Study Plan using these simple steps:

1. Go to **kaptestglobal.com/resources**.
2. Follow the onscreen instructions. Please have a copy of your book available.

Access to the Online Study Plan is limited to the original owner of this book and is nontransferable. Kaplan is not responsible for providing access to the Online Study Plan to customers who purchase or borrow used copies of this book. Access to the Online Study Plan expires one year after you register.

Step 2: Take a IELTS Practice Test

It's a good idea to take a practice test early on. Doing so will give you the initial feedback and diagnostic information that you need to achieve your maximum score.

You can use Practice Test 1 (in Part Six of this book) as your diagnostic test. This practice test, which includes full-length Listening, Reading, Writing and Speaking subtests, will give you a chance to familiarize yourself with the various question types. It also allows you to accurately gauge the content you know and identify areas for practice and review. (Print out a copy of the answer sheet from your Online Study Plan to use as you take this practice test. After completing the test, copy your answers from your answer sheet into the online answer grid available in your Online Study Plan. This will allow you to see a detailed breakdown of your performance. You may also enter your Writing and Speaking scores, which you will need to determine using the self-assessment rubrics available in your Online Study Plan.)

Review the detailed answer explanations to better understand your performance. Look for patterns in the questions you answered correctly and incorrectly. Were you stronger in some areas than others? This analysis will help you target your practice time to specific concepts.

Step 3: Create a Study Plan

Use what you've learned from your diagnostic test to identify areas for closer study and practice. Take time to familiarize yourself with the key components of your book and Online Study Plan. Think about how many hours you can consistently devote to IELTS study. We have found that most students have success with about three months of committed preparation before Test Day.

Schedule time for study, practice, and review. One of the most frequent mistakes in approaching study is to take practice tests and not review them thoroughly—review time is your best chance to gain points. It works best for many people to block out short, frequent periods of study time throughout the week. Check in with yourself frequently to make sure you're not falling behind your plan or forgetting about any of your resources.

Step 4: Learn and Practise

Your book and Online Study Plan come with many opportunities to develop and practise the skills you'll need on Test Day. Read each chapter of this book and complete the practice questions. Depending on how much time you have to study, you can do this work methodically, covering every chapter, or you can focus your study on those question types and content areas that are most challenging for you. You will inevitably need more work in some areas than in others, but know that the more thoroughly you prepare, the better your score will be.

Initially, your practice should focus on mastering the needed skills and not on timing. Add timing to your practice as you improve fundamental proficiency. As soon as you are comfortable with the question types and Kaplan Methods, take and review the additional full-length practice tests in your Online Study Plan.

You have two options for accessing the Listening tracks that accompany the chapters and practice tests in this book. You may listen to them in your Online Study Plan, or you may use the CD-ROM included with the book. This CD-ROM is compatible with devices that can read and play MP3 discs.

If you would like additional resources to help you prepare for the IELTS, visit us at **kaptestglobal. com/IELTS**.

Thanks for choosing Kaplan. We wish you the best of luck on your journey to English fluency.

An Overview of the IELTS

The International English Language Testing System (IELTS) is designed to measure English proficiency for educational, vocational and immigration purposes. The IELTS measures an individual's ability to communicate in English across four areas of language: listening, reading, writing and speaking.

The IELTS is administered jointly by the British Council, IDP: IELTS Australia and Cambridge English Language Assessment at over 1,000 test centres and 140 countries. These test centres supervise the local administration of the test and recruit, train and monitor IELTS examiners.

IELTS tests are available on 48 fixed dates each year, usually Saturdays and sometimes Thursdays, and may be offered up to four times a month at any test centre, depending on local needs. Go to the IELTS website at www.ielts.org to find a test centre near you and to check for upcoming test dates at your test centre.

Test results are available online 13 days after your test date. You can either receive your Test Report Form by post or collect it from the Test Centre. You will normally only receive one copy of the Test Report Form, though you may ask for a second copy if you are applying to the UK or Canada for immigration purposes – be sure to specify this when you register for IELTS. You may ask for up to 5 copies of your Test Report Form to be sent directly to other organisations, such as universities.

There are no restrictions on re-sitting the IELTS. However, you would need to allow sufficient time to complete the registration procedures again and find a suitable test date.

Which version of IELTS?

There are two versions of the IELTS: the Academic IELTS and the General Training IELTS. The Academic IELTS is taken by people who wish to enrol in undergraduate and postgraduate courses and those who wish to undertake work experience at a graduate or postgraduate level. The General Training IELTS is taken by people who wish to complete their secondary education or undertake work experience or training programmes in an English speaking country, and by people who are planning to emigrate to the UK, Australia, Canada or New Zealand.

This IELTS book covers both the Academic and the General IELTS. The Listening and Speaking modules are the same for the General and Academic IELTS, but there are different versions of the Reading and Writing modules for the IELTS General Training exam.

Which version of English?

Since the IELTS is used widely in the UK and Commonwealth countries, it is written in British English. Its vocabulary and syntax will be completely understandable to anyone who has studied English in an English-speaking country. You do not have to use British English in the Writing module. However, you should use only one type of English – that is, stick with either British or American English – throughout the exam.

IELTS Modules

Module	Total Time	Tasks
Listening	30 minutes	Listen to 4 tracks (2 conversations, 2 monologues). Answer 10 questions on each track.
Reading	60 minutes	Read 3 passages. Answer 13–14 questions on each passage.
Writing	60 minutes	Two tasks: Write a description of information in a chart, graph, table or diagram. At least 150 words. (20 minutes) Write an essay in response to an opinion or a question. At least 250 words. (40 minutes)
Speaking	11–14 minutes	Answer questions about yourself and common topics.

The Listening, Reading and Writing modules are always taken on the same day, in that order, without a break. These three modules take a total of 2 hours and 45 minutes. The Speaking module may be scheduled on the same day or up to a week before or after the other modules.

IELTS Scores

Each of the four modules of the IELTS is scored on a scale of 1.0 to 9.0, in half-point increments. These scores are then averaged together for the overall score. This overall score can either be a whole or half band. Each band corresponds to a global descriptor, summarizing each of the nine levels of English competence. Usually band scores required for entry onto a UK university course are in the region of 5.5 to 7.5

The statements below will give you a sense of the level of English required for each band level. These statements only give an overall view, there are more detailed descriptors available for speaking and writing competence which can be found at the following websites:

Writing Task One

https://takeielts.britishcouncil.org/sites/default/files/IELTS_task_1_Writing_band_descriptors.pdf

Writing Task Two

http://www.ielts.org/pdf/uobds_writingt2.pdf

Speaking

https://www.ielts.org/pdf/SpeakingBanddescriptors.pdf

Note: If the above links are no longer active, do an internet search for 'IELTS Writing band descriptors' or 'IELTS Speaking band descriptors' and double-check that the document you are using is from an official IELTS website (such as ielts.org or the British Council), to ensure you are using current and correct information.

OVERALL BAND SCORE DESCRIPTIONS
Band 9: Expert User Has complete control of the language: correct and effortless usage with complete understanding.
Band 8: Very Good User Has complete control of the language with few errors. Confusion may take place in new or atypical circumstances. Is able to formulate advanced, in-depth arguments.
Band 7: Good User Has advanced control of the language, though with a few errors of confusion in some circumstances. Uses sophisticated words and complex syntax and comprehends dense arguments.
Band 6: Competent User Has capable control of the language despite some errors and confusion. Can employ and comprehend moderately advanced language but mainly in routine and typical circumstances.
Band 5: Modest User Has limited control of the language. Is able to use plain statements in routine and typical circumstances. Commits numerous errors and occasionally has difficulty with the general meaning of conversations.
Band 4: Limited User Has low-level proficiency restricted to routine and typical circumstances. Uses only the most simplistic of words and syntax and occasionally has trouble following a relatively simple, common conversation.
Band 3: Extremely Limited User Cannot follow a relatively simple, common conversation, even with the most simplistic use of words and syntax.
Band 2: Intermittent User Can handle only plain words to express basic needs. Even the most simple phrases or syntax usage are not well understood. Struggles significantly with spoken or written English.
Band 1: Non User Knows a small number of random words. Has basically no understanding of English at all.
Candidates who do not attempt to answer any tasks score 0.

Scoring for the Listening and Reading Modules

In the IELTS Listening and Reading modules, there are 40 questions each. One mark is awarded for each correctly answered question, unless otherwise stated on the question paper. To obtain a score of Band 7, you must answer at least 30 questions correctly.

Answers must be transferred to the answer sheet to be marked. While you can use the question paper to make notes, only answers on the answer sheet will be marked.

The tests are marked by trained IELTS clerical markers who follow a model answer sheet. This includes all variations of the answer which are acceptable. It is vitally important to remember that words have to be spelled correctly to get the mark.

●● BRITISH
●● COUNCIL

Family name: _____

First name(s): _____

Are you: Female? ___   Male? ___

| Reading | Reading | Reading | Reading | Reading | Reading |

Module taken (shade one box):   Academic ▭   General Training ▭

#		Marker use only	#		Marker use only
1		✓ 1 ✗	21		✓ 21 ✗
2		✓ 2 ✗	22		✓ 22 ✗
3		✓ 3 ✗	23		✓ 23 ✗
4		✓ 4 ✗	24		✓ 24 ✗
5		✓ 5 ✗	25		✓ 25 ✗
6		✓ 6 ✗	26		✓ 26 ✗
7		✓ 7 ✗	27		✓ 27 ✗
8		✓ 8 ✗	28		✓ 28 ✗
9		✓ 9 ✗	29		✓ 29 ✗
10		✓ 10 ✗	30		✓ 30 ✗
11		✓ 11 ✗	31		✓ 31 ✗
12		✓ 12 ✗	32		✓ 32 ✗
13		✓ 13 ✗	33		✓ 33 ✗
14		✓ 14 ✗	34		✓ 34 ✗
15		✓ 15 ✗	35		✓ 35 ✗
16		✓ 16 ✗	36		✓ 36 ✗
17		✓ 17 ✗	37		✓ 37 ✗
18		✓ 18 ✗	38		✓ 38 ✗
19		✓ 19 ✗	39		✓ 39 ✗
20		✓ 20 ✗	40		✓ 40 ✗

| Marker 2 Initials | | Marker 1 Initials | | Band Score | | Listening Total | |

Scoring for the Writing Module

Two sets of criteria are used to assess your writing.

- **Task 1:** You must either write an analysis, normally involving a comparison of information in a table, graph or diagram, a description of a process in a diagram, or a comparison of two maps. You need to report the information from the graph accurately and, where appropriate, identify and compare the key features.
- **Task 2:** You are given a prompt in the form of a question or statement, and are required to formulate and express your point of view on this subject. You should support your ideas with relevant examples from your own experience.

For both of these Tasks, reading the question carefully and responding to that specific question are key factors in getting a good band score.

The Writing module is marked using the following criteria:

- **Task Achievement (in Task 1)** and **Task Response (in Task 2):** This assesses how well you have answered the question given.
- **Coherence and Cohesion:** This assesses how well you link ideas within a paragraph and how you organise the paragraph to create a clear progression of your ideas.
- **Lexical Resource:** To obtain a high score for this criterion, you must demonstrate flexibility in your use of vocabulary. You need to be able to use words appropriately and spell them correctly. Credit is given to candidates who use more advanced and imaginative vocabulary.
- **Grammatical Range and Accuracy:** You should use a variety of simple and complex grammatical structures accurately. You will also be assessed on your ability to punctuate your writing appropriately.

The Writing Tasks are marked by certificated IELTS examiners who are regularly monitored to ensure that the accuracy of their marks meet the IELTS Standard. Each task is given a mark in each of the four criteria above. The value of Writing Task 1 is worth half that of Writing Task 2; so make sure you do not spend more than 20 minutes on task one, leaving you 40 minutes for task two. Your final band score will be a weighted average of the 8 scores given.

Scoring for the Speaking Module

Your speaking will be assessed according to the following criteria:

- **Fluency and Coherence:** Your ability to express ideas and opinions clearly and coherently, without long pauses and hesitations.
- **Lexical Resource:** Your ability to use a wide range of vocabulary appropriately and naturally.
- **Grammatical Range and Accuracy:** Your ability to use a wide range of grammatical structures without making too many mistakes.
- **Pronunciation:** Your ability to speak clearly and use pronunciation features, such as word stress and sentence intonation, naturally.

The interviewer for the Speaking module will be a certificated IELTS examiner. Your interview will be recorded. The recordings are used mainly to ensure that the examiner is marking to standard. The recording is also used if you ask for an 'Enquiry on Results'. The examiner will assign a band score out of 9 for each of the above marking criteria, and your final Speaking Score will be an average of these.

What to Expect on Test Day

It's natural to be nervous on Test Day, but if you are well-prepared and organised you will be able to perform at your best:

- Carry out your online Test registration in advance, and make sure you know exactly where the Test centre is and how you are going to get there. If you are concerned about traffic it is worth doing a 'practice' run the week before. Remember, if you arrive late you will not be allowed to take the test.
- You are asked to arrive at the test venue 15 minutes before the start of the test. However, it is useful to arrive earlier, especially at test centres where there are a lot of candidates.
- Make sure you bring the identification documents you used when you registered for the test. If you do not have these documents, you will not be allowed to take the test.
- Before entering the examination room your identification will be checked. In some centres, the staff will take your photo and a record of your finger prints before the exam starts.
- You need to bring your own writing equipment. It is recommended to use a pencil for all the tests, so that you can erase anything you want to change. Make sure you have pencils, a pencil sharpener and an eraser.
- Bags and electronic devices, such as mobiles or tablets, are not allowed in the examination room. Be prepared to leave these outside. If you are concerned about the security of these, it is best to leave them at home.
- You will be assigned a seat which you keep throughout the test.
- You are not permitted to leave the examination room, so make sure that you go to the bathroom beforehand.
- You can make notes on any of the exam papers to help you. However, no exam papers or spare answer sheets can be taken from the examination room.
- You can ask for more paper for the Writing modulue by raising your hand.
- The examination room invigilators are not able to answer any questions you may have about the paper or any of the questions on it. So it is important that you are familiar with all the different question types.
- Although it is tempting, it is best not to try to do any revision the night before Test Day. Instead, you could watch your favourite English language film or get together with some English friends. Try to avoid spending the night reading books or doing online activities.

The Speaking module may take place the afternoon of Test Day or on a different day. It can also be in a different location.

- Make sure that you know where the Speaking interview is going to take place and, if necessary, do a trial run to ensure that you know how to get there.

- You will be given a time and you should arrive at least 15 minutes before that time. Ideally 30 – 45 minutes beforehand.
- Make sure that you bring all the appropriate identification documents with you. If you do not have then, you will be asked to go home and get them.
- Before entering the examination room your identification will be checked. In some centres photos are taken and/or finger prints recorded.
- If you arrive shortly after the time given for your interview you may have to wait until the next candidate has been interviewed.
- If you arrive more than 30 minutes after the time given for your interview the examiner is not obliged to conduct the interview. Although, depending on the circumstances, they may be prepared to do so.
- Bags, electronic devices such as mobiles and tablets are not allowed in the interview room. So be prepared to leave them outside. If you are concerned about the security of these it is best to leave them at home.
- You can take a small bottle of water into the interview and tissues if you need to.
- It is not advisable to chew gum during the interview.
- Be aware that the interviewer will have the recorder on from the moment you enter the room. Interviewers are not permitted to engage in 'small talk' so don't worry if they appear unfriendly.
- The examiner understands that many candidates will be very nervous and possibly be under great stress to perform well. Thus, they will do what they can to help nervous candidates relax.
- Don't let the recorder make you nervous. The main purpose of this is to check the performance of the examiner, not you.
- Finally, remember that the examiner, unlike a class teacher, is looking out for all the good things in your Speaking module, and not the things you do wrong. They want you to perform to the best of your ability!

How Do You Get Top Scores on the IELTS?

Firstly, for both the Reading and Writing modules, make sure you give an answer for every question. Even if you are well prepared for IELTS, you could find yourself missing some of the answers on the Listening module or running out of time in the Reading module –timing is very tight for the Reading module. If you have a few questions that you haven't been able to answer fully, it is better just to guess and gain a chance of picking up the marks, rather than leaving questions unanswered.

In the Writing module, make sure you read the question carefully, double check that you understand what you have been asked to do and make sure you answer the question as accurately and fully as possible. For example: If in Task 2 you are asked 'To what extent do you agree or disagree' you should discuss how much you, not other people, agree or disagree with the statement. Not answering the specific question given is one of the main reasons candidates are marked down. If you have a good level of English, you do not want to see your Writing band score (and thus your overall band score) go down because you failed to answer the question. On the plus side, if you do a good job of simply answering the questions that are asked, this will have the effect of boosting your score (for Task Achievement in Task 1 and

Task Response in Task 2), even if you are weaker in the other criteria, since you will score highly (closer to 9) in that first criterion.

In addition, you have to make sure that you write enough words. For Task 1, you must write at least 150 words and for Task 2, at least 250 words. If you write less than these amounts, you will be deducted marks.

Of all the modules, test-takers will often find the Speaking module to be the most challenging, because Speaking is the module that is most affected by your personality. You may be a quiet and shy person who doesn't say very much even in your mother tongue, so you may find the Speaking interview particularly challenging. Unfortunately, the examiner can't take this into consideration, so you need to speak as much as you can. It helps to remember that the examiner, unlike a teacher, is looking for the positives in your English, so the more you can say, the more chance you have to get a higher score. Some candidates feel that there is a 'right' or a 'wrong' answer and that they will be judged on this. This is not the case; the examiner is only interested in how you express your ideas in English – it doesn't matter what those ideas are.

The final tip for getting a top score in the IELTS is to make the most of this book. Learn the different types of questions and tips for the Listening and Reading modules. Practise the strategies for the Writing and Speaking modules. This book is loaded with Kaplan practice tests, which will allow you to become familiar with all the different types of questions. Take note of all the Kaplan top tips to maximise your scores and avoid pitfalls.

LISTENING INTRODUCTION

MODULE OVERVIEW

The Listening module consists of four recorded sections, each containing ten questions, and takes 30 minutes to complete. You will only hear each recording once so you must be prepared to know what to listen for. You are not expected to have any specialist knowledge, but you should be able to deal with a range of topics and a number of different voices and accents.

Each of the four sections in a Listening module may have up to three types of questions. Before each section, you will hear a short introduction about the speaker(s) and the situation. This introduction is not printed on the test paper. You are then given 30 seconds to look over the questions before the recording continues. You will have another short break (30 seconds) each time there is a new set of questions within the section, so you can look over the next set of questions before the recording continues.

Each section is played only once, and the questions always follow the order of the information presented in the recording. After each section, you are given 30 seconds to check your answers.

In any Listening module, there are always the same four section types, which always appear in the same order. The first two sections are from everyday contexts and the last two from educational contexts.

- **Section 1**: A conversation between two people in a real-life context, often involving customer service, in which information is exchanged.
- **Section 2**: A monologue in a real-life context, often involving directions, a description of a place, event, organisation or process.
- **Section 3**: A conversation, usually between two students, sometimes being guided by a tutor.
- **Section 4**: An extract from a lecture.

There are six main question types in the Listening module; you may see any or all of them in any given test paper. The fourth type combines several similar formats into a single question type; in this Kaplan IELTS book, we will consider examples and strategies for these individual formats. The table describes the different question types, and whether you are expected to write a letter, word(s) or a number.

	Question Type	Form of Answer
1	Multiple Choice	Choose the correct letter
2	Matching	Choose the correct letter
3	Plan, map, diagram labelling	Choose the correct letter or word
4	Form, note, table, flow-chart, summary completion	Write words and/or numbers
5	Sentence completion	Write words and/or numbers
6	Short answer	Write words and or numbers

For questions involving money or measurements, you should write the unit (e.g. £, cm, %) if it is not already given on the test paper. It is not necessary to write the full form (e.g.; pounds, centimetres, percentages); the abbreviated form or symbol is fine. Abbreviated forms (£12, 3 cm, 45%) count as a number.

Once you have heard all four sections, you will have a further 10 minutes to transfer your answers from the test paper to the answer sheet. You will only receive credit for answers that have been entered on the answer sheet. The examiners do not mark anything you have written on the test paper.

The Listening section always begins with an example, which you do not have to answer.

Listening Strategies

Read the instructions before the start of each recording, so you know how many words you should write. The word limit includes all articles and prepositions. Do not go above the word limit or your answer will be marked incorrect.

Underline the keywords in the questions and options before you listen. Underlining the keywords around each blank can help you listen more effectively.

Before each recording starts read the questions and information carefully to get the gist of the recording.

Ask yourself who is talking and what they are talking about.

Analyse the questions and decide what type of information is required for each blank. This may include information such as a price, name or time.

Eliminate options in multiple choice questions by putting a mark (such as a cross) next to them when you are sure they are wrong.

Try to re-phrase the notes and questions in your own words. This could help you to identify the moment when the speaker is about to give the correct answer.

Listen for any synonyms or paraphrases that have the same meaning as the information you expect to hear; sometimes you will hear the correct answer said in a different way.

Listen for any clue that the speaker is about to answer the questions. They will probably use different words than those in the question.

Do not write more than the maximum number of words you are asked for. Write only the words you hear, without changing them.

If you miss an answer, do not worry – keep listening. Otherwise, you will miss the next question, too!

Make sure you include an answer for every question. You will not lose marks for wrong answers.

As you copy your answers, check that the words you have written make sense in the context, are grammatically correct and are correctly spelt.

Do not copy anything printed on the test paper when transferring your answers to the answer sheet. You should copy only what you yourself have written.

You will have plenty of time during the Listening test to read the questions and check your answers, so don't panic.

Predict key points based on the main idea. Using your prediction skills makes listening easier. Once you have identified the topic it will help you to find out certain details. For example, a student who wants to talk about his term paper might have problems with his topic, organisation, due date, length, bibliography or a partner. Similarly, a professor who gives a lecture on bees might discuss their appearance, abilities, evolution, migration, reproduction, diet, the reasons for studying them, and so on. Knowing the possibilities makes it easier to understand what a speaker says.

Do not try to record everything in notes. If you decide to take notes during the exam, make sure they are effective and efficient. That means you need to determine the topic of the talk, study the questions and decide what type of information and what types of words are missing. Focus on noting down only those words. You can either leave out less important words or record them using symbols and abbreviations.

Be familiar with number conventions, such as:

Telephone numbers:

- These are usually spoken as individual numbers. For example, 273458 would be spoken as 'two seven three four five eight.'
- Sometimes, British or Australian speakers may say *double* or *triple* or *treble* when a digit is repeated in a phone number. For example, a British person might say the phone number 020 7766 3444 as 'oh two oh…double seven, double six… three, treble four.'
- When a group of a numbers is given, the intonation rises before the pause to indicate an unfinished group. At the end of the last group, the intonation of the speaker falls.

Decimal numbers:

- These are indicated with the word *point*, and then each decimal number is spoken individually. For example, the number 12.75 would be spoken as 'twelve point seven five.'

Prices:

- When talking about prices, the word *point* is not usually used. Instead, the decimal numbers are usually combined and indicated with *and*. For example, £15.99 would be spoken as 'fifteen pounds ninety-nine' or 'fifteen pounds and ninety-nine pence.'
- Sometimes, the currency is also left out. For example, £15.99 could be spoken as 'fifteen ninety-nine.'

Fractions:

- With the exception of 'a half,' 'a quarter' and 'a third,' fractions are expressed with –*th(s)* at the end. For example, the fraction 5/6 would be spoken as 'five-sixths' and 9/10 would be spoken as 'nine-tenths.'

Thousands:

- It is possible to express thousands as the equivalent number of hundreds. For example, 1,700 could be spoken as 'seventeen hundred,' 2,700 could be spoken as 'twenty-seven hundred' and 1,123 could be spoken as 'eleven hundred twenty-three.'

Dates:

There are several correct ways to write dates.

- In British English, the day comes before the month, and periods are often used to separate elements. For example, the date May 16, 1976 could be written as 16.05.76 or 16.5.1976.
- In American English, the month comes first, and slashes are often used to separate elements. For example, May 16, 1976 could be written as 05/16/76 or 5/16/1976.
- For IELTS Listening, Kaplan recommends writing dates as 4 July or 4 July 1776 (when it is necessary to include the year).

OBJECTIVES

By the end of this chapter, you will be able to:

- Listen for details, including numbers and spelling of names.
- Understand the context and speakers in a listening section.
- Recognise synonyms and paraphrases.
- Practise strategies for answering Short Answer, Form Completion and Multiple Choice questions.

Introduction

The first Listening recording you will hear will be a conversation between two people in a real-life context, often involving customer service, in which information is exchanged.

It is quite likely that you will have been in one of these situations so you will be familiar with the context and the type of language used.

The main types of question forms for this section are Short Answer, Form Completion and Multiple Choice questions.

To get a final IELTS band score of 5.5 or above, you should be aiming to get all the questions in this section correct.

SHORT ANSWER QUESTIONS

Strategies

- Check how many words or numbers you can include in each answer.
- Predict what the speakers will be talking about.
- Check whether any of the answers will be names or special numbers (such as prices, phone numbers or post codes).

How to Recognise Short Answer Questions

The question has a blank after the question mark (not within the question).
There is a question without a blank.
The instructions say 'Answer the questions' (rather than 'Complete the sentences').
The instructions may ask you to list 2 or 3 points. Each will be a separate answer.

Getting Ready to Listen

1. Before each of the listening texts, you will be given some information about the context.

   a. What is the 'context'?

   b. How can knowing about the context help you understand the listening?

   c. How can you identify the speakers?

   d. Why is it important to identify the speakers?

2. At the start of each recording, you will hear the introduction and then you will have 30 seconds to read the questions.

To develop your prediction and listening skills, complete each pre-listening exercise with a strict time limit of 30 seconds. Read the instructions first, then start the timer.

You should preview questions 1–6 below and answer the questions a–f within 30 seconds. Then, review the answers to questions a–f in the back of the book before listening to the track and answering questions 1–6.

   a. Can you write one word for an answer?

   b. Can you write two words and a number for an answer?

   c. Which question(s) need(s) numbers for an answer?

   d. Which question needs a place for an answer?

   e. Which question needs a price for an answer?

   f. Think of 4 different types of party they could be planning?

Listen

 Track 1 (Will and Emma)

Questions 1–6

Answer the questions below.

*Write **NO MORE THAN TWO WORDS AND/OR A NUMBER** for each answer.*

1. What type of party are they organising? ....

2. What does Will think costs too much? ....

3. How many people will be coming to the party? ....

4. How many chairs does Will have at his kitchen table? ....

5. How much did Will pay for attending last year's party? ....

6. What venue do they select? ....

Did you answer all of the questions in 30 seconds? Well done. Now check your answers at the back of the book. How did you do? Don't worry if you didn't get the answers in time. You will improve with practice.

KAPLAN TIP

Listening questions always appear in the same order as the correct answers in the script. So you will hear the answer to question 1 before the answer to question 2, for example.

Listening for Detail

This is one of the most important skills necessary to get a good score in your IELTS Listening test. Listen to Track 1 again and write *questions* for the following *answers*.

a. November

b. Christmas dinner

c. No, (he doesn't)

d. Next few weeks

e. Three/3

f. Christmas

KAPLAN TIP

It is a good idea to keep listening out for the answers to the next two or three questions so that if you do miss one answer you do not get totally left behind. Remember, there is plenty of time afterwards to go back and think about the missing answer.

Practice

Getting Ready to Listen

Before listening to the recording, look over questions 1–7 below and take 30 seconds to answer the questions a–f. Then, take a moment to review the answers for a–f at the back of the book before listening to the recording.

  a. What type of questions are these?

  b. How many numbers can you write for each answer?

  c. Can you write two words for each answer?

  d. Which questions will need a number in the answer?

  e. Which answer(s) will include a month?

  f. What other types of information are you listening for?

Listen

Now listen to Track 2 and answer questions 1–7.

 Track 2 (Woodland College)

Questions 1–7

Answer the questions below.

*Write **NO MORE THAN ONE WORD AND/OR A NUMBER** for each answer.*

1. What time does the painting class meet?

2. How much does the painting class cost?

3. When does the next painting class start?

4. What is the date of the last session?

5. What is Ruby's surname?

6. What is Ruby's postcode?

7. What is Ruby's phone number?

How did you do? Many listening recordings will include dates, addresses and phone numbers, which may include a lot of figures in formats that may sound unusual. You may wish to listen again to any recordings that include such items, so you can practise writing down the dates, addresses and phone numbers that you hear.

Improve Your Score – Different Types of Numbers

In the General Listening tips above we looked at some conventions for saying numbers, prices, dates, etc.

Look at the information below and practice saying them out loud as you would expect to hear them in an IELTS test. Record yourself if you can and then check the answers.

a. £3.50

b. 00 44 7560 160667

c. 7.30pm

d. £56.45

e. 13th April

f. 31st December

g. 11.15am

h. 0203 666 3351

Practise listening for numbers with TV or radio news reports in English. Weather reports, business and science stories also include different types of numbers, so they are good for listening practice.

Improve Your Score – Synonyms and Paraphrases

The ability to be able to recognise and use synonyms and paraphrases will help you to improve your band score in all of the four IELTS modules. In the Listening test, the question will probably use a synonym or a paraphrase of the words used in the audio.

Below are some phrases or sentences (1–14) from the two listening tracks you have heard. Match each sentence with one of the words or phrases (a–n) below and underline which word or phrase it could replace in the sentence.

1.	it's only a month away	**a.**	have
2.	what do we need to do?	**b.**	go on
3.	it's not connected with Christmas	**c.**	four weeks
4.	we could cook it ourselves	**d.**	right
5.	my table has only six chairs	**e.**	related to
6.	we can see about getting a booking at a restaurant	**f.**	half a dozen
7.	why don't we look at having a party at a pub?	**g.**	prepare
8.	there are a total of eight sessions	**h.**	what's
9.	seventy five pounds is the total charge	**i.**	reservation
10.	that's quite a good deal	**j.**	left
11.	there are two places available	**k.**	bargain
12.	it will continue into June	**l.**	consider
13.	may I take your name?	**m.**	cost
14.	yes, that's correct	**n.**	classes

As you can see from this exercise, synonyms and paraphrases do not always involve difficult vocabulary. However, the context is always very important. For example, left is not always a synonym for available, but in this context it is a perfect synonym. Being able to understand and use common words and phrases such as these flexibly throughout the IELTS tests will really improve your score.

FORM COMPLETION QUESTIONS

Strategies

- Check how many words or numbers you can include in each answer.
- Predict what sort of information you will need for each answer.
- Carefully check the order of the answers. Sometimes with a table the order may be horizontal.

How to Recognise Form Completion questions

- *The instructions will ask you to 'Complete the form below'*
- *This could include boxes or look like an official document*
- *There will be some information filled in*
- *You can use this information to help you follow the text as you are listening*

MULTIPLE CHOICE QUESTIONS

Strategies

- Read all the questions and answer choices carefully.
- Underline the keywords from each question and answer choice.
- If you have time, think of possible synonyms and paraphrases you may hear.

How to Recognise Multiple Choice Questions

- *There is a question or incomplete sentence, followed by a choice of answers*
- *There are usually three or four possible answers*
- *Usually, there is only one correct answer. Occasionally, you will be asked to choose two correct answers*

Getting Ready to Listen

Before listening to the recording, look over questions 1–4 below and take 30 seconds to answer the questions a–e. Then, take a moment to review the answers for a–e at the back of the book before listening to the recording.

a. What question type is this?

b. Can you write three words for an answer?

c. How many numbers can you write for an answer?

d. What kinds of answers are you going to listen for?

e. What is the job of the person who works for the university?

Listen

Now listen to Track 3 and answer questions 1–4.

 Track 3 (IT department)

Questions 1–4

Complete the form below.

*Write **NO MORE THAN TWO WORDS** for each answer.*

IT SUPPORT TRACKING FORM – UNIVERSITY CLUBS AND SOCIETIES	
Reason for call	Problem accessing **1** ....
Name of society	Rugby Club
Position of officer reporting the problem	**2** ....
Name of officer (first name and surname)	**3** .... Singh
Nature of the problem	**4** ....

Sometimes one Listening track will have two different types of questions. In this case, the recording will stop and you will be given another 30 seconds to look at the next set of questions.

Getting Ready to Listen

Before listening to the second part of the recording, look over questions 5–10 and take 30 seconds to answer the questions a–b. Then, take a moment to review the answers for a–b at the back of the book before listening to the recording.

    a. What type of questions are these?

    b. Underline the keyword(s) in each question.

Listen

Now listen to Track 4 and answer questions 5–10.

 Track 4 (IT department)

Choose the correct answer: A, B or C.

Questions 5–10

5   The error was due to the student misunderstanding what number?

   A   one

   B   six

   C   zero

6   What does the student initially suggest as a new password?

   A   offside

   B   tackle

   C   tap kick

7   What special symbol does the student include in the new password?

   A   asterisk

   B   dollar sign

   C   question mark

8   The longest video they would like to put on the website is

   A   less than a minute.

   B   under three minutes.

   C   more than three minutes.

9   The maximum size for a video posted to a university website is

   A   15 MB

   B   50 MB

   C   15 GB

10   In international rugby, the student supports

   A   Chile.

   B   England.

   C   Fiji.

> Don't worry if you see a question that needs a name for an answer.
> Names are usually spelled out, so as long as you know the sounds of
> the English alphabet you will be fine.

Improve Your Score – Listening for Detail

You can never do enough practice on synonyms and paraphrases, so listen again to Tracks 3 and 4 and find the synonyms or paraphrases for the following:

a. problem accessing

b. spelt wrong

c. sort it out

d. What exactly was the problem...

e. that's bad

f. sadly

g. place to start

h. in place of

i. Is that OK?

j. ...the people to help...

Takeaway

1. In your IELTS Listening module, you need to be able to identify the question types immediately. Without looking back, write the key characteristics of the following question types:
- Short answer questions
- Form completion questions
- Multiple choice questions

2. Why is it important to read the questions carefully? Give more than one reason.

3. Why is it important to know about synonyms and paraphrases?

Practice listening to dialogues: interviews, discussions of news stories or personal issues. Try National Public Radio from the US (www.npr .org) or BBC Radio 4 from the UK (www.bbc.co.uk/radio4). Listening to these will give you great practice in identifying speakers and content.

OBJECTIVES

By the end of this chapter, you will be able to:

- Listen for directions and descriptions of places.
- Understand information based on direction and movement words.
- Follow the steps involved in an action or a process.
- Practise strategies for answering Map Labelling, Flow-chart Completion and Note Completion questions.

Introduction

The second Listening recording you will hear is usually a monologue set in a real-life context, often involving directions, a description of a place, event, organisation or process.

It is likely that the speaker in the Listening recording will describe an event or process that you are already familiar with, such as starting at a new school or college.

The most common types of question formats in this section are Map or Diagram Labelling, Flow-chart Completion and Note Completion Questions.

If you want to get an overall IELTS Band Score of 5.5 or above you, need to get all or most of the questions in this section correct.

MAP LABELLING QUESTIONS

Strategies

- Check if it's a fill-in map (numbered blanks in the map) or a matching map (letters in the map).
- Look for any information on the map that will help you to find your way.
- Keep an eye on the list of labels – they will be listed in the order you will hear them in the recording.
- Use the features on the map to help you to find your way.

How to Recognise Map Labelling Questions

The questions include a map or plan.
The map contains some information, along with numbered blanks or letters.
The instructions say 'Label the map' or 'Complete the map.'
If the map contains letters, then there will be a numbered list of labels.

Improve Your Score – Direction and Movement Words

Directions can be difficult if you are looking at a map of an area you don't know. Because of this, it is important to look carefully at all of the information on the map: does it include main roads or landmarks such as important buildings, stations or parks? These can be very useful when you are following the directions given in the listening.

1. Look at the map of New Town. Ten important places are missing from the map. Read the ten directions below to identify where they are.

Handout C

A	Zoo	**B**	Post Office

Bay Street

Train Station	King Avenue	**C** Library **D**	Victoria Avenue	**E**	York Avenue
F		High School		**G** Baxter's Bakery	

Hill Street

Police Station	**H** **J** King's Arms Pub	City Hall
L	**K**	**M** Shep's Shoes

Spruce Street

N	**P**	Retro Records **Q**
Mia's Pizza		

1. To get to the courthouse from the train station, you leave the train station and go down King Avenue. Take the second left along Spruce Street. The courthouse is on your left.

2. I'm at the city hall, and I need to go to the pharmacy. I take Hill Street and then turn right into Victoria Avenue. The pharmacy is on the corner with Bay Street.

3. To get to Maison Blanche from Retro Records, turn right from Spruce Street into Victoria Avenue and go straight past Hill Street to the far end of Victoria Avenue. You will find Maison Blanche on the corner with Bay Street.

4. From the Post Office, you can get to Canoe Coffee by going all the way down York Avenue to Spruce Street and turn right. Canoe Coffee is on the corner of Spruce Street and King Avenue, beside Mia's Pizza.

5. The hospital is quite close to the high school. It is a block away at the junction of King Avenue and Bay Street.

6. How do I get to the fitness centre from the city hall? It's also on York Avenue, on the other side of Bay Street from the Post Office.

7. To get to the department store from the zoo, you can take either King Avenue or Victoria Avenue. Go past Hill Street, and the department store is on Spruce Street, between the two avenues.

8. Where do I park my car if I'm going to the train station? Oh, that's easy, the public parking is adjacent to the station.

9. The dance studio is in the same block as the pub, but it is across the street from the police station

10. I've got tickets for the cinema and I'm arriving by train, so I need to take King Avenue and then take the second left into Spruce Street. The cinema is on the other side of Victoria Avenue, next to Retro Records.

2. Now, underline all of the key 'direction words and phrases.'

Being able to understand the meaning of all these expressions is a key skill for Map Labelling Questions, so you should make sure that you know them all.

Getting Ready to Listen

Before listening to the recording, look over questions 1–5 below and take 30 seconds to answer the questions a–d. Then, take a moment to review the answers for a–d at the back of the book before listening to the recording.

a. How many numbers can you write for any answer?
b. Is there a train station on the map?
c. What is different about the blank for question 3?
d. What are the most important places a new student needs to know about?

Listen

Now listen to the recording and fill in the answers to questions 1–5 in the map below. Remember that in the IELTS test, you can make notes on the map before you write your answers on the answer sheet.

 Track 5 (Shipsbury)

Questions 1–5

Label the map below.

Write **NO MORE THAN TWO WORDS** for each answer.

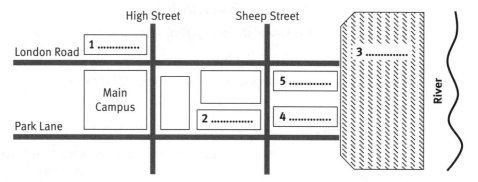

Check your answers for questions 1–5. How did you do? Hopefully you were able to anticipate which part of the map to look at before the answers for the next question were given in the recording. This is a skill you must practise, and it is an essential use of the 30 seconds to review each new map in the test paper.

Improve Your Score

When you encounter a set of Map Labelling questions, it is important to ask yourself during the 30 second thinking time: 'Where on the map will the recording start?'

Look at the map above again and identify the two clues that indicate where the recording will start.

Practice

Getting Ready to Listen

Before listening to the second part of the recording, look over questions 6–10 below and take 30 seconds to answer the questions a–c. Then, take a moment to review the answers for a–c at the back of the book before listening to the recording.

a. How is this map different from the one above?

b. What are some of the challenges of answering the questions here?

c. What must you remember about the numbering of the questions?

Listen

Now listen to Track 6 and answer questions 6–10 below.

 Track 6 (Shipsbury)

Questions 6–10

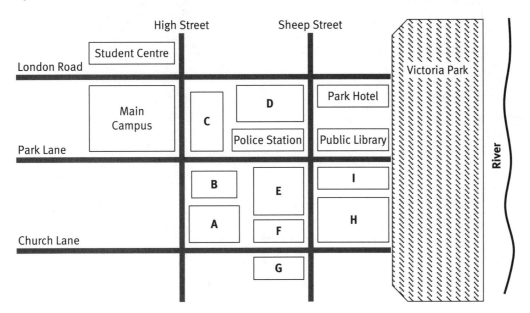

6. town hall ....

7. supermarket ....

8. post office ....

9. primary school ....

10. Wok 'n' Roll ....

Listening for Detail

1. Listen again and for each answer (6–10), note down the key phrase and underline the direction and movement words that you hear in the recording.

2. What do you notice about the position of the direction and movement words within each sentence?

Improve Your Score

It is important to learn which direction words to use when places are on the same side or different sides of the street.

Mark the following phrases 'S' for the same side and 'D' for different sides.

    a. next to

    b. between

    c. opposite

    d. just beside

    e. straight across

    f. on the other side

KAPLAN TIP

Look carefully at the map and identify the key reference points. If there are numbers on the map, find the reference point nearest to the first question to locate the 'start point'.

FLOW-CHART COMPLETION QUESTIONS

Strategies

- Check how many words or numbers you can include in each answer.
- Predict what sort of information you will need for each answer.
- Look for clues that will tell you when to move on to the next box in the flow-chart.

How to Recognise Flow-chart Completion Questions

- The instructions ask you to complete the flow-chart.
- The flow-chart usually includes a series of boxes or circles, connected by lines or arrows, with blanks inside.
- Some information is already filled in. Use this to help you identify what you are listening for.

Getting Ready to Listen

Before listening to the recording, look over questions 1–8 below and take 30 seconds to answer the questions a–f. Then, take a moment to review the answers for a–f at the back of the book before listening to the recording.

- **a.** Can you write a number for any answer?
- **b.** Can you write three words for any answer?
- **c.** How many stages are there to the process?
- **d.** Which three of the questions have verbs or verb forms as answers?
- **e.** Which one of the questions has an adjective as an answer?
- **f.** Predict what you think the answer to question 1 will be. What information did you use to help with your prediction?

Listen

Now listen to the recording and fill in the answers to questions 1–8 in the flow-chart.

 Track 7 (In the Kitchen)

Questions 1–8

Complete the flow-chart below.

*Write **ONE WORD ONLY** for each answer.*

How To Make Cirak (Slovak Cheese)

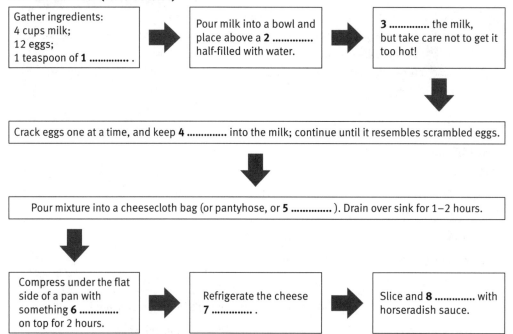

Gather ingredients:
4 cups milk;
12 eggs;
1 teaspoon of **1** ....

→ Pour milk into a bowl and place above a **2** .... half-filled with water.

→ **3** .... the milk, but take care not to get it too hot!

↓

Crack eggs one at a time, and keep **4** .... into the milk; continue until it resembles scrambled eggs.

↓

Pour mixture into a cheesecloth bag (or pantyhose, or **5** ....). Drain over sink for 1–2 hours.

↓

Compress under the flat side of a pan with something **6** .... on top for 2 hours.

→ Refrigerate the cheese **7** ....

→ Slice and **8** .... with horseradish sauce.

Take a moment to check the answers in the back of the book. Was your prediction for question 1 correct?

Did you spell all the answers correctly?

Improve Your Score – Spelling Verbs

In both the listening and the reading tests you only get a point if you spell the answer correctly. So if you wrote 'stiring' for question 4, although you got the idea correct, because the spelling was wrong you would not get the point.

It is useful to know when we double the final consonant at the end of the verb.

1. Complete the following rules with either **double** or **do not double**:

    1. If a verb ends in a single consonant and the stress falls on the final syllable you _____ the final consonant.

    2. If a verb ends in a single consonant and the stress does not fall on the final syllable you _____ the final consonant.

    3. If a verb is one syllable and ends in a single consonant with a single vowel before it, you _____ the final consonant.

    4. If a verb ends in a single consonant with two vowels before it, usually you would _____ the final consonant.

2. Now practice by writing the –ing form of the following verbs:

    1. admit
    2. hit
    3. tour
    4. cater
    5. refer
    6. visit
    7. heal
    8. stop

Improve Your Score – Compound Nouns

A compound noun is when two or more words are written together to form a third, different, noun. For example, in your language, you may say 'the leg of the table'. However in English we say 'table leg'. There are a lot of compound nouns in English and we use them frequently. They are especially important in Academic Writing tasks, as they enable you to include a lot of information in a few words.

Being able to recognise and use compound nouns in your IELTS exam will help you improve your band score.

1. Look back at the answers to the listening. Which two answers are compound nouns?

    There are three ways we can write compound nouns:

    1. As one word: saucepan

    2. As two or more words joined by a hyphen: sister-in-law

    3. As two words separately: table leg

2. Write these compound nouns in their correct forms

    A   break down

    B   check in

    C   word processing

    D   middle class

    E   T shirt

    F   work out

    G   some where

    H   post office

It is important to be aware of common compound nouns and to know how they are written. This could make a difference in some Listening questions.

KAPLAN TIP

Being able to recognise compound nouns is an essential skill for both the Listening and Reading tests. Additionally, being able to use compound nouns effectively both in your writing and your speaking tests will help you improve your score. IELTS Writing examiners and speaking interviewers will look out for compound nouns as a sign of your English level. As such, it is worth spending some time reviewing compound nouns.

NOTE COMPLETION QUESTIONS

Strategies

- Check how many words or numbers you can include in each answer.
- Predict what sort of information you will need for each blank.
- Look for clues that will tell you what to listen for, and when to move on to the next part of the notes.

How to Recognise Note Completion Questions

The instructions ask you to complete the notes.

The notes are organised in some format, often a table or box or bulleted list, with blanks inside.

Some information is already filled in. Use this to help you identify what you are listening for.

Practice

Listen

Now that you have had some practice of the different type of questions it's time to do a complete IELTS listening set of 10 questions. In this exercise, you will complete a full listening recording and answer all 10 questions just as you would on Test Day. Thus, there are no questions to answer before you begin the recording.

 Track 8 (Village fete)

Questions 1–5

Complete the notes below.

Write **NO MORE THAN THREE WORDS AND/OR A NUMBER** *for each answer.*

PLANNING NOTES – THIS YEAR'S FETE	
Date of the fete:	**1** ....
Expected weather:	22 degrees and **2** ....
Fundraising purpose:	In aid of the roof of the **3** ....
Fundraising goal:	£4000
Last year's tickets:	400 adult tickets at £5 each, plus **4** .... discounted tickets at £2.50 each
Total from ticket sales last year:	**5** ....
Amount needed from food and drink sales to reach overall target:	£1250 (assuming total from ticket sales is the same as last year)

Questions 6–10

Label the plan below.

*Write **NO MORE THAN THREE WORDS AND/OR A NUMBER** for each answer.*

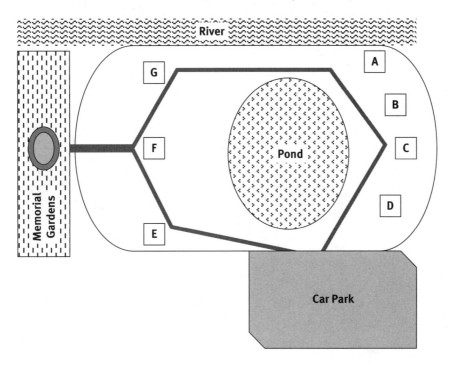

6   Raffle ....

7   Face painting ....

8   Band stand ....

9   Kids' games ....

10 Egg and spoon race ....

Now check your answers. How did you do?

1. Did you write the answers to questions 1 and 4 as words or numbers? Which do you think is best and why?

2. Why did you have to include the £ sign?

3. In the second part, did you write on the map what F and B are? What are they?

4. Why is it a good idea to write on the map all the places you can identify, even if they are not one of the questions?

Takeaway

In this section we've looked at Map labelling, flow chart and note completion questions.

Which parts of this section did you find most useful?

What have you learned that you will be able to use on Test Day?

OBJECTIVES

By the end of this chapter, you will be able to:

- Listen for connecting words.
- Follow the logical flow of a conversation.
- Determine the function of what a speaker is saying.
- Practise strategies for answering Table/Summary Completion, Sentence Completion and Matching Questions.

Introduction

The third Listening recording you will hear will usually be a conversation between two people, often university students, sometimes being guided by a tutor.

Even though you may not have ever discussed these exact topics before, you will have had similar styles of discussions with your classmates, college friends or work colleagues.

The most common question formats for this section are Table/Summary Completion, Sentence Completion and Matching questions.

If you want to get an IELTS band score of between 5.5 and 6.5, this can be achieved even if you get some questions wrong in this section.

TABLE/SUMMARY COMPLETION QUESTIONS

Strategies

- Check how many words or numbers you can include in each answer.
- Predict what sort of information you will need for each answer.
- For Table Completion: Check the order of the answers. Be ready to move through them in numerical order, regardless of where they appear.
- For Summary Completion: Look for clues that will tell you when to move on to the next sentence.

How to Recognise Table/Summary Completion Questions

The instructions ask you to complete the table or the summary.
A table may have several rows or columns, some of which will contain numbered blanks.
A summary may contain one or more paragraphs, with blanks included in some of the sentences.
Some information is already filled in. Use this to help you identify what you are listening for.

Improve Your Score – Connecting Words

1. Set a timer for 7 minutes to skim the two passages below ('Ada Lovelace' and 'Glastonbury') and underline all the connecting words you find. Check your answers in the Answer Key. How did you do?

2. Many of these connectives have the same function in the sentence. Look at the following categories and match the answers you underlined (in question 1) to each of the categories:

   - Addition
   - Comparison and Contrast
   - Time and sequence
   - Cause/effect and condition
   - Examples and emphasis
   - Conclusion

3. How can recognising and understanding connecting words help in the Listening and Reading modules of the IELTS?

4. How can being able to use connecting words effectively help in the Speaking and Writing part of the test?

Passage 1
Ada Lovelace

The child of the famous poet Lord Byron seems an unlikely candidate to be thought of as the first ever computer programmer, especially since this child was female, but Ada Lovelace was just that. Born in 1815 at a time when there were no recognised computer engineers, let alone female computer engineers, Ada helped shape the field.

Ada Lovelace came from a very wealthy background with a high position in society and a very intelligent mother, although her father left when Ada was just a month old. Her mother instilled in her a love of mathematics, hoping that she would not become a poet like her father. Despite her mother's best efforts, though, Ada continued to a have a passion for both science and poetry. Ada became Countess Lovelace after she married a man named William King in 1835. They had three children together and lived in London.

Ada's future career in computing first took flight when she was just 17 and was introduced to Charles Babbage at a friend's dinner party in London. Babbage was working in Cambridge on the first computer-like machine ever made. The two brilliant minds corresponded frequently by long distance letter throughout their partnership and Ada was very supportive of Babbage's ideas. In particular, she helped Babbage in the design of his second computing machine, called the Analytical Engine. Up until then, Babbage had been working with a mathematician in Italy to come up with some ideas for a new machine, which were published in a French journal. Babbage asked Ada to translate the French journal article so it could be published in England. Following this, Ada wrote to him with further suggestions and ideas, expanding the concept of the article even further than Babbage had. Indeed, she even came up with the steps needed to allow the machine to calculate Bernoulli numbers, a complex mathematical sequence. Ada's efforts here marked the beginnings of computer programming, as we know it today. Ada also predicted the future; she wrote that computers would eventually be used to create music and graphics.

So influential was this English mother of three, that the United States Defense Department named a software code after her. As a result of her remarkable achievements, Ada Lovelace is still celebrated today around the world on Ada Lovelace Day in October, which is a day to commemorate great women in science and technology.

Passage 2
Glastonbury

Everyone has heard of Glastonbury, although it is perhaps less familiar for its ruined abbey than for other reasons. Glastonbury Abbey was originally built in 712 and was almost completely destroyed by a fire in 1184. Throughout history, there have been many familiar stories about Glastonbury Abbey, including that it was visited by Joseph of Arimathea, the man who is depicted in the Bible as having donated his tomb so it could be used for the burial of Jesus. In the familiar story, Joseph of Arimathea travelled to England following the death of Jesus; upon arrival he proceeded to put his walking stick in the ground at Glastonbury, as a result a tree sprung from it and the abbey was built on that very site; this hawthorn tree is known as the 'holy thorn'. The story of Joseph coming to England is so popular that it is included in the first line of William Blake's *Jerusalem*: 'And did those feet in ancient time/Walk upon England's mountains green': the 'ancient feet' are commonly thought to belong to Jesus, who (according to a legend popular in Blake's time) visited England in his childhood with his uncle, Joseph of Arimathea. Thus, the holy thorn is linked directly to Jesus's visit to England. This tree remains so popular today that every Christmas morning, a posy from this hawthorn is sent to be displayed on the Queen's breakfast table.

However, recent research by archaeologists has complicated the history of Glastonbury. A team of 31 medieval archaeology specialists, under the direction of Professor Roberta Gilchrist of the University of Reading, discovered that there is no contemporary evidence for the story of Joseph of Arimathea prior to the 17th century. Despite the popularity of this legend, it has proven to be not more than 150 years older than William Blake himself, who was born in the mid-18th century. It is now thought that previous generations of scholars and church authorities either ignored or suppressed the evidence that would have disproved the myth of Joseph of Arimathea visiting Glastonbury.

Gilchrist and her team uncovered evidence of a medieval glassworks at the site of the abbey, which must have made the fragments of glass with elaborate, multi-coloured patterns found at the site dating back as early as the 7th century, prior to the construction of the first church at the abbey. The site also contains ceramic fragments which prove that, in addition to being the earliest known glassworks in Saxon England, the abbey had also imported wine from the continent even earlier than it made glass.

Gilchrist's research reveals that many of the concerns of the English during the Middle Ages (which dates to 500–1500) are not very different from our own. The fire that devastated the abbey in 1184 caused severe financial difficulties to the monks; it is now believed that the legends about Glastonbury were invented at this time, in order to help with fundraising to build a replacement for the original wooden church. The stone church whose ruins you can visit at the site in the present day was built thanks to this fundraising drive. Stories that circulated at the time include claims that the original church at Glastonbury was built by Jesus's disciples (which likely influenced the later legend that Jesus and Joseph of Arimathea had visited England and planted the holy thorn), and that King Arthur and Guinevere were buried nearby. This last legend had 'proof' in the form of a lead cross bearing a Latin inscription with the name of the king, now lost to history, which supported the idea that the legendary Avalon – Arthur's burial site – was right by Glastonbury Abbey. In fact, historians now agree that the monks at the abbey merely made up this claim, due to the popularity of stories about Arthur and Guinevere at the time of the fire in the late 12th century.

Getting Ready to Listen

Before listening to the recording, look over questions 1–8 below and take 30 seconds to answer the questions a–e. Then, take a moment to review the answers for a–e at the back of the book before listening to the recording.

a. What type of question is this?

b. How many numbers can you write for any answer?

c. Which question has a place as an answer?

d. Which questions have verbs or verb forms as answers?

e. Which questions have nouns as answers?

Listen

Now listen to the recording and answer questions 1–8 in the table below. Be careful to spell all the answers correctly.

 Track 9 (Sonia and tutor)

Questions 1–8

Complete the table below.

*Write **ONE WORD ONLY** for each answer.*

GLASS WORKS – TWO SIDES TO THE BUSINESS		
Industrial glass: for commercial customers (offices and **1** ....)	Artisanal glass: for homes (stained glass **2** .... and tableware)	
HOW TO 3 .... **GLASS**		
First, you must **4** .... it: Make a line, then break the glass along the line		
OPTION 1 **5** .... break (large sheets of glass)	OPTION 2 Use a **6** .... or pliers (smaller pieces)	OPTION 3 **7** .... method: Knock gently against the line, down its full length, then fold carefully along the line (best for **8** ....)

Check your answers for questions 1–8. How did you do? Being able to identify what types of words you are listening for will help you find the correct answers easily.

Improve Your Score – Silent Letters

Some words in English contain letters which we write but we don't say. These are called silent letters.

1. Which word in the answers to the Listening Track 9 contains a silent letter?

2. Look at the words below and underline the silent letter.

wrap*	Wednesday	receipt
knee	debt	wrong
sandwich	know*	write*

3. Why do you need to be careful with those words marked with an asterisk?

Quite often in the IELTS Listening test, one of the answers will be a word with a silent letter, so it's a good idea to become familiar with the common words with silent letters. Search online for 'words with silent letters' and you will find several lists of the most common words to learn and review.

Improve Your Score – Function

Function means the purpose, why we are saying what we are saying. For example the function of 'hello' is to greet someone. For the first, second and fourth Listening sections in the Listening module the function is usually very clear. However, in the third listening, which is usually a conversation between two students; sometimes with a tutor or between a student and a tutor, the function of the language is not always so obvious. Listening for the tone as much as the words will help you to identify the function.

Below is part of a conversation between two students who are discussing the arrangements for their end of term presentation. Match each sentence with the 9 common functions beneath, then underline the key function words.

   a. OK, let's move on to the room. Have you booked the multimedia room for us?

   b. Yes, I spoke with the administration office yesterday. We've got the large one on the fifth floor of the science block.

   c. Oh, that's great. That's definitely the best room.

   d. Now, they suggested that we hire some spare equipment in case something goes wrong with our laptops? Do you think we should?

   e. No, I don't think that's necessary.

   f. Yes, you're right, of course. But it is only twenty pounds.

   g. Twenty pounds, shouldn't that be ten pounds as we are undergraduates?

   h. Mmm, actually, they told me that they no longer give discounts for the undergraduates.

   i. That's completely outrageous. Do they think we are made of money?

1. agreeing
2. changing topics
3. confirming
4. correcting
5. disagreeing
6. rejecting
7. showing pleasure
8. suggesting
9. showing anger

SENTENCE COMPLETION QUESTIONS

Strategies

- Check how many words or numbers you can include in each answer.
- Predict what sort of information you will need for each blank.
- Check the wording before and after the blank, to ensure that your answer fits properly.
- Keep an eye on the next sentence, so you are ready to listen for its answer.

How to Recognise Sentence Completion Questions

The instructions say 'Complete the sentences below.'
Each sentence will include a blank. There is only one blank, even if you can write two or three words.
The instructions tell you how many words you can put in the blank.

MATCHING QUESTIONS

Strategies

- Look over the list of items with letters before the recording starts, so you know the options.
- Listen for each numbered item in turn. Write the corresponding letter next to it as soon as you hear the matching information in the recording.
- Keep an eye on the next numbered item, so you are ready to listen for its answer.

How to Recognise Matching Questions

There is a box of items with letters, followed by a list of numbered items (names, places, things, ideas).
The instructions say to choose the answers from the box and write the letter that goes with each question.
The instructions will not use the word 'matching,' but will contain a question that tells you what to listen for.

Example

Getting Ready to Listen

Now that you've had quite a lot of practice with different question types, here's an opportunity to do a complete IELTS listening script with two new question types.

You have 30 seconds before each section to answer questions a–f below before listening to the recording and answering the questions

Getting ready to listen to questions 1–5:

    a. How many numbers can you write for any answer?

    b. Can you write one word and two numbers for any answer?

    c. Which question will be answered by a verb? How do you know?

    d. Which question needs a plural noun as an answer? How do you know?

Getting ready to listen to questions 6–10:

    e. How many more 'answers' are there than questions?

    f. Read the 'answers': For each of the questions 6–10, write down the letters of the answers that you think may be possible. Don't worry if you don't have time for all of them.

Listen

Now listen to the recording and answer questions 1–10. Be careful to spell all the answers correctly.

 Track 10 (Tourism presentation)

Questions 1–5

Complete the sentences below.

*Write **NO MORE THAN TWO WORDS AND/OR A NUMBER** for each answer.*

1   The tutor said they should begin with a .... of the problem.

2   The primary reason for the decline in tourism is ....

3   The students will need three or four .... of how to make the town more welcoming for tourists.

4   The strongest point will be explained in .... of the presentation.

5   When they give the presentation in class, the students plan to ....

Questions 6–10

Choose FIVE answers from the box and write the correct letter, A-H, next to Questions 6–10.

A	install baby changing facilities
B	close the gates at sunset
C	improve road signs
D	add more toilets
E	clean thoroughly at night
F	add more lighting
G	collect rubbish once per week
H	eliminate entry fee

6   the old pier ....

7   Abbey Park ....

8   the beach ....

9   shops on The Strand ....

10   Royal Art Gallery ....

After listening to the recording and answering the questions, check all your answers. How did you do?

Improve Your Score

- Why in question 4 is it important to include 'the'?
- Is it important to know what a 'pier' is?
- For matching questions, why is it useful to check which answers could possibly match each question?
- All the answers in the Listening recording used synonyms of the 'answers' from the test. For each correct answer, write down each pair of synonyms.

KAPLAN TIP

When preparing for a Matching question, underline the key words in the 'answers' and think of possible synonyms.

Once you have used an 'answer' draw a line through it. This will make it easier to check the options that remain.

Practice

Listen

This time you are going to do a full IELTS listening set, with 10 questions in 2 different question types. This time there are no questions to help you get ready for the listening. You have to decide how best to use the 30 second pause before starting each group of questions.

 Track 11 (Robert and Millie)

Questions 1–4

*Choose the correct answer: **A, B** or **C**.*

1 The students are each preparing

    A an ecology presentation.

    B a report on recycling.

    C a talk about climate change.

2 In his work, Robert is focusing on

    A data from a nearby area.

    B rubbish collection figures.

    C national recycling statistics.

3 Meanwhile, Millie's focus is

    A why the local area is not recycling enough.

    B a policy of the local council that has failed.

    C efforts to grow the recycling rate.

4 As part of her research, Millie has talked to

    A opponents of the new recycling scheme.

    B people involved in the political process.

    C reporters and rubbish collectors.

Questions 5–10

Complete the summary below.

*Write **NO MORE THAN ONE WORD AND/OR A NUMBER** for each answer.*

Greenwood recycled 31% of all its waste last year, an improvement on its recycling rate of **5** ………….. from three years ago. However, the figure for the overall amount of **6** …………..
was up by 10%. This means that there was more recycling and less **7** ………….. . Also, the rate of paper and card recycling has **8** ………….. by 6%. The change is attributed to people reading newspapers and magazines on computers and **9** ………….. . Meanwhile, the amount of **10** ………….. recycled in Greenwood has increased by a quarter, thanks to the attention to recycling items such as drinks containers and carrier bags.

Now check your answers. How did you do?

If you got any questions wrong, go to the transcript at the back of the book and see if you can see where you made your mistake. We can often learn more from our mistakes than from getting questions correct. So don't be concerned if there are a few errors at this stage. Just learn from them.

Improve Your Score – Homophones

Look back at the answers to the Listening above. Can you see a word that can have a different spelling with a different meaning, but still sounds the same? What is the other word?
Words that sound the same but have different spellings and meanings are called homophones. In IELTS Listening the context will tell you which homophone is being used, but it is important that you spell the right word correctly.

Look at the pairs of homophones below. Match the meaning with the correct homophone and give the meaning for the other one.

a.	part of something	peace/piece	_____
b.	all of something	whole/hole	_____
c.	to listen	here/hear	_____
d.	a step	stair/stare	_____
e.	to slow down or stop	break/break	_____

Improve Your Score – Percentages

In the Listening module and also in the Writing module it is important to be able to understand and produce percentages correctly.

The key to percentages is in the prepositions that we use when talking about changes.

Look at the following information and then complete the sentences.

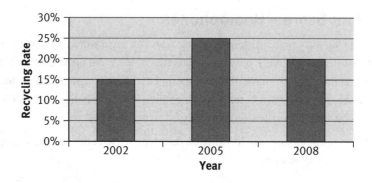

A   The recycling rate increased _____ 15% in 2002 _____ 25% in 2005.

B   The recycling rate decreased _____ 5% _____ 2005 and 2008.

Now complete the rules.

1.   We use the prepositions _____ and _____ when we talk about the actual percentages and how they change over time.

2.   We use the preposition _____ when we talk about the amount of change in percentages.

3.   We use the preposition _____ when we talk about the dates of the change.

Do these preposition rules apply if we are taking about other types of data such as number of sale, money earned, people who visited?

Takeaway

What have you learned in this part that will help you improve your score on Test Day?

How can you continue to practice and improve?

OBJECTIVES

By the end of this chapter, you will be able to:

- Follow a lecture or talk.
- Determine the main idea and supporting or contrasting ideas.
- Listen for words indicating examples and theories.
- Practise strategies for answering Short Answer, Multiple Choice and Note Completion questions.

Introduction

In the fourth Listening recording, you will hear an extract from a lecture.

You will have attended lectures before, so you will know what to expect in terms of structure. However, the subjects chosen are usually quite unusual. This is to give everyone a fair chance. So don't worry if, when you look at the question paper, it is clearly a subject you know nothing about.

In this section, the question formats can be any of the ones you have previously studied.

Even if you need to get an IELTS Band score of 7.5, you can still do that even if you get some questions wrong in this section.

We will not be looking at any new question formats in this chapter. However, there will be lots of practice on answering questions for the final listening script.

Improve Your Score – Topic and Main Idea

The final Listening recording is usually an extract from an academic lecture. The language used when someone gives a lecture is very different from when they are talking about their subject to students individually. To prepare for the final Listening section, you will listen to three short extracts from three different lectures.

 Track 12 (three extracts)

1. Listen to the three extracts from different lectures in Track 12. During each extract, try to make a note of the topic and the main idea of each lecture.

    - Topic: the subject matter of the talk (in Listening) or the passage (in Reading)
    - Main idea: the view or claim that the speaker/writer makes about the topic

2. How is topic different from main idea?

3. How can listening for topic and main idea help in the Listening module?

Take a few moments to check your notes of the topics and main ideas against those in the Answer Key. How did you do?

Getting Ready to Listen

The final listening recording is usually an extract from an academic lecture. The language used when someone gives a lecture is very different from when they are talking about their subject to students individually.

1. Look at the following list and tick the features that you would expect to hear in an academic lecture.

    - Higher level vocabulary
    - Lots of phrasal verbs
    - The word 'I'
    - Long noun phrases
    - Passive verbs
    - Explanations
    - Colloquial expressions
    - Clear signposting language

2. Before listening to the recording, look over questions 1–7 below and take 30 seconds to answer the questions a–d. Then, take a moment to review the answers for a–d at the back of the book before listening to the recording.

    a. What type of question format is this?

    b. Can you use numbers for your answer?

    c. Which answer is going to be a type of job?

    d. What type of word are all the answers going to be?

Listen

Now listen to the recording and answer questions 1–7. Be careful to spell all the answers correctly.

 Track 13 (sunken boats)

Answer the questions below.

*Write **NO MORE THAN THREE WORDS** for each answer.*

1 What does a fen contain in significant amounts? …………..

2 During what era were the boats sunk? …………..

3 Who originally used some of the boats? …………..

4 Which side of the boats did the water enter from? …………..

5 Some of the boats were only as thick as what part of the body? …………..

6 What will be injected into the boats, in order to preserve them? …………..

7 What is thought to have increased considerably, just before the boats were sunk? …………..

Don't forget that just like all the other Listening sections, you will hear the answers in the same order that the questions are given on the test paper. You will hear the answer for question 1 before the answer for question 2, and so forth.

How did you do? Don't worry if you didn't get them all correct. Review the listening script at the back of the book to check any words or phrases you did not understand.

Improve Your Score – Articles

The way the articles— *a*, *an* and *the*— are used in English can be quite confusing, so being able to use them correctly in your IELTS Speaking and Writing tests will really help you improve your score; you will often have to decide whether to include the article for a fill-in answer in the Listening test. Sometimes no article is required. The best way to learn how to use articles is to see how they are used in authentic speaking and writing.

Look back at the answers to the Listening and answer the following questions.

- **a.** Why is there no article in the answer to question 1?
- **b.** Why is the article in the answer to question 2 optional?
- **c.** Why is there no article in the answer to question 3?
- **d.** Which type of article is in the answer to question 4 and why is it necessary?
- **e.** Which type of article is in the answer to question 5 and why this type?
- **f.** Why is the article in the answer to question 6 linked with the adjective as being optional?
- **g.** Why is there no article in the answer to question 7?

Improve Your Score – Academic Language Synonyms

When someone gives a lecture, their language is more formal and academic. Thus, is it is important to become familiar with some of the most frequently used words in an academic context.

Look the words below and find as many synonyms as you can.

- **a.** benefit
- **b.** challenge
- **c.** interpretation
- **d.** conclusion
- **e.** finding (noun)
- **f.** explanation
- **g.** recommendation
- **h.** data

One way you can really help improve your IELTS band score is to increase your vocabulary by learning synonyms. Every time you learn a new word, find some synonyms and antonyms (words that have the opposite meanings) that go with it.

Getting Ready to Listen

You are now going to a listen to an IELTS part 4 listening track. Before you listen, take 30 seconds to answer questions a–b below.

- **a.** Underline one word in each 'answer' which could be replaced by a synonym in the Listening recording.
- **b.** Which type of words are unlikely to be replaced by synonyms?

Listen

Now listen to the recording and answer questions 1–6.

 Track 14 (ice cream)

Questions 1–4

*Choose the correct answer: **A**, **B** or **C**.*

1 The earliest Chinese ice cream consisted of

   A milk, flour and ice.

   B milk and rice, packed in snow.

   C snow and fruit juice.

2 The Roman emperors ate a frozen dessert that is similar to

   A a snow cone.

   B sherbet.

   C a fruit smoothie.

3 The European version of ice cream was developed over time by

   A mixing in fruits and nuts.

   B adding more and more milk.

   C replacing the ice with snow.

4 Which claim about the history of ice cream has no basis in historical fact?

   A George Washington spent a lot of money on ice cream.

   B The Washingtons liked to serve ice cream.

   C Martha Washington made ice cream by leaving cream outside overnight.

Questions 5–6

*Choose **TWO** letters, **A-E**.*

   A The cost of collecting snow or ice

   B The difficulty of mixing cream with ice

   C The cost of milk

   D The difficulty of storing it

   E The preference for baked desserts

How did you do? Don't worry if you didn't get them all correct. Review the listening script at the back of the book to check any words or phrases you did not understand.

Improve Your Score – Synonyms

Look at each correct answer and find the matching synonym in the Listening script at the back of the book.

Do all the questions have matching synonyms?

Were your predictions in Getting Ready to Listen correct?

KAPLAN TIP

When you see a multiple choice question that has more than one answer, underline the keywords in the question and look carefully at the answer choices – also underlining any keywords – before the recording starts. This will help you to avoid missing the correct answers.

Practice

Listen

This is your final listening practice. All 10 questions appear in the form of a table completion set. There is a lot of information given in the table to help you understand what the talk is about and what you are going to hear. Although you need to look at all 10 questions in the 30 seconds before the lecture begins, you can still learn a lot to help you answer the questions.

 Track 15 (exercise wheels)

Complete the notes below.

*Write **NO MORE THAN ONE WORD AND/OR A NUMBER** for each answer.*

WILD MICE AND EXERCISE WHEELS
Two traditional theories as to why mice run inside exercise wheels: • To relieve **1** .... : the activity has a psychological benefit. • It's a stereotyped behaviour: a repetitive activity without a **2** ....
Three criteria for a stereotyped behaviour: • The behaviour occurs only in animals in **3** .... , not in animals in nature. • The behaviour is recurring and always the same, with no clear purpose. • There is no external stimulus for the behaviour; for example, there is no **4** .... Traditionally, wheel running by captive mice has been understood as a stereotyped behaviour. • This is because they do it even in the absence of a stimulus. • This is similar to **5** .... in a cell pacing back and forth for no reason.
Two locations for the experiment involving wild mice: • An **6** .... area (a professor's back garden) • A rural area (a remote dune inaccessible to the public)
Results of the experiment: • The running wheels were used more than **7** .... times. • Later on, researches removed food from the boxes, yet the visits where the wheel was used increased by **8** .... • Scientists concluded that running in an exercise wheel is inherently **9** .... to wild mice. • This means that the first theory is effectively true: mice run in wheels because it is something that they **10** ....

How did you do?

Don't worry if you didn't get all of them correct. Remember this is the most difficult of the listening scripts and even if you need a band score of 7.5, you do not have to get all of them right. Check your incorrect answers by looking at the script at the back of the book.

Improve Your Score – Collocations

1. Do you know what a collocation is? Choose the correct explanation below.

    a. Language that is grammatically incorrect but generally accepted. For example: *He did good* (instead of *He did well*).

    b. Language that is 'from the street' where commons words are given meanings different from their original one. For example: *wicked* used to mean *fantastic*, rather than *evil*.

    c. Language that is made up of two more words; nouns, verbs or adjectives, which appear together regularly. For example: *tragic accident*, rather than *sad accident*.

2. How can knowing about collocations help you with IELTS?

3. Look at the following table and complete the collocations.

    a. traditional _____

    b. to _____ stress

    c. external _____

    d. no _____ _____

    e. an urban _____

4. There are another seven common collocations in the table from Track 15. How many can you identify? Underline each collocation in the table.

Takeaway

As the listening recordings get harder, synonyms and collocations become more important. Go back through all the listening scripts at the back of the book and compare them with the questions to identify as many synonyms as you can.

After searching for synonyms, read each script again and note any collocations you can see.

P.S. from Kaplan

There is no need to be nervous about the IELTS Listening test. Remember that you have plenty of time to get ready to listen by reading and analysing the questions on the test paper. Don't forget that the answers always come in the order of the questions. Most importantly, read the questions carefully and make sure you always have the correct number of words and/or numbers.

LISTENING ANSWER KEY

Listening Chapter 1

Getting Ready to Listen

1	**A**	The context is: who the people are, what they are talking about and why.
	B	Knowing the context can help you because you can use your own knowledge about the situation to help you identify the answers. For example, if someone is calling to book a holiday, you would expect them to talk about places, type of accommodation, dates, prices etc.
	C	Usually it is quite easy to identify the speakers from the information given in the introduction and how they address each other.
		If you identify the speakers it will help you to decide what sort of language they will be using. For example, if someone is calling to book a holiday, the travel agent will be asking questions about where the caller wants to go. While the caller will be asking questions about prices.
2	**A**	yes
	B	yes
	C	3 and 4
	D	6
	E	5
	F	*suggested*: Birthday, wedding, anniversary, graduation

Track 1

1 graduation

2 bowling

3 12, twelve

4 6, six

5 £30, thirty pounds, £30.00

6 Emily's house

Listening for Detail

A   When is the graduation?

B   What does everyone like?

C   Does Will want to cook the graduation dinner?

D   When will a lot of students be having their graduation parties?

E   Who have quite big houses near to our college

F   What is 'sorted'?

Getting Ready to Listen

A   Short Answer questions

B   one or none

C   no, only one

D   all but number 5

E   3 and 4

F   times, prices, postcodes, phone numbers and names

Track 2

1   6.30 pm

2   £75

3   11th April

4   30th May

5   Byrne

6   GR5 2MQ

7   07989 457015

Improve Your Score – Different Types of Numbers

A   Three pounds fifty pence/Three pounds fifty/three fifty

B   double zero/oh double four seven five six zero/oh one six zero double six seven

C   seven thirty pm/half past seven in the evening

D   fifty six pounds and forty five pence/fifty six pounds forty five/fifty six forty five

E   thirteenth of April

F   thirty-first of December

G   eleven fifteen a.m./quarter past eleven in the morning

H   zero/oh two zero/oh three triple six double three five one

Improve Your Score – Synonyms and Paraphrases

1	**C**	It's only <u>a month</u> away
2	**A**	What do we <u>need</u> to do?
3	**E**	It's not <u>connected with</u> Christmas
4	**G**	we could <u>cook</u> it ourselves
5	**F**	My table only has <u>six</u> chairs
6	**I**	We can see about getting a <u>booking</u> at a restaurant
7	**L**	Why don't we <u>look at</u> having a party at a pub?
8	**N**	There are a total of eight <u>sessions</u>
9	**M**	Seventy five pounds is the total <u>charge</u>
10	**K**	That's quite a <u>good deal</u>
11	**J**	There are two places <u>available</u>
12	**B**	It will <u>continue</u> into June
13	**H**	<u>May I take</u> your name?
14	**D**	Yes, that's <u>correct</u>

Getting Ready to Listen

A Form completion

B No, only 1 or 2

C No, numbers are not mentioned in the question

D what they can't access, the officer's position and first name and details of the problem

E to help student organisations with their IT problems

Track 3

1 email [account]

2 vice-president/vice president

3 Rakesh

4 wrong password

Getting Ready to Listen

A   Multiple choice questions

B   5   The error was due to the <u>student misunderstanding</u> <u>what number</u>?

   6   What does the <u>student initially</u> suggest as <u>a new</u> <u>password</u>?

   7   What <u>special symbol</u> does the <u>student</u> include in the <u>new password</u>?

   8   The <u>longest video</u> they would like to put on the website is

   9   The <u>maximum size for a video</u> posted to a university website is

   10   In <u>international rugby</u>, the <u>student supports</u>

Track 4

   5   C
   6   B
   7   A
   8   B
   9   B
   10 C

Improve Your Score – Listening for Detail

A   locked out of

B   spelt incorrectly

C   fix it

D   what exactly was the trouble

E   that's not good

F   unfortunately

G   a starting point

H   instead of

I   Will that do?

J   …..the ones to help…..

Takeaway

1 See shaded boxes in the chapter

2 A   So you know how many words and numbers you can write

    B   they will give you more clues about the context

    C   They can help you follow the recording in case you miss a question

    D   There are likely to be synonyms in the recording which will help you with the answers

3 Because many of the answers will use synonyms or paraphrases of the questions.

Listening Chapter 2

Improve Your Score – Direction and Movement Words

1	**K**	To get to the courthouse from the train station you leave the train station and <u>go down</u> King Avenue. <u>Take the second left</u> along Spruce Street. The courthouse <u>is on your left</u>.
2	**D**	I'm at the City hall and I need to go to the pharmacy. I take Hill Street and then turn right into Victoria Avenue. The pharmacy is on the corner with Bay Street.
3	**B**	To get to Maison Blanche from Retro records turn right from Spruce Street into Victoria Avenue and go straight past Hill Street to the far end of Victoria Avenue. You will find Maison Blanche on the corner with Bay Street.
4	**N**	From the post office you can get to the Canoe coffee shop by going all the way down York Avenue to Spruce Street and turn right. Canoe Coffee is on the corner of Spruce Street and King Avenue, beside Mia's Pizza.
5	**A**	The hospital is quite close to the High School. It is a block away at the junction of King Avenue and Bay Street.
6	**E**	How do I get to the fitness centre from the City Hall? It's also on York Avenue, on the other side of Bay Street from the Post Office.
7	**P**	To get to the department store from the zoo you can take either King Avenue of Victoria Avenue. Go past Hill Street and the department store is on Spruce Street, between the two avenues.
8	**F**	Where do I park my car if I'm going to the train station? Oh, that's easy, the public parking is adjacent to the station.
9	**H**	The dance studio is in the same block as the pub, but is across the street from the Police station
10	**Q**	I've got tickets for the cinema and I'm arriving by train so I need to take King Avenue and then take the second left into Spruce Street. The Cinema is on the other side of Victoria Avenue next to Retro Records

Getting Ready to Listen

A None, you must answer in words

B No, there are no 'tracks' shown

C It's not a building

D *Answers will vary*

Track 5

1 student centre/student center

2 Police Station

3 Victoria Park

4 public library

5 Park Hotel

Improve Your Score

Only two features are named on the map, the Main Campus and the river, so the recording will have to start with reference to one of those. However, question number 1 is next to the main campus, so the recording will start there.

Getting Ready to Listen

A It is bigger and includes more places.

B Places are marked with letters and the questions are numbered below.

C The recording will follow the numbers of the questions. Thus it will start with the town hall.

Track 6

6 I

7 C

8 D

9 H

10 A

Listening for Detail

1	**6**	straight across from the library
	7	just beside the police station in Park Lane
	8	opposite the Park Hotel
	9	between Sheep Street and the park, across the road from the church
	10	at the corner of Church Lane and the High Street
2		The direction and movement words always come before the places they relate to.

Improve Your Score

A S

B S

C D

D S

E D

F D

Getting Ready to Listen

A no

B no

C 8

D 3, 4, 8

E 6

F *Answers will vary.* The clues are 'teaspoon' and the fact that it is cheese, which is salty not sweet.

Track 7

1 salt

2 saucepan/pan

3 warm

4 stirring

5 tights

6 heavy

7 overnight

8 serve

Improve Your Score – Spelling Verbs

1	1	double
	2	do not double
	3	double
	4	not double
2	1	admitting
	2	hitting
	3	touring
	4	catering
	5	referring
	6	visiting
	7	healing
	8	stopping

Improve Your Score – Compound Nouns

1		2 (saucepan) and 7 (overnight)
2	1	breakdown
	2	check-in
	3	word processing
	4	middle class
	5	T-shirt
	6	workout
	7	somewhere
	8	post office

Track 8

1 19th/nineteenth
2 [plenty of] sunshine
3 village hall
4 300/three hundred
5 £2750
6 E
7 G
8 A
9 C
10 D

Questions following Track 8

1 It is always best to write numbers as it's quicker and you can't make a spelling mistake

2 Because it was not included in the question paper.

3 F: Jam making B: drinks stand

4 By doing this you can eliminate the letters that are not required for the answer. So if you do miss the correct answer you can at least guess it from your map.

Listening Chapter 3

Improve Your Score – Connecting Words

1	**Ada Lovelace**	Connectives in the text: especially; but; let alone; with; although; when; despite; after; and; in particular; up until then; following this; indeed; so (influential); as a result
	Glastonbury	Connectives In the text: although; throughout; including; upon arrival; as a result; according to; thus; however; despite; prior to; in addition; also; in order to; thanks to; and; this; now; due to; in fact

2 [connectives in brackets are suggested additional examples – the lists are not exhaustive]

Addition	and, also, in addition, including [in addition to, as well as, like]
Comparison and contrast	but, let alone, despite, although, however, [on the other hand, yet, despite this, whereas, except, unless, either… or]
Time and sequence	when, after, up until then, following this, throughout, upon arrival, prior to, now [then, first, second, next, last, later, earlier, before, after]
Cause/effect and condition	following this, as a result, thus, thanks to, due to [because, if, since, so that, resulting in, unless, in order to,]
Examples and emphasis	in particular, indeed, so (influential), in fact [for example, in fact]
Conclusion	thus, indeed, as a result, in fact, [to conclude, in conclusion, finally, to sum up]

3	Connecting words will help you to follow the steps in a process. They will also help you understand the relationship between ideas in a sentence and between ideas in a dialogue or paragraph.

4

The ability to write in a coherent and cohesive way (ie to link your ideas together within a paragraph and between paragraphs) is one of the key descriptors for both Writing Tasks. The better your writing shows 'progression' through your ideas the higher your score will be! Similarly, for speaking, if you are able to link your ideas clearly you will be more fluent and easier to understand and you will get a better score.

Getting Ready to Listen

1	**A**	Table Completion question
	B	None
	C	1
	D	3, 4 and 7
	E	1, 2, 5, 6 and 8

Track 9

1 factories

2 windows

3 cut

4 score

5 table

6 knife

7 tapping

8 curves

Improve Your Score – Silent Letters

1 knife – the k is silent.

2 A

<u>w</u>rap*

<u>k</u>nee

san<u>d</u>wich

We<u>d</u>nesday

de<u>b</u>t

<u>k</u>now*

receip<u>t</u>

<u>w</u>rong

<u>w</u>rite*

3   These words when spelled without the silent letter are completely different words with totally different meanings.

Improve Your Score – Function

A   OK, <u>let's move on to</u> the room. Have you booked the multimedia room for us? (changing topics)

B   <u>Yes,</u> I spoke with the administration office yesterday. We've got the large one on the fifth floor of the science block. (confirming)

C   <u>Oh, that's great</u>. That's definitely the best room. (expressing pleasure)

D   Now, they suggested that we hire some spare equipment in case something goes wrong with our laptops? <u>Do you think we should</u>? (suggesting)

E   <u>No, I don't think that's necessary</u>. (rejecting)

F   <u>Yes, you're right</u>, of course. But it is only twenty pounds. (agreeing)

G   Twenty pounds, <u>shouldn't that be</u> ten pounds as we are under-graduates? (correcting)

H   Mmmm, <u>actually</u>, they told me that they no longer give discounts for the under-graduates. (disagreeing)

I   <u>That's completely outrageous</u>. Do they think we are made of money? (showing anger)

Getting Ready to Listen

A   one

B   no (but you can write two words and one number)

C   5 because of the word 'to' – the answer will be a verb in the infinitive with to

D   3 because of the words 'three or four' in the sentence

E   3

F   [suggested] 6 ABDEF 7 ABCFG 8 EG 9 ACF 10 ADH

Track 10

1   summary

2   poor weather

3   examples

4   the end

5   take turns

6   **F**   (we want to put extra lights on the pier)

7   **B**   (they shoud just shut the park gates at sunset)

8	E	(The beach should have the rubbish collected and litter cleared every night – a total overnight cleaning)
9	A	(we need to put some baby-changing tables in the toilets at those shops)
10	H	(they should abolish the admission charge)

Improve Your Score

A for two reasons, the sentence doesn't make grammatical sense without some sort of determiner (a, the, etc) and in this context they are speaking about a specific 'end' (of their presentation)

B Of course it's helpful to know the meaning of the word 'pier' as it will help you understand which of the answers may or may not be possible. However it is not vital that you know what it means. You know it is some sort of 'place' as all of the questions are. So all you have to do is listen out for the word pier in the text. Very high level, specialist or technical words are not replaced with synonyms.

C By focusing on what answers could be possible it reduces the number of words/synonyms/paraphrases you need to look out for.

D	F	extra lights/more lighting
	B	shut/close
	E	total/thorough
	A	put….in/install
	H	abolish admission charge/eliminate entry fee.

Track 11

1 B (Working on my recycling report)
2 A (I'm looking at the statistics for recycling collected by the local council)
3 C (My report is all about what Greenwood Council are doing to increase the amount of rubbish that is recycled)
4 B (I've spoken to several councillors and local activists who have done a lot on this issue)
5 27%
6 waste
7 rubbish
8 dropped
9 tablets
10 plastic

Improve Your Score – Homophones

waste – waist

A   part of something – piece; peace – the opposite of war

B   all of something – whole; hole – an opening (e.g. button hole on a jacket)

C   to listen – hear; here – where you are now

D   a step – stair; stare – to look at something for a long time

E   to slow down or stop – brake; break – to destroy something or to stop something from working

Improve Your Score – Percentages

A   The recycling rate increased from 15% in 2002 to 25% in 2005

B   The recycling rate decreased by 5% between 2005 and 2006

C   We use the prepositions from and to when we talk about the actual percentages and how they change over time

D   We use the preposition by when we talk about the amount of change in percentages

E   We use the preposition between when we talk about the dates of the change.

Yes, these preposition rules apply whatever data we are talking about.

Takeaway

Connecting words – words with silent letters – homophones – prepositions we use with percentages

At this stage the best way for you to improve your knowledge is to listen to as much English as you can. Find English speaking radio channels on the internet or download podcasts. It is particularly helpful if you can find material that you can play many times. Set yourself small tasks; like looking for connecting words, or homophones. Listen to business news to hear people talk about increases and decreases and use percentages

Listening Chapter 4

Improve Your Score – Topic and Main Idea

1	**First extract**	Topic: The behaviour of lions
		Main idea: Why the social behaviour of lions is different from that of other big cats
	Second extract	Topic: Increases in childhood allergies
		Main idea: Whether the Hygiene Hypothesis explains the rise in childhood allergies
	Third extract	Topic: The impact of footwear on how well you run
		Main idea: Whether people should run barefoot instead of wearing shoes
2		The topic is more general and it is neutral – the topic does not indicate a view or claim, while the main idea expresses a view/claim.
3		If you listen for the topic and main idea, it can help to keep you focused in a Listening recording that is more challenging. Some lectures may be dry or may involve unusual or unfamiliar content, so listening for the topic and identifying the main idea will help you to pay attention. They will also likely relate to several of the details that you must listen for, so topic and main idea will lead to points in many (if not all) cases.

Getting Ready to Listen

1 You would expect to hear the following in an academic lecture:

Higher level vocabulary

Long noun phrases

Explanations

Clear signposting language

2	**A**	Short Answer
	B	No
	C	3
	D	nouns

Track 13

1 water

2 [the] Bronze Age

3 fishermen

4 the rear

5 a finger

6 [a special] wax

7 sea levels

Improve Your Score – Articles

A Water is an uncountable noun so doesn't have an article

B Bronze Age is a proper noun

C Fisherman is a plural noun being used generally to answer the question 'who?'

D This is the definite article and is used because it is referring to a specific part of the boat and is answering the question 'which?'

E This is the indefinite article. Finger is a singular uncountable noun so it needs to have a determiner (the finger, this finger, that finger etc). However as this is general it has to be 'a' the indefinite article. Without the article the answer would not make any sense.

F wax is a uncountable noun and so doesn't need an article. However as soon as the adjective 'special' is added it becomes a specific type of wax and needs an article. However because it is a general comment it is the indefinite article that is needed.

G Because it is plural and plural countable nouns when talked about generally do not take articles. For example: sea levels have risen dramatically in the last five hundred years however the sea levels in the southern hemisphere have risen even faster.

Improve Your Score – Academic Language Synonyms

Answers will vary. Suggested synonyms:

A advantage, profit

B difficulty, problem, test, task

C view, opinion, understanding, version

D summary, ending, closing, finishing

E result, conclusion, discovery

F reason, example, account, justification

G suggestion, proposition, reference, endorsement

H information, data, statistics, evidence

Getting Ready to Listen

A   Students' own answers (will be checked in Improve your score activity)

B   Countries, peoples, individual people,

Track 14

1	B	(The Chinese made a mixture of milk and rice, then packed the mixture in snow)
2	A	(some Roman emperors......snow.....flavoured with fruit juice....something more like a snow cone)
3	B	(This European version....was developed over the years, eventually adding larger amounts of milk)
4	C	(Of course this is pure legend...Martha Washington frequently served ice cream....no record of her ever having made it)
5	A/D	(A: ice or snow would have to be brought in.....could only be done at great expense.)
6	A/D	(D: the challenge of keeping the ice cream cold, once it is made.)

Improve Your Score – Synonyms

1   B: a dairy product/milk

2   A: none – snow cone

3   B: more and more/larger amounts

4   C: none

5/6   A: collecting/brought in; D: difficulty/challenge

Track 15

1   stress

2   goal

3   cages

4   reward

5   prisoners

6   urban

7   12,000

8   42%

9   rewarding

10   enjoy

Improve Your Score – Collocations

1 C Collocations are, usually, pairs of words that come together through regular use. There is no grammatical reason why they are together.

2 Good use of collocations can help you get a high score in both the Writing and the Speaking modules as they are considered an indication of a high level user of English. They can often help with the answers to questions in the Reading and Listening modules.

3 A traditional theories

B to relieve stress

C external stimulus

D no clear purpose

E an urban area

4 psychological benefits

stereotyped behaviour

experiment involving

a rural area

inherently rewarding

scientists concluded

effectively true

READING INTRODUCTION

MODULE OVERVIEW

The Reading module consists of 40 questions based on three passages, with a total of 2,000 to 2,750 words on average. You are advised to spend 20 minutes on each passage and its questions, and there is no time at the end to transfer your answers to the answer sheet. Answers must be written on the answer sheet within the 60 minutes given.

The IELTS Reading module tests a range of skills, such as skimming and scanning, understanding main ideas, reading for detail and understanding opinion and attitude. The passages come from books, magazines, newspapers and journals and are non-specialised. At least one passage contains a detailed argument. Although the texts are representative of reading requirements for undergraduate and postgraduate students, they are not discipline specific. The passages are usually presented in increasing order of difficulty. Each passage has 13–14 questions, usually broken into two or three sets of different question types.

There are 11 main question types in the Reading module; you may see any of them in a given test paper, but you are unlikely to see all of them in a single test paper. The ninth type combines several similar formats into a single question type; in the *Strategies* course, we will consider examples and strategies for these individual formats. The table below breaks out the different question types, and whether you are expected to write a letter, word(s) or a number.

	Question Type	Form of Answer
1	Multiple Choice	Letters
2	True/False/Not Given	Words
3	Yes/No/Not Given	Words
4	Matching Information	Letters
5	Matching Headings	Roman numerals
6	Matching Features	Letters
7	Matching Sentence Endings	Letters
8	Sentence Completion	Words and/or a number
9	Summary, Note, Table, Flow-chart Completion	Words and/or a number
10	Diagram Label Completion	Words and/or a number
11	Short Answer	Words and/or a number

Differences between the Academic and General Training Reading Modules

While the types of questions on the Academic and General Training Reading Modules are the same, the types of reading passages differ. The Academic Module will usually contain at least one passage organized as a logical argument, while the readings in the General Training module are likely to be more descriptive or instructive. The organization of non-argumentative texts may vary, but common organizational themes are categories, chronological description and describing a process.

The Academic Reading module involves reading three passages, with one passage per section. Texts come from books, magazines, newspapers and journals and are non-specialized. At least one passage contains a detailed argument.

The General Training Reading module involves reading three or four passages grouped into three or four sections. Section 1 usually deals with social survival – for example, public information leaflets. Section 2 focuses on subjects related to general training and usually consists of two texts which, for example, give information about a university or college and services or facilities provided. Sections 3 and 4 each consist of one longer text related to general training; these may test general reading comprehension on almost any subject.

Although the kinds of texts differ slightly, the types of questions in both the Academic and General Training Reading modules are the same. Therefore, Part Three features examples from both tests. The skills which you will learn in Part Three will help you to confidently answer questions about any type of text that you read.

OBJECTIVES

By the end of this chapter, you will be able to:

- Create a passage map.
- Skim a passage in three to five minutes.
- Identify the main idea of a passage and of each paragraph.
- Practise strategies for answering Multiple Choice, Matching Heading and Sentence Completion questions.

Introduction

This chapter will focus on how to create a passage map and how to skim a Reading module text in three to five minutes.

A passage map is a brief outline that you can use to quickly find information and answer questions. You should write four or five keywords or phrases to summarise each paragraph's main points.

Why is this important? Because you must work quickly; brief notes will make it easier to find the right paragraph quickly when answering questions. Long notes take longer to write and could be confusing later.

This chapter will also cover Multiple Choice questions and two types of fill-ins: Matching Headings and Sentence Completion questions.

Reading Strategies

In the IELTS Reading module, you need to read each of the 3 passages and answer the accompanying questions in 20 minutes. There is no extra time to transfer answers to the answer sheet.

1. If you take one minute to answer each question, how long do you have to read each passage? Hint: check the number of questions for each text in the Module Overview above.

2. You must read each passage quickly but thoroughly. Skim for the main idea and key details in each paragraph. Make a passage map – a note of a few brief words that summarises the topic or main idea in each paragraph. You might also underline the topic sentence, and circle or underline key words or phrases. You MUST practise so that you can skim and 'passage map' any text in 5 minutes or less on Test Day.

MULTIPLE CHOICE QUESTIONS

Strategies

- Look over all the multiple choice questions after reading the passage.
- Identify a keyword from each question—underline these on the test paper.
- If you have time, identify a keyword from each answer choice.

How to Recognise Multiple Choice Questions

There is a question or incomplete sentence, followed by three or more possible answers.

Most multiple choice questions have only three possible answers, but some will have four or five.

Usually, there is only one correct answer. Sometimes, you will be asked to select two correct answers.

Passage 1 – Getting Ready to Read

1. Review the Strategies for answering Multiple Choice questions above. Multiple Choice questions are fairly easy to identify, as they include three or more answer choices, each with a letter. Normally, there is one correct answer. Sometimes, you may be asked to select two correct answers – so read the instructions carefully!

   The passage you are about to read is a bit shorter than the average passage in the IELTS test. Shorter passages give you more chances to practise.

2. **a.** Have a look at the length of this first reading text. How long do you think it will take you to read this passage thoroughly?

   b. How quickly do you think you could skim the passage?

MAKING A PASSAGE MAP

Passage 1 – Practice

Take 4 minutes to read the text below and make brief notes for each paragraph – just 4–5 words or phrases per paragraph. Time yourself.

Passage 1 – The Isles of Scilly

The Isles of Scilly (pronounced *SILL-ee*) form an archipelago off the southwestern tip of Cornwall. They are comprised of 140 islands and islets, the most significant of which are St Mary's, Tresco, St Martin's (with White Island), St Agnes (with Gugh), Bryher (with Gweal), Samson, Annet, St Helen's, Teän and Great Ganilly. The total population of the Isles of Scilly is just over two thousand. Scientific evidence suggests that the isles were likely much larger in ancient times and that many of them would have been joined into one island. Rising sea levels over time have led to the current geography.

Up until the early twentieth century, the residents of the Isles of Scilly practiced subsistence living, raising their own livestock and crops and catching fish to eat. Today, things are quite different. The Isles are well known for their flowers, particularly daffodils, which are their chief agricultural product. Otherwise, the Isles today depend largely on food and other products imported from the mainland, though fishing remains a popular pastime, if not a significant source of income.

The main industry on the isles today is tourism, making up 85% of the islands' total income. The favourable summer climate, conducive to flowers and holidays, facilitate the large amount of tourism in the area. The bulk of tourists visit St Mary's, the only island with a significant road network and airport, though the island of Tresco also has a number of timeshare resorts and a heliport. The holiday season on the Isles of Scilly, unlike many other tourist destinations in England, extends through October, when the isles are a top destination for bird watchers who come to see the many exotic birds who make the first stop of their migration on the isles.

The dominance of the tourism industry on the island has caused some political problems. Sixty-three percent of the island's jobs come from the tourism industry, but the vast majority of these offer only seasonal or part-time work. Thus, the isles employ a number of guest workers. Currently, the average income on the islands is only 70% that of the national average in the UK, whereas housing prices are, on average £5,000 more expensive than in the rest of the country. These factors make life difficult for those who make the isles their home, though they continue to be very popular among tourists.

When the time is up, compare your passage map with the passage map in the Answer Key.

   a. Did you have more words (or quite a lot more words) than the example passage map?

   b. How many words do you think you need for a decent passage map?

Now, practise using your passage map to answer the following Multiple Choice questions. We will do the first two together.

Questions 1–6

*Choose the correct answer: **A**, **B** or **C**.*

1. The geography of the Isles of Scilly was shaped by

    A changing sea levels.

    B a decline in farming.

    C a rise in population.

    Answer: The geography of the Isles of Scilly is discussed in the first paragraph. The final sentence of this paragraph says that rising sea levels over time led to the current geography.

    Therefore Answer **A** is correct – changing sea levels shaped the isles' geography. As for the other answers: The second paragraph mentions a decline in farming, but this is not connected to the isles' geography, so **B** is incorrect. A rise in population is not mentioned in the passage, so **C** is incorrect.

2. A political issue on the islands is that there are not enough

    A placets for islanders and tourists to live.

    B full-time, year-round jobs.

    C roads and shops to accommodate the seasonal visitors.

    Answer: The second sentence of this paragraph says that 63% of the jobs on the isles come from the tourism industry, but the vast majority of these are seasonal or part-time jobs.

    Thus, there are not enough full-time, year-round jobs. Answer **B** is correct. As for the other answers: The final paragraph says that housing on the island is more expensive than in the rest of the UK, but it does not say there are not enough places for tourists and locals to live. Answer **A** is therefore incorrect. The third paragraph says that only one island has a significant road network, but that does not mean there are not enough roads for tourists. Answer **C** must also be incorrect.

Take 3–4 minutes to answer the following three questions on your own. When you finish, check your answers with those in the Answer Key. Remember: you do not need to identify the incorrect answers during the test – only to find the correct answers.

3. Today, the Isles of Scilly are renowned for producing and selling

    A fish.

    B livestock.

    C daffodils.

4. Houses in the Isles of Scilly are

    A   cheaper than houses in England.

    B   costlier than houses in the UK.

    C   owned mostly by part-time residents.

5. A chief reason that tourists visit the Isles of Scilly is to see

    A   the many airports and helicopters.

    B   the historical church on the main island.

    C   unusual birds that are passing through.

Let's work through the final question together. Question 6 asks for an appropriate title for the passage. The title would need to capture a sense of the main idea of the passage. Before you answer Question 6, ask yourself:

    a.   What is the main idea of the passage?

    b.   What will we find in the incorrect answers?

6. Which of the following is an appropriate title for the passage?

    A   The Pros and Cons of Island Tourism

    B   Reasons to Visit the Isles of Scilly

    C   The Geography of a British Archipelago

    D   Introducing the Isles of Scilly

    E   Island Life Before and After Subsistence Living

Let's consider what's wrong with each answer (or whether it is correct).

    A   It's too narrow – only the final two paragraphs discuss the pros and cons of tourism

    B   Again, too narrow – only the third paragraph covers reasons to visit the isles.

    C   The geography is only mention in the first paragraph – very narrow!

    D   CORRECT

    E   This answer is also too narrow – it's the main idea of the second paragraph.

KAPLAN TIP

Wrong answers will often feature other details from the passage, or will change details from the passage. Make sure you are picking the detail that answers the question being asked.

MATCHING HEADINGS QUESTIONS

Strategies

- Do not read the list of headings before starting on the passage.
- Read the paragraphs one at a time, making your passage map notes as you do so.
- Underline the topic sentence in each paragraph where you find one.
- Once you have made your passage map notes for a paragraph, check the list of headings and find the one that matches. Then repeat these steps for the following paragraph.

How to Recognise Matching Heading Questions

The headings will appear in a box, each with a lowercase Roman numeral.
The paragraphs will be labelled with letters, starting with A.
The headings will appear before the passage. They are the only question type to appear before the passage.
One or more paragraphs may already be matched with their heading, as an example.

Passage 2 – Getting Ready to Read

1. Matching Heading questions are the only question type that appears before the passage. However, do NOT read the headings until you have read the passage, as there will be several headings that are not correct answers.

   Instead, skim the passage, making a passage map or underlining the topic sentence in each paragraph where you find one.

2. Once you have your passage map (or underlined topic sentences), check the headings box to find the one that matches. Repeat these steps for the following paragraph.

We will use the Matching Headings questions and the passage below to practise the strategies outlined above. Read the text before you read the questions. We will work though matching the first two paragraphs and headings together.

Note that unlike all other Reading question types, Matching Heading questions appear before the passage that they accompany. We have printed them below to maintain the same sequence you will see on Test Day, but this means that our guidance for dealing with these questions follows the passage.

Passage 2 – Practice

*The reading passage on the following pages has eight paragraphs, **A-H**.*

Choose the correct heading for each paragraph from the list of headings below.

i	The problems with the Julian calendar
ii	The calendar in Eastern Europe
iii	Early adoption of the Gregorian calendar
iv	The problems with the early Roman calendar
v	Why some countries were late to change their calendars
vi	Priests and the calendar
vii	How the Julian calendar works
viii	The problem with the solar year
ix	Current rules for leap years
x	The development of the Gregorian calendar
xi	The length of a year

Examples	Answer
Paragraph **A**	**xi**

1   Paragraph B   ....

2   Paragraph C   ....

3   Paragraph D   ....

4   Paragraph E   ....

5   Paragraph F   ....

6   Paragraph G   ....

7   Paragraph H   ....

Passage 2 – Calendars Through the Years

A   How many days are there in a year? You might say 365, with an extra 'leap day' added to the end of February every four years. This averages out to a quarter of a day every year, so that every year is 365.25 days. This is because the actual length of a solar year – that is, the time it takes for the Earth to complete a full rotation of the Sun – is a little bit more than 365 days. Throughout history, most calendars have tried to match their year to the length of a solar year, with varying degrees of accuracy.

B   The calendar used in much of the world today is based on the one used by the Romans. Because Romans thought that even numbers were unlucky, the earliest Roman calendar had months of 29 or 31 days, with 28 days in February. Since the year had 355 days, they would add a leap month of 27 days between February and March every 3 to 5 years, as determined by priests called _pontifices_. As a ~Ancient Roman~ result, the average year was anywhere from 360 to 364 days, so it is no surprise that the calendar very quickly deviated from the solar year. ~diverge~

C   Julius Caesar decided that the calendar should be based on the solar year, following a special year of 445 days in 46 BC that readjusted the months to their proper seasons. From 45 BC onwards, the months were given the current lengths of 30 or 31 days, retaining 28 for February but adding the 29th February every four years to account for the accumulated extra quarter days. The names of the months used by the Romans remain in English today, either with a slight adjustment to spelling (e.g., they called it _Aprilis_, we call it April) or in the exact same form (e.g., they also called September, October, November and December by those very names).

D   The calendar used from 45 BC onwards – known as the Julian calendar, after the man who imposed it on the world – is far more accurate than any earlier calendar. Even so, the Julian calendar deviates from the solar year by 1 day every 128 years. This is because the exact length of the solar year is actually 365.2422 days, or about 11 minutes shorter than the 365.25 days calculated by the Romans. ~difference~

E   By the 16th century AD, the discrepancy between the solar year and the Julian calendar was notable enough that something had to be done. It took several decades of consultation among mathematicians and astronomers until it was finally decided to end the Julian calendar, and move to a new system of calculating leap years. Pope Gregory XIII decreed that the Julian calendar would end on Thursday 4th October 1582, and that the following day would be Friday 15th October. This would remove the 10 days that had been added in error by the Julian system for leap years, and readjust the calendar to the seasons in the solar year.

F   The Gregorian calendar was put into use immediately in Italy, Portugal, Spain, Poland and most of France, and in Austria, Hungary and much of Germany in the next few years. However, the new calendar was not implemented by the United Kingdom and its overseas territories, such as the colonies that are known today as Canada and the United States, until 1752. By then, the adjustment required was 11 days, so the Parliament decided that the British would go to bed at the end of the day on 2nd September 1752 and wake up the next morning on 14th September. Sweden followed the British in moving to the Gregorian calendar the next year.

G   An even longer adjustment was required when the Gregorian calendar was adopted by Japan in 1872, and in the early 20th century by China, Bulgaria, Estonia, Russia, Greece and Turkey. Many of these countries that were among the last to adopt the Gregorian calendar for civic purposes used the Byzantine calendar, a variant of the Julian calendar, prior to the change. Many people in these same nations continue to use the Eastern Orthodox calendar (also based on the Julian calendar) for religious feasts and festivals. Similarly, in China and Japan, a traditional calendar is still used to select dates for weddings, funerals and new ventures. These last two countries did not exactly delay the move to the Gregorian calendar; rather, they started using it once it became beneficial, due to the more extensive connections with other countries on that calendar.

H   As we can see from this brief history of calendars, one of the key challenges in making any calendar is the decision about how to account for the variations between the calendar year and the solar year, since the latter includes a fraction of a day. The Gregorian calendar improved considerably on the Julian calendar, limiting the discrepancy to one day every 3,336 years. While it is commonly believed that every fourth year is a leap year, the actual rule imposed in 1582 is slightly more complicated: we add a day to February in years that are divisible by 4, but not in years divisible by 100, unless they can be divided by 400. Thus, 1700, 1800 and 1900 were not leap years, but 1600 and 2000 were. This adjustment means that the average calendar year is only 26 seconds longer than a solar year, so it won't be an issue again until the year 4918.

KAPLAN TIP

A heading describes a paragraph's main idea. Incorrect headings may focus on details that are not the main idea, or they may distort details from the passage.

1. Take 30 seconds to skim the first paragraph. Time yourself. What is the topic sentence of the first paragraph?

   Answer: The topic sentence is very first sentence. Even though it is a question; the rest of the paragraph is the answer – there are slightly more than 365 days in a year. The correct heading is given in the example – it's **xi**, the length of a year. This is what we might have written in our passage map, either *length of a year* or *year = 365 days + a bit*.

2. Take another 30 seconds and skim the second paragraph. What is the topic sentence? Which heading matches Paragraph B?
   Answer: The topic sentence is the first sentence of the paragraph, but the key detail comes in the final sentence – due to the complicated method of determining leap years, the original Roman calendar varied significantly from the actual solar year.

   Which heading matches? Why isn't the answer **viii** (the problem with the solar year)?

   The answer is **iv,** the problems with the early Roman calendar – that's what this paragraph describes in some detail. It's not **viii,** as there isn't actually a problem with the solar year – the problem is how the Roman calendar was different from the solar year.

3. Now, read the rest of the passage in four minutes, from paragraph C to H. Underline the topic sentence of each paragraph, or make a passage map, or do a combination of the two. Time yourself. Select the heading that matches each paragraph as you work through the passage. Once you have finished, check your answers with those in the Answer Key.

4. What is wrong with the paragraphs that weren't used as correct answers? Compare your ideas to those in the Answer Key.

SENTENCE COMPLETION QUESTIONS

Strategies

- Check how many words or numbers you can include in each answer.
- Try to predict what sort of information you will need for each blank.
- Check the wording before and after the blank, to ensure that your answer fits properly.
- Where possible, use your passage map to find the relevant paragraph.

How to Recognise Sentence Completion Questions

The instructions say 'Complete the sentences below.'
Each sentence will include a blank. There is only one blank, even if you can write two or three words.
The instructions tell you how many words you can put in the blank.

Passage 2 – Practice

The questions below accompany the passage on calendars. Follow the guidance below the questions to complete this exercise.

Questions 8–15

Complete the sentences below.

*Write **NO MORE THAN THREE WORDS AND/OR A NUMBER** for each answer.*

8. A solar year is the time it takes for the Earth to make a .... of the sun.

9. Without a .... , the year in the earliest Roman calendar was 355 days long.

10. From 45 BC, the calendar year was based on the solar year, thanks to the intervention of ....

11. Unfortunately, the solar year is .... than the year in the Julian calendar.

12. When Pope Gregory XIII first instituted the new calendar, one change was to .... that were mistakenly added by the Julian calendar.

13. The British used the Gregorian calendar starting in ....

14. Russia and other nations continue to use the .... calendar for religious purposes.

15. Under current rules, years that are .... are not leap years, unless they can also be divided evenly by 400.

1. We will complete the first sentence together. First of all, re-read the instruction for the question.

   a. How many words numbers / go in each blank?

2. Now read incomplete sentence 8 above. Briefly answer the following questions in your book. Finally, compare your answers with the suggestions in the Answer Key.

   b. What clues to the missing information are found in the incomplete sentence?

   c. Which paragraph contains the correct answer?

   d. What words / numbers go in the blank?

3. Now read incomplete sentence 9 above. Briefly answer the following questions. Compare your answers with the suggestions in the Answer Key.

   a. What clues to the missing information are found in the incomplete sentence?

   b. Which paragraph contains the correct answer?

   c. Which words / numbers go in the blank?

4. Complete the rest of the sentences in 6 minutes. Time yourself. Then, check your answers in the Answer Key.

Takeaway

On the IELTS, you will have to read quickly and find the main idea of each paragraph. It is essential to be familiar with the question types, and to use your passage map or the topic sentences in each paragraph to help you find the correct answers.

Think about your answers to the following questions:

What did you learn in this lesson?

What questions do you have about Multiple Choice, Matching Heading and Sentence Completion questions?

Why is it important to be able to skim and make a passage map on Test Day?

IMPROVE YOUR SCORE

Practise by reading magazine articles on academic topics that appear frequently on the IELTS, such as business, science and history. Good reading sources include *The Economist* (www.economist.com), *New Scientist* (www.newscientist.com) and *BBC History Magazine* (www .historyextra.com). Pick an article of passage length (600–900 words) and make a passage map. Time yourself. Practise until you can skim an article of this length and map it out in less than five minutes.

OBJECTIVES

By the end of this chapter, you should be able to:

- Scan a passage for keywords that will help you answer questions.
- Find synonyms or paraphrases for information from the questions in the passage.
- Improve your speed at reading a passage and answering questions.
- Practise strategies for answering True/False/Not Given, Matching Information and Note Completion questions.

Introduction

This lesson provides practice on answering True/False/Not Given questions, as well as practice with Matching Information and Note Completion questions.

True/False/Not Given questions focus on factual information. They ask you to read statements and compare them to the information in a given passage. If the statement relates to the information given in the passage, but the passage does not actually agree or disagree with the statement, you need to select 'Not Given.'

The IELTS uses a wide variety of Matching questions. You may be asked to match pieces of textual or visual information to each other or to sections of a text. In the Academic Training module, these sections will be paragraphs from a single passage. In the General Training module, you might be asked to match pictures or statements.

Note Completion questions usually focus on the main ideas of part or all of a text. They may include headings, subheadings and numbers or bullet points.

TRUE/FALSE/NOT GIVEN QUESTIONS

Strategies

- Understand the meaning of True, False and Not Given.
- The information (for True/False items) appears in the passage in question order. This can help in determining if an item is Not Given.
- Identify keywords from each question, and scan for these keywords in the passage.

How to recognise True/False/Not Given Questions

The instructions ask if the statements agree with the information given in the passage.

You are told to write TRUE, FALSE or NOT GIVEN on your answer sheet.

The answers are found in the passage in question order.

True/False/Not Given Questions are fairly easy to identify, as the instructions say to write TRUE, FALSE or NOT GIVEN on the answer sheet.

Let's review the meaning of the answer choices:

- True: The statement is correct, based on the passage.
- False: The statement is not correct, based on the passage.
- Not Given: You can't tell if the statement is correct or incorrect, because the necessary information is not in the passage.

Passage 1 – Getting Ready to Read

In order to find answers quickly in a text it will be useful to have more practice with synonyms and paraphrasing.

1. Draw a line matching up the word or phrase on the left with the word or phrase on the right that has almost the same meaning. Take 2 minutes to complete this task. Time yourself. The goal is to get good at guessing synonyms and paraphrasing, so don't use a dictionary to help you with your choices. You won't be able to use one on the day of the test!

A	in the evening (8)	1.	characterised	
B	affect (5)	2.	interesting results	
C	fascinating outcomes (2)	3.	extremely worrying	
D	laptops, mobiles and tablets (9)	4.	an increased likelihood	
E	described (1)	5.	impact	
F	very troublesome (3)	6.	speeding up	
G	tricks our biological systems (12)	7.	adequate	
H	accelerating (6)	8.	before bed	
I	contents (10)	9.	electronic devices	
J	very thought-provoking (10)	10.	subject matter	
K	decent (7)	11.	highly mentally stimulating	
L	a greater chance (4)	12.	fools the body	

When you have finished, compare your answers with the Answer Key in the back of this book.

Passage 1 – Practice

Before we attack the questions, we need to review the passage.

1. Take 4 minutes to skim Passage 1 below and make a passage map. Time yourself.

    When you have finished, consider these questions:

    - What is the main idea of each paragraph?
    - What did you put in your passages map?
    - What is the main idea of the entire passage?

Compare your answers to these questions with the answers in the Answer Key.

2. Use your passage map to help you answer the True/False/Not Given questions below the passage.

Passage 1 – Bluebells in Britain

Every April and May, Britain welcomes spring with the blooming of bluebells, which appear in patches large and small across the nation. Indeed, almost half of all native British bluebells (*Hyacinthoides non-scripta*) worldwide are found in the UK. These bluebells, with their distinctive scent and colour, thrive in the damp habitat of British woodlands.

However, the British bluebell is at risk of extinction, and nowhere more than in London specifically and Southeast England generally, from a Spanish invasion. The Spanish bluebell (*Hyacinthoides hispanica*) has spread quickly through British cities in the last few decades, to the point where virtually all bluebells in London are hybrids (*Hyacinthoides x massartiana*) of the two varieties.

Hybridisation is a threat to our native bluebells not only in terms of the sheer number of hybrid flowers in our cities, but also in their appearance, which is very difficult to distinguish from those of the unmixed species, except just after the flowers have opened. At this time, native bluebells will have a distinctively sweet scent, with white pollen and stems leaning to one side; the petals are always a notably deep shade of blue-violet.

Compare this to the Spanish bluebell, which features blue pollen and usually stands upright, with petals ranging in colour from blue to pink to white (but never dark blue). A hybrid of British and Spanish bluebells can combine any features of the two, including colour, with one exception: whilst the petals of hybrids can be dark blue, they can never be the blue-violet of the UK species.

There is some good news for British bluebells: they continue to dominate non-native bluebells by a rate of 100-to-1 nationwide, as the Spanish variety does not grow well in woodland, limiting the risk of hybridisation to urban areas. We should not be complacent, though, as botanists agree that the hybrid bluebell is more common than the Spanish species; thus, it's likely that before long, without intervention, most bluebells in UK cities will show signs of hybridisation.

Questions 1–8

Do the following statements agree with the information given in the reading passage?

Write

TRUE	*if the statement agrees with the information*
FALSE	*if the statement contradicts the information*
NOT GIVEN	*if there is no information on this*

1   Bluebells bloom in Britain in the springtime.

2   Half of all bluebells in the world are found in the UK.

3   British bluebells grow only in woodland.

4   In a few years, the British bluebell will be extinct.

5   Most bluebells in London are Spanish bluebells.

6   Spanish bluebells do not have a distinctive scent.

7   A hybrid bluebell could have white pollen and pink petals.

8   Most hybrid bluebells in the UK are found in forests.

3.   For each True/False/Not Given statement ask yourself:

    a.   What are the key words in the statement?

    b.   Where in the passage you can find the answer (based on the passage map)?

    c.   Which answer is correct (True, False or Not Given) and why?

Let's consider these questions as they relate to statement 1. The keywords are *bloom*, *Britain* and *springtime*. The answer comes in the first paragraph. The first sentence is a close paraphrase of this sentence, so it is TRUE.

Think through the rest of your answers in the same manner, then compare your answers with those in the Answer Key.

KAPLAN TIP

When scanning for keywords, keep an eye out for related words, such as synonyms or paraphrases.

MATCHING INFORMATION QUESTIONS

Strategies

- Do not look at the statements until you have read the passage.
- Use your passage map to help find the relevant information.
- Scan for keywords from each statement – but be sure to check the entire passage for possible matches.

How to Recognise Matching Information Questions

The paragraphs are be labelled with letters, starting with A.

The instructions ask which paragraph contains the following information.

The questions are a list of statements – there are no blanks and no answer choices.

Passage 2 – Practice

1. You are going to skim Passage 2 and make a passage map in 5 minutes or less. Before you begin, you may notice that this passage is very long – it has nine paragraphs, and it is nearly double the length of the previous passage.

With a long passage like this one, you still need to skim the whole passage. However, you may wish to break long passages like this one into sections and passage map the sections instead of individual paragraphs.

2. Take 5 minutes to skim through the text and create a passage map. Time yourself. Stop after 5 minutes whether you have finished or not.

Look at the passage again. If you wanted to divide this long passage into three sections, where would you put the divisions? Compare your answer with the suggestions in the Answer Key.

3. If you can't finish reading (or skimming) the passage in 5 minutes, then you should move into the questions and scan the passage for keywords from the statements. This will be harder to do if you don't have a passage map and haven't looked through the whole passage, so it is important to improve your skimming speed!

> **KAPLAN TIP**
>
> Five minutes is the magic number in terms of time – that leaves you fifteen minutes to answer 13 (or 14) questions AND mark answers on the answer sheet. If you take longer than five minutes, you won't have enough time for the questions – or for recording the answers properly..

Passage 2 – Beware of the Danger to Bees

A In the last 10 years, the number of beekeepers in the UK has increased dramatically. According to the British Beekeeper Association (BBKA), the rise comes amidst growing international concern for the health of the global bee population. In 2007, the UK government proposed a budget cut that would defund the National Bee Unit, a group within the Department for Environment, Food and Rural Affairs that supports British beekeepers and is involved in the management of threats to bees.

B In response to this, the BBKA launched a campaign to save the National Bee Unit, simultaneously drawing attention to the swiftly declining bee population. In the end, the National Bee Unit succeeded in keeping its funding, and the membership of the BBKA more than doubled. There are now around 24,000 amateur beekeepers registered with the association, and that number continues to rise.

C At the same time that there has been an increase in the number of beekeepers in the UK, there has been a decline in the number of bees worldwide. Over the last decade, beekeepers in North America, South America, Europe and Asia have reported huge devastations to the bee populations in their hives. In 2007, former MP Lord Rooker predicted that the honeybee might be extinct in Britain within a decade.

D Perhaps most troubling is the fact that the cause of this rapid decline has been hard to identify. Scientists point to the varroa mite as one explanation. This virus-carrying parasite preys on bees and has been threatening bee populations since the 1960s. Recently, researchers at Harvard University have argued that insecticides may deserve more of the blame. Neonicotinoids, a range of insecticides used by many farms, can be deadly to bees; they exterminated the entire population of bees in one Chinese province in the 1980s, and were an initial suspect in the phenomenon known as 'colony collapse disorder.'

E Colony collapse disorder occurs when all the worker bees from a beehive previously thought to be well-functioning and healthy suddenly disappear. The phenomenon was first observed by scientists and beekeepers in North America in 2006, in which some beekeepers lost up to 90% of their hives. While pesticides were at first believed to have caused the disappearance of the bees, further research has shown that a combination of two infections – a virus and a fungus – are far deadlier for bees than either would be on its own.

F In this study, one hundred percent of collapsed hives were found to have traces of invertebrate iridescent viruses (IIV); however, since these are often found in strong colonies, IIV alone cannot be responsible for colony collapse. A variety of microbes that attack invertebrates were found in most of the collapsed colonies, but most could be eliminated as possible culprits, as they occurred in only a few collapsed hives.

G However, one fungus called Nosema, which consists of a single cell and targets bees specifically, was found in most of the collapsed colonies in the study. Scientists determined that Nosema is not likely to predict the likelihood of collapse when found in an otherwise healthy hive, absent any traces of IIV; conversely, the presence of both Nosema and IIV is a strong indicator of the likelihood of collapse, given the high correlation of the two in collapsed colonies in the study.

H   Declining bee populations are troubling for a multitude of reasons. Bees directly produce items that humans consume in large quantities, such as beeswax and honey. It is the indirect production of bees, however, that would cause the largest devastation. Virtually everything humans eat depends on pollination, and bees are hugely important to the pollination process. Although cross-pollination is achieved in some cases by wind, insects account for a much larger proportion of plant reproduction, and bees are arguably the most prolific agents of pollen transport among insects.

I   If bees go extinct, most fruits and vegetables would die off as well. Animals, such as cows and pigs, who consume plants that reproduce with the help of bees would also be affected. The survival of bees, therefore, is tied to our consumption of beef, pork and dairy. The literal 'fruits of the labour' of bees also often become vital ingredients in important medicines. In short, if bee populations disappear, there will be an immensely detrimental impact on the global economy and life as we know it.

4.   Matching Information questions only occur when the when the paragraphs are labeled with letters; they ask you to identify the paragraph that contains the information in each statement. The question presents a list of statements (rather than questions), with no blanks and no answer choices. Take a moment to look over the list of statements, then continue with the next step below.

Questions 1–7

The reading passage has nine paragraphs labelled A–I. Which paragraph contains the following information?

NB: *You may use any letter more than once.*

1   An explanation of a phenomenon in which bees disappear

2   The impact of bees on other plants and animals

3   The fate of the UK agency that protects bees

4   Some dangers that bees faced in the 20th century

5   Details of the combination of causes that indicate a hive is likely to collapse

6   The global decline in the number of bees

7   A fungus that is a particular threat to bees

5. Look at the first statement above. What are the keywords in the statement? Where in the reading passage above can we find the answer? How did you find it? From the passage map, or scanning for keywords, or both?

6. Let's consider the answer to question 1 together. In this statement, the key words are *bees disappear* and also *explanation*. The phenomenon in which bees disappear is mentioned briefly at the end of Paragraph D, but the explanation of this phenomenon comes in the next paragraph.

7. Go through the rest of the statements in this way. Then compare your answers with the answers in the Answer Key.

KAPLAN TIP

A paragraph may contain the information that matches multiple statements. You must continue checking the entire passage for each statement – including the paragraphs that held the answers to previous statements.

NOTE COMPLETION QUESTIONS

Strategies

- Check how many words or numbers you can include in each answer.
- Try to predict what sort of information you will need for each blank.
- Scan the passage for keywords that appear before or after the blank.
- Check that your answer fits properly.

How to Recognise Note Completion Questions

The instructions ask you to complete the notes.
The notes are organised in some format, often a table or box or bulleted list, with blanks inside.
Some information is already filled in. Use this to help you identify what you are scanning for.

Note Completion Questions are a common type of fill in the gap question. The format can vary; mostly the notes are within a box, which means that they can look quite similar to a table. Indeed, there's not much of a distinction between Note Completion and Table Completion Questions. The notes could also be in a bulleted list.

There will be a clear structure to the notes. Similar to an outline, including many of the ideas from the passage and key supporting points. The notes will always contain the numbered blanks in passage order.

Be sure to check the instructions carefully before you begin. Make sure you are clear about how many words/numbers to write in each blank. You must copy the EXACT words/phrases from the passage in your answer.

Passage 2 – Practice

1. Give yourself 5 minutes to answer the following questions, which accompany Passage 2:

Questions 8–13

Complete the notes below.

*Write **NO MORE THAN THREE WORDS AND/OR A NUMBER** for each answer.*

BEES IN THE UK AND AROUND THE WORLD
In the UK: • A threat to funding for the **8** ....   • Publicity saved the funding and led to growing interest in bees.   • The number of officially registered **9** .... is 24,000, and continues to rise.
Dangers to bees: • Sharp declines in bee populations around the world.   • In 2007, the honeybee was predicted to become extinct in the UK **10** ....   • The major problem is **11** .... , in which all the worker bees in a hive thought to have been healthy are suddenly no longer there.
Possible causes of collapsed hives: • IIV and microbes have been considered, but neither alone is the cause.   • A combination of Nosema, a **12** .... , and IIV indicate a likelihood of collapse.
Consequences of having fewer bees   • Less beeswax and honey   • Difficulty in growing food that depends on bees   • **13** .... may occur by wind, but depends on insects; bees are the most prolific.

2. When you have finished, compare your answers with those in the Answer Key.

Takeaway

On the IELTS, once you have skimmed the passage and made a passage map, you can use the keywords from the questions to help you scan and find correct answers quickly. Scanning for keywords is a valuable skill, as it can help you find answers even when you did not fully read or understand the passage.

IMPROVE YOUR SCORE

Whenever you read articles in a well-written newspaper or magazine, make a list of any words you do not recognise. Be sure to look up the meaning of these words, and note a synonym for each word. Building your vocabulary, and your confidence with unfamiliar words, will boost your performance on Test Day.

OBJECTIVES

By the end of this chapter, you should be able to:

- Find keywords that indicate a positive, negative or neutral tone.
- Identify the views and claims of the writer.
- Practise strategies for answering Matching Sentence Endings, Yes/No/Not Given and Summary Completion questions.

Introduction

This chapter provides further practice scanning for keywords, finding synonyms and paraphrasing. You will practise identifying positive/negative tone and identifying views and claims. You will also practise strategies for doing Matching Sentence Endings questions, Yes/No/Not Given questions, and Summary Completion questions.

In Matching Sentence Endings questions, you must use keywords from the unfinished sentences to find relevant detail, then find the sentence ending in the box that matches the detail. Look out for synonyms and paraphrases. You must also ensure that the sentence ending fits within the structure of the sentence, in terms of grammar as well as meaning.

In Yes/No/Not Given questions, you need to decide whether the statement agrees with or contradicts the writer's opinions, or whether there is no information relating to the statement in the passage. Many passages include the writer's views or claims (opinions) on a topic as well as providing factual information.

Finally, Summary Completion questions reflect the order of information in a text. The sentences will focus on key information from part or all of the passage. There are two types of Summary Completion tasks. You may be asked to complete a summary by taking words directly from the text or by choosing from a list of options.

MATCHING SENTENCE ENDINGS QUESTIONS

Strategies

- Scan the passage for keywords from each unfinished sentence.
- Check the box for any answers that match the information that you find in the passage.
- Look out for synonyms and paraphrases.
- Check the full list of sentence endings to ensure you don't miss out one that comes later.

How to Recognise Matching Sentence Endings Questions

The instructions say to complete the sentences, but there aren't blanks in the sentences. There is a numbered list of unfinished sentences, followed by a box of phrases with letters.

The instructions say to complete each sentence with the correct ending from the box.

Passage 1 – Getting Ready to Read

To begin with, you will practise determining whether a word has a positive or negative tone. This can help when are not sure of the exact meaning of a word.

1. Look at the following list of words. Give yourself 3 minutes to look through the list and decide whether each word is positive or negative. Note your choice on the page by placing a + or − sign beside each word.

incapable	straightforward
innovative	accommodating
dynamic	isolated
exploitative	misinterpret
forthcoming	rational
ignorant	unmotivated

2. Compare your answers with those in the Answer Key.

Passage 1 – Practice

Matching Sentence Endings Questions are fairly easy to identify, as the instructions say to complete the sentences, and there are no blanks in the sentences (as there would be for Sentence Completion Questions).

1. Before you attack the questions, skim the passage about Newton and Leibniz below. Take 4 minutes and make a passage map. Time yourself.

2. Before comparing your passage map to the one in the Answer Key, consider the following questions:

   a. What is the main idea of each paragraph?

   b. What did you put in your passage map?

   c. What is the main idea of the passage?

Passage 1 – Who Discovered Calculus – Newton or Leibniz?

Born in 1643 in Lincolnshire, Isaac Newton is best known for his contribution to physics, as he was the first to define many of the fundamental concepts that form the basis of this field. Newton pioneered the study of optics, the properties of light detectable by the human eye, with his insight that white light is made up of the same spectrum of colour as a rainbow. Newton was also the first to demonstrate that gravity was a universal physical force, applied to everything in the universe, in his groundbreaking 1687 study, *Mathematical Principles of Natural Philosophy*. Newton furthered the study of physics in this same work by explaining the three fundamental laws of classical mechanics for the first time. Newton always wrote in Latin, as this was the accepted scientific language of the time.

Following from insights developed by mathematicians over several centuries, Isaac Newton was the first to elucidate the fundamental theorem of calculus and the first to explore differential calculus, as well as its relation to integral calculus. Newton originally developed these concepts of calculus in a 1666 treatise that was not published in full until 1704.

There are two reasons that Newton's discovery of calculus remained unknown for so long. First, publishers in the 17th century were wary of texts in the field of theoretical maths, which were so unprofitable that they drove one specialist publisher to bankruptcy. Second, Newton was extremely tight-lipped about his highly original work in 'the method of fluxions and fluents' (as he called calculus), not mentioning it in print until a brief reference in *Mathematical Principles of Natural Philosophy*. What Newton called a fluxion is known today as a derivative of a function, one of the basic concepts of calculus. A derivative describes the way that the slope of a function changes over time, so it is focused on the differences in the graph of the function. This approach is known today as differential calculus.

After commencing study of differential calculus in the 1670s, Gottfried Leibniz, a German mathematician, developed many of the principles of calculus independently of Newton, and was initially given credit for its discovery, with a 1684 publication. Leibniz's work was very analytical, whereas Newton's was more geometrical. Leibniz focused on sequences of extremely similar values, which could then be integrated (added up) to find, for example, the area under the graph of a function. Integral calculus, as the approach developed by Leibniz is now known, is concerned with describing these small portions of the graph of a function.

However, it's not clear that Newton and Leibniz worked entirely independently, as they had many of the same friends (fellow mathematicians), and occasionally wrote to each other. Thus, it's possible that the two men were aware of each other's work, at the very least. Calculus as studied and applied today is more similar to the method developed by Leibniz, but Newton's work forms an essential part of calculus. Both men worked tirelessly at calculating infinitely small amounts, and our approach today – whether with the differential or the integral – starts with an understanding of the limits of maths, just as it did for them.

Questions 1–7

*Complete each sentence with the correct ending, **A–J**.*

1 The study of optics began from the insight that white light consists of

2 Newton's works are written in Latin because

3 Newton wrote up his discovery of calculus in 1666, but

4 In the 17th century, books of maths theory were not favoured by publishers because

5 Today, we know that a derivative of a function is

6 Leibniz's approach, now known as integral calculus, focused on analysing

7 Just like Leibniz and Newton, we come to calculus by starting from

A	one of the basic concepts of calculus.
B	it was a universal physical force.
C	it was not published until nearly 40 years later.
D	the same spectrum of colour as a rainbow.
E	the three fundamental laws of classical mechanics.
F	small portions of the graph of a function.
G	a brief reference in *Mathematical Principles of Natural Philosophy*.
H	it was very difficult to make any money from them.
I	it was the language used for science in that era.
J	an understanding of the limits of maths.

3. Review your answers, considering the following questions: What are the keywords in the first half of the sentence? Which statement in the text do these keywords lead to? Where is this information located?

In question 1, the keywords in the first half of the sentence are *optics* and *white light*. These keywords lead to the second sentence of the first paragraph. Newton saw that white light is made up of the same spectrum of colour as a rainbow. Answer **D** is therefore correct.

4. Work through questions 2 through 7 in a similar manner. Then compare your answers with those in the Answer Key.

KAPLAN TIP

Check the final words of the unfinished sentence, and compare to the first words of the possible endings. You can usually tell whether the ending should start with a verb or a noun – this will often be sufficient to eliminate most of the options.

YES/NO/NOT GIVEN QUESTIONS

Strategies

- Understand the meaning of Yes, No and Not Given.
- The information (for Yes/No items) appears in the passage in question order. This can help in determining if an item is Not Given.
- Identify keywords from each question, and scan for these keywords in the passage.

How to Recognise Yes/No/Not Given Questions

The instructions ask if the statements agree with the information given in the passage.
You are told to write YES, NO or NOT GIVEN on your answer sheet.
The answers are found in the passage in question order.

Passage 2 – Getting Ready to Read

1. Yes/No/Not Given questions require you to identify views or claims of the writer. Let's think about the following questions. Compare your thoughts with the suggested answers in the Answer Key.

   What is a view?

   What is a claim?

   What is the difference between a view and a claim?

2. Do you think the following statements are views or claims? Mark each statement as either a view or a claim. Then, compare your ideas with those in the Answer Key.

Statement	View	Claim
1. Your father is completely out of order.		
2. In the last few years, each summer has been longer and hotter than the one before.		
3. Henry VIII was interested in sport, but he did little as king to support artists and writers.		
4. The Royal Parks of London are a welcome breath of woodland in the heart of the congested city.		
5. We have found eight planets so far, but no one knows for sure exactly how many planets there are in our solar system.		
6. Van Gogh's *Starry Night* is composed with bold colours and simple brush strokes, and yet it is so deeply beautiful and moving.		
7. You get the best view of Scotland by visiting its castles.		
8. Chocolate ice cream tastes better than vanilla.		
9. More people prefer chocolate ice cream than any other flavour.		
10. My surname is relatively uncommon.		

Passage 2 – Practice

1. Before you answer the Yes/No/Not Given Questions, skim the reading passage below and make a passage map. Allow yourself 5 minutes to skim and make your notes. Because it is a long passage, you may wish to break some or all of the passage into sections, rather than making specific notes for each paragraph.

Compare your passage map with the example found in the Answer Key.

2. Yes/No/Not Given questions are fairly straightforward to identify, as the instructions say to write YES, NO or NOT GIVEN on the answer sheet. Let's review the meaning of each of these choices:

YES	*The statement agrees with the views or claims of the writer.*
NO	*The statement does not agree with the views or claims of the writer.*
NOT GIVEN	*The writer does not express a view or claim on this topic.*

Passage 2 – Bring Up the Bodies: Richard III and the Princes in the Tower

In 1483, King Edward IV died, leaving two sons, aged twelve and nine. The elder boy became King Edward V, with his uncle, Richard of Gloucester, as Protector. Richard soon deposed his nephew, installing himself as King Richard III and sending the young princes to the Tower of London. The princes were never seen alive again. Bones now accepted to be those of the princes were found at the Tower in 1674, and medical tests in 1933 showed that they likely died of suffocation. In Shakespeare's play *Richard III*, Richard organises the murder of the young princes, as they are the last obstacle (and the final victims) standing between him and the throne.

But did Richard III in fact order the deaths of the young princes? Shakespeare's play depicts Richard as sending James Tyrrell to kill the boys; in real life, Tyrrell did confess to the murders while imprisoned in the Tower during the reign of King Henry VII, who took the throne after Richard died in battle in 1485. However, Tyrrell's confession is the only direct evidence against Richard, and the confession was given under torture. Furthermore, Tyrrell was unable to locate the bodies of the princes – a fact he would presumably know had he killed them. Discrediting Tyrrell's confession – the key evidence against Richard – as unreliable, a 1997 'trial' at the Indiana University School of Law found Richard 'not guilty' of the princes' murder. This verdict itself does not prove Richard's innocence, but rather the ongoing fascination with the fate of the princes.

Most people think of Richard as a craven and unrelenting murderer, sending numerous enemies to their deaths, because of Shakespeare's play. But this horrific view of Richard ultimately traces back to 1557, nearly forty years before Shakespeare wrote his drama, when Thomas More depicted Richard very harshly in a book far too coloured by the politics of its day to be of historical value. More was heavily influenced by his role in the court of King Henry VIII, a descendant of Henry VII, the first Tudor king, who vanquished Richard III and ended many years of conflict between the houses of York (Richard III's family) and

Lancaster (Richard III's enemies), known as the Wars of the Roses. Living under the Tudors, it was easy to look back at the Wars of the Roses – nearly 100 years earlier – as a time of political strife and unnecessary brutality, and thus to cast Richard III as a prominent villain of his day. The popularity of these views in Shakespeare's day says more about the politics of the 1500s than the historical realities of the 1400s.

In any case, historians agree that Richard was responsible for the murder of the princes. They point out that, by the end of 1483, the princes were widely rumoured to be dead. As their protector, Richard might have brought out the boys to prove they were alive, but he took no such action; indeed, he never mentioned the boys publicly after they were sent to the Tower. In later years, a number of pretenders came forward, claiming to be the younger boy, also called Richard. But there is no evidence of any pretenders claiming to be Edward V, so it is safe to conclude that people widely assumed he was dead.

After taking the crown, Richard III ruled England for less than two years. He was an unpopular monarch, and his reign soon broke down into civil war. Richard was killed in 1485 at the Battle of Bosworth and buried at Greyfriars Franciscan friary, in what is now Leicester. Richard's death on the battlefield is famously, and relatively accurately, shown at the end of Shakespeare's play, as Richard bemoans the loss of 'my kingdom for a horse.' In fact, Richard III was the last English king to die in battle.

For centuries, the exact location of Richard's body was unknown, as the Greyfriars friary had long since disappeared. In 2012, an archaeological dig beneath a Leicester car park uncovered remains believed to be those of Richard III. The bones, which show evidence of wounds sustained in combat, were found in what would have been the choir area of the friary. The excavation was organised and funded by Philippa Langley, a longtime Richard III aficionado who believes that Richard III's character was unfairly maligned by Shakespeare. Using historical records of the friary, Langley and the team worked out the exact spot in the car park where Richard III was likely to have been buried. Amazingly, within an hour of digging in this very spot, the archaeologists had found the first of Richard III's bones. They had not expected to find anything, let alone on their first effort at excavation.

The skeleton, later confirmed by DNA evidence and radiocarbon dating tests to be Richard III, could contribute significantly to what is known of this controversial king. Most significantly, the remains have refuted Shakespeare's claim that Richard III was a hunchback. Instead, the skeleton found in Leicester suggests that the king instead suffered from severe scoliosis, which would have made his right shoulder appear higher than his left. On this detail, Richard's remains are consistent with many contemporary descriptions of him during his reign.

This discovery has also sparked a movement to rehabilitate the monarch's image. Langley and fellow supporters of Richard III have long protested that his reputation was tarnished by Shakespeare. Now that Richard III's remains have been found, there is a wider movement to restore Richard III to his rightful place among English kings. Perhaps unique among monarchs, Richard III never had a state funeral; his supporters have called for a funeral befitting a king, followed by reburial at Westminster Abbey. However, there is an equally vocal movement to deny this honour to the historically decisive ruler.

As a result, Richard III will be reinterred inside Leicester Cathedral, close to where he was originally laid to rest.

Questions 1–7

Do the following statements agree with the views or claims of the writer in the reading passage?

Write

YES	if the statement agrees with the views or claims of the writer.
NO	if the statement contradicts the claims of the writer.
NOT GIVEN	if it is impossible to say what the writer thinks about this.

1   The remains of the young princes were found at the Tower of London in the 17th century.

2   In 1997, a trial in Indiana determined that Richard III was not guilty of murdering the princes.

3   The Tudors were more political than the Yorks and the Lancasters.

4   It was commonly thought that Edward V was not alive.

5   Everyone expected to find the remains of Richard III in the car park.

6   Shakespeare was correct to depict Richard III as a hunchback.

7   Richard III should have a state funeral at Westminster Abbey.

3. Consider your answer to question 1. What are the keywords in this statement? Where in the passage can we find the answer? Is the statement a view or a claim?

Let's work through the first question together. The keywords in question 1 are young princes, Tower of London and 17th Century. These lead to the first paragraph, where the year 1674 is mentioned; that's when the bones now accepted as those of the princes were found in the Tower. Thus, there is a view on this passage, and the writer agrees – the answer is therefore YES.

4. Consider the rest of your answers in this manner. Then compare your ideas about each statement with those in the Answer Key.

KAPLAN TIP

Remember the nature of the task in Yes/No/Not Given questions. If the writer expresses a view or makes a claim on that topic, the answer is Yes or No. Not Given is only correct if the writer does not express a view or make a claim on the topic.

SUMMARY COMPLETION QUESTIONS

Strategies

- If there is a box: Take a moment to look over the choices before you start work on the summary.
- If there isn't a box: Check how many words or numbers you can include in each answer.
- Try to predict what sort of information you will need for each blank.
- Scan the passage for keywords that come before or after each blank.

How to Recognise Summary Completion Questions

The instructions ask you to complete the summary.

A summary may contain one or more paragraphs, with blanks included in some of the sentences.

There may be a box, containing a series of answer choices to complete the blanks.

Summary Completion questions are a common type of fill-in question. The summary itself will be a paragraph or several paragraphs, with fill-in blanks included. Most commonly, you will have to write words / numbers in the blanks.

Some Summary Completion questions will come with a box containing answer choices, as we see in the questions below. In this format, you should look over the choices briefly before you work on the summary.

Put an X next to each choice, or cross out the letter, once you have used it in the summary.

Passage 2 – Practice

1. Take 30 seconds to look over the choices in the box below. Ask yourself the following questions:

   a. What types of words do you see here?

   b. Which choices are nouns? Verbs? Adjectives?

   c. Which choices could be more than one part of speech, depending on the context?

Compare your answers to the above questions to the ideas in the Answer Key.

2. Take 5 minutes to complete the questions, which accompany Passage 2. Time yourself.

Questions 8–13

*Complete the summary below. Select a word from the box, **A–J**, for each blank.*

A	torture
B	controversial
C	concluded
D	tarnish
E	influenced
F	monarchy
G	suffocated
H	rehabilitate
I	contemporary
J	combat

Richard III became king of England after deposing his young nephew, and sending the prince and his younger brother to the Tower of London. The princes were never seen alive again, and later medical tests revealed that the princes had been **8** .... to death. James Tyrrell admitted to killing the boys, but he only confessed after being subjected to **9** .... , and was unable to say where the princes' bodies could be found. Shakespeare's play depicts Richard III as sending Tyrrell to murder the princes, but Shakespeare's view originated in the work of Thomas More, who was **10** .... by Tudor politics; the Tudors defeated Richard III and ended the Wars of the Roses.

In 2012, the remains of Richard III were found beneath a car park in Leicester. His bones indicated that he was wounded in **11** .... Richard's skeleton added much to what we know about the **12** .... king, including the fact that he was not a hunchback, but likely had scoliosis, with one shoulder higher than the other. Following this discovery, some people have moved to **13** .... the image of Richard III, arguing that his reputation was damaged by Shakespeare. These supporters of Richard III want him to be reburied at Westminster Abbey. However, another movement is just as strongly opposed to any honours for this long-lost monarch.

3.   When you have finished, review your answers. For each answer, identify the relevant support in the passage and how you found the answer. Finally, compare your ideas and answers with those found in the Answer Key.

Takeaway

On the IELTS, some questions will require you to identify views and claims. Finding positive and negative words is hugely helpful for these questions, and can help as well when there are vocabulary words you do not know, or whose exact meaning you do not recall.

IMPROVE YOUR SCORE

Build your vocabulary by reading novels in English. To get ideas, search for a high school reading list (USA) or GCSE reading list (UK). These lists will include novels that are accessible to a broad audience, yet also written to a high standard. As you read, make a list of any words you do not know, and be sure to look them up in the dictionary.

OBJECTIVES

By the end of this chapter, you should be able to:

- Identify the word types that belong in each blank.
- Read a passage and answer all its questions in 20 minutes.
- Practise strategies for answering Diagram Labelling, Short Answer and Matching Features Questions.

Introduction

This chapter provides further practice identifying word types, skimming and mapping passages, and answering specific question types. You will practise answering Diagram Labelling questions, Short Answer questions and Matching Feature questions.

Passages that describe mechanical devices or processes may include Diagram Labelling questions. This type of question requires you to read the paragraphs carefully and study the diagram at the same time. Some labels may already be provided to help you.

Short Answer questions usually focus on factual information. The questions reflect the order of information in the text, but the answers may be widely spaced in the text, so you need to use keywords in the questions to help you scan the text quickly. You must not change the form of words or use different words – the answers must come directly from the passage.

Most commonly, the 'features' in Matching Features questions are a list of names that appear in the passage, such as researchers, scientists, or experts. The questions will be a list of statements, and you must match the 'feature' that goes with statement. So if the features are experts, then you would identify the expert associated with each statement in the passage.

DIAGRAM LABELLING QUESTIONS

Strategies

- Look over the diagram and check the order of the numbered blanks.
- Find the part of the passage that contains the information needed to fill in the blanks.
- Check that you are using the correct words, and the correct number of words, for each blank.

How to Recognise Diagram Labelling Questions

There is a diagram or illustration, containing a series of numbered blanks.
The blanks may appear through any part of the diagram, in any order.
The correct answers will appear in the passage in numbered order.

SHORT ANSWER QUESTIONS

Strategies

- Check how many words or numbers you can include in each answer.
- Use keywords from the question to find the information in the passage.
- Omit words such as articles and auxiliary verbs (in most cases), as they may put you over the word count.

How to Recognise Short Answer Questions

The question has a blank after the question mark, or there is a question without a blank. The instructions say 'Answer the questions' (rather than 'Complete the sentences'). The instructions may ask you to list two or three points. Each will be a separate answer.

Passage 1 – Getting Ready to Read

1. Look at the list of words below. Take 5 minutes and identify the type of each word – e.g. noun, verb, adjective, adverb, etc. Time yourself. Each word may belong to more than one type, depending on the context – include all possible types for each word. When the time is up, compare your answers with those in the Answer Key.

1. current	**7.** tense
2. focus	**8.** highlight
3. temporary	**9.** radical
4. practice	**10.** analysis
5. fundamental	**11.** involved
6. likewise	**12.** acquire

2. Look again at the last three words on the list and answer the following questions. Then compare your answers with those in the Answer Key.

    a. What's the verb form of analysis?

    b. What's the noun form of involved?

    c. What's the noun form of acquire?

Passage 1 – Practice

One challenge with Diagram Labelling questions is that numbered blanks may appear anywhere within the diagram. Therefore, you will need to check the numbers and move through the blanks in that order so you can find the relevant information most efficiently. Remember, correct answers will appear in the passage in the numbered order.

1. Before you attack the questions, skim the passage about Pluto and the Kuiper Belt below. Take 4 minutes and make a passage map. Time yourself.

Passage 1 – Pluto and the Kuiper Belt

Pluto was considered the Solar System's ninth planet, and the furthest from the Sun, from the time of its discovery in 1930 until 2006, when the International Astronomical Union (IAU) voted to define *planet* for the first time. According to this definition, a planet has three characteristics: it must orbit the Sun, be of approximately round shape and have 'cleared its neighbourhood' – that is, it must be the only body of its size, other than its own satellites, in its region of outer space.

Because its orbit, which is eccentrically elliptical compared to those of the other planets, overlaps significantly with the orbit of Neptune – its nearest neighbouring planet in the Solar System – Pluto fails to meet the third criterion of the definition, and so it is no longer considered a planet, but instead a 'dwarf planet.' This decision by the IAU caused considerable controversy in the popular press at the time it was taken, due to the fact that generations of children had learnt in school that the Solar System includes nine planets; people often have difficulty facing reality when further scientific discovery complicates what they had previously thought to be settled, definite fact.

The IAU's decision to change Pluto's designation from planet to dwarf planet was not taken lightly, and became necessary due to the discovery of a number of objects in the Kuiper Belt. The Kuiper Belt is an asteroid belt that starts just outside the orbit of Neptune, and is thought to contain more than 70,000 objects, with 35,000 of these that are more than 100 kilometres in diameter. The Kuiper Belt covers a massive distance – it is 2.9 billion km wide, and its most distant point is 7.4 billion km from the Sun. Scientists believe there may be a further asteroid belt beyond the Kuiper Belt, named the Oort Cloud, which is thought to contain more than a trillion comets.

A space object discovered in the Kuiper Belt in 2003 and since named Eris (after the ancient Greek goddess of discord) has a greater diameter than Pluto, with 25% more mass; both Pluto and Eris are thought to consist of the same mixture of ice and rock. Scientists could not justify calling Pluto a planet and Eris a Kuiper Belt object; since Eris was larger than Pluto, why shouldn't it also be a planet?

The matter was further complicated by the fact that a second Kuiper Belt object, Makemake, discovered in 2005, is only slightly smaller than Pluto. Due to their significantly smaller mass and their resulting weaker gravitational pull, dwarf planets such as Pluto, Eris and Makemake are unable to clear other nearby space objects – either by repelling them, or by colliding and absorbing much of their mass, and thus growing larger and increasing their gravitational pull – and so are unlikely ever to become planets.

For these reasons, the IAU considered three options for defining planets at its meeting in 2006: the first would have increased the number of known planets to 12, keeping Pluto and adding Eris, Makemake and Ceres, long-known as the Solar System's largest asteroid; the second would have defined a planet as being one of the nine planets discovered as of 1930; the third was the definition ultimately approved.

Despite popular sentiment, scientists could not justify defining planets according to what was already known, as ongoing improvements in technology continue to allow us to observe the deepest reaches of the Solar System with increasing accuracy. The major problem with the first definition is that its broad nature could allow for an astonishing number of planets, once the expanse of the Kuiper Belt is further explored. NASA launched a spacecraft, New Horizons, in 2006 that will explore Pluto, its moons and the Kuiper Belt, where it will spend 5 to 10 years and send the first images of the many large objects in this faraway region of the Solar System.

Questions 1–6

Label the diagram below.

Write **NO MORE THAN TWO WORDS AND/OR A NUMBER** *for each answer.*

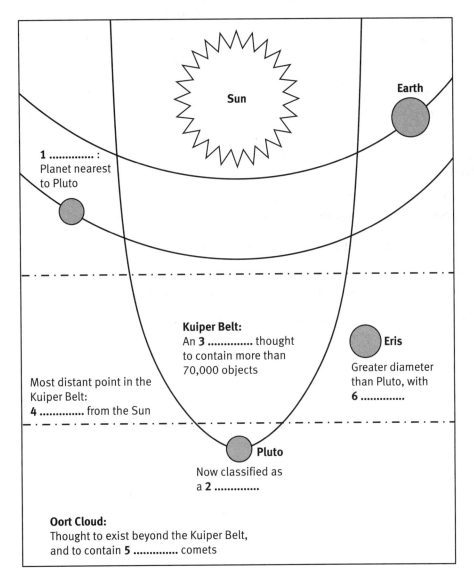

2. Let's work through the first Diagram Labelling question together. Where in the passage can we find the answer? Use your passage map, or scan for keywords, or both! What are the keywords that could be used to scan for each statement?

In Question 1, the keywords are *planet* and *nearest* to Pluto. These lead to the second paragraph, which states that Neptune is Pluto's nearest neighbour planet in the Solar System. Thus, the answer is Neptune.

3. Take 5 minutes and complete Questions 2–6 in the same way. Then, check your answers in the Answer Key.

The key with Short Answer Questions is to keep track of the number of words allowed for each answer, and to ensure your answers are not too long.

Use keywords from the question to help you find the information in the passage – either scan for keywords, or check the keywords against your passage map.

4. Take 5 minutes and complete the Short Answer Questions (Questions 7–10) below. Time yourself. When you finish, compare your answers to those found in the Answer Key.

Questions 7–10

Answer the questions below.

*Write **NO MORE THAN TWO WORDS** for each answer.*

7. What did the IAU vote to do for the first time in 2006? ....

8. What is the shape of Pluto's orbit? ....

9. What about Pluto and Makemake is weaker than it is for planets? ....

10. What will send images from the Kuiper Belt? ....

KAPLAN TIP

The answers for Short Answer questions are words in the reading passage. If you find there are too many words in the passage for the number of words allowed, check if you can leave out an article (the, a, an) or an auxiliary verb. Also, ensure that your answer gives enough words from the passage to answer the question.

Passage 2 – Practice

This final set will give you timed practice on a full Reading passage, including all 13 questions. You must try to complete this set in 20 minutes, just as you will have to on Test Day.

You will put into practice everything you have learned so far. This means you should aim to finish reading the passage and making a passage map in 5 minutes, then try to answer each question in one minute or less. This should leave you a couple of minutes at the end to check your work or transfer answers to the answer sheet.

1. Take 5 minutes to read and make a passage map for the passage below. Time yourself. If you do not create a passage map, be sure to underline keywords or the main idea of each paragraph.

2. Answer questions 1–5. For each question, quickly identify the paragraph the answer comes from and which answer is correct.

3. Answer questions 6–9. Identify the paragraph in the passage where each answer is found.

4. Answer questions 10–13. This is an example of a Summary Completion set that does not have a box.

5. When you have finished all 13 questions, compare your answers with those in the Answer Key.

Passage 2 – Changing Office Culture

In an article for the *Harvard Business Review*, John Coleman recently set out to understand the dynamics and importance of workplace culture. Coleman cites research that the culture of a firm 'can account for 20-30% of the differential in corporate performance when compared with "culturally unremarkable" competitors.' The culture of a workplace is not to be treated as incidental, then: it is fundamental to the performance of any business. Coleman identifies six elements that he sees as influencing the development and success of a workplace culture: vision, values, practices, people, narrative and place. 'Place' refers to the built environments in which people work and suggests that these have a huge impact on the way we work. Indeed, some organisations intentionally design open-planned offices so that individuals overhear one another conversations and are forced to run into one another regularly in order to encourage better collaboration between colleagues.

Chuck Cohn, CEO of Varsity Tutors, agrees that a strong corporate culture proceeds from a clear articulation by those at the top of an organisation of what the company stands for and what its vision is. Once this vision is clearly communicated, Cohn suggests, it is critical to have openness and accountability run throughout the organisation in order to maintain adherence to the stated goal. As time goes on and as a company grows, it will be necessary to invest in maintaining and renewing its culture accordingly. Above all, it is important for companies to take time in hiring people who will fit in well within the organisation's culture and who share similar values and modes of working. If you don't take deliberate actions to shape the culture of a firm, Ben Horowitz says, it will take shape by itself and you will lose control of one of your business's most valuable assets.

Jim Whitehurst of Red Hat sees 'meritocracy' as the key to a successful workplace culture. For Whitehurst, meritocracy means that everyone in an organisation is allowed to express their opinions and views freely with decisions being made on the basis of which of these views are best. It is now taken for granted that meritocracy in the workplace is a good thing: companies are quick to emphasise the importance they place on meritocracy when recruiting more junior members of the team, sending the message that, irrespective of your age and experience if you are capable you will ascend the organisation quickly. This is ironic, of course, since the term was initially coined as something of an insult. Michael Young invented the word in his 1958 book *The Rise of the Meritocracy* to satirically describe a United Kingdom governed by a culture favouring merit and intelligence more than anything else, even more than past achievements. Young looked unfavourably on such a culture, as in his view a meritocracy entrenches the powerful by limiting the educational and other opportunities of the lower classes.

Workplaces the world over have undergone a number of fundamental and dramatic shifts in recent years as a result of changes in attitudes to work and technological advancements. For example, it used to be that business was conducted face to face. Be it board meetings, client meetings or brainstorming sessions; all used to be done in the same office building. The internet and mobile communications revolutions have changed this and mean that some 79 per cent of workers are now part of virtual teams – conducting some (if not all) of their day to day business via social networking sites and online video conferencing services.

Some feel that mobile communications have blurred the lines between home life and work life. Possession of an iPhone or Blackberry for work means that you are deemed always contactable by your employer at any time of the day and therefore intrusions into your personal life have become more frequent. Others, however, see developments differently. Managed properly greater connectivity can mean more, not less, time spent at home with your family and loved ones. Business conference calls across time zones no longer need to be undertaken in the office; they can be done at home over the internet. While this flexible use of technology is generally beneficial to employees, it can also result in over-working, so it is important for companies to ensure that their practices regarding technology fit with their values. As Coleman argues, a company's values do not make much of a difference unless they are fully integrated into a company's everyday practices.

Some of the most profitable and high profile technology companies are investing millions and millions of dollars in making sure that they are harnessing all kinds of technological developments to ensure that they are attracting and retaining the very best talent. In a highly controversial move, Facebook and Apple recently offered their female employees up to $20,000 to pay for the option of having their eggs frozen in order to shield their female employees from making the traditional choice between work and motherhood. Now, they can become mothers later on in life and enjoy career advancement in the meantime.

Some have praised the move, saying that egg freezing gives women more control. Senior marketing executive Jennifer Tye said, 'When I turned 30, I had this notion that my biological clock was ticking, but I didn't know what my options were. These employers should be commended.' Others, however, see it differently – accusing the technology giants of attempting to 'play God' with one of the most important and intimate decision of a person's life. Writing in the *Daily Telegraph*, obstetrics and gynaecology registrar

Dr Irene Gafson voiced alarm at the lack of attention that has been paid to the medical facts. According to the evidence, Gafson explained, there is no guarantee that freezing of eggs will result in a live birth of a baby. According to the figures from the Human Fertilisation and Embryology Authority, there is a 12.5 per cent chance that a woman will have a child after undergoing a cycle of frozen egg IVF treatment. Thus, Gafson concludes, the tech giants are offering a benefit that is at best uncertain. As an alternative, she suggests freezing embryos, which have a much higher rate of resulting in a live birth after being unfrozen than an unfertilised egg.

Questions 1–5

Look at the following statements (Questions 1–5) and the list of people below.

*Match each statement with the correct person, **A, B, C** or **D**.*

***NB** You may use any letter more than once.*

A	Dr Irene Gafson
B	John Coleman
C	Michael Young
D	Chuck Cohn

1   Office culture can account for a significant proportion of a business's success or failure.

2   A company needs transparency and accountability at all levels if it is to reach its goals.

3   A meritocracy protects the position of the upper classes by controlling educational opportunities.

4   A company's day-to-day practices should fully reflect its values.

5   Women cannot rely on frozen eggs to result in the birth of a baby.

KAPLAN TIP

Each set of Matching Features questions will be given in passage order. Thus, the information corresponding to the first question will appear before the information corresponding to the second question, and so forth. Use this knowledge to help you when you have difficulty scanning for the information in the passage.

Questions 6–9

Choose the correct answer: A, B or C.

6 According to the passage, office architecture can result in

  A increased interactions with work colleagues.

  B little difference in the way we work.

  C a 30% change in corporate performance.

7 Ben Horowitz would agree that business that fail to set out a clear vision for their firm

  A can trust their employees to develop the correct vision.

  B will lose control of a precious asset.

  C will find that all their values have been compromised.

8 Why does the writer mention '79 per cent of workers' in the fourth paragraph?

  A to illustrate the prevalence of virtual working

  B to show why office buildings are no longer necessary

  C to explain a dangerous consequence of the internet revolution

9 Why are some companies offering to pay female employees to freeze their eggs?

  A to keep them from leaving for another job elsewhere

  B to encourage them to have children sooner rather than later

  C to protect them from a difficult decision

Questions 10–13

Complete the summary below.

*Write **NO MORE THAN THREE WORDS AND/OR A NUMBER** for each answer.*

In a recent article, John Coleman discussed six elements that are essential to the office culture of a successful business. These include vision, values, practices, people, **10** .... and place. It is essential for a company to set out a clear vision and, as the business grows, to ensure that it invests in **11** .... and renewing its culture. Thanks to technological advancements, there are fewer face-to-face meetings and **12** .... sessions; nowadays, many of these interactions take place online. Technology is also helping many of the largest companies in that sector to recruit and retain the strongest possible **13** .... This can include flexible working arrangements and other benefits; some companies are even paying for their women workers to delay having children by freezing their eggs.

Takeaway

On IELTS Test Day you must be prepared to skim each passage in 5 minutes or less, so that you will have enough time to answer the questions. You should also aim to spend no more than 1 minute on each question. Any longer and you will risk running out of time.

IMPROVE YOUR SCORE

As you prepare for Test Day, time yourself strictly in your Reading practice. You should aim to finish skim reading the passage and making a passage map in about 5 minutes, so you will have 15 minutes to answer the questions. This will allow about a minute per question, which should be sufficient to find the answers in the passage, using your passage map and your scanning skills.

READING ANSWER KEY

Reading Chapter 1

Passage 1

Getting Ready to Read

2 A   *Answers will vary.* It's a short passage, so you should aim to read it in 3–4 minutes.

B   By 'skimming' – reading quickly, for the main idea in each paragraph – you should be able to skim the passage AND complete a passage map in 4 minutes. That's about 1 minute to skim, and map, each paragraph.

Making a Passage Map

1   P. 1: geography of the isles

P. 2: agriculture, then and now

P. 3: tourism = main industry

P. 4: tourism = political problems

2 A   *Answers will vary.* Note how concise our passage map is!

B   You only need a few words for each paragraph, to give a sense of the main ideas covered there. You need to practise 'boiling it down' to the minimum words required to make a note of these main ideas. The more you practise, the easier it will be to make a passage map quickly and effectively.

Passage 1 Answers

3 C   The second paragraph discusses agriculture on the islands.

Today, the islands are well known for their flowers, particularly daffodils, which are their chief agricultural product.

The correct answer is therefore C.

As for the other answers: The final sentence of the second paragraph says that fishing is a popular pastime, but not a significant source of income. The same paragraph says that the islanders used to raise their own livestock, but things have changed. Thus, A and B are not supported by the passage.

4 B   Houses in the Isles of Scilly are mentioned in the final paragraph.

Houses in the Isles of Scilly are on average £5,000 more expensive than in the rest of the UK. The answer is therefore B.

As for the other answers: The passage does not mention the cost of houses in England, only in the rest of the UK. The passage never clarifies how many houses are owned / used by tourists or part-time residents as compared to full-time residents

5 C   Tourism is discussed in the third paragraph. The final sentence of this paragraph states that the isles are a top destination for bird watchers who come to see many exotic birds who make the stop in their migration on the islands Thus, answer C is correct. As for the other answers: There is one airport and one heliport on the islands, so it is not correct to say there are many of these. One island is called St Mary's, but the passage says nothing about an historical church there.

6 A   This passage is about the Isles of Scilly – it covers geography, agriculture, tourism and political problems. Thus, you could say the passage gives an overview or introduction to the history and current issues on the Isle of Scilly.

B   The wrong answers would either be on the wrong topic, or would be too narrow – touching on only one paragraph, rather that the whole passage.

Passage 2

Matching Heading Questions

3   Paragraph C vii

Paragraph D i

Paragraph E x

Paragraph F iii

Paragraph G v

Paragraph H ix

4		Heading ii does not work, as it is not the main idea of a paragraph; also, the calendar in Eastern Europe is mentioned in both Paragraphs F and G. There's the same problem with heading vi; priests are mentioned in Paragraphs B and E (the pope is a priest), but priests are not the main idea of either paragraph. Heading viii is not relevant as the solar year is mentioned frequently, but there aren't problems with the solar year – the problems are with the calendars.

Sentence Completion Questions

1	A	Each blank can contain up to three words and / or a number.
2	A	The clues are 'solar year,' 'the Earth' and 'a [blank] of the sun.'
	B	The answer is found in Paragraph A. The fourth sentence says that a solar year is the time it takes the Earth to complete a full rotation of the sun.
	C	The words 'full rotation' go in the blank. It would be wrong to write 'a full rotation' in the blank, since the 'a' is given before the blank.
3	A	The clues are 'Without a,' 'earliest Roman calendar' and '355 days long.'
	B	The answer is found in Paragraph B. The earliest Roman calendar had 355 days, and they would add a leap month of 27 days between February and March every 3 to 5 years. Without a leap month, then, the earliest Roman calendar was 355 days long.' fourth sentence says that a solar year is the time it takes the Earth to complete a full rotation of the sun.
	C	The words 'leap month' go in the blank.
4	10	The clues are '45 BC' and 'the intervention of [blank].' The answer is found in Paragraph C. Julius Caesar decided that the calendar should be based on the solar year, which was from 45 BC onwards. Thus it was Julius Caesar that intervened. The words 'Julius Caesar' should go in the blank.
	11	The clues are 'Unfortunately,' 'the solar year is [blank]' and 'the Julian calendar.' The answer is found in Paragraph D. The final sentence says that

the solar year is 365.2422 days, or about 11 minutes shorter than the Julian calendar. The word 'shorter' should go in the blank.

12   The clues are 'Pope Gregory XIII,' 'one change was to [blank]' and 'mistakenly added by the Julian calendar.' The answer is found in Paragraph E. The pope decreed that 4th October 1582 would be followed by the 15th October 1582, in order to remove 10 days added in error by the Julian calendar. The words 'remove days' or 'remove 10 days' o 'remove the 10 days' should go in the blank.

13   The clues are 'British' 'Gregorian calendar' and 'starting in [blank].' The answer is found in Paragraph F. The Unites Kingdom implemented the Gregorian calendar in 1752. The number 1752 should go in the blank.

14   The clues are 'Russia,' 'continue to use the [blank] calendar,' and 'religious purposes.' The answer is found in Paragraph G. Russia and other countries continue to use the Eastern Orthodox calendar for religious feasts and festivals. The words 'Eastern Orthodox' should go in the blank.

15   The clues are 'current rules,' 'years that are [blank] are note leap years' and 'divided evenly by 400.' The answer is found in Paragraph H. Years divisible by 100 are not leap years, unless they can be divided by 400. The words 'divisible by 100' should go in the blank.

Reading Chapter 2

Passage 1

Getting Ready to Read

1	A	in the evening = before bed
	B	affect = impact
	C	fascinating outcomes = interesting results
	D	laptops, mobiles and tablets = electronic devices
	E	described = characterised
	F	very troublesome = extremely worrying
	G	tricks our biological systems = fools the body
	H	accelerating = speeding up
	I	contents = subject matter
	J	very thought-provoking = highly mentally stimulating
	K	decent = adequate
	L	a greater chance = an increased risk

Passage 1 – Practice

1	Paragraph 1	Brit bluebells: spring; in woodland
	Paragraph 2	risk to Brit bb: Spanish bb; hybrid
	Paragraph 3	hybrid threat; appearance of Brit bb
	Paragraph 4	appearance of the Spanish & hybrid bb
	Paragraph 5	good news for Brit bb

The main idea of the passage is the risk to British bluebells from Spanish and hybrid bluebells, which is a real problem in the British Isles.

2

Q. 2: The keywords are half, world and UK. This statement is somewhat similar to the second sentence of the first paragraph. However, the sentence in the passage states that almost half of British bluebells worldwide are found in the UK. Q. 2 says something slightly different – it mentions half of all bluebells worldwide, which is a slightly larger amount (half versus 'almost half'), and Q. 2 talks about all bluebells in the world, not just British bluebells. Thus, the answer to Q 2 is NOT GIVEN in the passage, as Q. 2 is too different from this sentence in the passage to be true or false.

Q. 3: The keywords are British and woodland. The last sentence in the first paragraph says that British bluebells thrive in woodlands, but then the second paragraph mentions that they also grow in cities. Thus, this statement is FALSE.

Q. 4: The keywords are British and extinct. The second paragraph starts with a sentence that states that the British bluebell is at risk of extinction. There is no further information that this species will definitely be extinct, only more information about the risk. Thus, this statement is NOT GIVEN in the passage, as it is neither true nor false based on the passage.

Q. 5: The keywords are London and Spanish. The second paragraph explains that virtually all bluebells in London are hybrids of British and Spanish bluebells. This statement is therefore FALSE. Keywords that are capitalised are usually fairly easy to scan for.

Q. 6: The keywords are Spanish and distinctive scent. The distinctively sweet scent of British bluebells is discussed in the third paragraph, and the features of Spanish bluebells are described in the fourth paragraph. These include its blue pollen, the fact that it stands upright, and a range of petal colours – but nothing about whether or not it has a distinctive scent. The answer is NOT GIVEN.

Q.7: The keywords are hybrid, white pollen and pink petals. The fourth paragraph says that a hybrid of British and Spanish bluebells can combine any features of the two, including colour, with the exception that the petals of a hybrid cannot be blue-violet. A British bluebell has white pollen, and a Spanish bluebell can have pink petals, so a hybrid could have white pollen and pink petals. The statement is TRUE.

Q. 8: The keywords are hybrid, UK and forests. The final paragraph says that the Spanish bluebell does not grow well in woodland, so the risk of hybridisation is limited to urban areas. This means that hybrid bluebells are found in cities, not in woodland. This statement is therefore FALSE.

Passage 2 – Practice

2   Section 1 (P. A to P, C): bees ↓ beekeepers ↑

        Section 2 (P. D to P, G): possible causes of bee pop ↓

        Section 3 (P. H to P, I): problems due to bee pop ↓

Passage 2 – Matching Information Questions

Q. 2: The keywords are impact and other plants and animals. You should scan for examples of other plants and animals in the passage. The final paragraph mentions fruits, vegetables, cows and pigs, all of which depend on bees either for their pollination (for the plants) or their food source (the animals). The answer is I.

Q. 3: The keywords are fate and UK agency. UK is a capitalised keyword, so perhaps the easiest to scan for; it appears in Paragraphs A and C. Skimming again in this section (Section 1 in our passage map) reveals that the National Bee Unit is the UK agency that protects bees; it was nearly defunded in 2007, but Paragraph B says that this funding was saved, thanks to a campaign by the BBKA. Thus, the fate of the NBU is found in Paragraph B.

Q. 4: The keywords here are dangers and 20th century. Dates make for great keywords, as numbers will stand out from the words in the passage. We should look for any years starting with 19, since the 20th century is also referred to as the 1900s. The only such dates are the 1960s and 1980s, both mentioned in Paragraph D in relation to something that was 'threatening bee populations' (in the sixties) and that 'exterminated bee populations' (in the eighties). Those are certainly both dangers from the 20th century! The answer is D.

Q. 5: Our passage map shows that the causes of declining bee populations are discussed in Paragraphs D to G. The keywords here are combination of causes and likely to collapse. The words 'likelihood of collapse' appear in the final sentence of Paragraph G; skimming just before this, you will see that scientists found that a fungus called Nosema, in combination with IIV (a type of virus), is likely to cause collapse. Answer G is correct.

Q. 6: The keywords here are global decline. The decline in bee populations is discussed most generally in the first section, as Section 2 is more about causes and Section 3 is about problems. The first sentence of Paragraph C includes the words 'a decline in the number of bees worldwide,' which is a close paraphrase for this statement. The answer is therefore C.

Q. 7: The keyword fungus might sound familiar – we just came across it in answering an earlier question. Paragraph G mentioned a fungus called Nosema that was found in most collapsed hives in the study, and is believed to be part of the cause of colony collapse. This sounds like it is quite a threat to bees – so the answer is G.

Passage 2 – Note Completion Questions

Q. 8: A threat to funding for the **National Bee Unit**. The keywords threat and funding lead to Paragraph A, which mentions that the UK Government proposed a budget cut that would defund the National Bee Unit.

Q. 9: The number of officially registered **[amateur] beekeepers** is 24,000, and continues to rise. The keyword here is 24,000, which appears in the final sentence of Paragraph B. You would get the mark for this question whether or not you included amateur in your answer, but you would need to be sure to spell it correctly if you did!

Q. 10: In 2007, the honeybee was predicted to become extinct in the UK **within a decade**. The keyword 2007 appears in the final sentence of Paragraph C; Lord Rooker predicted that the honeybee would be extinct in Britain within a decade. In this case, you had to copy the exact words from the passage, so 'within ten years' would be incorrect.

Q. 11: The major problem is **colony collapse disorder**, in which all the worker bees in a hive thought to have been healthy are suddenly no longer there. This blank is in the Dangers to bees section of the passage, so it must correspond to Section 2 of our passage map. The part of the sentence after the comma is a close paraphrase of the first sentence of Paragraph E; the missing words therefore must be colony collapse disorder. This sentence repeats the definition of CCD from the passage.

Q. 12: A combination of Nosema, a **fungus**, and IIV indicate likelihood of collapse. The keyword Nosema is a great clue – we saw previously that it shows up in Paragraph G.

Q. 13: **Cross-pollination** may occur by wind, but depends on insects; bees are the most prolific. The keywords wind and insects appear in the final sentence of Paragraph H, which this sentence paraphrases.

Reading Chapter 3

Passage 1

Getting Ready to Read

1	1	incapable = negative; incapable means unable or helpless
	2	innovative = positive; innovative means groundbreaking or original
	3	dynamic = positive; dynamic means lively or active
	4	exploitative = negative; exploitative means unfair or abusive
	5	forthcoming = positive; forthcoming means approaching (imminent) or helpful
	6	ignorant = negative; ignorant means unaware or rude
	7	straightforward = positive; straightforward means easy or frank
	8	accommodating = positive; accommodating means helpful or cooperative
	9	isolated = negative; isolated means remote or lonely
	10	misinterpret = negative; misinterpret means misunderstand or misread
	11	rational = positive; rational means balanced or sensible
	12	unmotivated = negative; unmotivated means apathetic or uninterested

Practice

2	Paragraph 1	Newton's contribution to physics
	Paragraph 2	Newton: 1st to explain calculus
	Paragraph 3	Newton's calc unknown – 2 reasons; N's approach
	Paragraph 4	Leibniz also discovered calc; L's approach diff from N's
	Paragraph 5	Were they independent? Calculus today

The main idea of the passage is that Newton and Leibniz both discovered calculus, working largely independently and with different approaches.

3

Q. 2: The keyword is Latin. Latin is mentioned at the end of the first paragraph; Newton wrote in Latin because it was the accepted scientific language of the time. I matches this detail from the passage and completes the sentence correctly.

Q. 3: The keyword is 1666. This date appears in the final sentence of Paragraph 2. Newton originally developed his concepts of calculus in a 1666 treatise that was not published in full until 1704. The correct answer is C – it was not published until nearly 40 years later – as this is a paraphrase of the detail from the passage.

Q. 4: The keywords are 17th century and publishers. These keywords appear in the third paragraph. Texts in the field of theoretical maths were so unprofitable that they drove one specialist publisher to bankruptcy. This detail from the passage matches H – the books of maths theory were so unprofitable, meaning that you could not make money from them. Another good paraphrase, though it might be tough to spot at first because the words are so different – yet the meaning is exactly the same.

Q. 5: The keywords are today and derivative of a function. These appear together in the third paragraph. What Newton called a fluxion is known today as a derivative of a function, one of the basic concepts of calculus. Answer A matches the wording from the passage exactly, so it is correct.

Q. 6: The keywords are Leibniz's approach and integral calculus. According to our passage map, L's approach is found in Paragraph 4. These keywords lead to the final sentence of Paragraph 4: Integral calculus, as Leibniz's approach is now known, is concerned with describing small portions of the graph of a function. The correct answer is therefore F.

Q.7: The keywords are a bit more difficult here. The unfinished sentence mentions Leibniz and Newton, and also 'we come to calculus.' These keywords lead to the end of the passage, where the final sentence mentions Leibniz and Newton, as well as 'our approach today,' which starts with an understanding of the limits of maths, just as it did for them. Answer J is correct.

Passage 2

Getting Ready to Read

1   Answer: A view is an opinion. A claim is a statement made by the writer as if it is a fact. Views and claims are similar. The difference is that a claim is meant to be taken as a fact, while a view reflects personal opinion. If there are strong opinion words, then it's a view. If it sounds like something true or correct without opinion words, then it is a claim.

2   1   view; *completely out of order* indicates a strong opinion

     2   claim; *longer and hotter* indicate data, which can be checked

     3   claim; *was interested* and *did little* are facts, and can be checked against the historical record

     4   view; *welcome breath of woodland* and *congested city* indicate opinion

     5   claim; this statement is factually true (as of today)

6   view; *deeply beautiful and moving* indicate opinion

7   view; *best view* indicates opinion

8   view; *tastes better* indicates opinion

9   claim; *more people prefer* suggests it's a fact, which could be checked against data about the popularity of ice cream flavours

10   claim; although this is personal, *relatively uncommon* suggests it is a claim about data, rather than an opinion

Practice

1   The passage can be divided up into four sections.

Paragraph 1-4   R3 & young princess; did he murder them?

Paragraph 5   R3's death

Paragraph 6   R3's body rediscovered

Paragraph 7-8   consequences of rediscovery

Yes/No/Not Given Questions

Q. 2: The keywords are 1997, Indiana and not guilty. The keywords all appear in the second paragraph, which explains that a trial was held at an Indiana law school in 1997 that found Richard 'not guilty' of the princes' murder; in the next sentence, the writer asserts that this verdict does not prove Richard's innocence. Thus, the writer expresses a view on this topic, and he disagrees with the statement. The answer is NO.

Q. 3: The keywords are Tudors, Yorks and Lancasters. All the keywords are mentioned midway through the third paragraph. Thomas More, writing in the time of the Tudors, was coloured by the politics of his day in his depiction of Richard III, according to the writer. But then the writer says that the time of the Yorks and Lancasters was a time of political strife. So it is not clear whether the Tudors were more political than the earlier houses, or whether the writer has a view on this topic. The correct answer is NOT GIVEN.

Q. 4: The keyword is Edward V. He is mentioned in the final sentence of Paragraph 4. The writer states that it is safe to conclude that people widely assumed Edward V was dead because there is no evidence of pretenders claiming to be him. Q. 4 is a close paraphrase of this detail, and the writer agrees with the claim – so the answer is YES.

Q. 5: The keywords are everyone expected and car park. The discovery of Richard's body in the car park is discussed in the sixth paragraph. The final sentence says that the archaeologists had not expected to find anything, let alone on their first attempt; the previous sentence says that 'Amazingly,' they found his remains within an hour of starting to dig. 'Amazingly' reflects the writer's view, and it indicates that the writer is just as amazed as the archaeologists at their luck in finding the remains so quickly. However, this means that the writer disagrees with the statement in Q. 5. The answer is NO.

Q. 6: The keywords are Shakespeare and hunchback. These appear in Paragraph 7, which states that the remains have refuted Shakespeare's claim that Richard III was a hunchback. The writer disagrees with the statement in Q. 7, so the answer is NO.

Q. 7: The keywords Westminster Abbey lead to the final paragraph. Some people think that Richard III should have a state funeral there; others think he should be denied this honour. The writer does not express a view on this controversy; thus, the correct answer is NOT GIVEN.

Summary Completion Questions

1	**A**	There are nouns, verbs and adjectives.
	B	Monarchy is a noun. Concluded, influenced, suffocated and rehabilitate are verbs. Controversial and contemporary are adjectives.
	C	Torture, tarnish, and combat could be nouns or verbs, depending on context.

Q. 8: The princes were never seen alive again, and later medical tests revealed that the princes had been **suffocated** to death. These details come from the passage's first paragraph; the princes died of suffocation, according to medical tests in 1933. None of the other past tense words (ending in –ed) fits the meaning here – you cannot be concluded to death, or influenced to death. The answer is G.

Q. 9: James Tyrrell admitted to killing the boys, but he only confessed after being subjected **to torture**. These details are found in the second paragraph of the passage. None of the other nouns in the answer choices make sense here, and the context in the passage is fairly clear. The answer is A.

Q. 10: Shakespeare's play depicts Richard III as sending Tyrrell to murder the princes, but Shakespeare's view originated in the work of Thomas More, who was **influenced** by Tudor politics. These details appear in Paragraph 3. The context of the blank requires a verb in the past tense; the only other option is concluded, but that does not fit the meaning of the sentence. Answer E is correct.

Q. 11: His bones indicated that he was wounded in **combat**. These details are discussed in the passage in the sixth paragraph – the bones show evidence of wounds sustained in combat. The summary is a close paraphrase of the passage, so the match is relatively straightforward. The answer is J.

Q. 12: Richard's skeleton added much to what we know about the **controversial** king, including the fact that he was not a hunchback, but likely had scoliosis, with one shoulder higher than the other. These details appear in the passage's next-to-last paragraph. The first sentence there describes Richard III as 'this controversial king,' so the passage context is the key to finding the correct answer, B.

Q. 13: Following this discovery, some people have moved to **rehabilitate** the image of Richard III, arguing that his reputation was damaged by Shakespeare. The relevant details are found in the last paragraph of the passage, which mentions the movement to rehabilitate Richard's image. Answer H is correct.

Reading Chapter 4

Passage 1

Getting Ready to Read

1	**1**	current (N/ADJ)
	2	focus (N/V)
	3	temporary (ADJ)
	4	practice (N/V) – note that in UK spelling, the verb is 'practise'
	5	fundamental (N/ADJ)
	6	likewise (ADV)
	7	tense (N/V/ADJ)
	8	highlight (N/V)
	9	radical (N/ADJ)
	10	analysis (N)
	11	involved (V/ADJ)
	12	acquire (V)
2	**A**	analyze (or analyse)
	B	involvement
	C	acquisition

Passage 1 – Diagram Labelling Questions

Q. 2: The keywords are Pluto and now classified. The answer is found in the second paragraph. Pluto is no longer considered a planet, but instead a dwarf planet. The answer is dwarf planet.

Q. 3: An **asteroid belt** thought to contain more than 70,000 objects. The keywords are Kuiper Belt and 70,000. These appear in the third paragraph; the answer is found in the same sentence in the passage as the figure 70,000.

Q. 4: Most distant point in the Kuiper Belt: **7.4 billion** km from the Sun. This figure also appears in the third paragraph; the keywords are most distant point and from the Sun. This answer could also be written as 7,400,000,000 km, or the word kilometres or kilometers could be used instead of km. However, it is easiest and quickest just to copy the figure as written in the passage.

Q. 5: Oort Cloud: Thought to exist beyond the Kuiper Belt, and to contain **more than 1 trillion** comets. The keywords Oort Cloud lead to the end of the third paragraph. Note that this answer must be written as here, or with 1 trillion as a number (1,000,000,000,000); it cannot be 'more than a trillion' as that is three words and a number.

Q. 6: Eris: Greater diameter than Pluto, with **25% more mass**. The keyword Eris appears in the fourth paragraph; the detail for the blank follows the statement about Eris's diameter. Remind students that a percentage counts as a number; thus, this answer is two words and a number.

Passage 1 – Short Answer Questions

Q. 7: The keyword IAU appears in the first paragraph. In 2006, the IAU voted to define planet for the first time. The answer is **define planet**.

Q. 8: The keywords Pluto's orbit lead to the start of the second paragraph. Pluto's orbit is eccentrically elliptical compared to the orbits of the other planets. The answer here is **eccentrically elliptical**, though you could also write **elliptical**. Note that there is a trap answer in the first paragraph, if you look for the keyword shape – you might have written 'round' or 'approximately round' – this is incorrect, as it describes the shape of Pluto itself, not its orbit.

Q. 9: The keyword Makemake (pronounced MAHK-ay-MAHK-ay) appears in the fifth paragraph. Pluto, Eris and Makemake have significantly smaller mass, and, as a result, a weaker gravitational pull than other planets. Thus, the answer is **gravitational pull**.

Q. 10: The keywords Kuiper Belt and images lead to the last paragraph, which talks about the exploration of the Kuiper Belt. The passage's final sentence explains that a spacecraft called New Horizons that launched in 2006 and will spend 5 to 10 years exploring Pluto and the Kuiper Belt. The correct answer is **New Horizons**.

Passage 2 – Passage Map

Paragraph 1	6 elements of O.C.; 1 = place
Paragraph 2	2 = vision
Paragraph 3	3 = values; meritocracy pros & cons
Paragraph 4	4 = practices; tech changes
Paragraph 5	home vs. work
Paragraph 6-7	5 = people ('talent'); example of egg freezing

The topic of the passage is the six elements of office culture, and how these are changing today. There is a lot of attention to technology and how this affects working and retaining talent.

Passage 2 – Answers

Q. 1: The answer is found in the first paragraph. Coleman uses research showing that the culture of a firm can account for 20-30% of the differential in corporate performance, meaning whether the business succeeds or fails. Thus, the answer is B.

Q. 2: The answer appears in the second paragraph. It is critical to have openness and accountability run throughout the organisation in order to maintain adherence to the stated goal. Chuck Cohn is the one who says this, so the answer is D.

Q. 3: Meritocracy is discussed in the third paragraph. The final sentence there says that Young looked unfavourably on a meritocratic culture, as in his view a meritocracy entrenches the powerful by limiting the educational opportunities of the lower classes. Answer C is correct.

Q. 4: The keywords day-to-day practices lead to the end of Paragraph 5. As Coleman argues, a company's values do not make much of a difference unless they are fully integrated into a company's everyday practices. This sentence is a close paraphrase for Q. 4, so the answer is B.

Q. 5: The keywords frozen eggs appear in the final paragraph. Dr Irene Gafson explained that there is no guarantee that freezing of eggs will result in a live birth of a baby. Thus, the answer is A.

Q. 6: The keywords office architecture lead to the first paragraph. Open-planned offices encourage better collaboration between colleagues. The answer is A.

Q. 7: The keyword Ben Horowitz appears in the end of the second paragraph, which is about vision. Businesses that don't take deliberate actions to shape the culture of a firm will lose control of one of their most valuable assets. Answer B matches this detail, so it is correct.

Q. 8: The 79 per cent figure appears near the end of the fourth paragraph. The passage says that all work used to be done in the same office building, but that this has changed with internet and mobile communications; now, 79% of workers are part of virtual teams, conducting some or all of their work via these new technologies. The 79% figure is therefore mentioned to show how common it is for people to work virtually. The correct answer is A.

Q. 9: Companies offering to pay female employees to freeze their eggs are mentioned in the last two paragraphs. The next-to-last sentence of the sixth paragraph states that this is done in order to shield their female employees from making the traditional choice between work and motherhood. Answer C is therefore correct.

Q. 10: narrative. This answer appears in the fourth sentence of Paragraph 1.

Q. 11: maintaining. This answer is found in the third sentence of Paragraph 2.

Q. 12: brainstorming. This answer appears in the third sentence of Paragraph 4.

Q. 13: talent. This answer is found in the first sentence of Paragraph 6.

WRITING INTRODUCTION

MODULE OVERVIEW

The Writing module consists of two tasks that must be completed in a total of 60 minutes.

You are given one answer sheet for both Task 1 and Task 2 answers. It does not matter where on the answer sheet you write your answers. You can start with Task 1 and do Task 2 afterwards, or start with Task 2 and do Task 1 afterwards.

You may write your essay in pen or pencil. Pencil is recommended as it is tidier to make amendments.

Task 1 carries one-third of the marks, and Task 2 carries two-thirds of the marks. As such, you should give yourself 20 minutes for Task 1 and 40 minutes for Task 2.

You must complete both tasks in full sentences and paragraphs – do not answer in a list of notes or bullet points. You should write in a formal, neutral tone, and only include information that is directly relevant to the task.

In Task 1, you will be presented with visual information in the form of a chart, graph, table or diagram. You must write at least 150 words based on the information, discussing any key features and trends.

In Task 2, you are given an opinion or a statement, followed by a question. You must write at least 250 words in response, ensuring that you answer the question asked in the task. You may be asked to argue for or against an opinion or a statement, to explain a statement, to give your own view on two conflicting opinions, or to say how much you agree or disagree with a statement.

Writing Strategies

Be familiar with the types of questions that will be asked.

Know the vocabulary for description, comparison/contrast and opinion/argument.

Follow the Kaplan Method for Writing:

- **STEP 1:** Read the prompt carefully. Make sure you understand what you are required to write about.
- **STEP 2:** Brainstorm and note down your ideas. Do this on your question paper because no one will look at it after the test. At this stage your notes do not need to follow any logical order. Just write down anything that you think is relevant to the task.
- **STEP 3:** Plan your essay. Select, prioritise and group your ideas according to the task.
- **STEP 4:** Write your essay. Do this in pencil, so it is easier to make changes later.
- **STEP 5:** Review and improve your essay. Check for grammar and spelling mistakes.

You may not be able to correct all the mistakes you have made, so focus on locating and correcting your typical mistakes.

Stick to the suggested timing for the Kaplan Method for Writing:

- Steps 1 to 3 should take no more than 2 minutes for Task 1 and 5 minutes for Task 2.
- Step 4 should take no more than 15 minutes in Task 1 and 30 minutes in Task 2, provided you have done a productive job in the first 3 steps.
- Step 5 should take no more than 3 minutes for Task 1 and 5 minutes for Task 2.

For Task 2, follow the appropriate structure for an essay:

- Start with an introductory paragraph, with a general statement of the topic in your own words. If you copy the words in the question these will be deducted from your word count. Include a sentence which directly answers the question.
- The main body of your essay should consist of at least two paragraphs which discuss both views. Each should have a topic sentence and supporting evidence. Use specific ideas or examples to support the views from the task.
- In the last paragraph, you should summarise the main points discussed in the body of the essay and include a solution, prediction, result or recommendation. If appropriate you may include your point of view in the conclusion.
- If the task asks you to present both sides of an argument, or to choose a side, you have two options.

First option: Introduce the sides of the argument in the first paragraph, explain one side in more detail in each of the body paragraphs, then choose a side in the conclusion.

Second option: Briefly introduce both sides in the introduction and choose a side at the end of that paragraph, explain your reasoning in the first body paragraph, explain the arguments for the other side in the second body paragraph, then resolve the argument in favour of your side in the conclusion.

Follow a compressed structure for Task 1:

- Begin with a brief overview of the visual information and its purpose (introduction: 1–2 sentences).
- The body of your response should focus on how the visual information works, or significant differences and similarities within/across the visual information. Do not try to describe every detail of the information. Focus on the most important points, or on key trends.
- Conclude your description with a summarising statement.

OBJECTIVES

By the end of this chapter, you should be able to:

- Describe a chart, graph or diagram.
- Make notes and plan before you begin writing.
- Write a response that fully completes the task.
- Practise strategies for completing Writing Task 1.

ACADEMIC WRITING TASK 1

Strategies

- Read the task carefully. Make sure you understand what is required.
- Look over the visual information and make notes on your question paper.
- Plan your essay on the question paper, then write the essay on the answer sheet.

For many IELTS candidates IELTS Writing Task 1 may seem to be the most difficult part of the whole test. This is particularly true if you don't have much experience with charts and graphs or did not work with them at school. However, there is no need to worry: graphs and charts are just one way of showing information. With a bit of practice, you will learn how to read and analyse them.

Chart/Graph 1 – Getting Ready to Write

1. Look at the chart on the next page and answer the following questions

    A   What sort of chart is it?

    B   What information is it showing?

    C   Does it show a change in information over time?

    D   What unit of measurement does it use?

    E   Why is this information displayed in this way?

    F   Do the same number of people visit the cinema in 2000 and 2015?

2. One important skill for writing a good Task 1 answer is the ability to write the same information in different ways. Look at these percentages given in the pie charts and find another way of saying the same information: 5%; 12%; 51%. Example: 25% is one-quarter.

3. Before you start writing it is important to decide first *what* you are going to write. Take just 1 minute to look at the information in the pie chart and decide what you are going to say. It's a good idea to make some notes on the diagram itself. Don't forget that the question asks you to make comparisons!

The chart shows the number of visitors to a local cinema last year according to age. Summarise the information by selecting and reporting the main features, and make comparisons where relevant.

Write at least 150 words

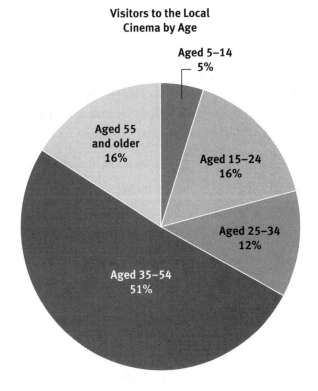

Visitors to the Local Cinema by Age

Aged 5–14
5%

Aged 55 and older
16%

Aged 15–24
16%

Aged 25–34
12%

Aged 35–54
51%

Chart/Graph 1 – Write

Set yourself 15 minutes to write out in full sentences the information you identified in step 3 above. At this stage, don't worry about word count, just focus on identifying and expressing the information.

When you have finished look at the answer. Did you include all those points?

Notice how each of those sentences contained comparisons.

Improve Your Score

When writing an IELTS Task 1 answer, it is very important to remember the following:

- Always support your statements with information from the graphs.
- Never give your opinion or speculate on the reasons for the information.

1. Look at the following list of sentences. Decide which would be acceptable (A) and which not acceptable (NA) for the answer to this task. Give reasons for all your decisions.

    A   The eldest group, 55 years and above, recorded the same percentage as the young adult group, 15–24 years.

    B   Adults between the ages of 35–54 were the largest group, accounting for 51% of the total.

    C   The reason older people represent such a small percentage is that they don't like the loud noise in the cinemas these days.

    D   Only 6% of the total is made up by children going to the cinemas.

    E   I like going to the cinema with my friends

One of the most common types of chart seen in IELTS Writing Task 1 is the line graph. It is important that you become comfortable with identifying and analysing the information contained in each graph.

> Only write about the information in the chart. Do not include any ideas of your own.

Chart/Graph 2 – Getting Ready to Write

1. Look at the graph on the next page and answer the questions

    A   What is being measured?

    B   How is this chart different to the pie chart in the previous exercise?

    C   Is there a time element to this information? If yes, what is it?

    D   Are two or more things being compared? If yes, what are they?

This graph is a very good example of an IELTS Writing Task 1 graph, as many of the graphs do not at first appear to show much information. At first, you may think that you are not going to find enough to write 150 words. But with a bit of practice, you will learn to analyse the graph in different ways to identify interesting information and comparisons to talk about.

2. Look at the graph for just one minute now, and then answer the following questions.

    A   What do you notice about pattern of visitor numbers to all the animals over the course of the year?

    B   What do you notice about the different number of visitors to each animal in January and November compared to July?

    C   What do you notice about the relative popularity of the pandas and the penguins for most of the year?

    D   What do you notice about the relative popularity of the animals in January and December compared to the rest of the year?

Chart/Graph 2 – Write

The graph below shows the number of visitors each month to the zoo's most popular exhibits. Summarise the information by selecting and reporting the main features, and make comparisons where relevant.

Write at least 150 words.

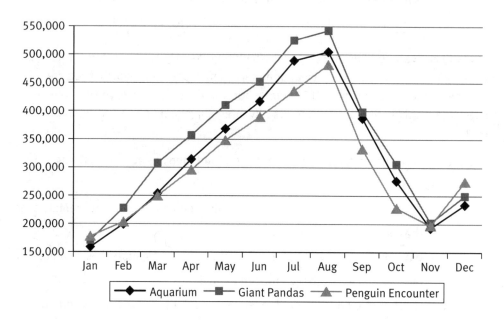

Now do the task. Take 15 minutes and write at least 150 words.

When you have finished check your ideas with the example in the Answer Key.

How did you do?

Improve Your Score

1. Look at the example again and answer the following questions:

   A What do the numbers 30,000, 60,000 and 20,000 represent?

   B How were these numbers obtained?

   C Why did the candidate include them?

   D Will including data such as this increase or decrease the candidate's score? Why?

2. The examiner will give your writing 4 marks. One of them is for Task Achievement; this means how well you answer the question. Let's look again at the wording of this Writing Task 1 question.

> *Summarise the information by selecting and reporting the main features and making comparisons where relevant.*
>
> *Write at least 150 words.*

   Complete the guidelines for a good score by filling in the gaps.

   A Give an overview of the _____ information.

   B Identify all the _____ relevant and significant _____.

   C Highlight the main _____ and similarities in the information.

   D Do not include your own _____ or _____ for the data.

   E Make sure you write _____ than 150 words.

Look for graphs and charts in newspapers and on the internet and practice identifying the key information, any changes and make comparisons.

Explain the graph to a friend and ask them to draw it. Then check how close it is to the original.

DIAGRAMS

Most IELTS Writing Task 1 questions are based on graphs or charts. However, occasionally the visual may be a diagram of a process or a map. In this first diagram, we are going to look at a process.

Diagram 1 – Getting Ready to Write

1. Look at the diagram and read the question, then answer the following questions

    A   What is not relevant and why?

    B   What does the diagram describe?

    C   How many stages are there?

    D   Which of the following verbs will be useful for your answer?

    - keep
    - hold
    - push
    - go
    - pump
    - throw
    - inject
    - combust
    - play
    - expel

2. Write the correct verbs from 1.D. above in the most appropriate place on the diagram. What do you notice about most of these verbs?

Diagram 1 – Write

The diagram below shows the structure of a basic rocket engine. Summarise the information by selecting and reporting the main features, and make comparisons where relevant.

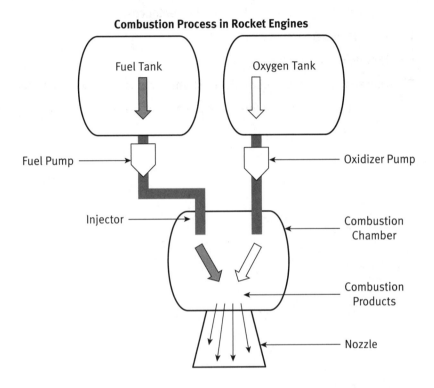

Take 15 minutes to write some sentences to describe the main features of the combustion process in rocket engines.

Now compare your ideas with those in the Answer Key.

Improve Your Score

1. Look again at the four sentences in the answer key and answer the following questions.

    A Which verb forms are used in 3 of the sentences?

    B Why is this verb form used?

    C How do you make this verb form?

    D One sentence uses a different verb form. What is it and why is it used here?

    E Why will using this verb form give you a higher score for IELTS Writing Task 1?

KAPLAN TIP

Using the present simple passive forms of verbs relevant to the process is the key to getting a high score for process diagram. The examiner will give you a mark for Grammatical Range and Accuracy, and correctly using the passive will impress the examiner

Diagram 2 – Getting Ready to Write

As well as using the passive form of key verbs, it is important to use good linking words when you are describing the process in order to make your writing coherent. As well as Task Achievement, another feature the examiner will mark you on is Coherence and Cohesion. Coherence is how easy it is to understand your writing and Cohesion is how well your ideas are connected together.

1. Put these words in the order you would expect them to appear in an essay describing a diagram that depicts a process: then, secondly, next, finally, after that, subsequently, firstly, later, at the end, at first.

2. Look carefully at the diagram. Don't worry if you don't understand it, or don't know all the words.

    A   Look at the information given and see how many verbs you can make to help you describe the process. Check your answers in the Answer Key.

    B   Now write these verbs in the present simple passive.

Diagram 2 – Write

The diagram below shows the life cycle of plastic bottles. Summarise the information by selecting and reporting the main features, and make comparisons where relevant.

Write at least 150 words.

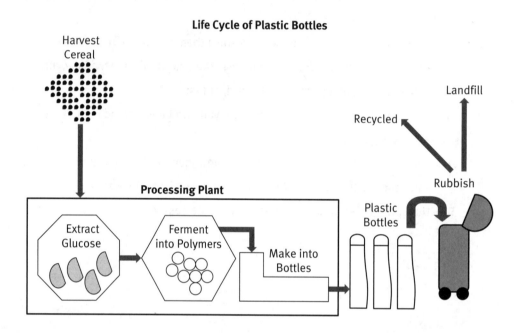

You have 15 minutes to write a description of the process. Remember to use good linking words and the present simple passive.

Now check your ideas with the Answer Key.

Improve Your Score

1.   Look again at the example answer and complete the following questions.

   A   What is important about the first sentence?

   B   Identify all the linking words.

   C   Identify all the verbs in the passive form.

Takeaway

There has been a lot of new information in this chapter. Without looking back, what are the most important things you can remember about Writing Task 1?

Check your ideas in the Answer Key.

KAPLAN TIP

Practise writing about processes by thinking of the steps of something you do every day. For example: making a cup of tea or coffee, or changing the paper in your printer. Think of the steps, then what verbs you need, and then write the process out using the passive form of the verb and good linking words.

OBJECTIVES

By the end of this chapter, you should be able to:

- Identify the key points your essay must address.
- Plan your argument or thesis before you begin writing.
- Write a response that fully completes the task.
- Practise strategies for completing Writing Task 2.

ACADEMIC WRITING TASK 2

Strategies

- Underline keywords in the task.
- Show clear links between the main argument and the supporting arguments.
- Develop the body of your essay.
- Provide a strong conclusion.

Writing Task 2 usually includes one or two statements about a topic of general interest, or provides a specific question to answer. It also tells you what types of ideas you need to include in your answer.

The most important thing you need to do before getting your ideas together is to understand the information given and be clear about what you have to do.

First Task 2 – Getting Ready to Write

1. Below (numbered 1–6) are some of the most common questions asked in IELTS Writing Task 2. Look at them carefully and then match them with statements a–e. Note: Some questions will match with more than one statement.

1 Discuss the advantages and disadvantages of such a proposal

2 Discuss both these views and give your own opinion

3 To what extent do you agree or disagree

4 Do the advantages outweigh the disadvantages

5 Has this become a positive or negative development

6 What do you think are the causes of this problem and what measures can be taken to solve them

a. In many countries, rates of diabetes are increasing and fitness levels decreasing.

b. Some countries are considering a tax on sugar in foods to help fight childhood obesity.

c. Social media has permanently changed the way people interact with each other.

d. Some people believe that children should be allowed to take up paid employment. Other people think that no child should have to work.

e. Some large cities in the world are charging car drivers to drive into the city centre.

f. Some people believe that children should be taught how to manage money at school.

2. Now look at the statements a–g regarding the first Writing Task 2 below and mark each statement true (T) or false (F).

a. This is about sports in schools.

b. This is about whether competition is good for children.

c. This is about children's health.

d. You only need to talk about what you think.

e. You need to discuss views that you may not agree with.

f. You shouldn't write anything about your personal experience.

g. There needs to be three parts to your answer.

3. Once you have understood the question fully, you should then brainstorm ideas for your answer. Look at the statements below and decide if they support the first view in the question (1) or the second view (2) regarding the first Writing Task 2 below

    a. It's just not fair if the same children win all the time.

    b. There's nothing wrong with a bit of healthy competition as long as no one takes it too seriously.

    c. Sometimes when we are adults things don't always go the way we want and we need to prepare our children for that.

    d. Some children will be made to feel inferior or not as good as the rest.

    e. Children need to be protected from the real world for as long as possible.

    f. Some children have other skills and they need to be nurtured as well.

First Task 2 – Write

You should spend about 40 minutes on this task.

Some people do not allow their children to participate in games, sports or competitions unless everyone gets a prize. Others think that children must learn to deal with winning and losing in order to be fully prepared for life.

Discuss both these views and give your own opinion.

Give reasons for your answer and include any relevant examples from your own knowledge and experience.

Write at least 250 words.

You will only have 40 minutes for this part of the Writing module. You need to understand the question and brainstorm your ideas quickly so that you have plenty of time left to write your answer.

For this practice you have just 30 minutes to write up your ideas. Try to write at least 250 words

Improve Your Score

1. Look back at your answer, have you done the following? Mark those that you have with a tick.

   a. I've restated the main ideas in my own words. ☐

   b. I've ended the first paragraph by saying what my opinion is. ☐

   c. I've discussed the idea that competition is bad for children. ☐

   d. I've given some reasons and examples about why competition is bad for children. ☐

   e. I've discussed the idea that competition is good for children. ☐

   f. I've given some reasons and examples about why competition is good for children. ☐

   g. In the final paragraph, I have explained my own opinion in more detail and given some reasons and examples. ☐

   h. I've written more than 250 words. ☐

2. How many did you tick? If it wasn't all of them, rewrite your answer to include all of the above points.

Sometimes it is easy to jump to conclusions about the Task, especially if the subject is one that we think we know a lot about or is something we have strong feelings for. It is important not to get too excited if we see such a subject, but to make sure we read the statements and the question carefully.

KAPLAN TIP

It is very important that you understand the question fully. You need to know what the statements mean and what question you are being asked. If you talk about a different subject or do not do exactly what the question asks you to do, you will not get a high score.

Second Task 2 – Getting Ready to Write

1. Look at the second Writing Task 2 below and answer the questions a–e, giving reasons for your answers.

    a. Is this a yes/no question?

    b. Do you have to discuss both points of view?

    c. Do you need to decide what the advantages and the disadvantages are?

    d. Do have you to get the advantages and disadvantages correct?

    e. Is this question asking you to develop your answer using reasons and examples?

2. In a question like this, you are being asked to discuss your own ideas and opinions. However, it is very important that these ideas and opinions are totally relevant to the question. You will lose marks if you include ideas that are not relevant to the question. Look at the list of sentences below and mark them *R* if they are relevant and *I* if they are irrelevant to the question.

    a. Social media is helping people all over the world to form new and different types of relationships.

    b. Some people are not aware of the dangers of putting too much information about themselves on social media.

    c. Social media companies make more money as more and more people use their services.

    d. Identity theft is becoming a major problem.

    e. Social media is being used by all age groups but for very different reasons.

    f. I really enjoy using social media.

KAPLAN TIP

At first 250 may seem like a lot of words, but if you break the answer down into the paragraphs then it will seem easier: Introduction and concluding paragraph about 50 words each. The two main body paragraphs 100 words each. Each of these paragraphs has to include at least 2 ideas (3 is better), as well as reasons for your ideas and an example to support one of them.

Second Task 2 – Write

Complete the task below.

Task 2

You should spend about 40 minutes on this task.

Social media is becoming increasingly popular amongst all age groups. However, sharing personal information on social media websites does have risks.

Do you think that the advantages of social media outweigh the disadvantages?

Give reasons for your answer and include any relevant examples from your own knowledge and experience.

Write at least 250 words.

Improve Your Score

1. Read over your answer. Have you done the following? Mark each one with a tick.

    a. I've restated the main idea in my own words. ☐

    b. I've answered the question clearly by writing something like: "*I believe that the advantages of social media outweigh the disadvantages*" or "*While there are many advantages to social media, I think that the disadvantages are much more important.*" ☐

    c. I've written a paragraph giving details of what I think are the advantages, including reasons and examples. ☐

    d. I've written a paragraph giving details of what I think are the disadvantages, including reasons and examples. ☐

    e. I've finished the essay by summarising these advantages and disadvantages and linking them to the answer I gave in the first paragraph. ☐

    f. I've written at least 250 words. ☐

2. How many did you tick? If it wasn't all of them, rewrite your answer to include all of the above points.

KAPLAN TIP

Be careful when you use examples! It is important that you include at least two – one for each side of the argument if appropriate – but no more. Sometimes candidates feel that they can fill out the 250 words by writing lots of examples. Even if these are well written, your mark will be reduced because you will not have fully answered the question.

Third Task 2 – Practice

It's time now to do a properly timed IELTS Writing Task 2.

You have 40 minutes to:

a. Make sure you understand the question.

b. Brainstorm ideas.

c. Write at least 250 words.

d. Check your work.

Task 2

You should spend about 40 minutes on this task.

Rates of diabetes and obesity are increasing in many countries around the world. Some people think that governments should ban soft drinks and sugary snacks from schools.

To what extent do you agree or disagree with this proposal?

Give reasons for your answer and include any relevant examples from your own knowledge or experience.

Write at least 250 words.

KAPLAN TIP

In IELTS Writing Task 2 questions, there are no correct or incorrect answers. All that matters is that your ideas fit the question and that you can express yourself clearly. You are not being marked on what your ideas actually are, just how well you explain them.

Improve Your Score

1. How did you do?

   - Look back at the check lists earlier in this chapter and write your own checklist for this task.
   - Did you do everything on your list?
   - Check your list with the list in the answer key.
   - Did you do everything on that list?

2. As you know, timing is very important in the IELTS Writing module. You need to pace yourself carefully so that you have time to do everything that you can to ensure you get the best score possible.

This means that you need to leave yourself 3–5 minutes after you have finished writing to check your answer. You are going to be marked on four different things. What aspects of your writing do you need to check for each of them? Complete the table.

Mark	Check
Task Response	
Coherence and Cohesion	
Grammatical Range and Accuracy	
Lexical resource	*Spelling*

Takeaway

There has been a lot of information in this chapter about Writing Task 2. Without looking back, write a list of the important things you have learned about how to get a good score in Writing Task 2. Then compare your ideas with those in the Answer Key.

KAPLAN TIP

You will get more marks for *trying* to do something clever with your writing. Perhaps a complicated grammar structure like a past perfect passive ('Before the new rules, children *had been made* to play sports competitively in my country') or some vocabulary you are not sure about ('sugary snacks and *fizzy drinks* should be banned in schools'). Always be ambitious in your writing: you will get more marks for trying, even if you get it wrong!

OBJECTIVES

By the end of this chapter, you should be able to:

- Compare and contrast information in graphs, charts and tables.
- Describe information in a map.
- Write accurately about data and visual information.
- Practise strategies for completing Writing Task 1.

ACADEMIC WRITING TASK 1

Strategies

- Concentrate on significant figures or key issues, rather than trying to describe everything.
- Look for trends and patterns.
- Vary your language. Use a range of vocabulary and structures.

Graph 1 – Getting Ready to Write

Writing Task 1 asks you to compare different information displayed in a visual form. Often the graph looks quite complex. This is a good opportunity for you to show your analytical skills by extracting information from the graph.

Look at the Writing Task 1 example below and then answer the following questions.

Task 1

The information below shows the number of customers and the number of popular fruits purchased in one greengrocers in England over one summer weekend. Summarise the information by selecting and reporting the main features, and make comparisons where relevant.

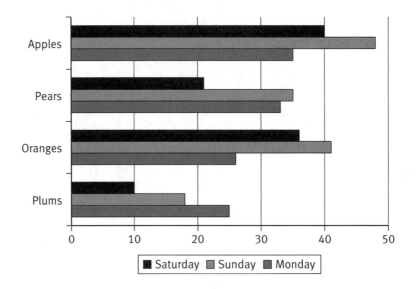

DAY	Saturday	Sunday	Monday
CUSTOMERS	776	1,253	984

1. Approximately how many apples were sold over the weekend?

2. Approximately how many plums were sold over the weekend?

3. What do you notice about the sales of apples on Monday, pears on Sunday and oranges on Saturday?

4. What are the highest and lowest daily sales, and what is the difference between them?

5. What is interesting about the sales of plums on Sunday?

6. What is interesting about the sales of apples and oranges?

7. What is noticeable about the sales of pears?

8. What percentage of fruit sold each day were plums?

9. What percentage of customers came to the greengrocer's on Monday

10. Why is it a good idea to sometimes use percentages in a question like this?

11. What are two disadvantages of using percentages in a question like this?

Graph 1 – Write

Now that you have had some time to analyse the chart, you have just 15 minutes to write and review your answer.

Improve Your Score

1. Looking at your answer, check that you have done the following:

   - I have restated the information in my own words.
   - I have only written about what is in the diagram.
   - I have not included personal opinions or reasons for the data.
   - I have included a comparison in every sentence.
   - I have included one sentence to describe all the information.

If you haven't ticked all of the points in the list above, rewrite your answer.

2. When there is a lot of information in a graph, some candidates feel that they need to describe everything. Look at the two sample answers below, then answer the questions that follow.

Sample Answer 1

The chart and table show the number of customers and the number of popular fruits purchased in one greengrocers in England over one summer weekend. On Sunday 1,253 people visited the shop and on Sunday 48 apples were bought.

On Saturday there were 776 customers and the most popular fruit was apples with 40 bought, then oranges with 36, followed by pears at 31 and plums were the least with 10.

On Sunday there were 1,253 customers and the most popular fruit was apples with 48 bought, then oranges with 41, followed by pears with 35 and plums were the least with 18.

On Monday there were 984 customers and the most popular fruit was apples with 35, then pears with 33, followed by oranges with 26 and plums were the least with 24.

(134 words)

Sample Answer 2

The chart and table show the number of customers and the number of popular fruits purchased in one greengrocers in England over one summer weekend. The fruits bought were apples, pears, oranges and plums.

40 apples were bought on Saturday. The most, 48, were bought on Sunday and the least, 35 were bought on Monday.

21 pears, the least number, were bought on Saturday. The most, 36, were bought on Sunday, and 34 were bought on Monday.

36 oranges were bought on Saturday, 41 on Sunday and the least, 26 on Monday.

10 plums, the least number, were bought on Saturday. 18 were bought on Sunday and the most, 25 were bought on Monday.

(114 words)

For both of the sample answers:

1. There is one really good thing in each answer. What is it?
2. Would this good thing, on its own, mean that these answers will get a good mark?
3. What is the problem with the first paragraph?
4. What is the problem with the paragraphs?
5. What is the problem with the comparisons?
6. What is the problem with the language used?
7. What is the problem with the data given?
8. What is the problem with the word count?
9. What is missing?

KAPLAN TIP

Although it is tempting to write a description of the visual information, you will lose marks if you:

- use language repetitively.
- list the information rather than analyse it.
- include all the data without thinking about it.
- don't include an overall comment on the information.

Graph 2 – Getting Ready to Write

Occasionally, the charts given will show information that is predicted for the future. Do not be alarmed by this as it is a good opportunity to show off your language skills.

Look at Task 1 below and answer the following questions.

You should spend about 20 minutes on this task.

The graph below gives information about Northcom's revenue from selected products in 2000, 2015 and future projections for 2030. Summarise the information by selecting and reporting the main features, and make comparisons where relevant.

Write at least 150 words.

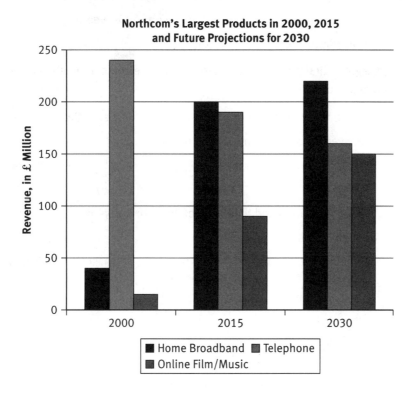

1. What is different about telephone sales compared to the sales of the other two products?

2. How would you describe the increase in sales of home broadband between 2000 and 2015?

3. How would you describe the predicted increase in sales of home broadband between 2015 and 2030?

4. How would you describe the increase in sales of online film/music between 2000 and 2030?

5. Can you say anything about the pattern of sales over the period of telephones and online film/music?

Graph 2 – Write

Now that you've had some time to analyse the chart, you have just 15 minutes to write 150 words to answer the question.

Improve Your Score

1. Look at your answer and check that you have done the following:

    A I have given an overview of the information.

    B I have identified all the most relevant and significant information.

    C I have highlighted the main differences and similarities in the information.

    D I haven't included my own ideas or reasons for the data.

    E I have written more than 150 words.

When we have a graph that predicts the future, we can use some interesting and impressive grammar constructions.

2. Complete the following sentences from a sample answer to this question by putting the verb in brackets into the correct form:

    A By 2030, sales of telephones _____(decline) by about £80million from 2000.

    B In 2030, it is predicted that sales of home broadband _____(reach) about £220million.

    C By 2030, sales of online film/music _____(increase) to £150 million.

Which form of the verb have you used and why?

KAPLAN TIP

Practise reading graphs and working out how you would analyse them. Take time to decide what verb forms you would use to describe data that covers time.

Maps 1 – Getting Ready to Write

1. Sometimes the information you are given is in the form of maps or ground plans. Often these are not difficult to understand and they always take place over time. Look at the maps in the next Task 1 below and then answer the questions (A–F) that follow.

Task 1

The maps below show Harrison's Stables in 1920 and in 2010. Summarise the information by selecting and reporting the main features and making comparisons where relevant.

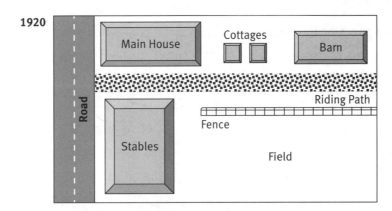

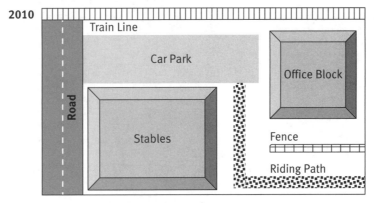

A   What can you compare between these two maps?

B   Why is it important to be able to use prepositions of place in a map question?

C   What is at the top right hand corner of the map in 1920?

D   What is at the top right hand corner of the map in 2010?

E   What four things are in both pictures?

F   What new buildings or features are there in 2010?

2. Match the following verb with features from the two maps. One or more answers may be possible.

   A build

   B enlarge

   C move

   D run

   E demolish

   F shorten

   G built on

3. Now complete the sentences with the correct preposition of place

   A The cottages are _____ the main house and the barn.

   B the riding path is _____ the fence.

   C The stables are _____ of the field.

   D The main house is at the _____ of the map.

   E The car park is _____ the train line.

   F The office block is _____ of the car park

Maps 1 – Write

Now that you have had some time to think about the maps in detail, take just 10 minutes to write an answer for the Task 1 above.

Improve Your Score

1. Read your answer and check that you have done the following:

   - I have restated the information in my own words.
   - I have included a sentence to describe the information overall.
   - I have made comparisons in every sentence.
   - I have correctly described where buildings and features of the maps are in relation to each other.
   - I have included all the important details.

2. Describing maps gives a good opportunity to use some complex verb structures.

   Complete the following sentences with the correct form of the verb in brackets.

   1 The stable block _____ (extend).

   2 A train line _____(built)

   3 The cottages _____(demolish)

   4 A car park _____(build)

   5 The fence and riding path _____(move)

3. Which verb form is used and why? Do you think using this verb form will improve your Grammatical Range and Accuracy score?

KAPLAN TIP

Don't panic if you get a map question for your Writing Task 1. All you need to remember is your prepositions of place and the present perfect passive.

Maps 2 – Getting Ready to Write

As you have had plenty of practice looking at charts, process and maps, you now have only 3 minutes to look at the two maps and decide what you are going to write about. Remember you can write on the question paper, so feel free to make notes as you analyse the maps.

Task 1

The maps below show the Grange House property in 1800 and in 2000. Summarise the information by selecting and reporting the main features and making comparisons where relevant.

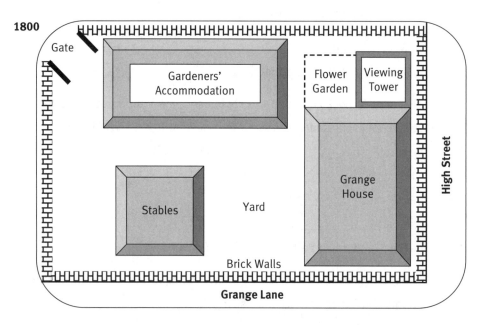

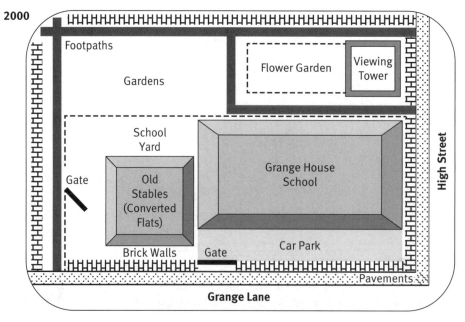

Maps 2 – Write

Spend only 15 writing your answer.

When you have finished take 2 minutes to check over your writing.

Improve Your Score

1. Read your answer and check that you have done the following:

- I have restated the information in my own words.
- I have included a sentence to describe the information overall.
- I have made comparisons in every sentence.
- I have correctly described where buildings and features of the maps are in relation to each other.
- I have included all the important details.

2. Complete the sentences below with the correct feature and location.

A One of the buildings that has remained since 1800 is the _____ which is now _____.

B Another feature that has remained the same since 1800 is the _____ and is situated at the _____ of the map.

C There is now a _____ in the middle of the _____ which runs along the _____ of the map next to Grange Lane.

D According to the 1800 map, there is _____ at the top of the map but by 2000 it had been replaced by a _____.

E A new feature is the _____ which has been built along the _____ and _____ of the map with another part between the _____ and the _____.

KAPLAN TIP

As you can write on the question paper, it is a good idea to circle, underline or highlight the points you want to write about. It can also be helpful to number them according to which you think is most important.

Remember the more you plan *what* you are going to write about, the easier it is to write about it and also have time to think about your grammar and spelling.

WRITING CHAPTER 4

OBJECTIVES

By the end of this chapter, you should be able to:

- Assess and improve the language used in your response.
- Understand some of the key areas that make a good Writing Task 2.
- Practise strategies for completing Writing Task 2.

Task 2 – Example

In this chapter you are going to analyse in detail a sample answer to a Writing Task 2 question and look at ways you can improve it.

Look carefully at the question and read the sample answer below:

Task 2

Some people do not allow their children to participate in games, sports or competitions unless everyone gets a prize. Others think that children must learn to deal with winning and losing in order to be fully prepared for life.

Discuss both these views and give your own opinion.

Give reasons for your answer and include any relevant examples from your own knowledge and experience.

Write at least 250 words.

Some people think children should ever have to loose and this means they will never win. Because you can't have winners without losers. It is true that its bad for children to here they are losers or stupid but its just as wrong to send a message they are winners or smart and nobody likes somebody who is smart and makes a big deal about it anyway. Children need to be praised and rewarded for efforts, not results, because their efforts all they can control.

Other people think winning and losing teaches important lessons to children, and it is. But children need to learn that if they feel good about there effort, they can enjoy winning without always being perfect and they can lose without being zero. Parents are in charge of how children see winning and losing, and the parents behaviour is just as important as what happens in games. If parents make a big deal out of when they win or lose kids will too. "Monkey see monkey do" is how it really works.

The best way for parents to teach self worth is to have some. Children need support in their efforts so they are not caught up in being winners or losers. Parents' thinking of winning and losing effect their kids much more than prizes that get handed out.
I think anybody needs to learn to value themselves and they're efforts and that is the best way to raise kids to understand about winning and losing. [250 words]

1. Writing Task 2 is given four marks for different aspects of the work. Complete the marking categories below:

   A _____ response

   B Coherence and _____

   C Grammatical _____ and _____

   D _____ resource

You're now going to analyse the writing for each one of the criteria above.

2. Let's now look at the writing and how it responds to the question. Read the Sample task again and answer the questions:

   A Does the essay discuss both of the views given in the question?

   B Does the writer give their opinion?

   C Are the ideas fully developed?

   D Do you agree or disagree with the writer's ideas?

   E How could the writer have improved their Task Response?

3. The second marking criteria looks at how well the writing is organised. Read the Sample task again and answer the questions:

   A Does the writing 'flow'? For example, does it have a 'beginning, middle and end'?

   B Are the paragraphs clearly identifiable and logical?

   C Do the ideas in the first paragraph follow logically?

   D What do the following pronouns refer to?

   - 'it' (2nd paragraph, 1st line)
   - 'they' (2nd paragraph, 2nd line; occurs twice)
   - 'their' (3rd paragraph, 3rd line)
   - 'that' (3rd paragraph, last line)

   E Are these pronouns correctly referencing nouns? Is this important?

   F How could the writer have improved their Coherence and Cohesion?

4. The third marking criteria looks at word choice and spelling. Look at the words in the sample task and answer the following questions:

   A Find four words that have been spelled incorrectly and correct them. What do you notice about these words?

   B Do these spelling mistakes make it difficult to understand what the candidate wants to say?

   C On two occasions, the candidate writes a word that is totally opposite to the word he wants to use. Which words are these, what should they be, and do these mistakes make the answer difficult to understand?

D   Can you see any mistakes with prepositions?

E   There are some good collocations (connections), phrasal verbs and expressions in this text. Underline all those that you can find. Comment on the importance of these

F   One of these expressions is used twice. How do you think this will affect the mark?

G   There is one expression that doesn't really 'fit' into the text. What is it and how do you think it will affect the mark?

H   Look carefully at the descriptors for Lexical Resource in 1b above. Do you think that this answer deserves a band 6 score? Why/Why not?

I   How could the candidate have improved their Lexical Resource score?

5.   Finally, let's have a look at how the candidate manages grammar and punctuation. Look again at the sample Task and answer these questions:

A   The candidate has some problems with punctuation. Can you identify their mistakes?

B   Do these mistakes make the answer difficult to understand?

C   Are there any mistakes with any of the following:
Verb tenses?
Subject verb agreement (i.e. singular subject with singular verb)?
Word order in sentences?

D   There is a big problem with one of the sentences in the first paragraph. What is it and how can it be improved?

E   Is there a relative clause in the text? If yes, identify it. Why are relative clauses important in IELTS writing?

F   Are there any sentences with no grammatical mistakes?

G   How could the candidate have improved their Grammatical Range and Accuracy?

Well done for working through all those exercises! What you have just done is exactly what the examiner will be doing when they mark your paper.

KAPLAN TIP

Time yourself every time you write a practice essay. Always allow a few minutes before time is up to check your work for spelling mistakes, wrong words and any other problems with your grammar or phrasing.

Task 2 – Write

You have just done a lot of work on analysing an IELTS Writing Task 2 answer, which will have given you a very clear idea of the things that examiners are looking for.

Now set your timer for 40 minutes and do the following task. Remember:

1. Before writing, decide your position.

2. Note down ideas to support your position.

3. Think of any examples you can include to support your position.

4. While writing: Remember to clearly state your position in the introduction.

5. Make sure your ideas are clearly expressed and follow a logical progression.

6. End with a concluding paragraph that sums up your position.

7. After writing: Check your work for basic spelling and grammatical mistakes.

Task 2

You should spend 40 minutes on this task.

One of the consequences of improved technology is that many jobs that used to be done by people can now be completed by robots or computers.t

Do you think the advantages of this development outweigh the disadvantages?

Give reasons for your answer and include any relevant examples from your own knowledge and experience.

Write at least 250 words.

Takeaway

From all the analysis that you did you may have learned some things that surprised you.

Is there anything that you have learned that will encourage you during the exam?

KAPLAN TIP

It is a good idea to print out a copy of the IELTS Writing Task 1 and 2 public writing descriptors from the internet to see what the descriptors are for the band score you need to get. You can then assess your practice essays against these descriptors. Download the current versions from takeielts.britishcouncil.org.

WRITING ANSWER KEY

Writing Chapter 1

Chart/Graph 1 – Getting Ready to Write

1	**A**	pie chart
	B	the number of people who visited a cinema last year according to age.
	C	No. It is showing information at one fixed point in time
	D	percentages
	E	Because we are interested in how one figure (the number of people who visited the cinema in one year) is divided among different groups. We are not interested in the actual numbers of people.
	F	We don't know because the pie charts only record the percentages not the actual numbers.
2	**5%**	one twentieth, a very small amount, a tiny minority
	12%	just over a tenth.
	51%	a little over half. Just over half

Chart/Graph 1 – Write

Some of the key features you should have identified.

1 The age group 35–54 has 51% of the visitors, more than the rest of the groups put together.

2 Equal numbers of cinema visitors, 16%/almost a fifth, are aged 15–24 and aged 55 and over

3 The two smallest groups with only 5% and 12% respectively are for children aged 15–24 and adults aged 25–34.

Improve Your Score

A	**Not acceptable.**	Although this is a good sentence with a good comparison it does not include any data
B	**Acceptable.**	Includes a comparison – largest – and gives data – 51%
C	**Not acceptable.**	This is an opinion
D	**Not acceptable.**	It is true and there is some data but there is no comparison
E	**Not acceptable.**	This has nothing to do with the chart

Chart/Graph 2 – Getting Ready to Write

1	**A**	The number of people who visit different parts of a zoo.
	B	This chart gives absolute numbers, not percentages.
	C	Yes, it shows the information over one year for each month.
	D	Yes, there are three things. Aquarium, Giant Pandas, Penguins.
2	**A**	The numbers ALL rise during the spring and summer months and then decline in the winter
	B	In Jan. and Nov. the numbers for each animal are about the same, but in July there is quite a big difference between all three.
	C	For most of the year, pandas are the most popular and penguins the least.
	D	Jan. and Dec. are the only months when penguins are the most popular.

Chart/Graph 2 – Write

In the chart, for all three animals, the monthly number of visitors increases each month from January when there are just over 150,000 to August, when visitor numbers reach a peak between 470,000 and 550,000. After this, the number decreases each month until November when there are about 200,000 visitors for each animal. In December, the visitor numbers increase again by 30,000 for the aquarium and 60,000 for the penguins.

Overall, the Giant Pandas are the most popular exhibit attracting the most visitors every month from February to October. In July they attracted almost 100,000 more visitors than the penguins. However the penguins are slightly more popular in January and December, with about 20,000 more visitors than the giant pandas.

Early in the year, especially in February and March, visitor numbers to the aquarium and penguins are about the same; around 200,000 in February and 250,000 in March. Subsequently the aquarium becomes increasingly more popular until in July it is attracting about 70,000 more visitors than the penguins. From August to October the decline in visitor numbers to both of these attractions is almost the same.

(186 words)

Improve Your Score

1 A   They represent the difference in visitor numbers between Nov. and Dec. for the aquarium (30,000) and Nov. and Dec. for the penguins (60,000). The difference in visitor numbers between the penguins and giant pandas in Jan and Feb. (20,000)

B   By subtracting the lower number on the graph from the higher number.

C   Because the information is interesting, relevant and is clearly a comparison.

D   Introducing new data extracted from the information on the chart to talk about interesting information or to show comparisons will **increase** your mark as it shows that you can interpret the graph to get the information you want.

2 A   Give an overview of the **main** information (summarise the information)

B   Identify all the **most** relevant and significant information (select and report the main features)

C   Highlight the main **differences** and similarities in the information (make comparisons where relevant)

D   Do not include your own **opinions** or **reasons** for the data.

E   Make sure you write **more** than 150 words

Diagram 1 – Getting Ready to Write

A   'comparisons' are not relevant as this diagram describes a process and thus there is nothing to compare anything with.

B   The combustion process in rocket engines

C   four

D   keep, hold, pump, inject, combust, expel

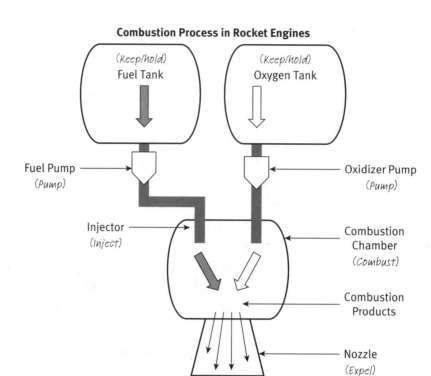

Combustion Process in Rocket Engines

Diagram 1 – Write

The diagram shows the combustion process for a rocket engine. The left hand side of the diagram shows fuel being fed from a fuel tank into a fuel pump and then injected into a combustion chamber. The grey arrow hoes the progression of the fuel.

Simultaneously, oxygen in the oxygen tank on the right hand side travels through the oxidiser pump and meets the fuel in the combustion chamber. The white arrow represents the oxygen.

In the combustion chamber, the fuel and oxygen meet, and react with each other in a way that causes combustion products to be created. These combustion products exit through the nozzle of the rocket engine, producing the power to move the rocket upwards.

(118 words)

Improve Your Score

A the present simple passive

B because we are not interested in the 'agent' of the verb (what is actually doing the action) but what is happening.

C the verb 'to be' + the past participle of the main verb

D   the third sentence uses the present simple because in this case it is the subject of the sentence 'mixture' which is the agent of the verb 'combusts'

E   Being able to use the passive appropriately and correctly is the key to getting a good mark in a Process question for IELTS Writing Task 1.

Diagram 2 – Getting Ready to Write

1   First/at first

Secondly/next/then/after that/subsequently/later

Finally/at the end

2   A   to harvest

to extract

to ferment

to make

to recycle

B   is/are harvested

is/are extracted

is/are fermented

is/are made

is/are recycled

Diagram 2 – Write

The diagram shows the process in which plastic bottles are made, and also what happens to them during their life-cycle. The first step in the process is when cereal is harvested. Once this stage has been completed, the cereal is then taken to a processing plant.

Next, at the processing plant, several steps are required finish making the plastic bottles. Initially, the glucose is extracted from the cereals. Once this step has been completed, the glucose is then fermented into polymers. Finally, these polymers are shaped into bottles, and the plastic bottles are ready for use. The bottles are then taken away from the processing plant to be used.

After the plastic bottles have been used and are no longer needed, they are thrown away in the rubbish. At this point there are two options. Either the waste bottles can be taken to landfill sites where they are buried or they are sent off to be recycled.

(157 words)

Improve Your Score

1	**A**	It describes the diagram but it doesn't use the same words as the question. If you repeat the same words exactly as given on the question paper these words will be deducted from your word count.
	B	The first step, next, initially, once, finally, when, at this point,
	C	are made, is harvested, is taken, are required, is extracted, has been done, is fermented, are made, are taken away, are no longer needed, are thrown away, are taken, are burned, are sent off.

Takeaway

If it is a chart or a graph, take some time to fully understand what information is being shown. Pay attention to the units and if there is any time period involved.

Only write about what you see in the diagram. Do not include personal opinions or reasons for the data

For charts and graphs try to include a comparison in every sentence.

There are no comparisons in a process diagram

In a process diagram, use the information given to find good verbs to help you describe the process.

Use the past simple passive where appropriate

Use good linking words to give your process description coherence and cohesion

Writing Chapter 2

First Task 2 – Getting Ready to Write

1	**1**	b, e
	2	d
	3	c, f
	4	b, e
	5	c
	6	a
2	**A**	F
	B	T
	C	F
	D	F
	E	T
	F	F
	G	T

(1: one view; 2: the other view; 3 your opinion)

3	**A**	1
	B	2
	C	2
	D	1
	E	1
	F	1

First Task 2 – Write

Recently, children's participation in sports and activities has been increasingly encouraged by parents and teachers. In an effort to motivate children of all abilities to enjoy and participate In games, sports and competitions, some adults believe it is necessary to award all of the children a prize, regardless of their performance.

The argument for this is that if every child feels rewarded by their participation, they are more likely to continue to take part in such activities. Also, if there are no losers in such games, sports and activities then it reduces the chance of children being bullied or made to feel bad about their performance, and therefore protect children's feelings and self-esteem.

However, one argument against such treatment is that such endeavours do not accurately represent real life. Once children have grown up, or even at their current age but in different, less parentally supervised games, these children will eventually be exposed to the sensation of losing, and all of the unpleasant feelings which accompany such loss. As such, parents and teachers can only be said to be postponing these unpleasant sensations, and not eliminating them entirely.

It could also be argued that the sooner a child learns to accept losing as a part of life, and finds ways to cope and deal with not being the best at everything, the sooner they will be able to integrate themselves into society in a useful and healthy way. In the long run, therefore, children will surely be better off if they are exposed to the possibility of loss and the benefits of winning from a young age, as it is inevitable that they will have to face these aspects of life eventually.

(282 words)

Second Task 2 – Getting Ready to Write

1	**A**	Yes, it is a yes/no question. You could answer the question effectively by saying "Yes, I do" or "No, I don't" But you would not get a very good mark.
	B	No, this is not a 'points of view' task
	C	Yes, before you start writing you need to think about which advantages and disadvantages you want to discuss.
	D	No, there is no 'right' or 'wrong' answer in IELTS Task 2 writings.
	E	Yes, this question is asking for just your opinion and the reasons why you hold this opinion and any examples you may have to support it.
2	**A**	R
	B	R
	C	I
	D	I (The sentence doesn't include any reference to social media so it could relate to anything, for the sentence to be relevant it needs to link directly to information given in the question
	E	R
	F	I (there needs to be more information in the sentence to make it relevant. Just saying that you enjoy something doesn't discuss any advantages or disadvantages.

Second Task 2 – Write

Since the invention of social media, many people have been better able to connect with each other and also to keep up to date with the lives of their friends, families, co-workers and even celebrities, to such a degree which was previously impossible.

However, social media has its risks. As people of all ages have access to social media, children can be exposed to adult content, and are themselves vulnerable to be approached by strangers with unknown intentions. Even if children are sure of who they're talking to on social media, social media's issues are not completely eliminated. Cyber bullying is frequently reported in the news, and occurs on social media between children and schoolchildren. This is problematic, as it means even when children are at home, remote from their bullies they can still be bullied when they're inside their own homes.

Social media can be problematic for adults, too. People often feel comfortable posting things on social media that they wouldn't say in real life. This can indirectly cause a bad impression on other people, and if employers judge the nature of the content prospective employees post on social media to be inappropriate, it can affect their chances of attaining or keeping jobs.

As long as people are aware of the risks of using social media, and are careful to post only respectful and respectable content, then the advantages of social media far outweigh the disadvantages, and children and adults alike should be allowed to benefit from such technology.

(250 words)

Improve Your Score (following Third Task 2)

1   Checklist example (your own checklist may vary)

A	I restated the statement in my own words
B	I said how much I agreed or disagreed with the proposal
C	I wrote a paragraph in support of the proposal
D	I included reasons and one example
E	I wrote a paragraph against the proposal
F	I included reasons and one example
G	I finished by giving more reasons for my answer and linking this to the information in the 2nd and 3rd paragraphs.

2

Mark	Check
Task Response	Have I understood the question?
	Have I directly answered the question in the first paragraph?
	Are all my ideas relevant to the question?
	Do have good reasons and some examples?
Coherence and Cohesion	Have I used pronouns properly?
	Does each paragraph have a topic sentence, and supporting sentences?
	Does the introduction give a clear indication about what I am going to say?
	Does the final paragraph summarise the ideas in the previous 2 paragraphs?
	Are my ideas easy to follow?
Grammatical Range and Accuracy	Have I used a range of grammatical structures:
	Verb tenses, passives, verb + verb structures?
Lexical resource	Spelling
	Uncommon or unusual words

Takeaway

- Fully understand the information given in the question
- Fully understand what the question is asking you to do
- Spend 5 or so minutes brainstorming your ideas and making a plan
- Spend 30 minutes writing at least 250 words
- Check that in the first paragraph you have re-stated the information in the question and given your answer
- Make sure that the body paragraphs match the question and contain only relevant information
- Include examples from your own experience if appropriate
- Include a concluding paragraph which rephrases your position.
- Make sure you have clear signposting and linking words

Writing Chapter 3

Graph 1 – Getting Ready to Write

1 125

2 53

3 They are all roughly the same at around 35-36

4 Plums on Saturday – 10 and apples on Sunday 48 difference of 38

5 All the other fruits had their greatest sales on Sunday which matched the greatest number of visitors. But the most plums were sold on Monday

6 The sales follow a similar pattern which doesn't match those of the number of customers

7 It matches the pattern of customers

8 Saturday: just under 10%; Sunday: about 12%; Monday 20%

9 About 33%

10 To show the examiner that you understand the information given

11 It can take a lot of time to calculate the percentages. It can be confusing if you move between real numbers and percentages.

Graph 1 – Write

The table below the graph shows that Sunday was the busiest day at the greengrocers, as they had the most customers; this is reflected in the sales of apples, pears and oranges, which all sold in the highest quantities on Sunday. However, although more plums were sold on Sunday than on Saturday, the highest number of plums were sold on Sunday, despite the greengrocer's having less customers on Monday than on Sunday.

On Saturday, more apples were sold than any other fruit. 40 apples were sold on Saturday, which is almost the same as the amount of oranges sold on Sunday.

Around 1/3 of the total visitors came to the greengrocers on Monday, and on Monday the sale of plums accounted for 20% of the total sales of the recorded fruit. In comparison, on Saturday, plums made up only 10% of the total sales.

(150 words)

Improve Your Score

1 The English is perfect; there are no grammar or spelling mistakes.

2 No. Each answer must display excellence according to all of the criteria in the Writing band descriptors to get a good mark.

3 It copies the information given in the question, so those words will be taken off the word count. The second sentence in each introduction doesn't give any useful analysis or overall statement about the information.

4 There is no clear paragraphing. Each sentence is given a new paragraph. This will mean marks are deducted.

5 Apart from the use of most and least, there are no comparisons and thus marks will be deducted.

6 The language is repetitive so although it is correct it will not get a high score as there is no 'range' in the grammar nor 'flexibility' in the vocabulary.

7 There is too much data given, it is given repetitively and with no analysis or comparison.

8 There are not enough words and even less when the copied words from the introduction are deducted. This will results in marks being taken off.

9 There is no 'overall' statement to describe the graph. Without this you will not get a mark of 6 on Task Achievement.

Graph 2 – Getting Ready to Write

1 Telephone sales are decreasing over the period.

2 dramatic, spectacular, rocketed,

3 slow, slight, small

4 steady, significant, regular

5 The decrease in sales of telephones is as steady/regular as is the increase in the sales of online film and music

Improve Your Score

1 *Answers will vary*

2 A   will have declined

　 B   will have reached

　 C   will have increased

　　　　　 The verb tense is future perfect. It is used because
　　　　　 you are talking about a information in the future that
　　　　　 is related to information in the past.

Maps 1 – Getting Ready to Write

1 A   The location of different buildings and features. The appearance or disappearance of different buildings and features. The size and or shape of the same building or feature

   B   So that you can be precise in your analysis of the maps

   C   a barn

   D   an office block

   E   the riding path, the stables, the fence and the road

   F   car park, office block, train line.

2 A   office block / car park / railway line

   B   stables

   C   fence / footpath

   D   train line

   E   main house / cottages / barn

   F   riding path

   G   field

3 A   between

   B   next to

   C   to the left of

   D   top right

   E   below

   F   to the right of

Maps 1 – Write

The two maps show Harrison's stables in 1920 and 2010. In 1920, the cottages are between the main house and the barn, whereas in 2010, the main house, cottages and barn have all been destroyed and a train line has been built above where they once were. In 2010, the main house and the barn have been replaced by a car park, and the barn has been replaced by an office block.

The office block in Harrison's stables in the 2010 map has also been built over where the footpath once crossed in 1920. In 2010, the footpath has been removed completely and a riding path has been created to the right of the stables and below the office block. The fence in 2010 is shorter and appears lower. In 2010 than the fence in 1920. In 2010, the fence is between the office block and the riding path.

The stables remain in the same place in both maps, but the stables are bigger in 2010 than they were in 1920.

(172 words)

Improve Your Score

1   *Answers will vary*

2   1   has been extended

    2   has been built

    3   have been demolished

    4   has been built

    5   have been moved

3   The verb tense is the present perfect passive. It is used because we do not know who or what did the extending/building/demolishing etc., and it is not important. It is also not important when these actions were done in the past. What is important is that they happened in the past and have an effect now. Yes, if you can use the present perfect passive accurately in a map question the examiner will be very impressed and will give you a good score for Grammatical Range and Accuracy. Especially if you have got your prepositions of place correct.

Maps 2 – Write

The two maps show the Grange House property in 2000 and also 200 years earlier. In 2000, the gardener's accommodation present in the 1800 map at the top left, next to the gate, has been replaced by gardens, and the flower garden to the right of the gardener's accommodation has been expanded from 1800 to 2000. Grange House itself has been replaced by Grange House School, which is larger than Grange House was in 1800, and also has a car park between it and the south side of the brick wall.

The structure of the stables from 1800 are still present in 2000, but have been converted into flats with a school yard installed above them (south) and a gate to the left of them (west). In 2000, there is also a gate in the middle of the south side of the brick wall that did not exist in 1800, and the gate that was present in the top left of the map in 1800 has been removed by 2000.

(169 words)

Improve Your Score

1 *Answers will vary*

2 A   Stables/converted flats

   B   Viewing tower/top right (hand corner)

   C   Gate/brick wall/bottom

   D   Gardeners' accommodation/garden

   E   Footpath/top/left hand side/school/flower garden

Writing Chapter 4

Example

1	**A**	Task response
	B	Coherence and Cohesion
	C	Grammatical range and accuracy
	D	Lexical resource
2	**A**	It is difficult to say: The second paragraph continues the ideas of the first paragraph rather than make completely different ones.
	B	Yes, in the final paragraph "I think….."
	C	Not fully, but the writer does give some good support to their ideas ('their efforts are all they can control' "parents' behaviour is just as important as what happens in the games"
	D	What the examiner thinks about the writers' idea doesn't matter. All that is important is that they are well explained. These are quite well explained and easy to understand.
	E	The candidate needs to make the second paragraph clearer so that it can be seen that these ideas are completely separate to those of the first paragraph and not just a continuation of them

Additionally it would be helpful to clearly state their opinion in an introductory paragraph. Key phrases for introducing your opinion are:

In my opinion

I believe that

Personally, I think ……

It is very important to use these phrases early on in the answer so that the examiner knows that you have given your opinion and answered the question

Also, the writer could have added an example from his own experience. Not putting in examples will not reduce your mark, but including a good one will help you improve your band score.

3	**A**	Not really, although there is some good signposting ("some people" "other people") the ideas of the second paragraph are a bit confusing and don't seem to follow logically within the context of the question.
	B	Yes,
	C	Yes, There is an excellent progression here from the idea that if you can't have losers you can't have winners, which the author then links to the bad things about being a loser and also, the bad things about being a winner, concluding with an idea that effort should be valued, not results
	D	it – winning and losing

they – children

the children's

that – valuing themselves |
	E	Yes, all the pronouns are correctly referencing nouns. This is important as poor pronoun use makes it very difficult to follow a text and will reduce the score for coherence and cohesion
	F	There are occasions where they could have used pronouns in the text rather than repeating nouns
4	**A**	Loose/lose, Here/hear, There/their, They're/their. They are all words that sound the same (homophones) but the candidate has chosen the wrong word to spell. These mistakes are very common so it is important that you learn the meaning and spelling of all of this regularly used words
	B	No. When examiners are marking a Writing task the most important criteria is 'can I understand what the writer is saying?'
	C	Ever/never, anybody/everybody. The first one, (ever/never) is clearly a mistake and doesn't really make the meaning difficult to understand – it is however a careless mistake. The other mistake (anybody/everybody) does make the sentence seem a bit confusing but it's still easy to see what the candidate means and the meaning of 'any' is quite complex.

D	No, there aren't any.	
E	The main ones are:	To send a message
		Make a big deal out of
		rewarded for efforts
		Are in charge of
		Self-worth
		Caught up in being
		Get handed out
		To raise kids up

Using collocations, phrasal verbs and fixed expressions accurately is something that the examiners like to see and you will get higher marks for this. There is a very good range of high level vocabulary here, all accurately used so this will get a good score for vocabulary.

F	It is not good to repeat expressions, especially if they are incorrectly used. Too many repetitions could reduce your mark. In this case the language is very informal and not really appropriate for academic writing.
G	"monkey see, monkey do". It is not clear why the candidate has used this American expression as it doesn't seem to fit in with the argument he is making.
H	The essay would get a score of band 4 or band 5. There are too many issues of poor wording and wrong word choice for it to score higher than 5.
I	This criteria could be improved by not repeating 'make a big deal out of' and 'smart' to give the examiner further evidence of the candidate's knowledge. Also the language is not always in an appropriate academic style.
5 A	The main problem with the punctuation is the lack of apostrophes. It should be it's instead of its. However the candidate has put a possessive apostrophe in the correct place for parents' which is very good indeed.
B	No
C	Verb Tenses: No
	Subject Verb Agreement: No

Word Order: No

D "It is true that its bad for children to here they are losers or stupid but its just as wrong to send a message they are winners or smart and nobody likes somebody who is smart and makes a big deal about it anyway." This sentence is much too long and contains too many ideas. It needs to be divided into at least two sentences.

E "nobody likes somebody **who is smart and makes a big deal about it anyway**" Relative clauses are important as they form part of 'complex' sentences and you need to have at least one complex sentence in your writing to get a 6.

F Yes.

G Firstly the candidate needs to understand when to use apostrophes with its and it's. Secondly, it would be helpful if there were a greater range of verb tenses. One advantage of including examples is that they are often stories about something that happened in the past and therefore need past tense structures. Finally, some more complex sentences would help.

Task 2 – Write

As technology progresses, machines are increasingly able to accomplish tasks which would once have been done by people. For the most part, this frees up our own time, and allows us to accomplish more as individuals. Household appliances such as washing machines, dishwashers and blenders have vastly reduced the amount of time necessary to 'keep house' and could even be seen as a contributing factor for the increase in married women who work – if less time needs to be spent doing household chores, both partners in a relationship can earn an income.

However, many people worry that increasing the amount of jobs done by technology and decreasing the amount of jobs done by people could result in poverty for many, as if machines are better able to carry out jobs than the people who were previously doing these jobs, then these workers will most likely be replaced by the machines and become unemployed. One example of this can be seen in the deployment of 'self-service' tills in supermarkets, which reduces the number of cashiers who need to be employed.

Although increasing the amount of jobs done by technology will undoubtedly reduce the amount of jobs available to people in the short term, and will also result in immediate unemployment for some, it is less certain that an increase in technology will cause long-term unemployment on a large scale. As noted above, replacing jobs which formerly had to be done by humans with technological devices and appliances, allows us to create more jobs, and get more done with people. Technology is designed to help us with one specific aspect of our lives, but the human brain is diverse and continually learning. As such, if machines replace the job we were previously doing, it is yet possible for us to learn to do something else instead.

(305 words)

Takeaway

Answers will vary.

However, one key point is that there can still be a lot of mistakes in the writing for it to get a good score. The most important thing is that the examiner can understand what you are trying to say.

SPEAKING INTRODUCTION

MODULE OVERVIEW

The Speaking module is conducted by an IELTS examiner who will meet with you for a one-to-one session. The total time required for the Speaking module is 11–14 minutes, and consists of three parts. The examiner is responsible for timing all parts of the test.

In Part 1 and Part 2, the examiner follows a script with instructions and questions. During Part 3, the examiner will paraphrase question prompts to match them to your proficiency level. Each test is recorded for security and monitoring purposes.

Details of the three parts of the Speaking module are given in the table below.

Part 1: Introduction and Interview

- Lasts 4–5 minutes.
- Examiner asks questions based on topic frames.
- Topics are general, such as your home, family or interests.

Part 2: Individual Long Turn

- Lasts 3–4 minutes.
- You are given a topic card and one minute to prepare notes.
- You speak a monologue based on the topic card.

Part 3: Two-Way Discussion

- Lasts 4–5 minutes.
- Examiner asks you questions based on the topic from Part 2.
- You may be asked up to seven questions, which the examiner adapts to your proficiency level.

Assessment Criteria

You are assessed according to the following criteria:

Fluency and Coherence

- Your ability to express ideas clearly and coherently without long hesitations.
- Lexical Resources
- Your range of vocabulary and
- how appropriate your use of vocabulary is.
- Grammatical Range and Accuracy
- The range of structures you use and
- The number of errors you make.

Pronunciation

- How easy it is to understand what you are saying.
- Your ability to use features of English pronunciation (intonation, stress and connected speech) naturally.
- Note that accents are *not* taken into consideration.

Speaking Strategies

Strategy 1: Don't memorise long answers. Anything the examiner thinks has been memorised will not be assessed.

Strategy 2: Use your imagination in your answers. Remember that the examiner is testing your ability to speak English, not your views or general knowledge.

Strategy 3: Use varied and advanced vocabulary. You must show that you have enough vocabulary to discuss non-personal topics.

Strategy 4: You can stall, but not for long. If you cannot think of an answer to the examiner's question right away, you can say some 'filler' phrases to acknowledge the question and to show the examiner that you are thinking about your answer However, avoid waiting for too long before you speak. Some examples:

- 'That's a good question!'
- 'OK, well, let me see…'
- 'I've never thought about this before…'
- 'Hmm, let me think…'

Strategy 5: Make your voice heard. You should speak loudly enough for the examiner to hear you and for the tape recorder to capture what you are saying.

OBJECTIVES

By the end of this chapter, you should be able to:

- Describe a familiar topic using specific examples.
- Pace yourself while speaking in order to give a full, natural response.
- Use the proper tense when speaking about the past, present and future.
- Practise strategies for answering Introduction and Interview questions.

SPEAKING PART 1 – INTRODUCTION AND INTERVIEW

The examiner introduces himself or herself and verifies your identity by checking your valid ID or passport. The examiner asks you questions covering up to 3 familiar topics. The first topic, for example, may be about your work or studies. The second could be about activities that you like doing in your free time. The third topic could be about your views on public transport in the area where you live.

None of the topics will require any prepared answers. The main aim in Part 1 of the IELTS Speaking is to get you warmed up and ready to talk.

Strategies

- Be prepared to make a good impression from the moment you enter the room.
- Maintain eye contact with the examiner and be mindful of your body language.
- Practise answering questions about familiar topics (people, places, things, activities).

Getting Ready for Speaking Part 1

It is useful to work on giving 30 second answers to questions in Part 1 of the IELTS. You will likely need at least 3 sentences to fill 30 seconds. You could need more, depending on the length of your sentences.

The questions in Part 1 will be on familiar topics such as those given below. Time yourself. Try to speak for at least 30 seconds on each of these subjects.

MY FAVOURITE _____

1. activity
2. book
3. film
4. food
5. holiday
6. place

Practice – Speaking Part 1

The examiner will begin the test by introducing himself or herself, stating the time, date, and location of the test (for the recording), and checking your identity. She or he will then ask you some questions about yourself based on everyday topics.

Here are some examples of questions the examiner may ask on the everyday topic of 'food':

- Let's talk about food.
- What do you like to eat?
- Do you prefer to cook, order takeaway food or eat at restaurants? [Why?]
- What types of food are popular in your country?
- What food have you encountered when travelling that you cannot get at home?

After 3 or 4 questions, the examiner will move on to another familiar topic. Here are some examples of questions the examiner may ask you on the topic of your 'daily routine':

- What do you usually do in the morning?
- Where do you spend most of your time during the day?
- What do you like to do in the evening?
- What do you do at the weekend which you would not normally do during the week?

1. Record yourself. Practise answering the questions above, speaking calmly, clearly and correctly. Try to spend about 30 seconds answering each question. This group of questions should take you 2–3 minutes to answer, slightly less than the time that you will be given during Part 1 of the Speaking module.

2. When you have finished, ask yourself the following questions:

    How did it feel?

    Which questions were easy? Which questions did you struggle with?

    What strategies are useful in Part 1, particularly when you are not sure what to say next?

3. Finally, review the Part 1 Strategies listed above.

KAPLAN TIP

Don't memorise answers to Speaking questions. Even though some topics come up frequently, you should answer spontaneously and imaginatively. If the examiner thinks you are giving a memorised answer, you will receive a very low mark.

Further Practice – Speaking Part 1

This practice session includes more questions than the previous practice, similar to the actual number of questions you will need to answer on the day of the test.

1. Practise answering the questions below, speaking in a calm, clear voice. Record yourself. Try to spend about 30 seconds answering each question. The questions about your family and your studies should take about 4–5 minutes in total to answer. This is the amount of time you will be required to speak for during Part 1 of the test.

2. When you have finished, listen to the recording and ask yourself the following questions:

   Does it sound like you are speaking spontaneously?

   Are there any long hesitations in your answers? If so, review Speaking Strategy 4 in the introduction to Part Five.

Introduction to Interview (4–5 minutes):

The examiner will begin by introducing himself or herself and checking your identity. She or he will then ask you some questions about yourself based on everyday topics.

- Can you tell me your full name, please?
- Thank you. And what should I call you?
- Okay. Can I see your identification, please?
- Thank you. That's great.
- Now, in the first part, I'd like to ask you some questions about yourself.
- Let's talk about what you do for fun.
- What do you enjoy doing, when you are not working or studying?
- Have you done an activity, such as a sport or a musical or artistic activity that requires a lot of practice? [How much?/How often?]
- What activities have you and your family enjoyed doing together?
- What do you like to do for fun that you can only do rarely or occasionally, such as when you are on vacation?
- Now let's talk about life in your country.
- What do you like best about living in your country?
- Is there a special holiday or festival that is celebrated in your country?
- What is a common misperception or misunderstanding about your country?
- Would you ever consider leaving your country and living somewhere else? [Why/Why not?]

Further Practice – Verb Tenses

Here is an exercise to help practise varying the verb tenses when speaking.

1. Let's review what we mean by past, present and future tense.

    PAST: formed with verb ending in –ed or irregular form (*sat* for *sit*); may include have, has, or had; was or were; used to.

    PRESENT: may be formed with am/are/is, possibly with verb ending in –ing

    FUTURE: will/shall; going to

2. Now, practise switching verb tenses. Say three sentences about each topic below: one in the past tense, one in the present tense, and one in the future tense.

    TELL ME ABOUT _____

    1. where you live

    2. what you like to eat

    3. how you travel to work or school

    4. your family

    5. where you like to relax

    6. how you exercise

Takeaway

In the Speaking module you must be ready to make a good impression from the moment you enter the room. You can practise for this, and practise answering questions on familiar topics.

KAPLAN TIP

Ask a friend or family member to help you practise the IELTS speaking tasks. Record yourself answering their questions, so you can play it back and check whether you have used varied and advanced vocabulary.

You should also count every time you use 'filler,' and keep practising so you can get it down to zero by Test Day.

Further Practice – Speaking Part 1

Have someone ask you these questions, and practise good eye contact and body language when answering them.

Part 1

Introduction to interview (4–5 minutes): The examiner will begin by introducing himself or herself and checking your identity. She or he will then ask you some questions about yourself based on everyday topics.

- Can you tell me your full name, please?
- Thank you. And what should I call you?
- Okay. Can I see your identification, please?
- Thank you. That's great.
- Now, in the first part, I'd like to ask you some questions about yourself.
- Let's talk about your family.
- How often do you get to see your family? [Why?]
- Who in your family would you say that you get along with the best?
- Is there a certain time or event that you usually spend with your family?
- How do you like living with your family?
- Now let's talk about your studies.
- Which subject did you like best when you were at school?
- Which subject are you planning to study/did you study at university? [Why?]
- Do you prefer to study from books, or using computers and websites? [Why?]
- Which subject do you wish you had studied more? [Why?]

OBJECTIVES

By the end of this chapter, you should be able to:

- Make notes that will help you speak on a familiar topic for 1–2 minutes.
- Use appropriate connecting words and avoid unnecessary filler.
- Answer wrap-up questions thoroughly and thoughtfully.
- Practise strategies for the Individual Long Turn.

SPEAKING PART 2 – INDIVIDUAL LONG TURN

This part of the test will last for 3–4 minutes. The examiner will give you a card containing a topic and some bullet point prompts. Before speaking you will have 1 minute to prepare and make notes on a sheet of paper. You will then be required to speak for 1–2 minutes. When you are finished speaking, the examiner will ask 1 or 2 follow-up questions.

You will not be allowed to bring any pens, pencils or paper into the examination room – these will be provided by the examiner. The notes are not marked and will be collected and destroyed after the test. You cannot take them out of the room. While you are making notes, the examiner will not talk to you.

Strategies

- Read the task card carefully.
- Make brief notes about each point on the card.
- Practise brainstorming and taking notes, to ensure you will have enough ideas to speak for 1–2 minutes

Getting Ready for Speaking Part 2 – Connecting Words

Connecting words link ideas, showing how these ideas are related. They can be used to:

- add something (and)
- make a contrast (but, however)
- explain cause (because)
- introduce an example (for example), or
- give a sense of time or order (first, next, in those days, now)

They are very useful when you want to add more detail, give another example, or explain your thoughts more fully. All these strategies can be useful for giving a longer, more fluent, coherent and complete answer, which is an essential skill in the IELTS Speaking module.

1. Practise speaking for a minute about each of the following topics. Try to use as many of the connecting words (listed above) as possible to connect your sentences. Record yourself. Count how many connecting words you used for each topic.

    A MEMORABLE _____

    A. meal

    B. event

    C. show/programme

    D. photo

    E. trip

    F. sight/view

2. When you have finished, ask yourself the following questions:

    How did it feel?

    Which questions were easy? Which questions did you struggle with?

    What strategies are useful in Part 1, particularly when you are not sure what to say next?

3. Finally, review the Part 2 Strategies listed below.

Further Strategies – Speaking Part 2

A common problem in the IELTS is how to speak for a longer period of time. Sometimes it can be difficult to think of enough things to say. To speak for longer, you will need to add details or further points. You could do this by adding new ideas, or by expanding upon ideas you have already mentioned.

To come up with further ideas, here are a few strategies you might employ:

*   Check your notes.
*   Review the task card.
*   Check the question again.
*   Think of an example to expand on a point you already made.
*   Try to think while you talk.

Practice – Speaking Part 2

1. Review the example task card below. Take 1 minute to think about what you are going to say and write your notes. Time yourself, or have a friend time you. Try to speak for 2 full minutes. Record yourself. Try to use as many of the connecting words above as possible in the two minutes.

2. When the time is up. Listen back to your recording and consider the following questions:

    Was it easy or difficult to talk for 2 full minutes?

    How many connecting words were you able to use?

    Can you think of other connecting words you might have used to make your answer longer?

3. Review the options of what to do if you are not sure what to say next.

Example

Candidates' task card instructions:

Task Card

Please read the topic below carefully. You will be asked to talk about it for 1–2 minutes. You will have one minute to think about what you are going to say. You can make some notes to help you if you wish.

Describe a place you have visited. You should say:

- *Where it was and when you went there*
- *Whether anyone went with you*
- *What happened during your visit.*

Also, explain what you liked or didn't like about that place.

The examiner may then ask you a couple of brief questions to wrap up this part of the test. Further questions:

- *What do you like about visiting different places?*
- *Do you like to visit faraway places, or do you prefer to stay closer to home? [Why?]*
- *What place would you like to visit that you haven't been to yet? [Why?]*

Speaking Part 2 – Taking Notes

There are different approaches to taking notes, but it is essential that you practice taking notes during Part 2 of the Speaking module, and that you do so on Test Day. This will help to ensure that you don't run out of things to say before the time is up. Aim to speak for 2 minutes or more.

1. Have a look at the notes that you took while practising the long turn in the previous exercise.

   Do they conform to any of the following styles of note-taking?

   - an outline
   - a list
   - a spider's web (main topic in the centre; talking points radiating outward)

   Or have you developed a different/unique style of note taking?

2. It is important that you find the approach that words best for you. You need to be able to brainstorm and make the notes quickly and efficiently in one minute. You also need to ensure you have something to say about each point on the task card.

3. Try experimenting with different types of note-taking as you work through the example Task cards below.

Practice – Speaking Part 2 – Taking Notes

1. Review the first task card below. Take 1 minute to think about what you are going to say and write your notes. Time yourself, or have a friend time you. Try to speak for 2 full minutes. Record yourself. Try to use as many of the connecting words above as possible when giving your answer.

2. Review the options of what to do if you are not sure what to say next.

3. Repeat these steps for the second task card below.

Task Card 1

Please read the topic below carefully. You will be asked to talk about it for 1–2 minutes. You will have 1 minute to think about what you are going to say. You can make some notes to help you if you wish.

Describe your dream job when you were a child. You should say:

- *How old you were, and what your dream job was at that age*
- *Why that job appealed to you*
- *What type of work you thought was involved in that job*

Also, explain whether it is still your dream job, and why it is or isn't.

The examiner may then ask you a couple of brief questions to wrap up this part of the test. Further questions:

- *What was your first job?*
- *Do you prefer working on a team, or working alone? [Why?]*
- *What would you do if you didn't have to work?*

Task Card 2

Please read the topic below carefully. You will be asked to talk about it for 1–2 minutes. You will have 1 minute to think about what you are going to say. You can make some notes to help you if you wish.

Describe an animal you encountered. You should say:

- *What type of animal it was*
- *Where you encountered the animal, and whether anyone was with you*
- *What happened during the encounter?*

Also, explain what you liked or didn't like about the animal.

The examiner may then ask you a couple of brief questions to wrap up this part of the test. Further questions:

- *What is your favourite type of animal? [Why?]*
- *If you could have any animal as a pet, which would you choose? [Why?]*
- *Is there a type of animal that frightens you? [Why/Why not?]*

Takeaway

In the Speaking module, you must be ready to speak for 1–2 minutes on the Individual Long Turn. You can practise for this, and practise answering questions on familiar topics.

KAPLAN TIP

Practise making notes and speaking for 2 minutes. Use the task cards in your IELTS course materials, or find more task cards online. Try making notes in different styles, to determine which works best for you.

Further Practice – Speaking Part 2

Time yourself strictly, or have a friend or family member to time you and ask the wrap-up questions.

Part 2

Individual long turn (3–4 minutes): Candidates' task card instructions:

Task Card

Please read the topic below carefully. You will be asked to talk about it for 1–2 minutes. You will have 1 minute to think about what you are going to say. You can make some notes to help you if you wish.

Describe an activity you do to relax. You should say:

- *Where and when you like to do the activity*
- *What is involved in the activity?*
- *Why you find it relaxing*

Also, explain why you think others would enjoy the activity.

The examiner may then ask you a couple of brief questions to wrap up this part of the test. Further questions:

- *How did you get started in the activity?*
- *Is there a cost to the activity?*
- *Where is the most relaxing place you have been?*

OBJECTIVES

By the end of this chapter, you should be able to:

- Discuss your opinion on an abstract topic.
- Explain the extent to which you agree or disagree.
- Use strategies to expand your answers.
- Practise strategies for answering Discussion questions.

SPEAKING PART 3 – TWO-WAY DISCUSSION

This part lasts 4–5 minutes. The examiner will ask you to discuss some abstract, non-personal questions. Depending on your level of English and performance, you might be asked up to 7 questions on a variety of themes related to the same topic that you discussed in Part 2. You are not required or expected to ask the examiner any questions.

Strategies

- Use key phrases to introduce your opinion and connecting words to link ideas.
- Express your opinions with confidence and justify them with relevant examples.
- Speak at length, but stay on topic.

Getting Ready for Speaking Part 3

It does not matter if you agree or disagree. But whichever side you choose, you must be sure to use examples to illustrate and support your opinion.

1. Look at the following list of questions. For each question, say whether you agree or disagree and explain why. Record yourself. Try to say 4–5 sentences for each response.

   DO YOU AGREE or DISAGREE?

   Would you agree that young people should read more books?

   Would you agree that everyone should learn a foreign language?

   Would you agree that a university education should be free for everyone?

   Would you agree that people shouldn't smoke?

   Would you agree that health care should be free for everyone?

Remember that agreeing or disagreeing is not simply a matter of picking one side. You also need to be ready to express the degree to which you agree or disagree. There are five possible options. Beside each option are phrases that you can use to indicate that level of agreement.

STRONGLY AGREE – You are exactly right/That's absolutely correct.

SOMEWHAT AGREE – I agree up to a point/I would generally agree, but...

NEITHER AGREE NOR DISAGREE – I can see both sides/It depends on the situation.

SOMEWHAT DISAGREE – In most cases, no/Sometimes, perhaps, but I would say...

STRONGLY DISAGREE – I don't agree at all/No, that is never the case.

2. Practise answering the questions above again. This time, chose a different level of agreement and say 4–5 sentences to support this level of agreement. Record yourself. When you listen back, do you sound convincing?

KAPLAN TIP

Remember, the examiner is only interested in your level of English, not whether or not you agree or disagree on a specific issue. You do not have to express your real opinion in order to show how well you make a point. However, expressing your real opinion might make the task easier.

Practice – Speaking Part 3

1.   It is best to practise for IELTS Speaking Part 3 by having someone read you the questions below. If you do not have a partner to work with, read the questions below yourself, and record your answers on a phone/computer. Try to give full answers (4–5 sentences) for each question.

2.   Listen to your recording. How would you rate yourself according to the four criteria (fluency, vocabulary, grammar, pronunciation) listed in the introduction to Part Five?

During Part 3 of the Speaking module, the examiner will ask you further questions related to your topic in Part 2. If your Long Turn topic related to 'city life,' your follow-up discussion questions might be...

Let's talk about living in a big city:

- *Do you think living in a big city is better than living in a small town? [Why?]*
- *What are some of the advantages of living in a big city?*
- *Would you agree that life in a big city can be too crowded and too expensive? [Why/Why not?]*

Finally, let's talk living in a small town:

- *Would you prefer to live in a small town that is close to a big city, or one that is far from the city? [Why?]*
- *What are some of the disadvantages of living in a small town?*
- *Would you agree that a small town is better for families with young children? [Why/Why not?]*

Further Strategies – Speaking Part 3

In Speaking Part 3, you will often be asked to discuss abstract ideas. By 'abstract' ideas, we mean any ideas that are intangible or complex. Something you can't see, or that is difficult to explain, is abstract. These ideas can be more challenging for non-native speakers to talk about because they involve more advanced vocabulary and phrasing than actual/concrete ideas, such as people, places and things. Thus, it is essential that you practise talking (and thinking) about abstract ideas in English, so that you are fully prepared for Test Day.

Practise answering the following questions involving abstract ideas. Have someone ask you the questions, or read them yourself and record your answers.

1.   Why do you think young people these days are waiting longer to get married?

2.   Does it really make a difference to the environment if one person recycles?

3.   Should everyone learn a new language?

4.   People are afraid of failure. Describe a situation where 'failure' is a good thing.

Further Practice – Speaking Part 3

1. If you do not have a partner to work with, read the questions below yourself, and record your answers on a phone/computer. Try to give full answers (4–5 sentences) for each question.

2. Listen to your recording. How would you rate yourself according to the four criteria (fluency, vocabulary, grammar, pronunciation) listed in the introduction to Part Five?

Let's talk about selfies (photographs you take of yourself with a smartphone or webcam):

- *Do you like to take selfies? [Why/Why not?]*
- *Would you agree that some people take too many selfies? [Why/Why not?]*
- *What would you do if you saw someone taking a selfie at an inappropriate time or place, such as a funeral or a war memorial? [Why?]*

Finally, let's talk about photographs more generally:

- *Do you prefer to take photographs with your phone, or with a camera? [Why?]*
- *Why do you think people like to keep photographs throughout their lifetime?*
- *Would you agree that there should be limits to the kinds of photographs that can be shared on social media? [Why/Why not?]*

Takeaway

In the Speaking module, you must be ready to make clear the extent to which you agree / disagree, and your ability to explain abstract ideas. Think about any particular questions that were difficult or challenging.

IMPROVE YOUR SCORE

Questions in Speaking Part 3 may touch on topics that have been in the news, such as recent world events or developments in technology. Read a newspaper or magazine at least once a week, so you can be familiar with these issues and any relevant English expressions. New words related to technology appear every year, so be sure that you are up to date with your pop culture technology (for example, *dotcom*, *selfie*, *unplugged*). Using common, current vocabulary correctly in your Speaking module is not required, but it can help you earn a higher mark.

Further Practice – Speaking Part 3

Have someone ask you these questions, and practise good eye contact and body language when answering them.

Part 3

Two-way discussion (4–5 minutes): In Part 3, the examiner will ask you further questions related to the topic in Part 2.

Let's talk about school:

- What was your favourite year at school? [Why?]
- How is school different for children today from how it was when you were a child?
- Would you agree that all children should attend school until the age of 18? [Why/Why not?]

Finally, let's talk about education more generally:

- Do you prefer to learn from a printed book, or from online resources on tablet or computer? [Why?]
- Would you agree that a university education should be provided free of charge to everyone? [Why/Why not?]
- Do you think that schools and universities prepare young people well for future employment? [Why/Why not?]

SPEAKING CHAPTER 4

OBJECTIVES

By the end of this chapter, you should be able to:

- Deal with common problems that arise during the Speaking module.
- Improve your pronunciation and intonation.
- Avoid repetition and filler.
- Practise strategies for all three parts of the Speaking module

THE SPEAKING MODULE

This lesson will cover some of the key issues around scoring for the IELTS Speaking module and give you a chance to practise the full module.

Getting Ready for the Speaking Module

The following are common problems that candidates may have during the IELTS Speaking module:

- not hearing the question
- not understanding the question
- making a mistake in your answer
- not knowing how to answer the question
- not having enough to say or not being able to think of enough points to cover.

1. Review these General Speaking module strategies:

   - Use your imagination in your answers
   - Remember that the examiner is testing your English, not your views or general knowledge
   - Use varied vocabulary. You will get marks for your attempts, even if you make mistakes.
   - Use a mixture of simple and complex sentence structure

2. Other problems and difficulties will be due to issues in using the right words and correct phrasing, and in speaking clearly and pronouncing and intoning words correctly.

Speaking Practice – Pronunciation and Intonation

Take turns asking and answering these questions with a partner. If there is no partner available, read the questions yourself and record your answers. Listen to your partner, or to the recording. Does pronunciation make any words difficult to understand? Note those words and practise their pronunciation.

1. Websites with photos and videos of cats are more popular than news sites. Is that a good thing, or a problem?

2. There's an old saying: Good fences make good neighbours. Do you think that's true?

3. People don't exercise as much as they used to. Why do you think that is?

4. The world does not do enough to help after a natural disaster. Do you agree?

KAPLAN TIP

Speak loudly and clearly. Be sure to pronounce your words correctly and vary your intonation. Most importantly, ensure that you are loud enough so that the interviewer can hear you, and the recorder can pick up your voice.

Speaking Practice – What would you do if . . .

Don't worry. Everyone feels stress about the speaking module, no matter how much you prepare. The key is to have strategies in place that you can use.

1. Review the General Speaking strategies in the introductory section of this module. Look these over as you practise, and again prior to the Speaking module – perhaps the night before, if not the same day.

2. Brainstorm answers to the following question before checking the answers below.

WHAT WOULD YOU DO IF . . .

- you didn't understand the question?
- you did not hear one or more of the words in the question?
- you made a mistake?
- you couldn't think of something to say?
- you had an idea of what to say, but couldn't think of the right words in English?

If you do not hear or understand the question, you can ask the examiner to repeat it. Another way to check is to repeat the question in your own words.

If you make a mistake, correct yourself. If you use a wrong word or phrase, go back and use the correct expression. If the mistake throws you off, say, "Excuse me. Let me start over."

When you make a mistake don't panic. It is common to talk faster when you are nervous, but try to speak at a comfortable, even pace.

We have discussed many strategies for what to do if you can't think of what to say. Review them and think about which you might find most useful.

If you can't think of the right words in English, then you might want to go on to a different example or different point. Perhaps the right English words will come to you while you are saying something else.

Practice – Speaking Module

All three parts of the IELTS Speaking module will take 11–14 minutes to complete. Try to practise the module with a friend or partner who will act as the examiner, asking the questions and timing the three parts of the module. If there is no one available to help, read the questions loud and record your answers on a phone/computer.

Part 1

Introduction to interview (4–5 minutes): The examiner will begin by introducing himself or herself and checking your identity. She or he will then ask you some questions about yourself based on everyday topics.

- *Can you tell me your full name, please?*
- *Thank you. And what should I call you?*
- *Okay. Can I see your identification, please?*
- *Thank you. That's great.*
- *Now, in the first part, I'd like to ask you some questions about yourself.*

- *Let's talk about your accommodation.*
- *Do you live in a house or a flat?*
- *How long have you lived there? Do you like it? [Why/Why not?]*
- *Do most people in your home town live in houses or in flats?*

- *Now let's talk about shopping.*
- *Do you like shopping?*
- *What kinds of things do you like buying?*
- *Do you prefer shopping online, or going out to the shops? [Why?]*

Part 2

Individual long turn (3–4 minutes): Candidates' task card instructions:

Task Card

Please read the topic below carefully. You will be asked to talk about it for one to two minutes. You will have one minute to think about what you are going to say. You can make some notes to help you if you wish.

Describe a city or town you have enjoyed visiting. You should say:

- *when you visited the city or town*
- *whether you made the visit alone or with others*
- *what you did there*
- *how long you stayed there*

Also, explain why you enjoyed the visit

The examiner may then ask you a couple of brief questions to wrap up this part of the test. Further questions:

- *Would you like to visit the place again?*
- *Has anyone you know visited the city/town?*
- *What would you recommend that a first-time visitor must see or do?*

Part 3

Two-way discussion (4–5 minutes): In Part 3, the examiner will ask you further questions related to the topic in Part 2.

Let's talk about travel and tourism:

- *Would you agree that people travel more nowadays than they did in the past? [Why/ Why not?]*
- *What can you learn from travelling to other countries?*
- *Do you think people will travel more, or less, in the future? [Why?]*

Finally, let's talk about tourism, travel and the environment:

- *What positive or negative effects does tourism have on a local economy?*
- *What effects does travel have on the environment?*
- *What can countries do to promote tourism?*

Takeaway

In the Speaking module, you must be prepared for a variety of different speaking activities. All the topics will be familiar, so you can focus on showing your grammatical and lexical abilities, while maintaining good eye contact and body language to communicate your confidence to the examiner.

IMPROVE YOUR SCORE

Listen to the intonation of native English speakers, and pay attention to where they place the emphasis on certain words and phrases, and where their voices rise and fall. Podcasts or radio programmes are a good source for this. You might try listening to different accents from the English-speaking world (American, Australian, Canadian, English, and Scottish) to increase your exposure to different intonations, and prepare yourself for Test Day.

Further Practice – Speaking Module

Part 1

Introduction to interview (4–5 minutes): The examiner will begin by introducing himself or herself and checking your identity. She or he will then ask you some questions about yourself based on everyday topics.

Let's talk about families.

- *Would you say that your family is large family, or a small family?*
- *Is there a holiday or festival when your family gets together?*
- *Which of your relatives would you say that you are closest to? [Why?]*

- *Now, let's talk about television.*
- *Do you like watching television? [Why/Why not?]*
- *Do you prefer to get your news from TV, or from other sources, such as a newspaper? [Why?]*
- *What kinds of TV programmes did you like to watch when you were a child?*

Part 2

Individual long turn (3–4 minutes): Candidates' task card instructions:

Task Card

Please read the topic below carefully. You will be asked to talk about it for one to two minutes. You will have one minute to think about what you are going to say. You can make some notes to help you if you wish.

Describe a skill (for example, driving, cooking, golfing) you have learned successfully. You should say:

- *which skill you have learned*
- *why you learned it*
- *who helped you learn it*
- *how long it took to learn it*

Also, explain what helped you to become good at the skill

The examiner may then ask you a couple of brief questions to wrap up this part of the test. Further questions:

- *How often do you get to use this skill?*
- *Do you know anyone else who is good at this skill?*
- *Could you teach this skill to someone else?*

Part 3

Two-way discussion (4–5 minutes): In Part 3, the examiner will ask you further questions related to the topic in Part 2.

Let's talk about skills and everyday life:

- *What skills are valued most in your country?*
- *Can you compare the skills that are important nowadays with the skills that were important 20 or 30 years ago?*
- *What everyday skills are the most difficult to learn? [Why?]*

Finally, let's talk about skills and training:

- *Which qualities does a good trainer need to have?*
- *Why do many companies invest a lot of money in training?*
- *Would you agree that it is easier to teach yourself a new skill, or to learn from a trainer? [Why?]*

PART SIX

IELTS
Practice Tests

LISTENING MODULE

 Practice Test 1, Track 1 (Track 16)

Section 1: Questions 1–10

Questions 1–4

Complete the notes below.

Write NO MORE THAN TWO WORDS AND/OR A NUMBER for each answer.

Write your answers in boxes 1–4 on your answer sheet.

NOTES ON COURSES AVAILABLE

Example:

Number of language courses per week: ...10...

Languages

- Modern European Languages: French, Spanish, German, Dutch, Polish
- Ancient Languages: Latin and **1** ....
- Asian Languages: Hindi and **2** ....

Cost £25.00 per person per term

Notes: Bulk booking (more than two courses for **3** .... terms) 10% discount.

To reserve a place in a language class, telephone Mrs Johnson on extension **4** ....

Questions 5–10

Complete the table and information below.

Write NO MORE THAN TWO WORDS AND/OR A NUMBER for each answer.

Write your answers in boxes 5–10 on your answer sheet.

Monthly Computer Courses

Date	Subject	Places Available	Cost per Person
1st February	**5**	24	£40.00
March	Excel	**6** .... only	£45.00
April	Outlook	19	**7** ....
3rd **8**	Word	**9**	£55.00

To book a place on a computer course, call Mary Jones before **10** ....

Practice Test 1, Track 2 (Track 17)

Section 2: Questions 11–20

Questions 11–16

Complete this summary of the welcoming speech.

Write NO MORE THAN TWO WORDS AND/OR A NUMBER for each answer.

Write your answers in boxes 11–16 on your answer sheet.

Dear Joe,

You missed the Welcome meeting. We were greeted by the principal of Donleavy
11 .... , who explained how the university has **12** .... campuses.

He told us where all the important buildings on this campus are and also explained
which subjects are studied on the other two. The principal's **13** .... is on our
campus. Weekly **14** .... are held in the Office and Administration Block every
Tuesday at 1:30 p.m., and we are encouraged to attend. The university shop sells all
the **15** .... and stationery we might need, and you can find it next to the cafeteria.

Remember, we must carry our **16** .... to get into the campus.

Regards,

Rebecca

Questions 17–20

Complete the labels on the buildings in the map.

Write NO MORE THAN TWO WORDS AND/OR A NUMBER for each answer.

Write your answers in boxes 17–20 on your answer sheet.

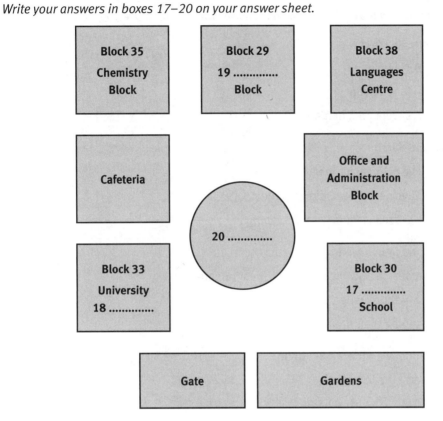

🎧 **Practice Test 1, Track 3 (Track 18)**

Section 3: Questions 21–30

Choose the correct letter: A, B or C.

Write your answers in boxes 21–30 on your answer sheet.

21 Bill was ill. What was wrong?

   A A cold

   B A food allergy

   C A severe pain in his head

22 Bill and Sarah

   A live near each other.

   B have never worked on a project together.

   C have plans for later that evening.

23 Bill and Sarah have to

   A research and write a survey questionnaire.

   B ask shopkeepers questions.

   C submit their project via the internet.

24 What does Sarah want Bill to do?

   A Visit the library

   B Write a list of questions

   C Use a computer

25 Which of the following items will be included in Bill and Sarah's research?

   A Deodorants and cosmetics

   B Electrical goods

   C Food and clothing

26 With what aspect of the project does Bill express concern?

   A Meeting the project's timeline

   B Invading people's privacy

   C Finding enough reference material

27 What does Bill plan to do for the rest of the day?

    A   Review the notes from the previous week

    B   Prepare for his next meeting with Sarah

    C   Find people to participate in the research

28 What does Sarah do for Bill?

    A   Lets him borrow her book

    B   Gives him a copy of her notes

    C   Promises to help him study

29 What does Sarah have to do at the library?

    A   Research

    B   Meet Bill

    C   Collect some books

30 Where do Bill and Sarah agree to meet the next day?

    A   In the library

    B   In class

    C   In the laboratory

Practice Test 1, Track 4 (Track 19)

Section 4: Questions 31–40

Questions 31–32

Choose the correct letter: A, B or C.

Write your answers in boxes 31–32 on your answer sheet.

31 Who is giving this talk?

    A An artist

    B An art critic

    C A curator

32 Why did the speaker choose to speak about Joan Miró?

    A Because a new work by Miró was recently added to the gallery

    B Because he thought Miró would appeal to people with different tastes

    C Because he felt everyone would be familiar with Joan Miró's art

Questions 33–35

Which THREE features below are mentioned by the speaker as characteristic of Joan Miró's art? Choose THREE letters: A–G.

Write your answers in boxes 33–35 on your answer sheet.

    A Themes from Spanish history

    B The use of primary colours

    C Influence of surrealism

    D Complex geometric forms

    E Large paintings

    F Equal number of sculptures and paintings

    G Birds and trees

Questions 36–40

Complete this table with information from the listening.

Write NO MORE THAN TWO WORDS AND/OR A NUMBER for each answer.

Write your answers in boxes 36–40 on your answer sheet.

THREE OF MIRÓ'S GREAT WORKS

TITLE	DATE	LOCATION	DETAILS
Woman and **36**	1982	A **37** .... in Barcelona	Tall sculpture, covered in **38** ....
Woman	**39**	National Gallery of Art, Washington, D.C.	Large canvas, bright colours
Seated Woman II	1939	Guggenheim Museum, New York	Painted when Miró was influenced by the **40** .... in Spain

ACADEMIC READING MODULE

Reading Passage 1

*You should spend about 20 minutes on **Questions 1–14**, which are based on Reading Passage 1 below.*

Gender selection—the choosing of a baby's gender prior to birth—occurs in many parts of the world. In China and India, for example, a baby's gender is considered to be of vital importance to the family, and male babies are often preferred over females for cultural reasons. In Western countries as well, there are many reasons why a family might want to choose a baby's sex. Often, parents wish to have a mix of both boys and girls in the family. There are also health reasons for gender selection: many diseases affect children of only one sex, and a family that is susceptible to these diseases may wish to choose a baby's gender to avoid having an affected child.

This demand for gender choice by parents has led scientists worldwide to investigate gender selection prior to conception. Conventional wisdom states that the father's sperm is the main determinant of a child's gender, but recent research has begun to reveal a number of other possible determining factors.

Elissa Cameron's research, conducted in 2007 at the University of Pretoria, South Africa, investigated the effects of diet on sex ratios at birth. In one experiment, she changed the blood sugar level of female mice prior to conception by putting a chemical in the animals' water. Mice that received the additive saw their blood sugar levels fall from 6.47 to 5.24 millimols/litre. A separate control group of mice received pure water, without the additive. After a few days, the two groups of mice were allowed to mate. In the control group, 41% of the mice were born female, as compared to 47% in the group that received the additive—a disparity that Dr Cameron ascribed to the differences in the mothers' blood sugar levels.

Interestingly, the idea that blood sugar levels affect a baby's sex follows traditional wisdom. It has long been believed that mothers should eat more red meat and salty foods—which raise blood sugar for a long period—if they want to have a boy; they are advised to eat chocolates and sweets—which raise blood sugar levels for a short time—if they want a girl.

Another researcher in this field, Fiona Matthews of the University of Exeter, England, has come up with further evidence in support of the effect of diet on the sex of the unborn child. Her study followed 740 pregnant women who kept detailed records of their diets before conception. Her study found that mothers who consumed high-energy foods prior to conception were slightly more likely to have boys. The food with the greatest effect seemed to be breakfast cereals, which tend to be high in energy and often high in sodium content as well. Among women eating cereals on a daily basis, 59% had boys, compared with 43% of women who ate less than one bowl of breakfast cereal per week. These results are said to echo those seen in other animals, for example horses and cows, which statistically bear more males when well-fed.

The eating habits of women in rich Western countries could explain the slight fall in male births that has been reported over the past several years. In the UK, male births are falling by 1 per 1,000 births per year. This decrease could be ascribed to the decline in the number of adults and adolescent girls eating breakfast on a regular basis. In addition, the popularity of low-calorie diets for females of child-bearing age could also be a factor contributing to the reduction in male births.

The recent decline in male births in Western countries appears to make sense if one looks at it from an evolutionary standpoint. Historically, more boys tend to be born in times of food plenty, while females tend to be born in times of scarcity. One explanation is that when food is scarce, it is better for the survival of the species for female children to be born—as one male can father offspring by many females. Lower-calorie diets among Western women could be biologically echoing the effects of scarcity—hence, the decline in male births.

So what can we conclude from this complicated picture? If you would like to have a son, it might be a good idea to eat a breakfast that includes cereal. On the other hand, if you would prefer to give birth to a daughter, then cut out breakfast and continue a weight reduction diet, at least until after conception.

Questions 1–8

Do the following statements agree with the information given in Reading Passage 1?

In boxes 1–8 on your answer sheet, write

TRUE	*if the statement agrees with the information*
FALSE	*if the statement contradicts the information*
NOT GIVEN	*if there is no information on this*

1 Mothers in India eat cereal for breakfast so that they will have male babies.

2 New drugs have been developed that allow parents to choose the sex of their child.

3 People used to think that the father was responsible for the sex of the baby.

4 Elissa Cameron used both humans and mice in her research.

5 The majority of research on gender selection is happening in Europe.

6 People in the United Kingdom often do not eat breakfast.

7 Some people think that drinking tea has an effect on the sex of a baby.

8 High-calorie diets have been shown to increase the likelihood of female births.

Questions 9–13

*Complete each sentence with the correct ending, **A-K**, below.*

Write your answers in boxes 9–13 on your answer sheet.

9   In Western countries, gender selection

10   Elissa Cameron

11   Fiona Matthews

12   Eating breakfast cereal on a daily basis

13   Evolution seems to support

A   artificially decreased the blood sugar levels of mice.

B   is often based on cultural preferences.

C   asked patients to write down everything that they ate and when they ate it.

D   the influence of food scarcity upon sex ratios at birth.

E   that adding sodium to food affects the sex of a baby.

F   is an American scientist.

G   sometimes occurs for health reasons.

H   an equal balance between male and female children.

I   conducted research on horses and cows.

J   is more common in the UK than in other Western countries.

K   seems to increase the likelihood of male births.

Question 14

Choose the correct letter: A, B, C, D or E.

Write your answer in box 14 on your answer sheet.

14   Which of the following is the most suitable title for Reading Passage 1?

   A   Eating Cereal Is Good for Pregnant Women

   B   Research Says Mice Make Better Mothers

   C   Diet May Influence the Sex of Your Baby

   D   Asian Research Influences Western Medicine

   E   Gender Selection Research Sparks Scientific Debate

Reading Passage 2

*You should spend about 20 minutes on **Questions 15–27**, which are based on Reading Passage 2 below.*

The Disease Multiple Sclerosis

A Multiple sclerosis (MS) is a disease in which the patient's immune system attacks the central nervous system. This can lead to numerous physical and mental symptoms, as the disease affects the transmission of electrical signals between the body and the brain. However, the human body, being a flexible, adaptable system, can compensate for some level of damage, so a person with MS can look and feel fine even though the disease is present.

B MS patients can have one of two main varieties of the disease: the relapsing form and the primary progressive form. In the relapsing form, the disease progresses in a series of jumps; at times it is in remission, which means that a person's normal functions return for a period of time before the system goes into relapse and the disease again becomes more active. This is the most common form of MS; 80-90% of people have this form of the disease when they are first diagnosed. The relapse-remission cycle can continue for many years. Eventually, however, loss of physical and cognitive function starts to take place, and the remissions become less frequent.

C In the primary progressive form of MS, there are no remissions, and a continual but steady loss of physical and cognitive functions takes place. This condition affects about 10-15% of sufferers at diagnosis.

D The expected course of the disease, or prognosis, depends on many variables: the subtype of the disease, the patient's individual characteristics and the initial symptoms. Life expectancy of patients, however, is often nearly the same as that of an unaffected person—provided that a reasonable standard of care is received. In some cases, a near-normal life span is possible.

E The cause of the disease is unclear; it seems that some people have a genetic susceptibility, which is triggered by some unknown environmental factor. Onset of the disease usually occurs in young adults between the ages of 20 and 40. It is more common in women than men; however, it has also been diagnosed in young children and elderly people.

F Hereditary factors have been seen to have some relevance. Studies of identical twins have shown that if one twin has the disease, then it is likely that the other twin will develop it. In addition, it is important to realise that close relatives of patients have a higher chance of developing the disease than people without a relative who has MS.

G Where people live can be seen to have a clear effect, as MS does not occur as frequently in every country. It commonly affects Caucasian people, particularly in North America, Europe and Australia. It has been recognised that MS is more common the further the country is away from the equator, and the incidence of

MS is generally much higher in northern countries with temperate climates than in warmer southern countries.

H Three things, which do not normally occur in healthy people, happen to people who have MS. First, tiny patches of inflammation occur in the brain or spinal cord. Second, the protective coating around the axons, or nerve fibres, in the body start to deteriorate. Third, the axons themselves become damaged or destroyed. This can lead to a wide range of symptoms in the patient, depending on where the affected axons are located.

I A common symptom of MS is blurred vision caused by inflammation of the optic nerve. Another sign is loss of muscle tone in arms and legs; this is when control of muscle movement, or strength in the arms or legs, can be lost. Sense of touch can be lost so that the body is unable to feel heat or cold or the sufferer experiences temperature inappropriately; that is, feeling heat when it is cold and vice versa. Balance can also be affected; some people may eventually have to resort to a wheelchair, either on a permanent or temporary basis. The course of the disease varies from person to person.

J A diagnosis of MS is often confirmed by the use of a magnetic resonance imaging (MRI) scan, which can show defects in the brain and spinal cord. Once diagnosed, MS is a lifelong disease; no cure exists, although a number of medical treatments have been shown to reduce relapses and slow the progression of the disease. It is important that patients with the disease are diagnosed early so that treatment, which can slow the disease, can be started early.

Questions 15–19

Reading Passage 2 has ten paragraphs labelled A–J. Which paragraph contains the following information?

Write your answers in boxes 15–19 on your answer sheet.

NB: *You may use any letter more than once.*

15   The main types of the disease

16   Loss of the sense of feeling

17   The progress of the disease

18   Treatments for the disease

19   The effects of geography

252

Questions 20–27

Complete this table below.

Choose NO MORE THAN THREE WORDS from the passage for each answer.

Write your answers in boxes 20–27 on your answer sheet.

Main Types of **20**		
21 .... 80–90% of sufferers	Primary Progressive Form **22** .... of patients	
Causes are unclear.		
23 .... **24** .... people are more often affected than other races. There is a higher incidence where the weather is **25**	Hereditary If one **26** .... is affected, the other is likely to develop MS.	
Three effects of MS:		
Inflammation in the brain and/or **27**	Coating of nerve fibres damaged.	Axons themselves damaged.

Reading Passage 3

*You should spend about 20 minutes on **Questions 28–40**, which are based on Reading Passage 3 below.*

Surge Protection

With more devices connecting to the world's electrical networks, protecting electrical systems and devices from power surges—also known as distribution overcurrent—has become more important than ever. Without adequate overcurrent protection, interruptions to electrical service can have catastrophic effects on individuals, cities and entire nations.

In a normal electrical system, customers are supplied with a steady electrical current—a predetermined voltage necessary to operate safely all electrical equipment connected to that system. This steady electrical supply is subject to minimal variations—variations that are imperceptible to the consumer and do not normally harm electrical devices. An overload current is any surge that exceeds the variances of this normal operating current. The higher the overcurrent, the more potential it has to damage electrical devices. One of the most important principles of overcurrent protection, therefore, is that the higher the magnitude of the overload current, the faster the overcurrent must be disrupted.

How do overcurrents occur? Most overcurrents are temporary and harmless, caused when motors start up or transformers are energised. Such things as defective motors, overloaded equipment or too many loads on one circuit, however, can cause harmful, sustained overcurrents, which must be shut off quickly to avoid damaging the entire distribution system. An inadequately protected system can cause damage ranging from electrical shocks to people coming in contact with electrical equipment, to fires caused by the thermal ignition of electrical materials on the overloaded circuit.

Electrical storms and lightning are among the biggest causes of major distribution overcurrent worldwide. In the United States alone, 67 people are killed every year by these types of storms (including those killed by falling trees and power lines—not only surges). The intense current of a lightning discharge creates a fleeting, but very strong, magnetic field. A single lightning strike can produce up to a billion volts of electricity. If lightning strikes a house, it can easily destroy all the electrical equipment inside and damage the distribution system to which that house is connected.

To protect people and devices adequately, overcurrent protection needs to be sensitive, selective, fast and reliable. IN the interest of conservation, most power systems generate different loads at different times of day; overcurrent protection must therefore be sensitive enough to operate under conditions of both minimum and maximum power generation. It also needs to be selective so that it can differentiate between conditions that require immediate action and those where limited action is required; in other words, it should shut down the minimum number of devices to avoid disrupting the rest of the electrical system. Overcurrent protection also needs to be fast; it should be able to disconnect undamaged equipment quickly from the area of overcurrent and thus prevent the spread of the fault. Of course, the most basic requirement of protective equipment is that it is reliable, performing correctly wherever and whenever it is needed.

When an overcurrent occurs at a major electricity supply point such as a power station, the resulting surge, if it is not checked, can damage the entire distribution system. Like a flooding river—which breaks its banks and floods smaller rivers, which in turn flood streets and houses—the extra voltage courses through the network of wires and devices that comprise the distribution system until it discharges its excessive energy into the earth. This is why each piece of equipment within the electricity manufacturing and distribution system must be protected by a grounding or earthing mechanism—the grounding mechanism allows the excess electricity to be discharged into the earth directly, instead of passing it further down the distribution system.

Within the distribution system, surge protection is provided by overcurrent relays. Relays are simply switches that open and close under the control of another electrical circuit; an overcurrent relay is a specific type of relay that operates only when the voltage on a power line exceeds a predetermined level. If the source of an overcurrent is nearby, the overcurrent relay shuts off instantaneously. One danger, however, is that when one electrical circuit shuts down, the electricity may be rerouted through adjacent circuits, causing them to become overloaded. At its most extreme, this can lead to the blackout of an entire electrical network. To protect against this, overcurrent relays have a time-delay response; when the source of an overcurrent is far away, the overcurrent relays delay slightly before shutting down—thereby allowing some of the current through to the next circuit so that no single circuit becomes overloaded. An additional benefit of this system is that when power surges do occur, engineers are able to use these time delay sequences to calculate the source of the fault.

Fuses and circuit breakers are the normal overcurrent protection devices found in private homes. Both devices operate similarly: they allow the passage of normal currents but quickly trip, or interrupt, when too much current flows through. Fuses and circuit breakers are normally located in the home's electrical switch box, which takes the main power coming into the house and distributes it to various parts of the home. Beyond this level of home protection, it is also advisable to purchase additional tripping devices for sensitive electrical devices such as computers and televisions. While many electrical devices are equipped with internal surge protection, the value of these devices usually warrants the additional protection gained from purchasing an additional protective device.

The modern world could not exist without reliable electricity generation and distribution. While overcurrents cannot be entirely avoided, it is possible to mitigate their effects by providing adequate protection at every level of the electrical system, from the main power generation stations to the individual home devices we all rely upon in our daily lives.

Questions 28–33

Choose the correct letter: A, B, C or D.

Write your answers in boxes 28–33 on your answer sheet.

28 In a normal electrical system,

    A   voltage differences are usually quite small.

    B   overcurrent protection is mainly provided by circuit breakers and fuses.

    C   different amounts of electricity are generated at different times of day.

    D   some circuits constantly experience a certain level of overcurrent.

29 The writer suggests that most overcurrents

    A   are harmless and temporary.

    B   affect all levels of the distribution system.

    C   are triggered by electrical storms.

    D   can be instantaneously controlled by relays.

30 What does the writer state is the most basic requirement of overcurrent protection equipment?

    A   Speed

    B   Selectivity

    C   Sensitivity

    D   Reliability

31 What is an essential safety requirement for every device in an electrical system?

    A   A grounding mechanism

    B   The ability to shut down quickly

    C   Sensitivity to variances in the electrical system

    D   Internal surge protection

32 In which of the following circumstances might the shutdown of an overcurrent relay be delayed?

    A   If the source of an overcurrent is nearby

    B   If an overcurrent is caused by an electrical storm

    C   If an entire electrical network experiences blackout

    D   If the source of the overcurrent is far away

33 The writer suggests that most household electrical devices

    A   are adequately protected by the home's electrical switch box.

    B   should be protected from overcurrent by additional devices.

    C   produce strong magnetic fields that can sometimes cause surges.

    D   are designed to shut off after a short time delay.

Questions 34–40

Do the following statements agree with the information given in Reading Passage 3?

In boxes 34–40 on your answer sheet, write

    TRUE   *if the statement agrees with the information*

    FALSE   *if the statement contradicts the information*

    NOT GIVE   *if there is no information on this*

34 All variations in electrical voltage are potentially damaging and must be prevented.

35 Electricians must use special tools to fit fuses.

36 The most common cause of overcurrents is the presence of too many loads on one circuit.

37 Over 100 people are killed by electrical storms worldwide each year.

38 Effective overcurrent protection systems shut down as few devices as possible.

39 The effects of overcurrents are magnified when electricity comes in contact with water.

40 Overcurrents course through the entire distribution system unless they are discharged into the earth.

ACADEMIC WRITING MODULE

Writing Task 1

You should spend about 20 minutes on this task.

The chart below shows the results of a recent survey into the causes of poor school attendance in the UK. Summarise the information by selecting and reporting the main features, and make comparisons where relevant.

Write at least 150 words.

CAUSES OF POOR ATTENDANCE IN UK SCHOOLS

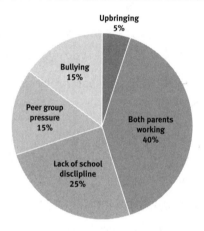

Writing Task 2

You should spend about 40 minutes on this task.

> *Some people think that the government should provide unemployed people with a free mobile phone and free access to the internet to help them find jobs.*

To what extent do you agree or disagree with this opinion? Give reasons for your answer and include any relevant examples from your own knowledge and experience.

Write at least 250 words.

SPEAKING MODULE

Time: 11–14 minutes

Part 1

Introduction to interview (4–5 minutes): The examiner will begin by introducing himself or herself and checking your identity. She or he will then ask you some questions about yourself based on everyday topics.

- Let's talk about the place where you live now.
- Describe the place where you live now.
- Were you born there?
- Do you live on your own or with your family?
- Has the place changed much over the time you have lived there? (How?)

Part 2

Individual long turn (3–4 minutes): Candidates' task card instructions:

Task Card

Please read the topic below carefully. You will be asked to talk about it for one to two minutes. You will have one minute to think about what you are going to say. You can make some notes to help you if you wish.

Describe a musical event you enjoyed attending. You should say:

- *What the event you attended was*
- *Where it took place*
- *Who was with you*

Also, explain why you enjoyed attending the event.

The examiner may then ask you a couple of brief questions to wrap up this part of the test. Further questions:

- Do you play music yourself?
- What instruments can you play?
- What kind of music do you most enjoy? What do you like about it?

Part 3

Two-way discussion (4–5 minutes): In Part 3, the examiner will ask you further questions related to the topic in Part 2.

Let's consider listening to music:

- How expensive is it to attend a concert in your country?
- Is it better to listen to live music or to listen to music on the television or radio? Why is one way better?
- Do you think there is too much music available now? Why/Why not?

Finally, let's talk about famous musicians:

- Why do you think people are so interested in the personal lives of musicians?
- Is that interest stronger now than in the past?
- What are some things that can affect the image and popularity of musicians?

GENERAL TRAINING READING MODULE

Time: One hour

Section 1

You should spend about 20 minutes on questions 1–14.

Questions 1–7

Read the text below and answer questions 1–7.

First Floor		Second Floor	
Emergency Services		**Ophthalmology**	
Reception	101	Reception	200
Treatment Rooms	102–110	Dr. Ana Boto	201
Waiting Room	111–113	Dr. Jina Williams	202
		Dr. Geoff Foreman	203
		Dr. Susan Widden	204
		Waiting Room	205
Internal Medicine		**Tropical Diseases**	
Reception	114	Reception	211
Waiting Room	115	Waiting Room	212
Dr. Ben Keran	116	Quarantine	213
Dr. Janet Goldsmith	117	Dr. Viet Nguyen	214
Dr. Christopher Sherin	118	Dr. Pongsambulnar Cutler	215
Dr. Rashmi PandiDr	119	Dr. Luisa Doyle	216
Dr. Mabel Chew	120	Dr. Lea Kynaston	21
Dr. Donald Tuffy	121		
General Practice		**Heart Disease Unit**	
Reception	122	Reception	221
Dr. Mary Garcia	123	Dr. David Parker	222
Dr. Helena Ho	124	Dr. Neil Kennedy	223
Dr. Jackie Jimenez	125	Dr. Julian Crosby	224
Dr. Tania Cherrin	126	Dr. Alison Cussons	225
Dr. Toshio Nishima	127	Dr. Fiona Darby	226
Dr. Ross Smith	128	Waiting Room	227
Waiting Room	129		

Services		Surgical Unit	
Toilets	130 and 131	Reception	230
Cafeteria	132	Surgeries	231–238
Banking and Telephoning Service	133	Recovery Room	239
		Waiting Room	240
Children´s Play Room	134		
Florist and Gift Shop	140		

Notices

When you arrive at the hospital, please go to reception in the relevant specialty area and register with the receptionist. You will then be shown to the waiting room where you will be asked to wait until your name is called. The waiting time varies according to the number of patients, and we ask for your patience and understanding. The reception staff will be able to give you information regarding how many people are ahead of you, but will not be able to give you an exact time for seeing the doctor.

If you have ten or more people ahead of you, you may wish to leave the waiting room and relax in other areas of the hospital (cafeteria, gardens or children's play room). In this case, ask the receptionist for a pager; you will be paged when there are fewer people ahead of you. Please come straight back to the reception area when paged.

While in the waiting room, please switch off your mobile phone, keep noise to a minimum, refrain from eating and drinking (except water from the coolers provided), do not smoke and ensure that children are kept close at all times (you may wish to take them to the play room).

Any discourteous or aggressive treatment of hospital staff or other patients will be dealt with immediately.

Questions 1–6

Read the questions below and write the appropriate room number in boxes 1–6 on your answer sheet.

Which room will you go to when you

1 want a cup of coffee?

2 are waiting to see Dr. Kynaston?

3 need treatment in an emergency?

4 want to see a doctor about your heart condition?

5 have bored, noisy children with you?

6 have an appointment with a general practitioner?

Question 7

Which of these things can you do in the waiting room? Write the words in box 7 on your answer sheet.

Page a doctor
Drink coffee
Eat snacks
Drink water
Use your phone

Questions 8–14

*Read the accommodation information on this page. Select the best accommodation for each student on the list below and write the correct letter, **A–H**, in boxes 8–14 on your answer sheet.*

NB: There are more offers of accommodation than there are students.

Student Accommodation

A   Four students living in five-bedroom house, looking for one more student to share. We are all serious, hard-working students who don't have much time for fun. We usually work in our rooms or in the library, but we have dinner together most nights. Share cooking and cleaning work.

B   Homestay—Family with two children want student to live with them, share family meals, etc. Own room and access to family areas of house. International student preferred so that children can learn about another culture.

C   St. Michael´s College has vacancies for about 20 students. All-male college. All meals provided. Cleaning service included. First-year students share room; all others, own room.

D   Single female looking for female flatmate. Vegetarian, relaxed approach. Share cooking and cleaning.

E   Rex Student Hostel—Rooms available for students. Dinner provided on request; also kitchen and dining room where students can prepare own meals. Option of own or shared room. Non-smoking. Quiet, hard-working atmosphere. Weekly cleaning service provided.

F   Three-bedroom house, one bedroom available. Three students in 20s share large, comfortable living space, meals, and housework. Want someone sociable who likes sharing meals, watching TV, listening to music, etc.

G   Two-bedroom flat with one large double bedroom available. Owners are Mike and Sue—student and dentist—looking for single or couple to share. $150 a week. Non-smokers.

H   Small one-bedroom flat available for rent, $300 a week. Suits single or couple, no kids or pets. Access to communal garden and washing area.

8 Jenny, non-smoker, vegetarian. Looking to share a flat with just one other. Likes jazz and blues, walking and going to the beach.

9 Paul, 22-year-old engineering student, likes parties. Doesn't know how to cook and clean and doesn't want to learn! Only studies at exam time. Works in a gym part-time.

10 Ella, 20 years old, international student. Doesn't know anyone yet, would like to meet people. Wants accommodation where she can cook for herself. Has never shared housing with anyone except her parents.

11 Henry, 40-year-old mature student. Studying medicine, so has to study most of the time. Works part-time from home (on computer, consulting) and likes cooking in his free time. Budget: $100 a week. Smoker.

12 Cherie, 18, international student, first time away from home. Missing her family, especially younger brothers and sisters. Doesn´t know how to cook or clean, etc. Will go back to China for the holidays.

13 Robert, 23, master's student. Sociable, has shared flats before, likes cooking. Goes out a lot. When home, likes to play video games and watch TV—and study.

14 Sally and Paul, young married couple from country town. Want own flat or share with another couple. Both study hard (vet science) and like to relax at home when not working—reading, dinner parties and music. Budget: $200 pw.

Section 2

You should spend about 20 minutes on questions 15–27.

Questions 15–21

*Look at the information in the Service Guide for the University of Northwestern Australia below, and answer the questions using **NO MORE THAN THREE WORDS**. Write the answers in boxes 15–21 on your answer sheet.*

University of Northwestern Australia Service Guide

Here you will find a list of the full range of services offered to students at Northwestern. For further information, see our website at www.northwestern.co.edu.au.

Health Services

Located on the Hartley campus, there is a clinic available to all students. It is open only during term time (during holiday periods, you must go to Casualty in town). To use the service, please ensure that you have both your student card and your Medicare card with you at all times. On presentation of these cards, treatment is free. There is a doctor and a nurse in attendance from 7 A.M. to 9 P.M. on weekdays and from 7 A.M. to 12.30 P.M. on Saturdays. At all other times, please use the town hospital.

Transport

At first, Northwestern may feel a little isolated—especially if you are used to living in the centre of town. The site, chosen for its natural beauty and the peacefulness of the area, is one of our most important assets. However, if you wish to enjoy the attractions of the local towns, don't despair—the public bus service is frequent and reliable, and additional university shuttle buses are available at peak times. To go to Thurile, catch the 45 bus from outside the Hartley main gates. It runs every 30 minutes on weekdays. If you wish to go to Gundini, catch the 67 bus from the Little campus—the stop is just near the football field. Both towns also have mini-cab services that offer competitive rates—so don't worry if you miss the buses once in a while!

Student Centre

The student centre is the heart of the university. Located on the Hartley campus, it comprises three buildings, and it is here that you will find a great variety of student services and leisure facilities. There is a career and job advisory service, where you can obtain advice regarding your chosen degree field; this service will also help you to find a part-time job.

The two restaurants and three cafés in the student centre, as well as a reading room and games room, make it a comfortable home-from-home between classes. For those who wish to combine leisure with work, there is a computer centre for student use; additional computers are available in the library. And finally, the student centre is where the Students' Union has its offices and information boards. All students automatically become members of the union when they pay their fees, so it's worth paying a visit to the union to find out more about what it can offer you.

International Student Office

Not to be confused with the student centre, this is where international students can go for information and advice regarding their academic or residential status. A team of academic experts here can help with solutions to such problems as difficulties with English or essay writing; they can also offer advice about future courses of study. A lawyer is also available three days a week to help with visa and immigration solutions.

> **Shopping Information**
>
> Every item basic to a student's needs can be found here at the shops on the Hartley campus. There is a stationer's, which sells computer software as well as the usual pens, notebooks, etc., and there is also a mini-market where you will find a wide range of food and drink, as well as cleaning products and basic medical supplies.
>
> For other consumer needs, you may need to go into the nearest towns. Thurile has the biggest range of shops, most of them located on the main street. There you will find a supermarket, a boutique, an Asian food store and several good, reasonably priced restaurants. Gundini, too, has a small supermarket, as well as a book store and video store. On Saturday mornings there is a wonderful farmers' market in Gundini, where you can find all sorts of fresh produce from the local farms and gardens.

15 Where should a student go to look for a part-time job opening?

16 Which bus would a student who wants to go to the bookshop take?

17 On which day can locally grown vegetables be purchased?

18 Where should a student go for help renewing a visa?

19 Where can a student who gets sick on a Sunday go for medical help?

20 There is a computer room in the student centre. Where else can students find a computer to use?

21 If you wish to talk to a representative of the Students' Union, to which area should you go?

Questions 22–27

*Read the course information for veterinary science below and complete the summary given. Use **NO MORE THAN THREE WORDS** for each answer.*

Course Information and Entry Requirements for Studying Veterinary Science at Northwestern Australia University

Course duration	5 years full-time
Units	96
Campus	Hartley
Course code	VTR101

Minimum education requirements, prerequisites	Western Australia year 12 or equivalent, English, mathematics, chemistry, physics. International students must also meet English language requirements (see international student website) and may be required to complete a foundation year at this or a related university
Visa requirements	To be eligible for an Australian student visa, you must enrol in this programme full-time on campus at NWAU. A student visa requires a minimum attendance rate of 80%.
Fees	Enrolment fee of $220 (non-refundable). Total course cost $37,800.
Closing date	Applications must be lodged through the Western Australian Tertiary Admissions Centre. In order to commence study in Semester 1, 2010, the closing date for admission is September 30, 2009.
Enquiries	For further information, please call the admissions office at (61) 8 96873954 or see our website www.nwau.edu.au/int/enquiry.

Questions 22–27

Summary

If you wish to study veterinary science at Northwestern Australian University, you need to have completed schooling until Western Australia year 12 **22** ....
You must have evidence of English language level proficiency (as outlined on the course website), and your school education must have included the following
23 .... : English, maths, chemistry and physics. An Australian student visa is essential for this course of study—to be **24** .... for a student visa, you must enrol full-time for five years. You must attend **25** .... 80% of classes on a student visa.

The course costs $37,800, including a non-refundable admission fee of $220.

You must apply to the Western Australian Tertiary Admissions Centre **26** ....
September 30 if you wish to begin studying in Semester 1, 2010. If you require
27 .... , you can call or see the university website.

Section 3

You should spend about 20 minutes on questions 28–40, which are based on Reading Passage 3 below.

Food for Thought

A   Have you ever eaten a food that might kill you? That's what thousands of Japanese and Koreans do every year when they sit down to a delicious meal of *fugu* fish.

B   *Fugu* is known in English as *puffer fish*, and there are over 120 species of puffers in the world's oceans. They are relatively small, generally grey— sometimes with spots—and they have spikes that pop up when they sense danger. Through these spikes they can inject a deadly venom into their attackers, and it is this venom which makes the *fugu* such a potentially dangerous dish.

C   The venom, called tetrodotoxin, is mainly concentrated in the internal organs of the fish, though it is also found in the ovaries and the skin. Ingesting this poison causes damage to the nervous system, leading to symptoms ranging from numbness of the mouth to total paralysis. 'The first sensation is numbness of the tongue and lips', says Dr. Yuko Honda, a biologist at the Kansai Marine Institute. 'This is soon followed by headache and dizziness, and often nausea and fatigue. The next symptom—and the most serious—is difficulty breathing, leading to paralysis'.

D   It is in Japan that *fugu* fish is most prized. Japanese law decrees that it must be prepared by a specially licensed *fugu* chef, who is legally bound to taste every dish before it is served. The chef is also required to dispose of the poisonous waste in a locked box. However, *fugu* is not as rare a dish as some people might think—in Tokyo alone it is served in some 3,000 restaurants, and it is also available at many supermarkets, sold in special trays with a security seal guaranteeing its safety.

E   *Fugu* is usually eaten as sashimi, very thinly sliced and accompanied by rice and sake. It can also be eaten in nabe or hotpots—a kind of fish soup—and even battered and fried. '*Fugu* is a fish with quite a delicate flavour', says

Hiroshi Takamura, *fugu* chef at the popular Kintatsu restaurant in Tokyo, 'so it's perfect for making sushi, which allows the flavour to be savoured. It needs to be cut very thinly, because it has quite firm flesh—I like to cut it so thin that the light shines right through it, though there are some chefs who cut it thicker'. Asked about the dangers of eating *fugu*, Takamura becomes quite serious. 'Obviously fugu must be prepared by a chef who knows how to do it', he says. 'If the chef is licensed and careful, then there is no danger at all'. And the poisonings we hear of sometimes? 'That's when people buy the fish and try to prepare it themselves. Sometimes people are even sold *fugu* disguised as salmon or trout, which is a very dangerous practice'.

F   While the poison of *fugu* is known to be extremely toxic, there are still those who wish to try it. And why do people want to try such a dangerous toxin? Japanese food writer Naotaro Kageyama explains that it is 'because of the sensation they get on their lips and tongue from the poison. It's a kind of tingling numbness that is really quite strange . . . not unpleasant at all. This is one of the aspects of *fugu* that is most attractive to the true connoisseur'.

G   While there are those who wish to try the poison, every year many people are sickened or killed by the poison accidentally. Kazuko Nishimura is one such victim. 'Yes, I tried *fugu* just once. I didn't really want to, but my uncle had caught the fish and prepared it as a special treat, so we all sat down to a meal. At first, it was just my mouth, but then my head started to ache, and then I couldn't breathe. They took me to hospital where I was in intensive care for a few days and they treated me for the poisoning, helping my body to breathe while I was paralysed'. 'Kazuko was very lucky to survive', says Doctor Harumi Matsui at the Kansai University hospital. 'Fewer than 50 per cent of victims of *fugu* poisoning survive, and it is not a very pleasant death. But Kazuko's family brought her to the hospital immediately, and we were able to keep her breathing while the poison wore off'. Luckily no one else who shared the meal was affected—a single *fugu* has enough poison to kill up to 30 people, so the situation could have been much worse. It seems that Kazuko was the only one to eat a portion that contained the poison.

H   If, after reading all this, you still wish to try *fugu*, you may have to travel a long way: Japan, Hong Kong, Korea and the US are the only places that allow licensed chefs to prepare the dish. *Fugu* is completely illegal in Europe and the rest of Asia and America. But if you can't travel that far to try it, you're in good company—the emperor of Japan is not allowed to eat it either, forbidden by royal decree.

Questions 28–32

*Look at the following descriptions (questions 28–32) and the list of people below. Match each description with the correct person: **A, B, C, D** or **E**. Write the correct letter in boxes 28–32 on your answer sheet.*

28   *fugu* chef at Kintatsu

29   victim of *fugu* poisoning

30   biologist who studies *fugu*

31   doctor who treated *fugu* victims

32   food writer

List of People

A   Yuko Honda

B   Hiroshi Takamura

C   Naotaro Kageyama

D   Kazuko Nishimura

E   Harumi Matsui

Questions 33–36

Do the following statements agree with the information in Reading Passage 3? In boxes 33–36 on your answer sheet, write

TRUE	*if the statement agrees with the information*
FALSE	*if the statement contradicts the information*
NOT GIVEN	*if there is no information on this*

33   A *fugu* chef must taste each dish before serving it to his customers.

34   More than 30 people die each year from *fugu* poisoning.

35   *Fugu* is popular because it has such a strong flavour.

36   The venom of the *fugu* is mainly concentrated in its skin.

Questions 37–38

*Use the information given in the passage to answer questions 37–38 below. Write the answers in boxes 37–38 on your answer sheet. Use **ONLY ONE WORD** for each space.*

37   What are the two types of places you can obtain *fugu* in Japan?

Restaurants and ....

38   In which four places are chefs licensed to prepare *fugu*?

Japan

Hong Kong

....

US

Questions 39–40

From the list of headings 1–7 below, choose the most suitable heading for Paragraph E and for Paragraph G. Write the appropriate number in boxes 39–40 on your answer sheet.

   1.   Innocent Victims of the *Fugu*

   2.   Physical Reactions

   3.   Medical Treatment

   4.   Dishonest Fishermen

   5.   Many Ways to Eat *Fugu*

   6.   *Fugu* Chefs Are Well Trained

   7.   A Dangerous Practice

GENERAL TRAINING WRITING MODULE

Writing Task 1

You should spend about 20 minutes on this task. Write about the following topic:

Last Tuesday you flew from New York to Paris. When you arrived home, you discovered that you had left your cabin bag on the plane. Write a letter to the airline. In your letter, you should explain:

- Where and when you lost your bag
- What your bag looks like
- What its contents were

Write at least 150 words. You do not need to write an address. Begin your letter with Dear Sir *or* Madam.

Writing Task 2

You should spend about 40 minutes on this task. Write about the following topic:

Some people are concerned that children spend too much time on computers—playing games, chatting and watching videos. But all this time is actually good preparation for children, who will have to spend many hours working on computers throughout their education and their working lives.

To what extent do you agree or disagree with this statement? Give reasons for your answer and include any relevant examples from your own knowledge and experience
Write at least 250 words.

LISTENING MODULE

 Practice Test 2, Track 1 (Track 20)

Section 1: Questions 1–10

Questions 1–3

Complete the form below

*Write **ONE WORD OR A NUMBER** for each answer.*

University Accommodation Dept.

Customer Information

Example:

The caller wants accommodation for *international* students.

Student Name: Maria Teresa **1** .... Vila

Student Number: **2** ....

Faculty: Modern **3** ....

Starting: September 1

Questions 4–7

Complete the table below.

*Write **ONE WORD AND/OR A NUMBER** for each answer.*

Name of Block	Location	Rent
The Trigon	Located near **4** .... and main campus	£ **5** .... per week
The Cube	Located near **6** .... entrance to campus	**7** .... room options -1 bedroom = £180 per week -2 bedrooms = £110 per week per person

Questions 8–10

*Choose **THREE** letters, **A-E**.*

*Which **THREE** of the following are features of accommodation at The Cube?*

    A   parking garage

    B   laundry room

    C   ensuite bathroom

    D   kitchen

    E   study bedroom

Practice Test 2, Track 2 (Track 21)

Section 2: Questions 11–20

Questions 11–16

Complete the notes below.

*Write **NO MORE THAN TWO WORDS AND/OR A NUMBER** for each answer.*

Barker's Country Safaris

Established: **11** .... years ago by John and Nancy Barker.

As teens the Barkers enjoyed:

climbing

kayaking

white-water rafting

pot-holing

12 ....

At university they organized:

motor trips

13 .... tours

5 years ago they **14** .... their regular jobs

15 .... years later they began running activity tours

1 year ago they started activities for **16** .... groups

---

Questions 17–20

Complete the table below.

Write **NO MORE THAN THREE WORDS AND/OR A NUMBER** *for each answer.*

Tour Options

Name	Size	Times
Woodland tour and trail	10 jeeps **17** .... people per jeep	Morning: 8 AM Afternoon: **18** .... PM to 6PM Evening: 7–11 PM
Family **19**	1 jeep/jeeps if **20** .... party	Whole Day From 10 AM till 11 PM

Section 3: Questions 21–30

Questions 21–27

Choose the correct answer: A, B or C.

Write your answers in boxes 21–27 on your answer sheet.

21 Jess wants to start the meeting by

   A organizing his notes

   B taking a photo

   C reviewing the objectives for the project

22 What are Matt and Jess planning to study?

   A different species of insects

   B different species of plants

   C old photos

23 How far apart are the plots supposed to be?

   A 12 feet apart

   B 10 meters apart

   C 10 miles apart

24 Where can the bamboo sticks be purchased?

   A department stores

   B toy shops

   C gardening centres

25 One person throws the frame and the other person

   A turns on the spot

   B smiles and waves

   C marks out the squares

26 The instructions sound complicated because

   A they are in writing

   B there is so much turning around

   C there are so many squares

27 Jess thinks Matt should do the throwing because

   A he has more experience

   B he has a stronger arm

   C he is more accurate

Questions 28–30

What do Matt and Jess decide about each of the possible locations?

Write the correct letter, A, B, or C, in boxes 28–30 on your answer sheet.

      A   they will go there

      B   they might go there

      C   they will not go there

Locations

      28 the lowland around the marsh _____

      29 behind the beach _____

      30 behind the headland near the bay _____

Practice Test 2, Track 4 (Track 23)

Section 4: Questions 31–40

Questions 31–34

Choose the correct answer: A, B or C.

Write your answers in boxes 31–34 on your answer sheet.

31 Compared to other industries, tourism has

    A the most young customers.

    B the biggest impact on people.

    C only indirect impact.

32 In global tourism there is a

    A 97% economic leakage.

    B a 9 in 10 chance of failure.

    C about 9% economic failure.

33 Some countries with high levels of tourism still have

    A poor accommodation.

    B great poverty.

    C large national debt.

34 Geo-tourism is all about

    A reducing pollution from industry.

    B increasing numbers of travellers.

    C providing a fair reward for service.

Questions 35–40

Complete the notes below.

*Write **ONE WORD AND/OR A NUMBER ONLY** for each answer.*

Project with World Bank

Developing technology platform

brings grassroots products to locals

avoids **35** ………….. men

Volunteering

many teens schedule **36** ………….. -year between school and university

volunteering organizations charge up to £ **37** …………..

Geo-Tourism

customers are looking for organizations that can suggest **38** ………….. projects

organizers would charge flat **39** …………..

this would make for a good **40** ………….. for each customer

ACADEMIC READING MODULE

Reading Passage 1

*You should spend about 20 minutes on **Questions 1–13** which are based on Reading Passage 1 below.*

What Makes Us Happy?

Do you seriously want to be happy? Of course you do! But what does it take to be happy? Many psychologists are now using scientific methods to try to understand the nature and origins of happiness. Their results may surprise you.

Surprisingly, happiness has been shown to be a constitutional trait. The study of different types of twins; identical and non-identical, has enabled scientists to calculate that 50–60% of self-identified happiness – and what other sort is there? – is down to genes. Of course, there is no one specific gene that determines happiness, but a great many and they tend to overlap with the genes that determine personality. People who are emotionally stable, sociable and conscientious, tend to be happier according to the research.

Now, many people believe that money makes us happy. However, there is no clear relationship between wealth and happiness. Once out of poverty, increases in wealth do not automatically turn into relative increases in happiness. For example, winning the lottery may give a rush of joy and excitement but does not ensure long-term contentment. In fact, studies have shown that lottery winners take less pleasure in everyday events following their win. It seems that they soon get habituated to their money, while at the same time they have distanced themselves from their former lives and identities by leaving jobs, friends and lifestyle.

Nor does a steady increase in income make for greater happiness. The more we have, the more we seem to want, so we are always stuck at the same level of satisfaction/ dissatisfaction. The perception of wealth is a relative thing: we are discontented when those who we compare ourselves with are better off than ourselves. This goes someway to explain why, in most Western countries, average incomes have increased considerably but without any increase in the average levels of happiness.

If wealth does not bring happiness, what about spending it? There is no doubt that shopping gives us a short lived burst of pleasure – but very little more than that. The only type of shopping that might provide longer term happiness is when we buy things for other people.

Nor does happiness does not come in liquid or tablet form. A couple of drinks at a party may lighten our mood and be good for us medically and mentally, but alcohol abuse destroys our body, mind and relationships. Similarly drugs like cocaine and ecstasy give brief bursts of joy but there is a massive price to be paid when the high is over.

So, what can we do to improve our sense of well-being? First we need to realise that we are not passive victims of external events. We can and should take control of our life to make it rewarding and satisfying. We should adopt a positive attitude, and overcome feelings of worthlessness and build our own self-confidence and self-esteem.

We should try to reduce the burden of unnecessary worry. If there is something that can be done about a problem we are worrying about then we should do it, and stop worrying. And of course there is no point in worrying about things we can't change. A sense of humour is good protection against adversity and a strong antidote to depression. One of the key symptoms of depression is the loss of the ability to laugh.

A key feature of happy and contented people is that they have a sense of meaning and purpose in life. Rather than just drifting through life, they have a clear set of values and goals that they are trying to achieve. This could be associated with faith, humanitarianism and family values, artistic or scientific aspirations and career ambitions. All these things provide a sense of identity as well as something to work towards or look forward to.

Happiness is a positive by-product of keeping active. But not just being busy, we need to be doing things that raise self-esteem and bring us satisfaction; controlling our own schedule and prioritising activities that satisfy our own needs. And saying 'no' to other people if necessary. Of course, this doesn't mean we have to be selfish. Being active members of the community or volunteering for a charity or helping your family can all create happiness – particularly for older people.

So, should we actively pursue happiness? Curiously, the happiest people seem to be those who do not actively see it – indeed the 'pursuit of happiness' may be counterproductive. To a large extent, happiness emerges as a by-product of who we are and what we do. Conversely, people who focus on making others happy usually make themselves happy in the process.

Questions 1–3

Choose the correct letter A, B, C or D.

Write the correct letter in boxes 1–3 on your answer sheet.

1   The main topic discussed in the text is:

   A   the danger of worrying about things beyond our control

   B   the difficult task of identifying what makes us happy

   C   key indicators of depression

   D   activities which can make us happy

2   A study of different types of twins suggests

   A   happiness is mostly a genetic trait.

   B   'happiness' and 'personality' are not related.

   C   identical twins are more emotional than non-identical twins.

   D   scientists are not happy people.

3 According to the text, a steady rise in income

    A increases anyone's level of happiness.

    B creates a steady decline in happiness.

    C happens frequently in Western cultures.

    D does not necessarily lead to greater happiness.

Questions 4–6

Complete the sentences below.

Choose **NO MORE THAN TWO WORDS** *from the passage for each answer.*

Write your answers in boxes 4–6 on your answer sheet.

    4 Observation of lottery winners suggests that there is no relationship between happiness and _____.

    5 When we compare ourselves to others we discover that the concept of 'wealth' is _____.

    6 The types of purchases which are most likely to provide us with happiness are those purchased for _____.

Questions 7–9

Do the following statements agree with the information given in Reading Passage 1?

In boxes 7–9 on your answer sheet write

    YES   *if the statement agrees with the claims of the writer*

    NO   *if the statement contradicts the claims of the writer*

    NOT GIVEN   *if it is impossible to say what the writer thinks about this*

    7 We are all unwilling participants in events beyond our control.

    8 A crucial determiner of happiness is starting each day by writing a 'to-do' list.

    9 'Happiness' has a strong relationship with our actions and attitudes.

Questions 10–13

*Complete the summary using the list of words, **A–I**, below.*

*Write the correct letter, **A–I**, in boxes 10–13 on your answer sheet.*

A	lifestyle
B	important
C	by-product
D	related
E	independent
F	relevant
G	scientific
H	selfish
I	exclusive

In this article, the author gives us a discussion of 'happiness' from a **10** .... perspective. The investigation into the influence of money on happiness suggests that the two are not **11** .... We should be able to say 'no' to other people, but this doesn't require us to be **12** .... The author concludes that happiness is the **13** .... of activity focused on making others happy.

Reading Passage 2

*You should spend about 20 minutes on **Questions 14–26** which are based on Reading Passage 2 below.*

The Business of Space

Up until very recently space travel and exploration were solely the preserve of governments, most notably the Russian and American. However, with the decline of government wealth and the dramatic increase in personal wealth, the whole landscape of space travel is changing.

The first tentative steps into the commercialisation of personal space travel began when billionaire Dennis Tito paid $20 million to ride on a Russian Soyuz spacecraft for a week's holiday on a space station. Since then, there have been seven space tourists who have paid large sums of money for a space experience. Yet, collectively, their financial contribution is minute, and certainly would not appear to represent a feasible business.

Richard Branson, billionaire and entrepreneur, has formed Virgin Galactic, a spaceship company with some very ambitious plans for space travel. Surprisingly, he is not alone; there are some 12 or 13 other space organizations worldwide with similar plans. Of course, there are setbacks, but Virgin Galactic plan to have paying flights beginning in late 2017, with tickets at $250,000 each. Expensive? Yes! But there are over 20,000 people who have expressed interest, despite the tragic death of a co-pilot during a test flight accident.

It seems that people who want to take short zero gravity suborbital flights are fully aware of the dangers and are willing to take the risk. It is also worth noting that there were almost 2000 billionaires in the world in 2016, and that number is growing. So entrepreneurs like Richard Branson may represent the tip of the iceberg of young rich investors who want to make their childhood dreams of space travel come true.

Obviously, the key to the success of any business venture is to ensure that the price of the product maximises sales and to reduce the very high costs of the vehicles and rockets needed to do this. Currently, space vehicles can only be used once, so the race is on to develop reusable space vehicles. It is this reusability that will break the 'cost-barrier' and bring this activity into the price bracket where middle class and moderately wealthy people can afford it.

So what would you pay for a zero-gravity sub-orbital space trip? A recent, unscientific study, amongst US millennials (people who became adults around the year 2000) suggested that if the price of the flights was reduced by a factor of five – a figure entirely possible given the progress being made with reusable vehicles – the yield would be about $20 billion a year of revenues for the space tourism industry.

Twenty billion dollars is an interesting figure, as it is about the same amount generated each year by the film industry in the US through ticket, DVD and other sales. So now it is possible to make an analogy between the business model of Hollywood and space travel. Which do you think is more expensive? A Hollywood blockbuster, or the cost of a space launch? Back in the 1960s and 1970s, a space launch cost hundreds of times more than a Hollywood film. But as more money came to be spent on Hollywood movies, the cost of space travel has been decreasing. One particularly illustrative example is the comparison between the film *Avatar*, a movie about life on an 'exomoon,' and the Kepler spacecraft. Both of these cost about $400 million dollars. So for about half a billion dollars you can either get a film about life on other planets, or you can pay for a mission, which may actually find earth-like worlds. As a scientist, which is the better deal?

So what really is in the future for space travel? Probably offers of suborbital travel by companies like Virgin Galactic will become fairly common after the initial teething phase is over. Other companies are developing space hotels, so people who can afford more than just the space trips, can spend their money holidaying in space. All the technologies allowing this to happen are advancing very rapidly and most of this is happening in the private sector.

Space is going to get commercialised and this may not be a good thing. Do we really want to see massive advertising signs in space? The moon littered with commercial rubbish? If this happens it will be very hard to regulate. While there is in existence a Treaty of the Moon, to acknowledge that no one can own the Moon or Mars, not one space faring country has signed it.

The future of space travel has never been more exciting than it is now. Young children with pictures of planets and space rockets on their bedroom have a greater chance than ever of actually going into space than ever before. But at what cost?

Questions 14–18

Choose FIVE letters, A–I.

Write the correct letters in boxes 14–18 on your answer sheet.

NB   *Your answers may be given in any order.*

Below are listed some popular beliefs about commercial space travel.

Which five of these are reported by the writer of the text?

    A   Space travel today is no different than space travel in the 1960's.

    B   To date, the amount of space travel undertaken by private individuals could not sustain a business.

    C   Richard Branson's plans for commercial space travel may be described as 'daring.'

    D   It is not surprising that Branson's company is not the only company interested in commercial space travel.

    E   Virgin Galactic's proposed fares will be highly affordable to many.

    F   Individuals who want to fly into space are gamblers.

    G   Parallels can be drawn between space travel and the Hollywood movie industry.

    H   The rise of companies like Virgin Galactic is unconditionally positive.

    I   Laws governing space travel will be difficult to enforce.

Questions 19–26

Do the following statements agree with the information given in Reading Passage 2?

In boxes 19–26 on your answer sheet write

TRUE	*if the statement agrees with the information*
FALSE	*if the statement contradicts the information*
NOT GIVEN	*if there is no information on this*

19 Space travel today remains under the control of the Russian and American governments.

20 The first commercial space passenger was Richard Branson.

21 The Virgin Group was established by Richard Branson in 1970.

22 Space vehicles are presently capable of being used more than once.

23 $20 billion is the amount that millennials currently spend on space travel.

24 The film 'Avatar' cost about $400 million to make.

25 It is unlikely that recycling will become common practice on the moon.

26 Children today have a better chance of realizing their dreams of space travel than children in the 1960's did.

Reading Passage 3

*You should spend about 20 minutes on **Questions 27–40** which are based on Reading Passage 3 below.*

Questions 27–32

Reading Passage 3 has seven paragraphs, A–G.

Choose the correct heading for paragraphs B–G from the list of headings below.

Write the correct number, i–x, in boxes 27–32 on your answer sheet.

List of Headings
i The prevalence of numerical 'codes' in modern life
ii How RSA works
iii A brief history of keeping things safe
iv 'New math' vs 'medieval math'
v Proof that RSA is effective
vi The illusion of security
vii Cryptography: the modern key for the lock
viii Why RSA is effective
ix In defence of medieval security systems
x A new approach to system security

Example	Answer
Paragraph **A**	**iii**

27 Paragraph B

28 Paragraph C

29 Paragraph D

30 Paragraph E

31 Paragraph F

32 Paragraph G

Using Mathematics to Secure Our Money

A Up until very recently people's wealth, mostly coins and jewels, was kept safe under lock and key. Rich medieval families would keep a strong box with a large key, both of which were carefully hidden in different places. Later the box may have been kept in a bank. In either case, potential thieves would need to find both the box and the key. A similar principle was used for sending secret diplomatic and military messages. The messages were written in code with both the sender and the receiver having the key to the code. Thus, while the message could be discovered its meaning could only be found if the 'key' was also known. And so began a long-running battle between code-makers who tried to make better keys, and code-breakers who sought ways of finding them.

B Nowadays, cryptography is central to how our money is kept secure, even though we may not be aware of it. Our money is no longer in a tangible form, but in the form of information kept with our banks. To keep everyone involved happy, the messages initiated by our plastic cards have to be sent and received safely and the entire operation must be carried out with a high level of confidentiality and security.

C On a practical level, it is clear that the work of code-makers has been introduced into our daily financial lives. Our credit cards have 16-digit numbers on the front and a 3-digit number on the back. They also contain a 'chip' that can do all sorts of mysterious operations with these numbers. Finally, we also have a Personal Identification Number which we all need to memorize. All these numbers form a type of cryptographic key. However, as we shall see, the modern crypto systems are very different in the way the keys are used.

D The main feature of the traditional systems was that only one key was needed by both the sender and the receiver to understand the message. However the main problem was that the key itself needed to be communicated to both parties before they could use it. Obviously a major security risk. A very different approach was developed in the 1970s, based on a different way of using the keys. Now the main idea is that the typical user, let us call him Amir, has two keys; a 'public key' and a 'private key'. The public key is used to encrypt messages that other people wish to send to Amir, and the private key is used by Amir to decrypt these messages. The security of the system is based on keeping Amir's private key secret.

E This system of public-key cryptography, known as RSA – from the names of the developers (Ronald Rivest, Adi Shamir and Leonard Adleman) – was developed in the late 1970s and is based on a collection of several mathematical algorithms. The first is a process that allows the user, Amir, to calculate two numerical keys: private and public, based on two prime numbers. To complete the RSA system, two more algorithms are then needed: one for encrypting messages and one for decrypting them.

F   The effectiveness of RSA depends on two things. It is efficient, because the encryption and decryption algorithms used by participants are easy, in a technical sense they can be made precise. On the other hand, it is believed to be secure, because no one has found an easy way of decrypting the encrypted message without knowing Amir's private key.

G   When the RSA system was first written about in *Scientific American*, the strength of the system was shown by challenging the readers to find the prime factors – the two original numbers – of a certain number with 129 digits. It took 17 years to solve this problem, using the combined efforts of over 600 people. So clearly it is a very secure system. Using mathematics in this way, scientists and technologists have enabled us to keep our money as secure as the rich medieval barons with their strong boxes and hidden keys.

Questions 33–36

Complete the notes below.

*Choose **NO MORE THAN TWO WORDS** from the passage for each answer.*

Write your answers in boxes 33–36 on your answer sheet.

Through the use of cryptography banks keep money **33** ....

The way credit cards work is an example of the influence of **34** ....

Crypto systems developed in the 1970's relied on 2 keys: the **35** .... and the **36** ....

Questions 37–40

Do the following statements agree with the views of the writer in Reading Passage 3?

In boxes 37–40 on your answer sheet, write

> **YES**   *if the statement agrees with the views of the writer*
>
> **NO**   *if the statement contradicts the views of the writer*
>
> **NOT GIVEN**   *if it is impossible to say what the writer thanks about this*

37   Online banking makes most people nervous

38   The way keys are used in modern cryptograph is quite different from the past

39   The main problem with traditional cryptography systems is that neither party can decode the message.

40   The RSA system represents the most secure cryptography we are ever likely to develop.

ACADEMIC WRITING MODULE

Writing Task 1

You should spend about 20 minutes on this task.

The table below gives details of world electricity production by renewable sources in the four years between 2009 and 2012.

Summarise the information by selecting and reporting the main features and making comparisons where relevant.

You should write at least 150 words.

World electricity production by renewable sources in Trillion Watt Hours (TWh)

Source	2009	2010	2011	2012
Geothermal	67.4	68.5	69.3	70.4
Wind	276.4	351.2	451.5	534
Solar	21	33.5	53.1	104.5
Hydraulic	3329	3514.3	3530.8	3663.4
Bio-mass	246.8	288.9	307.6	326.2

Writing Task 2

You should spend about 40 minutes on this task.

Discuss both these views and give your own opinion.

Childhood obesity is becoming a problem throughout the developed world. Because of this, some people think that adverts for fast food, sweets and sugary snacks should not be allowed in schools and colleges.

To what extent do you agree or disagree with this?

Give reasons for your answer and include any relevant examples from your own knowledge or experience.

You should write at least 250 words.

SPEAKING MODULE

Time: 11–14 minutes

Part 1

Introduction to interview (4–5 minutes) [This part of the test begins with the examiner introducing himself or herself and checking the candidate's identification. It then continues as an interview.]

Let's talk about where you live.

- *Do you live in a house or a flat?*
- *Which is your favourite room in your house/flat?*
- *How much time do you spend in this room? (why?)*
- *Why do you like it?*

Let's move on to talk about parks and public spaces.

- *Are there many parks and public spaces near where you live?*
- *Did you often go to a park or public space when you were a child?*
- *What do people like to do in parks or public spaces? (why?)*
- *What makes a park or public space a nice place to be?*

Let's now talk about flowers.

- *Do you like flowers?*
- *When did you last buy flowers? (why?)*
- *Why do people like to decorate places with flowers?*
- *Why do some people prefer artificial flowers?*

Part 2

Individual long turn (3–4 minutes): *Candidate's Task Card*

Task Card

Please read the topic below carefully. You will be asked to talk about it for one to two minutes. You will have one minute to think about what you are going to say. You can make some notes to help you if you wish.

Describe a meal that you enjoyed

- *Where and when did this meal take place?*
- *Who was at the meal?*
- *Why did you enjoy this meal?*

The examiner may then ask you a couple of brief questions to wrap up this part of the test.

Rounding off questions:

- *Do you often eat out at restaurants/at friends' houses?*
- *What sort of food do you enjoy most?*
- *Do you enjoy cooking?*

Part 3

Two-way discussion (4–5 minutes): In Part 3, the examiner will ask you further questions related to the topic in Part 2.

Let's talk about celebrations.

- *Do people in your country prefer to have celebration meals in homes or in restaurants? Why?*
- *Do young people and old people prefer to celebrate occasions in different ways? How?*
- *How do you think celebration meals will change in the future?*

Now let's talk about the hospitality industry.

- *Is the hospitality industry important in your country?*
- *Do you think it is a good industry to work in? Why/Why not?*
- *Do you think the hospitality industry will grow in your country in the future?. Why/ Why not?*

GENERAL TRAINING READING MODULE

Reading Passage 1

*You should spend about 20 minutes on **Questions 1–14** which are based on Reading Passage 1 below.*

Read the text below and answer Questions 1–7.

Li Heng from Hong Kong is organising a trip to Manchester for a group of family and friends. He has selected 4 hotels for them to choose from. Here are his notes:

Hotel (price per night)	Dining options	Facilities	Comments
A Manchester Hotel & Spa £113	Award winning restaurant specialising in seasonal dishes. An extensive vegetarian selection. ***** Steak and rib house with finest Scottish beef, grilled over a charcoal barbeque ***** B&B and Half board packages available	Full spa facilities, nail bar, relaxation room, thermal suite including sauna, steam room and ice shower. **** Each room has satellite TV, fridge, wi-fi, tea and coffee making facilities	Located in the thriving music and theatre district of central Manchester. Generally good reviews on the internet.
B Atrium Aparthotel £58	None	Each apartment has fully equipped kitchen. Stylish lounge with TV and wi-fi. Bathroom with luxury toiletries	Close to the metrolink station and nightlife area Excellent reviews on the internet
C Football Hotel £130	Café Football, international informal dining: burgers, pizzas, pasta, salad. Buffet breakfast included in the room rate.	Meeting and conference rooms with presentation facilities. Each room has air-conditioning and wi-fi and TVs with a collection of video games.	Next door to Old Trafford Football stadium. Tours can be booked through reception. Not close to main shopping and entertainment districts. Mixed reviews on the internet

| D
The Grand
£212 | Fine dining in an elegant and formal setting.

****
Afternoon tea in the Octagon lounge with live piano every Friday and Saturday.

******
B&B packages available | Each room contains a wealth of period detail from marble fireplaces to ceiling cornicing and traditional style ceiling lamps. Recently refurbished to a high standard to return it to its original glory from 1856. | Located near to the conference and exhibition centre and the museum and gallery district.
Good reviews on the internet especially for high quality service. |

Questions 1–4

Look at the four hotels A, B, C and D.

For which hotel are the following statements true?

Write the correct letter A, B, C or D in boxes 1–4 on your answer sheet.

> **1** This hotel does not have a dining room.
>
> **2** This hotel was recently refurbished.
>
> **3** This hotel is located next door to a football stadium.
>
> **4** This hotel provides food options for vegetarians.

Questions 5–7

Answer the questions below.

*Choose **NO MORE THAN THREE WORDS** from the text for each answer.*

Write your answers in boxes 5–7 on your answer sheet.

> **5** Where would you go to arrange a tour at the Football Hotel?
>
> **6** What type of beef does the Manchester Hotel and Spa feature?
>
> **7** Which meal is included in the room rate at the Football Hotel?

Questions 8–14

Read the text below and answer questions 8–14.

Li Heng is also researching travel insurance and these are his notes for the group:

From: Li Heng

To: Manchester Group

Subject: Insurance for our trip to Manchester

Hi Everyone,

As discussed I've done a bit of research into what sort of insurance we need for our trip to Manchester.

As Hong Kong has no reciprocal arrangement with the UK in respect of health care we need to take out travel insurance for medical coverage, as well as coverage for cancellation and belongings. I've looked into a number of policies and believe that we should have the following coverage:

Cancellation: I know we have all committed to this trip however there may be some unforeseen circumstances that mean that one, some or all of us have to cancel. We need insurance that will cover any non-refundable deposit and other costs we have paid for should we have to cancel for reasons 'outside our control'. However insurance to provide cover if we change our mind or our travel plans would be too expensive.

Belongings: Although we are not going to be taking anything that is very valuable I think it is important we include insurance for our belongings. This would cover loss or theft of our everyday belongings. For example the current value of items stolen – although for this you would need to be able to provide receipts. Additionally laptops, tablets and smartphones can be covered as long as they are specifically listed when we take out the policy.

Medical: We need to be covered for a serious illness or an accident while we are away. Also, I think it's important to include the cost of a flight back to Hong Kong with accompanying medical staff if necessary. However, we will not be able to get insurance cover for all pre-existing medical conditions. So we need to make sure that we check with the company before about any long-term illness or disabilities that any of us have.

Please confirm that you are happy with this and then I can start looking for a good policy for the group – we may be able to get a group discount. Do let me know if you think I've left anything out.

Best,

Li

According to Li's notes, classify the following as being:

A   covered by insurance on belongings

B   covered by medical insurance

C   covered by insurance for cancellation

D   not covered by insurance

Write the correct letter, A, B, C or D, in boxes 8–14 on your answer sheet.

8   Loss of a laptop that is not specifically listed on the policy

9   Loss of a non-refundable deposit

10   A flight back to Hong Kong in the event of serious illness

11   Cancellation of the trip for reasons out the control of travellers

12   The current value of lost or stolen items

13   Treatment for an existing medical condition

14   Loss or theft of everyday items

Reading Passage 2

*You should spend about 20 minutes on **Questions 15–27** which are based on Reading Passage 2 below.*

Questions 15–20

Read the text below and answer questions that follow.

Reducing Production Waste in an Industrial Bakery

Production waste is one of the main problems faced by manufacturers of all types of products and today we are looking at the case of a local family-owned bakery in Lincoln.

Concerned about the impact this waste was having on company profits Lincoln Breads called in specialist advisors to find out how they could reduce production waste.

Work on tracking the waste had already been carried out, but the figures were inconsistent and showed no obvious trends to help explain the causes of the waste generated.

Following initial discussions, it was decided that the project should be divided into two phases.

1. To identify key waste drivers throughout the various parts of the factory.
2. To determine actions targeted at reducing this waste with the involvement of the factory floor team.

The advisory team worked with the factory production staff to collect data from the various waste streams over different production shifts. This data was then used to understand the key drivers of waste. They then produced a report containing actions for waste improvement that would allow Lincoln Breads to focus their efforts on the key areas to reduce their production waste.

Lincoln Breads have now implemented a number of changes based on the recommendations, including:

1. Re-training of personnel
2. Engineering work to correct or modify machinery and equipment

Making these changes alone is predicted to significantly reduce waste and will save the company about £30,000 per annum. Other recommendations are still to be implemented and therefore waste figures at Lincoln Breads should reduce even further.

Complete the sentences below.

*Choose **NO MORE THAN TWO WORDS** from the text for each answer.*

Write your answers in boxes 15–20 on your answer sheet.

15 Lincoln Breads is a family-owned .... in Lincoln.

16 The company hired .... to help them determine causes of waste.

17 Lincoln Breads' own efforts to track waste were ....

18 The first .... of the project was to identify waste drivers within the factory.

19 After collecting data, the advisory team produced ....

20 To improve the efficiency of machinery, Lincoln Breads have arranged for ....

Questions 21–27

Read the text below and answer questions 21–27.

Flexible Work Arrangements: Guidelines for Employees

Employees who are interested in having a Flexible Work Arrangement (FWA) should remember that the arrangement depends on a partnership between the supervisor and employee. This is to ensure that the needs of both the employee and the company are being met.

Considering a Flexible Work Arrangement

If you wish to have a FWA then you need to prepare a proposal to submit to your supervisor. As you develop the proposal we recommend that you consider the following questions:

1. Is a Flexible Work Arrangement right for my job?
   - *Can my job be done at hours outside the range of traditional working hours?*
   - *Will your clients' needs (internal and external) continue to be met?*
   - *How will the performance be measured?*
   - *What are the differences from your current schedule, including your proposed work days, start and end times, hours of work,*
   - *How will your proposed FWA improve your performance?*
   - *What are the tasks or responsibilities you have that are unpredictable or variable?*

2. Is a Flexible Work Arrangement suitable for you?
   - *Are you a highly motivated can work independently?*
   - *Have you demonstrated your ability to solve problems without supervisor intervention?*
   - *Are you able to manage your own time?*

Requesting a FWA

To request a FWA you should meet with your supervisor. You are encouraged to use the "Is FWA right for me?" worksheet available from the HR department. The worksheet will help to guide the discussion.

Following the request, you supervisor will review your FWA proposal, taking into consideration the operational needs of the department.

The supervisor will be responsible for communicating the decision to approve or deny such a proposal.

If approved, the supervisor and employee agree an introduction plan. In the event that a request for a FWA is declined, the employee can appeal to HR.

The details of the arrangement must be agreed upon by both the employee and the supervisor.

Participating in a Flexible Work Arrangement

- Employees with flexible work arrangements are more inclined to practice self-management, work productively and experience improved morale. In order to achieve these results, special attention should be paid to the following:
  - Communication. All department employees need to be kept informed of their colleagues schedules. This calls for extra attention to communication for the first few weeks until everyone is familiar with any new arrangement.
  - Availability. Employees working a flexible work arrangement may be expected to structure their work schedule to ensure there are no disruptions to the departments operations.

Answer the questions below.

*Choose **NO MORE THAN THREE WORDS** from the text for each answer.*

Write your answers in boxes 21–27 on your answer sheet.

21 Whose needs should a flexible work arrangement meet?

22 What must be submitted to your supervisor if you would like to arrange a FWA?

23 Where may a copy of the "Is the FWA right for me?" worksheet be obtained?

24 Who makes the decision to approve or deny a FWA proposal?

25 If a FWA proposal is denied, who should an employee appeal to?

26 How is the morale of employees with flexible work arrangements affected?

27 Which areas need special attention when a FWA is agreed upon?

Reading Passage 3

*You should spend about 20 minutes on **Questions 28–40** which are based on Reading Passage 3 below.*

Questions 28–33

*The text below has eight sections, **A–H**.*

*Choose the correct heading for sections **C–H** from the list of headings below.*

*Write the correct number, **I–xi**, in boxes 28–33 on your answer sheet.*

List of Headings

  i   How the dogs are trained

  ii   Benefits of using dogs to diagnose malaria

  iii   Project funding

  iv   Other animals that are suitable for the task

  v   The symptoms of malaria

  vi   Reasons why rich people don't get malaria

  vii   Reasons why dogs are suitable for the task

  viii How food choices can help prevent malaria

  ix   The conditions which promote malaria

  x   Some background on the disease

  xi   Problems with current methods of diagnosis

Examples:

Section **A**   **x**

Section **B**   **v**

---

28 Section C

29 Section D

30 Section E

31 Section F

32 Section G

33 Section H

Medical Detection Dogs: Sniffing Out One of the World's Most Dangerous Diseases

For many years man's best friend has been helping blind people with their daily lives but now, as well as assisting with lives, they may be able to save them!

A   Malaria kills about half a million people a year. That's about 1400 people every day or 1 person every minute. The vast majority of these are children under 15 in some of the poorest countries in the world. There is no cure for malaria and no vaccine to prevent the most vulnerable children catching the disease. It can kill within 24 hours of infection and some children in Africa can be infected up to 13 times a year. Spending on malaria accounts for about 40% of the public health budget in countries that can ill-afford it.

B   When the malaria parasites from infected mosquitos enter the blood stream they infect and destroy red blood cells. This leads to flu like symptoms such as sweating, headache, fever, tiredness, nausea, vomiting and diarrhoea. Because these symptoms are so non-specific it is not always clear that the patient is a victim of malaria which can delay identification.

C   There is no vaccine for malaria and the conditions that encourage the spread of the disease, such as high population density and high mosquito density, are frequently found in the countries of sub-Saharan Africa. However, if any of these conditions are substantially reduced then malaria can be eradicated and this has happened in North America, Europe and parts of the Middle East. However until it is totally eliminated from the whole world malaria could easily become re-established.

D   One of the most important weapons in the fight against malaria is early detection of the disease. However, currently diagnosis involves finger-prick blood tests that are then screened in a laboratory. This is both time-consuming and very expensive and health authorities have real difficulties identifying who is carrying the malaria parasite in communities where the disease is present at a low level. This is where the dog's come in.

E   Using dogs to identify malaria carriers has the advantage that it is not invasive, the 'testing' can be done anywhere and it doesn't require a laboratory. Also a large number of people can be tested at the same time. The idea is to train dogs to be able to identify malaria victims by their scent.

F   Dogs have an incredible ability to detect minute odour traces created by diseases. Because they are able to detect tiny odour concentrations, around one part per trillion. This is the equivalent of one teaspoon of sugar in two Olympic-sized swimming pools. Thus, they are potentially able to detect diseases, such as malaria, much earlier than is currently possible with traditional methods. This pioneering work with dogs could help to speed up the diagnosis process and impact on thousands of lives.

G   To train the dogs, sweat samples will be collected from 400 Gambian children. Of the samples, 15 per cent will be collected from children known to be have the malaria parasite, so that the dogs can be trained to distinguish positive from negative samples. If the first phase of the trial is successful, then the project may be able to continue if sufficient grand funding is made available.

H   So far the project has already received sufficient funds from the Bill and Melinda Gates foundation to cover the costs of the initial training and studies. So if it is successful – and there is good reason to suppose it will be – there is every likelihood that the foundation will continue its support.

Questions 34–40

Do the following statements agree with the information given in the text?

In boxes 34–40 on your answer sheet write:

TRUE	*if the statement agrees with the information*
FALSE	*if the statement contracts the information*
NOT GIVEN	*if there is no information on this*

34   The majority of people killed by malaria are children under the age of 15.

35   Malaria always kills people within 24 hours of infection.

36   The symptoms of malaria make it easy to identify.

37   Scientists have been working of a vaccine for malaria since the 1920's.

38   Current methods of diagnosing malaria are expensive.

39   Dogs will identify carriers of malaria by their scent

40   If the project is successful it is not likely to receive further funding from the Gates Foundation.

GENERAL TRAINING WRITING MODULE

Writing Task 1

You should spend about 20 minutes on this task.

You recently bought a smartphone from a specialised store, but it is not working properly. You have called the shop several times but no action has been taken.

Write an email to the shop manager. In your letter

- *Give details of the mobile phone you purchased and when you bought it.*
- *Describe the problems you are having with the smartphone*
- *Explain what happened when you called the shop*
- *Tell the manager what you would like him to do.*

You should write at least 150 words.

Begin your letter as follows:

Dear Sir or Madam,

Writing Task 2

You should spend about 40 minutes on this task.

Discuss both these views and give your own opinion.

Today tourism is one of the world's biggest industries and many poorer countries are depending more and more on tourism for their economy.

What are some of the advantages and disadvantages of having a large number of tourists visiting a country?

Give reasons for your answer and include any relevant examples from your own knowledge or experience.

You should write at least 250 words.

LISTENING MODULE

 Practice Test 3, Track 1 (Track 24)

Section 1: Questions 1–10

Questions 1–6

Complete the form below, using **NO MORE THAN TWO WORDS AND/OR A NUMBER** for each answer.

EXPENSES CLAIM INFORMATION – GB AIRLINES

Customer name: Mr **1** …………..

Date of Departure: **2** ………….. 2016

Flight Number: GB1011

Flight: From **3** ………….. to London Heathrow, UK

Departure Time: **4** ………….. p.m.

Expenses Claimed: **5** ………….. Hotel, 73 euros

Taxis, **6** …………..

Questions 7–10

Complete the sentences below with **NO MORE THAN TWO WORDS AND/OR A NUMBER**.

7 The customer had the ………….. option for his previous flight.

8 There are three meal options without meat: vegetarian, vegan, and ………….. .

9 The vegan option doesn't contain any ………….. , eggs, fowl, or honey.

10 The meal option for the customer's flight to Kiev must be changed ………….. before the departure time.

Practice Test 3 Track 2 (Track 25)

Section 2: Questions 11–20

Questions 11–14

You are going to hear a radio interview with a self-publishing expert.

*What **FOUR** things does she say new writers need to make sure they have before they self-publish?*

  A   an impeccably edited novel

  B   another finished novel

  C   a budget

  D   a solid marketing plan

  E   a new novel in progress

  F   a lot of money on the side

  G   a good understanding of grammar

Questions 15–17

*Choose the correct letter, **A**, **B** or **C**.*

Write your answers in boxes 15–17 on your answer sheet.

15   Patricia Abaddon's first novel

  A   was a commercial success.

  B   had mediocre sales.

  C   performed terribly.

16   For the first year after his novel's publication, Patricia Abaddon

  A   avoided checking how many copies he sold.

  B   was depressed about the results.

  C   was relatively happy with how the novel was doing.

17   Patricia Abaddon subscribed to writing magazines because

  A   she wanted to find out about writing competitions.

  B   it was a good way to build a fan base.

  C   she wanted to read advice from professionals.

Questions 18–20

Complete the sentences below with ***NO MORE THAN THREE WORDS***.

18   Patricia Abaddon published her second novel under a .... because she didn't want her readers to know about her first novel.

19   Patricia Abaddon used her website and her pages on .... to promote her second novel.

20   By the time her second novel was out, Patricia Abaddon wanted her third novel to be ....

🎧 **Practice Test 3, Track 3 (Track 26)**

Section 3: Questions 21–30

Question 21

Which graph shows what students reported feeling after a year at school?

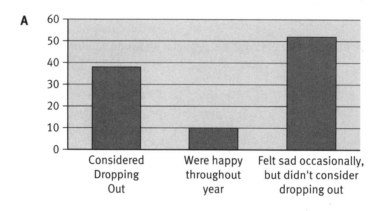

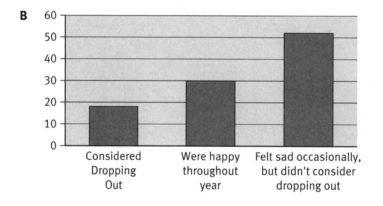

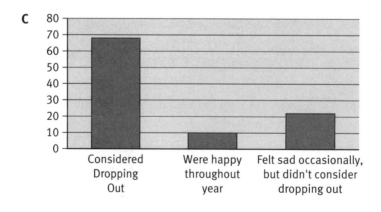

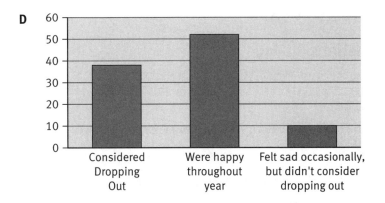

Questions 22–25

Which student will present which information?

    A   Gale

    B   Lindsay

    C   Kevin

Write the correct letter, A, B or C, in boxes 22–25 on your answer sheet

    22   the research focus   ....

    23   the focus group of the research   ....

    24   how the students acquired access to the focus group   ....

    25   the structure of the survey used in the research   ....

Questions 26–30

*Complete the sentences below. Write **NO MORE THAN TWO WORDS AND/OR A NUMBER** for each answer.*

    26   The number of males and females participating in the study was ....

    27   .... per cent of the participants came from Europe.

    28   The vast majority of the participants were 20 or 21 years old, and only .... per cent were 19.

    29   Most participants reported missing home and/or suffering from .... at the start of their course.

    30   The students examined the .... of the previous two years to ensure the numbers in their research were as accurate as possible.

Practice Test 3, Track 4 (Track 27)

Section 4: Questions 31–40

Questions 31–37

Answer the questions below.

*Write **NO MORE THAN THREE WORDS AND/OR A NUMBER** for each answer.*

31 How many English speakers are there around the world today? ....

32 Aside from French, which other language does the speaker say was more widely spoken than English in the 19th century? ....

33 Who does the speaker believe will determine the future of English? ....

34 What is the alternative name for English pidgin and creole languages? ....

35 What does "longi" mean? ....

36 According to the speaker, which language has a history which is very similar to English? ....

37 What kind of languages are Spanish, French, and Italian? ....

Questions 38–40

*Choose the correct letter, **A, B,** or **C.***

Write your answers in boxes 38–40 on your answer sheet.

38 The speaker says that Jamaican and South African English

    A are very traditional languages.

    B have greatly influenced the English language.

    C were created very recently.

39 According to the second theory mentioned by the speaker, English

    A might lose some of its more complex features in a global level.

    B might become even more complicated than it is now.

    C might be called 'Globish'.

40 English is a unique language because

    A it has the largest number of speakers in the world.

    B it hasn't changed much throughout human history.

    C it's spoken by a larger number of non-natives than any other language.

READING MODULE

Reading Passage 1

*You should spend about 20 minutes on **Questions 1–14**, which are based on Reading Passage 1 below.*

Synaesthesia

A   Imagine a page with a square box in the middle. The box is lined with rows of the number 5, repeated over and over. All of the 5s are identical in size, font and colour, and equally distributed across the box. There is, however, a trick: among those 5s, hiding in plain sight is a single, capital letter S. Almost the same in shape, it is impossible to spot without straining your eyes for a good few minutes. Unless, that is, you are a grapheme–colour synaesthete—a person who sees each letter and number in different colours. With all the 5s painted in one colour and the rogue S painted in another, a grapheme–colour synaesthete will usually only need a split second to identify the latter.

B   Synaesthesia, loosely translated as "senses coming together" from the Greek words syn ("with") and aesthesis ("sensation"), is an interesting neurological phenomenon that causes different senses to be combined. This might mean that words have a particular taste (for example, the word "door" might taste like bacon), or that certain smells produce a particular colour. It might also mean that each letter and number has its own personality—the letter A might be perky, the letter B might be shy and self-conscious, etc. Some synaesthetes might even experience other people's sensations, for example feeling pain in their chest when they witness a film character get shot. The possibilities are endless: even though synaesthesia is believed to affect less than 5% of the general population, at least 60 different combinations of senses have been reported so far. What all these sensory associations have in common is that they are all involuntary and impossible to repress, and that they usually remain quite stable over time.

C   Synaesthesia was first documented in the early 19th century by German physician Georg Sachs, who dedicated two pages of his dissertation on his own experience with the condition. It wasn't, however, until the mid–1990s that empirical research proved its existence, when Professor Simon Baron–Cohen and his colleagues used fMRIs on six synaesthetes and discovered that the parts of the brain associated with vision were active during auditory stimulation, even though the subjects were blindfolded.

D   What makes synaesthesia a particularly interesting condition is that it isn't an illness at all. If anything, synaesthetes often report feeling sorry for the rest of the population, as they don't have the opportunity to experience the world in a multisensory fashion like they do. Very few drawbacks have been described, usually minimal: for instance, some words might have an unpleasant taste (imagine the word "hello" tasting like spoilt milk), while some synaesthetes find it distressing when they encounter people with names which don't reflect their personality (imagine meeting a very interesting person named "Lee", when the letter E has a dull or hideous colour for you—or vice versa). Overall, however, synaesthesia is widely considered more of a blessing than a curse and it is often linked to intelligence and creativity, with celebrities such as Lady Gaga and Pharrell Williams claiming to have it.

E   Another fascinating side of synaesthesia is the way it could potentially benefit future generations. In a 2013 study, Dr Witthoft and Dr Winawer discovered that grapheme–colour synaesthetes who had never met each other before experienced strikingly similar pairings between graphemes and colours—pairings which were later traced back to a popular set of Fischer–Price magnets that ten out of eleven participants distinctly remembered possessing as children. This was particularly peculiar as synaesthesia is predominantly considered to be a hereditary condition, and the findings suggested that a synaesthete's environment might play a determining role in establishing synaesthetic associations. If that was true, researchers asked, then might it not be possible that synaesthesia can actually be taught?

F   As it turns out, the benefits of teaching synaesthesia would be tremendous. According to research conducted by Dr Clare Jonas at the University of East London, teaching people to create grapheme–colour associations the same way as a synaesthete may have the possibility to improve cognitive function and memory. As she put it, 'one possibility is guarding against cognitive decline in older people—using synaesthesia in the creation of mnemonics to remember things such as shopping lists.' To that end, researchers in the Netherlands have already begun developing a web browser plug–in that will change the colours of certain letters. Rothen and his colleagues corroborate the theory: in a paper published in 2011, they suggest that synaesthesia might be more than a hereditary condition, as the non–synaesthetic subjects of their study were able to mimic synaesthetic associations long after leaving the lab.

G   There is obviously still a long way to go before we can fully understand synaesthesia and what causes it. Once we do, however, it might not be too long before we find out how to teach non–synaesthetes how to imitate its symptoms in a way that induces the same benefits 4.4% of the world's population currently enjoy.

Questions 1–7

The reading passage has 7 paragraphs, A–G. Which paragraph contains the following information?

Write the correct letter, A–G, in boxes 1–7 on your answer sheet.

   1   some of the disadvantages related to synaesthesia

   2   what scientists think about synaesthesia's real–life usefulness

   3   a prediction for the future of synaesthesia

4   an example of how grapheme–colour synaesthesia works

5   a brief history of synaesthesia

6   some of the various different types of synaesthesia

7   information about a study that suggests synaesthetic symptoms aren't arbitrary

Questions 8–11

Do the following statements agree with the information given in Reading Passage 1?

In boxes 8–11 on your answer sheet, write

TRUE	*if the statement is true according to the passage*
FALSE	*if the statement is false according to the passage*
NOT GIVEN	*if the information is not given in the passage*

8   There are 60 different types of synaesthesia.

9   Before Professor Simon Baron-Cohen's research, synaesthesia was thought to be a myth.

10   A lot of celebrities are affected by synaesthesia.

11   Most scientists believe that synaesthesia runs in families.

Questions 12–14

Complete the summary.

Choose ONE WORD ONLY from the passage for each answer.

Write your answers in boxes 12–14 on your answer sheet.

Synaesthesia is a unique neurological condition that causes different senses to get mixed. Recent research has suggested that teaching synaesthesia to non-synaesthetes can enhance **12** ………….. and guard against the deterioration of cognitive **13** ………….. ; unfortunately, it might be a while before we come up with a beneficial way to **14** ………….. it to the general population.

Reading Passage 2

*You should spend about 20 minutes on **Questions 15–28**, which are based on Reading Passage 2 below.*

The Taman Shud Case

It has been more than 65 years since the Taman Shud case was first opened, but this notoriously bizarre murder mystery from Australia continues to baffle scientific investigators and crime aficionados from around the world today.

On the morning of 1st December 1948, the body of an unidentified man was discovered propped against a rock wall on Somerton beach in Adelaide, opposite the Crippled Children's home. The man was around 40–45 years old, had an athletic figure and was dressed in a smart suit and tie. He had no form of ID on him and all the labels on his clothes had been removed. The only things found on his body were an unused 10:50 a.m. ticket from Adelaide Railway Station to Henley Beach for the 30th November, a packet of chewing gums, an aluminium comb, a packet of cigarettes, a box of Bryan & May matches, sixpence and a small piece of paper with the words "Tamám shud" printed on it—which means "ended" or "finished" in Persian. To make matters more interesting, the autopsy revealed that his death had been unnatural, but determined no cause of death: although he had clearly died of heart failure, his heart had been healthy and no signs of violence or poisoning were discovered in his system.

The case garnered media attention almost immediately, with dozens of people with missing friends and relatives travelling to Adelaide to have a look at the Somerton man's body—but none of them being able to positively identify him. The next piece of evidence came when a journalist named Frank Kennedy discovered that the piece of paper with the printed words had been ripped from the last page of *The Rubáiyát of Omar Khayyám*, a book of collected poems by Omar Khayyám, an 11th century Persian poet. Following pleas by the police for the public to check their copies of *The Rubáiyát* for any missing pages, a local man brought in the correct copy, which he reported having found in the back seat of his car six months earlier, around the time the corpse had been discovered.

This is where things get even more complicated: in the back of the book, police discovered five lines of letters that appeared to be some sort of secret code. In the back cover, they also found a phone number which led them to a 27–year–old woman known as "Jestyn" who lived on Moseley Street, a stone's throw from the crime scene. Jestyn denied any knowledge of the man and was generally guarded and non–committal throughout the police interview. Nevertheless, the police decided not to pursue the lead. As for the code? Despite years of research by cryptology experts and students, no one has managed to crack it to this day.

It's not just the mysterious code, however, that makes this case so popular with crime fans. It's been more than half a century since the man's death, but his identity is still a mystery. Although copies of the victim's fingerprints and photograph, as well as the name "T. Keane" (which was written on some labels found in his suitcase) were sent around the world to all Commonwealth countries, the search turned up no results. Some theories regarding the man's origins have arisen over the years, with many believing that he was American due to the predominantly US way the stripes slanted on his tie, his aluminium comb (rare in Australia at the time) and the belief that Americans were far more likely to chew gum than Australians in the 1940s. Others also theorise that he was Jestyn's lover, and perhaps even a Soviet spy agent—although this all still remains just speculation for now.

Interest in the case was rekindled in 2013, following an interview on the show *60 Minutes* with Kate Thompson, the daughter of "Jestyn"—whose actual name was revealed to be Jo Thompson. Kate Thompson claimed that her mother had lied to the police about not knowing the Somerton Man. She also said her mother was a Soviet spy with a "dark side" and that she might've been responsible for the man's murder. Also participating in the show were Roma and Rachel Egan, wife and daughter respectively of Kate Thompson's late brother Robin, whom many believe to have been the Somerton man's son. The two women have backed a request to get the man's body exhumed in the interest of proving this claim, which they also believe to be correct. A similar bid had been rejected previously in 2011 by Attorney–General John Rau, citing insufficient "public interest reasons". There is currently a petition on Change.org, as well as an Indiegogo campaign to raise funds in support of solving the case.

Questions 15–20

Complete the timeline below.

*Choose **NO MORE THAN THREE WORDS** from Reading Passage 2 for each answer.*

*Write your answers in boxes **15–20** on your answer sheet.*

1948, November 30th—The Somerton Man misses a train to **15** ....

1948, December 1st—The Somerton Man's body is discovered on Somerton beach

1948, December 2nd—Post mortem reveals no **16** ....

1949, January 14th—Adelaide Railway Station discover deceased man's suitcase

1949, July 22nd—A businessman from Somerton hands in copy of poem book that contains the **17** .... and Jestyn's **18** ....

1949, July 25th—Police visit Jestyn at her house on **19** .... to speak with her – she remains **20** .... during questioning

Questions 21–24

Complete each sentence with the correct ending A–G below.

Write the correct letter, A–G, in boxes 21–24 on your answer sheet.

> **A** believes her daughter is related to the Somerton man.
>
> **B** has tried to solve it for decades with no results.
>
> **C** was revealed by her daughter in 2013.
>
> **D** inadvertently assisted the police in their investigation.
>
> **E** was only named as "Jestyn".
>
> **F** remains a mystery.
>
> **G** revealed that Jo Thompson was a cruel Soviet spy.

21 The code written on the back of *The Rubáiyát of Omar Khayyám*

22 Journalist Frank Kennedy

23 The identity of the woman to whom the phone number belonged

24 Kate Thompson's sister-in-law

Questions 25–28

Choose the correct letter, A, B, C or D.

Write your answers in boxes 25–28 on your answer sheet.

25 According to the autopsy on the Somerton man

    A his heart failed for no reason.

    B there were traces of poison in his system.

    C he was physically fit.

    D there was nothing wrong with his heart.

26 The copy of *The Rubáiyát of Omar Khayyám* with the missing page

    A was discovered in a local man's garage.

    B was in a local man's possession for six months after the murder.

    C was discovered by a local man six months after the murder.

    D was found by journalist Frank Kennedy.

27 One of the reasons many believe that the Somerton Man was American is that

    A   he wasn't found in any database in Commonwealth countries.

    B   he had been chewing a gum before his death.

    C   his tie had an American pattern of stripes.

    D   the name "T. Keane" was found in his suitcase.

28 Roma and Rachel Egan

    A   are critical of attempts to exhume the Somerton man's body.

    B   disagree that Robin Thompson was the Somerton man's son.

    C   backed the request that was rejected in 2011 by Rau.

    D   voiced their beliefs on the same programme as Kate Thompson.

Reading Passage 3

*You should spend about 20 minutes on **Questions 29–40**, which are based on Reading Passage 3 below.*

Coinage in Ancient Greece

A   There are more than 170 official national currencies currently in circulation around the world—and while they may differ greatly in value, most show a high degree of commonality when it comes to their design. Typically, a coin or banknote will feature the effigy of a notable politician, monarch or other personality from the country of origin on one side and a recognisable state symbol (e.g. a building or an animal) on the reverse. This pattern, which has been around for more than 21 centuries, originated in ancient Greece.

B   Prior to the invention of legal tender, most transactions in the ancient world took the form of trading a product or service for another. As sea trade grew in the Mediterranean, however, the once popular barter system became hard to maintain for two reasons: firstly, because it was tricky to calculate the value of each item or service in relation to another, and secondly, because carrying large goods (such as animals) on boats to do trade with neighbouring cities was difficult and inconvenient. Therefore, the need soon arose for a commonly recognised unit that would represent a set value—what is known today as a currency. As Aristotle explains in *Politics*, metal coins naturally became the most popular option due to the fact that they were easy to carry, and didn't run the risk of expiring. According to ancient Greek historian Herodotus, the first coins were invented in 620 BC in the town of Lydia, although some theorise that they actually originated in the city of Ionia. (Coins had already existed for nearly 400 years in China, unbeknownst to Europeans.)

C   Much like with every other form of ancient Greek art, the history of ancient Greek coins can be divided into three distinct chronological periods: the Archaic (600–480 BC), the Classic (480–330 BC) and the Hellenistic Period (330–1st century BC). As ancient Greece was not a united country like today, but rather comprised of many independent city–states known as *poleis*, each state produced its own coins. The island of Aegina was the first to mint silver coins, perhaps adopting the new system upon witnessing how successfully it had facilitated trade for the Ionians. Aegina being the head of a confederation of seven states, it quickly influenced other city–states in the Mediterranean and the new method of trade soon became widespread. Up until approximately 510 BC, when Athens began producing its own coin, the Aegina coin — which featured a turtle on its surface— was the most predominant in the region.

D   The tetradrachm, Athens's new coin bearing the picture of an owl on its obverse as a tribute to the city's protector, the goddess Athena, brought with it a shift in the world of coinage. Prior to the tetradrachm, Athenians had been using simple iron rods known as 'obols' for currency. As the average human hand could grasp about six obols, that number soon came to represent a 'drachma' (from the Greek verb 'dratto', which means 'to grasp')—so the new tetradrachm had the same value as 24 obols. With Athens continually growing in power, the tetradrachm soon replaced the Aegina 'turtle' as the most preponderant coin in the region. It was around that time that an agreement akin to way the EU's euro currency functions also appeared, with different coins from all over the Mediterranean being made to the same standards as the Athenian coin (albeit with each city's own symbols on them) and being used interchangeably among the trading city–states.

E   Coinage soon spread beyond those city–states. Romans abandoned the bronze bars they'd been using in favour of coins around the year 300 BC, and Alexander the Great and his father King Philip of Macedonia began to produce massive quantities of coins to fund their military escapades around the same time. It was with the death of the latter, in 336 BC, that the Hellenistic Period began. Two things characterise the Hellenistic Period: the introduction of a "type" (the design that coins were stamped with) on the reverse of the coins, and mass production, which mostly took place in kingdoms beyond the Greek city–states, such as Egypt, Syria and the far east. Another new feature, which was heavily criticised by the Greeks, was the introduction of profiles of kings and other important living figures as stamps in lieu of the traditional symbols of animals and buildings. Athens, still a powerful city at the time, eschewed these designs and continued to produce its own tetradrachm coins, even introducing a new–style coin characterised by broad, thin flans—a design which became popular across the Aegean and lasted until the spread of Roman rule over Greece.

F   It's not difficult to see why ancient Greek coins continue to fascinate coin collectors and historians today. They marked the beginning of a new era in business and introduced a model of trade in Europe that is still present nowadays; they greatly influenced the design of modern coinage, with symbols such as the owl (which can be seen on the Greek version of the euro today) and portraits of important personalities; and, since they were hand–made to high technical standards representative of ancient Greek perfectionism, many are even remarkable in their own right, as tiny metal works of art.

Questions 29–34

The reading passage has six paragraphs, A–F. Choose the correct heading for paragraphs A–F from the list of headings below. Write the correct number, i–ix, in boxes 29–34 on your answer sheet.

List of Headings

i	The beginning of the Archaic period
ii	The Athenian obol replaces the turtle
iii	How product exchange became insufficient
iv	Roman and Macedonian coins
v	The relevance of ancient Greek coins today
vi	New cities introduce new design rules
vii	A precursor of the modern euro
viii	The difference between Ionian and Lydian coins
ix	Modern coin designs and their origin

---

29 Paragraph A   —

30 Paragraph B   —

31 Paragraph C   —

32 Paragraph D   —

33 Paragraph E   —

34 Paragraph F   —

Questions 35–38

Answer the questions below with words taken from Reading Passage 3.

*Use **NO MORE THAN TWO WORDS** for each answer.*

35 What were the ancient Greek city–states commonly known as? ....

36 Which type did the Aegina coin use? ....

37 What was the value of a drachma in ancient Athens? ....

38 What did the Romans use prior to the introduction of coins? ....

Questions 39–40

Choose the correct letter, A, B, C or D.

Write your answers in boxes 39–40 on your answer sheet.

39　The Athenian Hellenistic–period tetradrachm coin

    A　replaced the owl type with the profile of a king.

    B　was a thin, wide metal disk.

    C　remained popular under Roman rule.

    D　was massively produced in Syria and Egypt.

40　Ancient Greek coins

    A　are still a method of trade in Europe nowadays.

    B　are remarkably different from modern coins.

    C　are a fine example of ancient Greek art.

    D　were a tribute to the goddess Athena, protector of Athens.

WRITING MODULE

Writing Task 1

You should spend about 20 minutes on this task.

The table below gives information about a bakery's average sales in three different branches in 2015.

Summarise the information by selecting and reporting the main features, and make comparisons where relevant.

You should write at least 150 words.

Average	London Covent Garden	London Oxford Circus	London St John's Wood
Number of Transactions	642	538	269
Transaction Value	£7.58	£4.51	£5.01
Number of Eat–in Transactions	304	247	150
Number of Take–Away Transactions	338	291	119
Most popular Item	Croissant	medium latte	strawberry tart

Writing Task 2

You should spend about 40 minutes on this task.

> *Some people think that developed countries have a higher responsibility to combat climate change than developing countries. Others believe that all countries should have the same responsibilities towards protecting the environment.*

Discuss both these views and give your own opinion.

You should write at least 250 words.

Give reasons for your answer and include any relevant examples from your own knowledge or experience.

SPEAKING MODULE

Time: 11–14 minutes

Part 1

Introduction to interview (4–5 minutes) [This part of the test begins with the examiner introducing himself or herself and checking the candidate's identification. It then continues as an interview.]

Let's talk about your family and friends.

- *Do you live with your parents?*
- *Do you often spend time with your family?*
- *What do you like to do when you go out with your friends?*
- *Do you like to spend time alone?*
- *Do you have any hobbies that you share with your family or friends?*

Let's move on and talk about your childhood.

- *Where did you grow up? What kind of house did you live in?*
- *Did you have your own room when you were a child?*
- *How often did you get in trouble as a child?*
- *Did you use to argue with your parents? What did you argue about?*
- *Which family member were you closest to when you were growing up? Is it still the same now?*

Part 2

Task Card

Please read the topic below carefully. You will be asked to talk about it for one to two minutes. You will have one minute to think about what you are going to say. You can make some notes to help you if you wish.

Describe one of your fondest memories as a child. You should say:

- *when it was*
- *where you were, and with whom*
- *what you were doing*

Also, explain why it's such an important memory for you.

Individual long turn (3–4 minutes): *Candidate's Task Card*

The examiner may then ask you a couple of brief questions to wrap up this part of the test.

Rounding off questions:

- Have you told the people involved in your memory how important it is for you?
- Do you think this memory has influenced who you are today at all?

Part 3

Two-way discussion (4–5 minutes): In Part 3, the examiner will ask you further questions related to the topic in Part 2.

Let's talk about memory for a moment.

- *Why do people find it so important to remember what happened in the past?*
- *Has recent technology changed how well our memory works?*
- *How might new technological advances affect memory in the future?*
- *How will it affect society if science finds a way to edit or implant memories?*
- *Would you ever buy someone else's memories, if possible? If so, whose?*

Now let's talk about technology.

- *Do people use technology a lot in your country? What kind of technology is popular?*
- *Do you think technology might eventually make some jobs obsolete? How should we respond to this as a society?*
- *Is cybercrime an issue in your country? What can we do to prevent cybercrime?*
- *How has technology affected education? How do you think it will affect education in the near or distant future?*

LISTENING MODULE

 Practice Test 4, Track 1 (Track 28)

Section 1: Questions 1–10

Questions 1–6

Complete the form below, using **NO MORE THAN TWO WORDS AND/OR A NUMBER** *for each answer.*

PET PROTECT UK

PET DETAILS

Type of pet:

☑ dog ☐ cat ☐ rabbit

Pet's name: 1 ....

Pet's D.O.B.: 2 .... , 2013

For Dogs Only

Is the dog a guide dog? ....No...............

Has the dog been neutered? 3 ....

Type of dog: 4 ....

CUSTOMER DETAILS

Name: Peter 5 ....

Address: 27 Cherry Drive, NW8 2HD

Phone Number: 6 ....

Questions 7–10

Complete the table below, using **NO MORE THAN ONE WORD OR A NUMBER** *for each answer.*

Type of Insurance	Fees
Basic	£8 p.c.m.
Premium	**7** £ .... p.c.m. for first 6 months, then up to £18*
Ultimate Premium	£15 p.c.m. for first 6 months, then up to £20
*(if expenses claimed do not exceed £300 the fee drops to £ **8** ....) Please be advised that your pet's documents and **9** .... must be checked before we proceed with an insurance agreement. All three insurance plans cover **10** .... fees.	

Practice Test 4, Track 2 (Track 29)

Section 2: Questions 11–20

Questions 11–14

You are going to hear an induction given to a group of students at a summer school.

Complete the sentences below.

*Write **NO MORE THAN THREE WORDS** for each answer.*

11 Jasmine Climb founded her school on a quiet and isolated site because she appreciated the .... of such places.

12 When the school was first founded, it had neither trees nor a ....

13 The students listening to the speech will be staying at the school for ....

14 The programme for the students' first day will culminate with a ....

Questions 15–20

*Complete the plan below using **NO MORE THAN TWO WORDS** for each answer.*

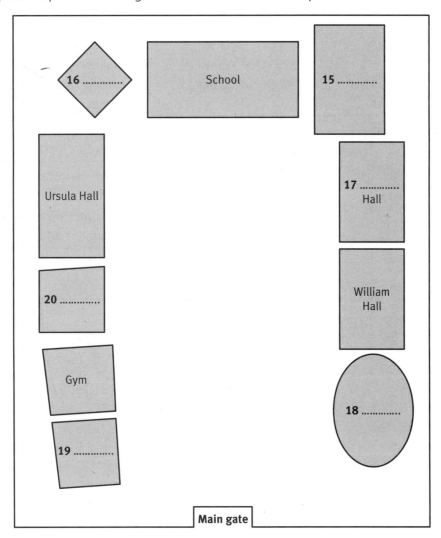

Practice Test 4, Track 3 (Track 30)

Section 3: Questions 21–30

Questions 21–30

Complete the table below.

Write **NO MORE THAN THREE WORDS AND/OR A NUMBER** *for each answer.*

	Management Scheme Interviews	
	Carol	**James**
Interview Subject:	Manager from **21**	Manager from **22** ....
How easy it was to schedule the interview:	Manager had a **23** .... — rescheduled 3 times	No issues
Recruitment process:	**24** .... process: panel interview and trial day – 3 months probationary period	Internal and external recruitment/three individual interviews – **25** .... probationary period
Training provided:	Trainees learn **26** .... and move up the ladder, starting at the bottom	Trainees receive external training and do courses – also sent to **27** .... for a semester
Length of scheme:	3 years	2 years for full–time/ **28** .... for part–time
Overall impression:	Manager friendly and knowledgeable Scheme very helpful, but not enough **29**	Manager eager and friendly Well–structured scheme, but duration **30** ....

Practice Test 4, Track 4 (Track 31)

Section 4: Questions 31–40

Questions 31–33

Complete the sentences below.

*Use **NO MORE THAN TWO WORDS AND/OR A NUMBER** for each answer.*

31 There are a few ………….. about being a foreign correspondent, but they are the wrong reason to choose it as a career.

32 The dangers of being a foreign correspondent lead to the death of ………….. per year.

33 Every journalist needs to possess certain media skills and ………….. .

Questions 34–37

*What **FOUR** pieces of advice does the speaker give to aspiring foreign correspondents?*

    A   to assimilate their target country's culture

    B   to get work experience around the world

    C   to travel as much as possible

    D   to examine the past of their target country

    E   to learn how to speak impeccable English

    F   to create an impressive CV before they leave their home country

    G   to study other languages

Questions 38–40

Choose the correct letter, A, B or C.

Write your answers in boxes 38–40 on your answer sheet.

38 Because of recent technological advancements

    A   international journalism is becoming less common.

    B   newspapers are loath to hire journalists on a contract.

    C   newspapers have started to opt for independent foreign correspondents.

39 If foreign correspondents want to earn enough money

    A   they need to learn how to network.

    B   they need to have a second job.

    C   they need to start at the bottom.

40 The speaker's ex–student found which of the following pieces of advice very useful?

    A   "You need to remember to renew your passport."

    B   "You need to learn how to deal with failure."

    C   "You need to remember that failure is inevitable."

Reading Module

Reading Passage 1

*You should spend about 20 minutes on **Questions 1–13**, which are based on Reading Passage 1 below.*

A   Recent years have seen a barrage of dystopian Young Adult novels grow in popularity almost overnight—from *The Hunger Games* to *The Maze Runner*, *Divergent*, and *The Knife of Never Letting Go*. These novels, set in post-apocalyptic, totalitarian or otherwise ruthless and dehumanising worlds, have gained such momentum that the trend has seeped into the film and TV industry as well, with multimillion dollar movie adaptations and popular TV series gracing the big and small screen. But what is it about dystopian stories that makes them so appealing to readers and audiences alike?

B   Dystopias are certainly nothing new. The word "dystopia" itself, meaning "bad place" (from the Greek *dys* and *topos*), has been around since at least the 19th century, and Huxley's *Brave New World* (1932) and Orwell's *1984* (1949), commonly regarded as the first dystopian novels that fit firmly into the genre, were published more than 75 years ago. Even the first YA dystopian novel is older than 20—Lois Lowry's *The Giver*, which came out in 1993. While these are individual examples from previous decades, however, one would be hard-pressed to find a YA shelf in any bookstore nowadays that isn't stocked with dozens of dystopian titles.

C   According to film critic Dana Stevens, it is the similarities that can be drawn between dystopian settings and the daily lives of teenagers that make YA dystopian stories so captivating: the high school experience involves the same social structure as the *Hunger Games* arena, for example, or the faction-divided world of *Divergent*. Teenagers might not literally have to fight each other to the death or go through horrendous trials to join a virtue-based faction for the rest of their lives, but there's something in each story that connects to their own backgrounds. The "cutthroat race for high school popularity" might feel like an "annual televised fight", and the pressure to choose a clique at school bears a strong resemblance to Tris's faction dilemma in *Divergent*.

D   Justin Scholes's and Jon Ostenson's 2013 study reports similar findings, identifying themes such as "inhumanity and isolation", the struggle to establish an identity and the development of platonic and romantic relationships as alluring agents. Deconstructing a score of popular YA dystopian novels released between 2007–2011, Scholes and Ostenson argue that the topics explored by dystopian literature are appealing to teenagers because they are "an appropriate fit with the intellectual changes that occur during adolescence"; as teenagers gradually grow into adults, they develop an interest in social issues and current affairs. Dystopian novels, according to author and book critic Dave Astor, feel honest in that regard as they do not patronise their readers, nor do they attempt to sugar-coat reality.

E   All of this still does not explain why this upsurge in YA dystopian literature is happening now, though. Bestselling author Naomi Klein, offers a different explanation: the dystopian trend, she says, is a "worrying sign" of times to come. What all these dystopian stories have in common is that they all assume that "environmental catastrophe" is not only imminent, but also completely inevitable. Moral principles burgeon through these works of fiction, particularly for young people, as they are the ones who will bear the brunt of climate change. YA author Todd Mitchell makes a similar point, suggesting that the bleak futures portrayed in modern YA literature are a response to "social anxiety" brought forth by pollution and over–consumption.

F   The threat of natural disasters is not the only reason YA dystopian novels are so popular today, however. As author Claudia Gray notes, what has also changed in recent years is humanity's approach to personal identity and young people's roles in society. Adolescents, she says, are increasingly dragooned into rigid moulds through "increased standardised testing, increased homework levels, etc." YA dystopian novels come into play because they present protagonists who refuse to be defined by someone else, role models who battle against the status quo.

G   So, how long is this YA dystopian trend going to last? If *The Guardian* is to be believed, it's already been replaced by a new wave of "gritty" realism as seen in the likes of *The Fault in Our Stars*, by John Green. Profits have certainly dwindled for dystopian film franchises such as *Divergent*. This hasn't stopped film companies from scheduling new releases, however, and TV series such as *The 100* are still on air. Perhaps the market for dystopian novels has stagnated—only time will tell. One thing is for certain, however: the changes the trend has effected on YA literature are here to stay.

Questions 1–7

Reading Passage 1 has seven paragraphs, labelled A–G. Choose the correct heading for paragraphs A–G from the list of headings below. Write the correct number, i–ix, in boxes 1–7 on your answer sheet.

List of Headings	
i	Teens are increasingly urged to conform
ii	The dystopian model scrutinised
iii	Dystopian novels now focus on climate change
iv	The original dystopias
v	Dystopian literature's accomplishments will outlive it
vi	A score of dystopian novels has taken over YA shelves
vii	The roots of dystopia can be found in teenage experiences
viii	Dystopia is already dead
ix	Dystopias promote ethical thinking

1   Paragraph A   —

2   Paragraph B   —

3   Paragraph C   —

4   Paragraph D   —

5   Paragraph E   —

6   Paragraph F   —

7   Paragraph G   —

Questions 8–12

Answer the questions below with words taken from Reading Passage 1.

*Use **NO MORE THAN THREE WORDS** for each answer.*

8   According to the writer, what was the first dystopian novel?

9   According to the writer, which author initiated the YA dystopian genre?

10   How does Dave Astor describe dystopian novels?

11   According to Naomi Klein, which element is present in all dystopian novels?

12   According to Claudia Gray, things like increased standardised testing and homework levels are a threat to what?

Question 13

Choose the correct letter, A, B, C or D.

13   Which is the best title for Reading Passage 1?

   A   A history of YA dystopian literature

   B   The wane of the dystopian phenomenon

   C   How dystopian fiction has shaped the world

   D   The draw of YA dystopian fiction

Reading Passage 2

*You should spend about 20 minutes on **Questions 14–27**, which are based on Reading Passage 2 below.*

Plant Wars

Mention the words "chemical warfare" or "deployed armies" in any conversation, and your interlocutor might immediately assume you're talking about wars between humans. In reality, however, there are other kinds of wars out there where these techniques are employed far more frequently and in a far more intricate manner: those waged in the plant kingdom.

We might not normally think of plants this way, but much like humans and animals, they too have to fight for survival on a daily basis. Nutrients, light and water are the three things any plant needs in order to grow; unfortunately, none of these is ample in supply, which means that the competition between plants can grow fierce. Some plants and trees are at an architectural advantage: taller trees have greater access to natural light, while plants with deeper roots have the ability to absorb more water and nutrients. Others, though, manage to defend their territory through "allelopathy", or chemical warfare.

So how does this chemical warfare work exactly? As Dr Robin Andrews explains, plants convert the nutrients they absorb from the ground to energy with the aid of a type of organic compound known as metabolites. These metabolites can be divided into two categories: primary and secondary. Primary metabolites are what allows a plant to live, playing a direct role in its growth and development, and are thus present in every plant. Secondary metabolites, on the other hand, can vary from plant to plant and often play the role of a defence mechanism against neighbouring competitors.

Out of these secondary metabolites, there are two that are incredibly interesting: DIBOA and DIMBOA. These two cyclic hydroxamic acids were at the forefront of a study conducted by Sascha Venturelli and colleagues in 2015, which found that once they are released into the soil by the plants that produce them, they degenerate into toxic substances that have the power to inhibit growth in nearby plants once they soak them up. As Dr Claude Becker notes, "the phenomenon" itself "has been known for years", but we now finally understand the "molecular mechanism" behind it—and its supreme intricacy would put to shame any chemical bombs created by humans.

But plants do not just fight wars against other plants; chemical warfare also comes into play in their defence against herbivores. As Brent Mortensen of Iowa State University describes, plants "actively resist" attacks made by herbivores through qualitative and quantitative chemical defences. What's the difference? Qualitative defences can be lethal even in small doses, and are often employed to protect "young" or "tender leaves or seeds". They can also be recycled when no longer necessary. Quantitative defences, in contrast, are only effective "in larger doses", but unlike qualitative defences, can protect the plant against all herbivores. Quantitative defences are also not as immediately lethal, as they usually lead to indigestion, pain, irritation of the mouth and throat, and inflammation or swelling in the skin.

And what about the "deployed armies" I mentioned before? Well, chemical attacks are not the only way plants elect to defend themselves against herbivores. Some plants, such as the African acacia, also recruit armies to assist them in their war. As Angela White of the University of Sheffield explains, the acacia tree has "hollowed-out structures" which invite ant colonies to build a home in them by providing not just shelter, but also food in the form of a special nectar. In return, ants protect them against herbivores—and this includes not just the small ones like bugs, but also the ones as big as giraffes.

At this point, of course, you might be wondering what all this has to do with you. The territorial nature of plants might be fascinating in its own right, but what is its application in real life? Well, Dr Venturelli of the 2015 study mentioned before has an answer for you: apparently, certain allelochemicals—the aforementioned chemical compounds that are responsible for stunting growth in plants—have been found to have an effect on human cancer cells, too. According to Michael Bitzer and Ulrich Lauer of the same study, "clinical trials at the University Clinics Tübingen currently assess the efficacy of these plant toxins in cancer patients". This means that comprehending the way plants defend themselves against the enemies in their environment might not just be of interest to plant biologists alone, but to medical researchers as well.

Questions 14–20

Complete the sentences below.

*Choose **NO MORE THAN THREE WORDS** from Reading Passage 2 for each answer.*

*Write your answers in boxes **14–20** on your answer sheet.*

14   Plants are very similar to .... as they also struggle to stay alive every day.

15   The height of a tree or plant can affect how much .... it receives.

16   Chemical warfare in plants also goes by the name of ....

17   Water and nutrients are both taken from the soil, and the latter is later turned into

....

18   Secondary metabolites are an .... that functions as a defence mechanism for

plants.

19   DIBOA and DIMBOA are two types of secondary metabolites that can ....

once absorbed by a plant.

20   The 2015 study by Sascha Venturelli and colleagues examined the .... of

chemical warfare in plants.

Questions 21 – 25

Complete the diagram below.

*Choose **NO MORE THAN TWO WORDS** from Reading Passage 2 for each answer.*

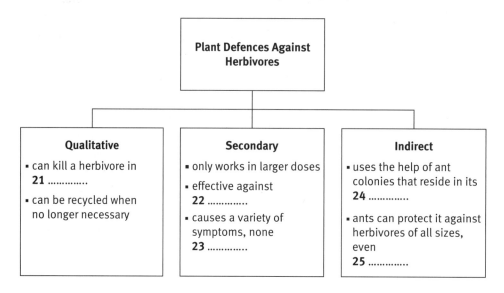

Plant Defences Against Herbivores

Qualitative
- can kill a herbivore in 21 ....
- can be recycled when no longer necessary

Secondary
- only works in larger doses
- effective against 22 ....
- causes a variety of symptoms, none 23 ....

Indirect
- uses the help of ant colonies that reside in its 24 ....
- ants can protect it against herbivores of all sizes, even 25 ....

Questions 26–27

Do the following statements agree with the information given in Reading Passage 2?

*In boxes **26–27** on your answer sheet, write*

TRUE	*if the statement is true according to the passage*
FALSE	*if the statement is false according to the passage*
NOT GIVEN	*if the information is not given in the passage*

26 Allelochemicals are secondary metabolites.

27 Plant biologists and medical researchers are currently cooperating to assess the efficacy of plant toxins in preventing the growth of cancer cells.

Reading Passage 3

*You should spend about 20 minutes on **Questions 28–40**, which are based on Reading Passage 3 below.*

Deafhood

A   At this point you might be wondering: what does 'deafhood' mean? Is it a synonym for 'deafness'? Is it a slightly more politically correct term to express the very same concept you've grown accustomed to—a person who lacks the power of hearing, or a person whose hearing is impaired? What's wrong with terms like 'hard of hearing' or 'deafness'? Have they not represented the deaf community just fine for the past few centuries? Who came up with the term 'Deafhood' anyway, and why?

B   The term 'Deafhood' was first coined in 1993 by Dr Paddy Ladd, a deaf scholar in the Deaf Studies Department at the University of Bristol in England. First explored through his doctoral dissertation in 1998, and later elaborated on in his 2003 book, '*Understanding Deaf Culture – In Search of Deafhood*', the idea behind Deafhood is twofold: first, it seeks to collect everything that is already known about the life, culture, politics, etc. of Sign Language Peoples (SLPs); secondly, it attempts to remove the limitations imposed on SLPs through their colonisation from hearing people.

C   In order to understand what Deafhood represents, it's first important to understand what is meant by colonisation. To do that, we need to examine two terms: Oralism and Audism. Oralism is a philosophy that first emerged in the late 19th century, and which suggests that a reduced use of sign language would be more beneficial to SLPs, as it would allow them to integrate better to the hearing world. In that respect, sign language is dismissively regarded as a mere obstacle to listening skills and acquisition of speech—treated, in effect, in the same manner as the languages of other peoples who were oppressed and colonised, e.g. the Maori in New Zealand, or the Aborigines in Australia. Audism, however, is an even more sinister ideology: first coined in 1975 by Dr Tom Humphries of the University of California in San Diego, it describes the belief that deaf people are somehow inferior to hearing people, and that deafhood—or, in this case, we should say 'deafness'—is a flaw, a terrible disability that needs to be eliminated. It is the effect of these two ideologies that Deafhood seeks to counter, by presenting SLPs in a positive light, not as patients who require treatment.

D   But even if we understand the oppression that SLPs have suffered at the hands of hearing people since the late 1800s, and even if we acknowledge that 'deafness' is a medical term with negative connotations that needs to be replaced, that doesn't mean it's easy to explain what the term Deafhood represents exactly. This is because Deafhood is, as Dr Donald Grushkin puts it, a 'physical, emotional, mental, spiritual, cultural and linguistic' journey that every deaf person is invited—but not obligated—to embark on.

E   Deafhood is essentially a search for understanding: what does being 'Deaf' mean? How did deaf people in the past define themselves, and what did they believe to be their reasons for existing before Audism was conceived? Why are some people born deaf? Are they biologically defective, or are there more positive reasons for their existence? What do terms like 'Deaf Art' or 'Deaf Culture' actually mean? What is 'the Deaf Way' or doing things? True Deafhood is achieved when a deaf person feels comfortable with who they are and connected to the rest of the deaf community through use of their natural language, but the journey there might differ.

F   Aside from all those questions, however, Deafhood also seeks to counter the effect of what is known as 'neo–eugenics'. Neo–eugenics, as described by Patrick Boudreault at the 2005 California Association of the Deaf Conference, is a modern manifestation of what has traditionally been defined as 'eugenics', i.e. an attempt to eradicate any human characteristics which are perceived as negative. Deaf people have previously been a target of eugenicists through the aforementioned ideologies of Audism and Oralism, but recent developments in science and society—such as cochlear implants or genetic engineering—mean that Deafhood is once again under threat, and needs to be protected. The only way to do this is by celebrating the community's history, language, and countless contributions to the world, and confronting those who want to see it gone.

G   So, how do we go forward? We should start by decolonising SLPs—by embracing Deafhood for what it is, removing all the negative connotations that surround it and accepting that deaf people are neither broken nor incomplete. This is a task not just for hearing people, but for deaf people as well, who have for decades internalised society's unfavourable views of them. We should also seek recognition of the deaf community's accomplishments, as well as official recognition of sign languages around the world by their respective governments. Effectively, what we should do is ask ourselves: how would the Deaf community be like, had it never been colonised by the mainstream world? And whatever it is it would be like, we should all together—hearing and Deaf alike—strive to achieve it.

Questions 28–34

The reading passage has seven paragraphs, A–G.

Which paragraph contains the following information?

Write the correct letter, A – G, in boxes 28–33 on your answer sheet.

28   Examples of other groups treated the same way as deaf people

29   Why the word 'deafness' is no longer appropriate

30   The definition of the word 'deaf'

31   Why deaf people might sometimes think negatively of themselves

32   How one can attain deafhood

33   Where the word 'deafhood' came from

34   Why deafhood is currently imperilled

Questions 35–37

Choose the correct letter, A, B, C or D.

Write your answers in boxes 35–37 on your answer sheet.

35 According to Dr Paddy Ladd, Deafhood

    A is a more appropriate term than 'hard of hearing'.

    B doesn't colonise SLPs as much as 'deafness' does.

    C strives to get rid of the effects of colonisation.

    D contributes positively to the life and culture of deaf people.

36 Oralism suggests that

    A SLPs have no use for sign language.

    B SLPs don't belong in the hearing world.

    C hearing people are superior to SLPs.

    D SLPs are unable to acquire speech.

37 Aborigines in Australia are similar to deaf people because

    A eugenicists also tried to eradicate them.

    B they were also considered inferior by their oppressors.

    C their languages were also disrespected.

    D their languages were also colonised.

Questions 38–40

Answer the questions below with words taken from Reading Passage 3.

*Use **NO MORE THAN TWO WORDS** for each answer.*

38 What should deaf people use to communicate with each other, according to deafhood?

39 Who has used oralism and audism to attack the deaf community?

40 What does the deaf community strive to achieve for sign language worldwide?

WRITING MODULE

Writing Task 1

You should spend about 20 minutes on this task.

The graphs below show the trends in three boys' and girls' names which are currently popular in the UK.

Summarise the information by selecting and reporting the main features, and make comparisons where relevant.

Write at least 150 words.

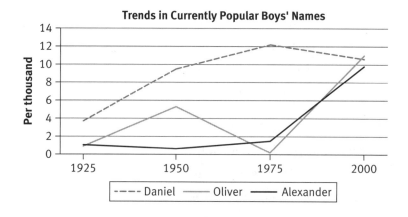

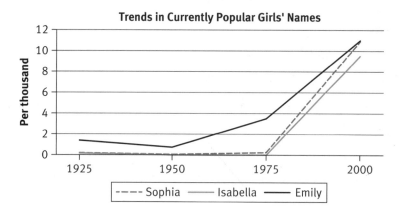

Writing Task 2

You should spend about 40 minutes on this task.

The number of children that read books for fun has dropped dramatically in recent years. What are the reasons for this? How can we encourage children to read more?

Write at least 250 words.

SPEAKING MODULE

Time: 11–14 minutes

Part 1: Introduction and interview (4–5 minutes)

[This part of the test begins with the examiner introducing himself or herself and checking the candidate's identification. It then continues as an interview.]

Let's talk about your home town.

- *Do you come from a big city or a small town?*
- *Do you study or do you work?*
- *What options are there for entertainment in your home town?*
- *Is your home town popular with tourists?*
- *Is your hometown more industrial or rural?*

Part 2: Individual long turn (3–4 minutes)

Candidate Task Card

Task Card

Please read the topic below carefully. You will be asked t talk about it for one to two minutes. You will have one minute to think about what you are going to say. You can make some notes to help you if you wish.

Describe the last time you went to the cinema or theatre. You should say:

- *where you went, and with whom*
- *what you saw or watched*
- *why you chose it*

Also, explain whether you liked it or not and why.

Rounding off questions

- What were your expectations before you saw the film or play? Did it live up to them?
- Would you recommend it to others? Why (not)?

Part 3: Two-way discussion (4–5 minutes)

Let's talk about theatre for a moment.

- *Why do you think people enjoy going to the theatre?*
- *In ancient times, the theatre was an educational tool. Is it still an educational tool today?*
- *Do you think the theatre might one day disappear? Why (not)?*
- *William Shakespeare once wrote, "All the world is a stage." Do you think that's true?*

Now let's talk about entertainment.

- *Which forms of entertainment are most popular in your country? Why do you think that is?*
- *Do you think entertainment programmes today are more violent due to shock value?*
- *Should there be any limitations when it comes to art and entertainment? If so, what kind of limitations?*
- *Has quality in entertainment declined in the last few decades in your opinion? Why (not)?*
- *What could be the future of entertainment?*

LISTENING MODULE

 Practice Test 5, Track 1 (Track 32)

Section 1: Questions 1–10

*Complete the form below, using **NO MORE THAN TWO WORDS AND/OR A NUMBER** for each answer.*

Write your answers in boxes 1–10 on your answer sheet.

The George and Dragon
BOOKING FORM

DETAILS

Name: Carla **1** …………..

Phone Number: 2 …………..

Type of event: retirement party

Date: 3 …………..

Number of people: 16–17 (*Please note that the upstairs room has a capacity of no more than **4** ………….. people*)

MENU

Seven **5** …………..

Two ham and cheese and two **6** …………..

7 ………….. platters

One Caesar and one **8** ………….. salad

PRICE

*Venue will be needed for a total of **9** …………..hours*

Final price: **10** £ …………..

🎧 **Practice Test 5, Track 2 (Track 33)**

Section 2: Questions 11–20

Questions 11–15

You are going to hear a speech given at a poetry award ceremony.

Complete the sentences below.

*Write **NO MORE THAN TWO WORDS AND/OR A NUMBER** for each answer.*

11 Antonia Watson's parents instituted the Antonia Watson Memorial Poetry Award in ....

12 The Antonia Watson Memorial Poetry Award's second prize is £ ....

13 Thomas is one of Antonia Watson's ....

14 The name of the first poem Antonia Watson published was ....

15 After her grandfather passed away, Antonia suffered from ....

Questions 16–18

Choose the correct letter, A, B or C.

16 Between 1999 and 2003, Antonia

    A wrote a few theatre plays and painted self–portraits.

    B published several poems in her college's journal.

    C remained ardent about poetry despite her break from writing.

17 The speaker and Antonia met in Sheffield, where

    A they both studied English Literature at the University of Sheffield.

    B they shared a room in a centrally located flat for a year.

    C they became friends with each other despite having no common friends.

18 Antonia's self–published poem collection

    A was named after a poem about her birthday.

    B was released a few months before her death in 2005.

    C led to her signing a contract with a literary agent.

Questions 19–20

Complete the summary below.

*Write **NO MORE THAN TWO WORDS AND/OR A NUMBER** for each answer.*

Write your answers in boxes 19–20 on your answer sheet.

The Antonia Watson Memorial Poetry Award has dealt with a variety of themes over the years, all falling under the scope of a general theme reflecting Antonia's personal belief that all humans are **19** .... Next year's competition is no exception, with its theme of **20** ....

Practice Test 5, Track 3 (Track 34)

Section 3: Questions 21–30

Questions 21–24

Label the chart below.

Choose your answers from the box below and write the correct letters in boxes 21–24 on your answer sheet.

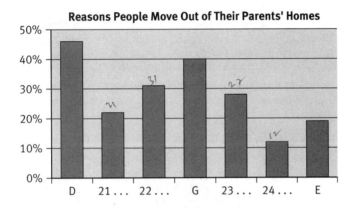

Reasons People Move Out of Their Parents' Homes

D   21 . . .   22 . . .   G   23 . . .   24 . . .   E

A	relationship/marriage
B	emancipation
C	need for freedom
D	studies
E	conflict with parents
F	pressure from parents
G	new job
H	need for space and privacy
I	abuse

Questions 25–29

Which student will present which information?

    A   Melanie

    B   Chris

    C   Both

Write the correct letter, A, B, or C, in boxes 26–29 on your answer sheet.

    25   the 18–20 group   . . . .

    26   the 20–24 group   . . . .

    27   the under–18 group   . . . .

    28   the 25 and over group . . . .

    29   the group that still live with parents . . . .

Question 30

Which graph shows what problems people who moved out of their parents' house faced in their first few months living alone?

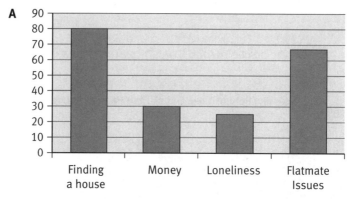

A

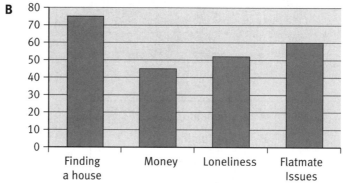

B

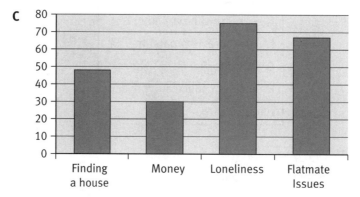

C

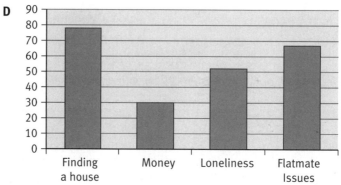

D

Practice Test 5, Track 4 (Track 35)

Section 4: Questions 31–40

Questions 31–33

*What are the **THREE WAYS** in which turbellaria differ from other flatworms, according to Dr Baker?*

- **A**   they are not parasitic
- **B**   80% of their nutrition comes from platyhelminths
- **C**   they have a simpler structure
- **D**   they're less intelligent
- **E**   they have eyes
- **F**   their sensory system is more elaborate
- **G**   their sensory organs are chemical

Questions 34–38

Complete the sentences below.

*Write **NO MORE THAN THREE WORDS AND/OR A NUMBER** for each answer.*

34   Turbellaria are able to .... thanks to the structure of their bodies.

35   Any part of a turbellarian's body that isn't occupied by organs is filled with a ....

36   While turbellaria are hermaphrodites, they don't ....

37   Most turbellaria's natural habitat is ....

38   Turbellaria expel all undigested food from their ....

Questions 39–40

Choose the correct letter, A, B or C.

Write your answers in boxes 39–40 on your answer sheet.

39   Fission is the ability of

- **A**   two worms to grow out of one if you split it in the middle.
- **B**   flatworms to procreate by breaking into smaller flatworms.
- **C**   flatworms to regenerate organs they've lost.

40   Fission in flatworms is an important phenomenon for scientists because

- **A**   it might help them find a way to do the same to human cells.
- **B**   it has been found to put a break on the human aging process.
- **C**   it technically means that flatworms can live forever.

READING MODULE

Reading Passage 1

*You should spend about 20 minutes on **Questions 1–13**, which are based on Reading Passage 1 below.*

A Brief History of London Underground

It is a staple of not just the capital of the UK, but of British culture in general. It is used by more than 1.3 billion people per year, and it is more than 400 kilometres long. It has survived fires, floods, terrorist attacks and two world wars, and it has been described as a "form of mild torture", a "twopenny tube" and a system of "padded cells". It is London Underground, and it has been around for more than 150 years. But how did it all start?

The idea of an intricate train network running underneath a vibrant and heavily populated city like London might not be such a novelty in contemporary society, but it certainly was one back in the early 19th century when it was first conceived. In fact, the only reason such a notion—at the time described by *The Times* as an "insult to common sense"—was even entertained in the first place was pure desperation: during the Victorian era, London roads were insufferably overcrowded, and a Royal Commission of 1846 meant that central London was out of bounds for railway companies, whose mainline railways all had to stop just outside the City and West End. A way to connect Paddington, Euston and King's Cross was therefore a necessity to relieve the congested streets, and Charles Pearson, the man who originally envisioned a Fleet Valley rail tunnel just fifteen years after the first steam passenger service was opened in 1830, couldn't have come up with his plan for what was to become London Underground at a better time.

And so the story begins, in 1863, with the opening of the Metropolitan Railway, which ran between Paddington (called Bishop's Road at the time) and Farringdon, serving a total of eight stations. Five years later, in 1868, the first section of the Metropolitan District Railway (now incorporated into the District and Circle lines) followed, running from South Kensington to Westminster. Within the first fifty years, much of what is known as Zone 1 of the London Underground system today would be built, all funded by private developers. (Unfortunately for them, none would get the financial returns they had been promised.)

People nowadays might complain about the atmosphere in London Underground, particularly in the summer, but it is nothing compared to the conditions the Metropolitan Railway's passengers had to weather during the first years of its operation. So foul was the smell in the tunnels that spread under the city that drivers were allowed to grow beards, in hopes that this would protect them from inhaling the billowing smokes. (According to the account of a civil servant from that time, the stink in the underground was comparable to that of a 'crocodile's breath'.) Nevertheless, the line was a smashing success from the very beginning, with more than 11 million passengers in just the first year.

The second spate of construction works arrived with the development of electric traction at the end of the 19th century, which meant that trains no longer had to run through shallow tunnels to allow room for the steam produced by the engines to escape. Instead, new tunnels could now be dug, cutting deeper into the belly of the city. The first deep-level electric railway was opened in December 1890 by the City and South London Railway, connecting King William Street to Stockwell. In the following fifty years, the existing tube lines would systematically be extended, branching into London's various suburbs. Surprisingly, it would take until 1968 for an entirely new line to open again: the Victoria Line (provisionally named the Viking Line), which was followed by the Jubilee Line eleven years later.

As I mentioned above, London Underground's first lines were built by private developers, meaning that each line was owned by different companies. This changed in 1933, when all of those companies were nationalised and merged to form the London Passenger Transport Board, which controlled London's railway, tram, trolleybus, bus and coach services. (Coincidentally, 1933 was also the year the first diagram of the iconic Underground map was first presented by Harry Beck.) The London Passenger Transport Board itself was nationalised in 1948.

The next wave of changes came at the turn of the 21st century, and has continued to unfold well into its second decade: in 2003, the famous Oyster card was introduced—a wireless travel card that can be charged up with money to be used for single fares or weekly, monthly, and yearly travel tickets. Busking was also legalised the same year. In 2007, London Underground achieved its next important milestone, reaching 1 billion passengers per year, and in 2009 it was named the best Metro system in Europe. In early 2016, a new Crossrail line named after Queen Elizabeth II was announced, which is due to open in late 2018. This will be the first new line in nearly forty years. And the story goes on.

So, there you have it. The underground system that every Londoner loves to hate, but without which London never would have become the sort of financial hub and melting pot it is today. A history spanning across three centuries, all of which contributed to the creation of not just a transport system, but a unique, daring brand, and a cultural phenomenon the likes of which the world had never seen before. Perhaps it is, as its critics contend, too busy, too hot, too pricey and too grimy. But it is also a remarkable achievement, for Londoners and non-Londoners alike, and it should be treasured regardless of its shortcomings.

Questions 1–6

Do the following statements agree with the information given in Reading Passage 1?

*In boxes **1–6** on your answer sheet, write*

TRUE	*if the statement is true according to the passage*
FALSE	*if the statement is false according to the passage*
NOT GIVEN	*if the information is not given in the passage*

1   More than a billion commuters use London Underground every day.

2   London Underground would not be considered a unique concept were it to be build today.

3   In the 19th century, railway companies were not allowed to build stations within central London.

4   Charles Pearson's London Underground plan was a precursor of his Fleet Valley rail tunnel idea.

5   The first section of the Metropolitan District Railway, opened in 1868, took five years to complete.

6   The British government promised great financial returns to private investors to convince them to fund London Underground.

Questions 7–10

Choose the correct letter, A, B, C or D.

Write your answers in boxes 7–10 on your answer sheet.

7   During the first year of its operation, the Metropolitan Railway

    A   encouraged passengers to grow beards to block the smell.

    B   was not particularly successful.

    C   had more than 11 million passengers.

    D   was as bad as it is nowadays during the summer months.

8   At the end of the 19th century,

    A   London Underground stopped using shallow tunnels.

    B   a new London Underground line was completed.

    C   a new method of moving trains with electricity was invented.

    D   the City and South London railway was established.

9 The Victoria Line

    A was originally named the Viking Line.

    B was the first London Underground line to use electric traction.

    C was the fourth London Underground line to be built.

    D was built more than 70 years after its predecessor.

10 The London Passenger Transport Board

    A replaced the private companies that previously owned London Underground.

    B released the first diagram of the Underground map in 1933.

    C was established by private developers.

    D controlled most of London's transport services.

Questions 11–13

Complete the sentences below.

*Choose **NO MORE THAN TWO WORDS** from Reading Passage 2 for each answer.*

Write your answers in boxes 11–13 on your answer sheet.

11 Since 2003, London commuters have been able to listen to **11** .... in and outside London Underground stations.

12 London Underground not only attracted a lot of business to London, but also helped it to become a **12** ....

13 London Underground does have its **13** .... but it's still a unique and important cultural phenomenon.

Reading Passage 2

*You should spend about 20 minutes on **Questions 14–28**, which are based on Reading Passage 2 below.*

The Pioneer Anomaly

A   It's been more than four decades of incessant theorising and perplexed head–scratching for scientists, engineers and astronomy fans across the globe, but thanks to a recent study published in the journal *Physical Review Letters*, we finally have some answers to what has been causing the deceleration of NASA's Pioneer 10 and 11 spacecraft—otherwise known as the "Pioneer Anomaly".

B   Pioneer 10 and 11 were launched in 1972 and 1973 respectively, and were the first spacecraft to travel beyond the solar system's main asteroid belt. Their claim to fame, however, changed the moment they skirted past Jupiter and began their journey towards Saturn, as it was at that point—by then already the early 1980s—that scientists and navigators discovered something had gone terribly awry: the two spacecraft seemed to be slowing down.

C   As Bruce Betts of The Planetary Society explains, the scientists involved in the project had anticipated most of the slowing down due to "the gravitational pull of the Sun and other massive objects in the solar system". In fact, when the deceleration was first observed, it was so small that it was dismissed as an insignificant, temporary phenomenon, and attributed to the effect of dribbles of leftover propellant still in the fuel lines after controllers had cut off the propellant. It would take until 1998 for a group of scientists led by John Anderson of Jet Propulsion Laboratory (JPL) to confirm that, even at 13 kilometres from the sun, the two Pioneer spacecraft were still losing speed at a rate of approximately 300 inches per day squared (0.9 nanometres per second squared). The first theories of what might be the cause followed soon thereafter.

D   The late 1990s were an important time for the field of astrophysics, with the Hubble Space Telescope observations of distant supernovae having only in 1998 confirmed that the universe is expanding at an accelerating rate. Anderson et al's confirmation of the Pioneer Anomaly the same year seemed to offer a demonstration of the very same phenomenon of expansion within our own solar system—a theory that plenty of scientists quickly embraced. Others yet ascribed the deceleration to dark matter, while some suggested the spacecraft, as Toth and Turyshev put it, might've "unearthed the first evidence of extra dimensions". The possibility that a new law of physics directly contradicting Einstein's general theory of relativity might be to blame was also considered.

E   In 2004, Turyshev decided to get to the bottom of the Pioneer anomaly. Since the two spacecraft had stopped communicating with earth (Pioneer 11 first in 1995, and Pioneer 10 less than a decade later in 2003), all he could depend on were old communications and data; so, with the monetary aid of the Planetary Society and its eager, dedicated members, he began to gather the data from a number of different sources. There were two types of data that he needed to procure for his research: the "housekeeping data" engineers had used in order to monitor spacecraft operation, and Doppler data.

F   The data came in all sorts of forms: some were in digitised files offered by JPL navigators (a lucky find, as punch cards were still the preferred method of data storage back in the 1970s), while others were in magnetic tapes accidentally discovered under a staircase in JPL. All in all, there were more than 43 gigabytes of data—an admirable result, considering that at the time the two Pioneer spacecraft were launched there had been no formal requirement that NASA archive any of the records collected, and it had only been due to sheer luck and a former Pioneer team member's diligence that any telemetry data had been saved at all.

G   Once all the data had been collected, the formidable task of going through the volumes of information began. It was neither quick nor easy, and it required the assistance of a variety of people, including JPL engineers and retired TRW engineers who had worked on the Pioneer project, who had to consult with each other in order to interpret old blueprints and reconstruct the probes' 3D structure. In the end, however, the team's perseverance paid off, and Turyshev's suspicions—which had initiated the study—were confirmed: it was the electrical subsystems and the decay of plutonium in the Pioneer power sources that were to blame for the spacecraft's bizarre trajectory—more specifically the heat they emitted. This was corroborated by the discovery that other spacecraft with different designs had not been affected in the way Pioneer 10 and 11 had.

As Turyshev said, speaking of the study, "the story is finding its conclusion because it turns out that standard physics prevail. While of course it would've been exciting to discover a new kind of physics, we did solve a mystery."

Questions 14–20

The reading passage has seven sections, A–G. Which section contains the following information?

Write the correct letter, A–G, in boxes 14–20 on your answer sheet.

14   The contemporary context of John Anderson's study

15   How Turyshev's study was conducted

16   A description of the journey of the Pioneer aircraft

17   How data was normally cached at the time of the Pioneer launch

18   Why Turyshev's study couldn't rely on new information

19   The name of a scientific publication

20   The original theories for the Pioneer anomaly

Questions 21–25

Complete each sentence with the correct ending A–H below. Write the correct letter, A–H, in boxes 21–25 on your answer sheet.

A	played a pivotal role in Turyshev's study.
B	coincided with another scientific breakthrough in its field.
C	leftover propellant had been expected to cause issues.
D	contradicted contemporary theories about the Pioneer spacecraft.
E	ceased communication later than its predecessor.
F	was inspected by former TRW engineers to confirm its authenticity.
G	exceeded all expectations in terms of quantity.
H	external factors had been taken into account in the planning stage.

21 NASA's Pioneer 10 spacecraft

22 The Planetary Society

23 Some of the spacecraft's deceleration was not a surprise because

24 John Anderson's study

25 The data Turyshev used in his study

Questions 26–28

*Choose **THREE** letters A–H. Write your answers in boxes 26–28 on your answer sheet.*

***NB** Your answers may be given in any order.*

Which THREE of the following statements are true of Turyshev's study?

A Former Pioneer team members were recruited to help to understand the data.

B It was an initiative by the Planetary Society that instigated it.

C It provided us with the first proof of extra dimensions.

D It identified calefaction caused by the Pioneer design as the culprit behind the anomaly.

E Parts of the Pioneer spacecraft were recreated to help with the study.

F The analysis stage of the study was particularly time–consuming.

G It proved that spacecraft with design similar to the Pioneer 10 and 11 faced similar issues.

H Turyshev was unhappy with the result of his investigation.

Reading Passage 3

*You should spend about 20 minutes on **Questions 29–40**, which are based on Reading Passage 3 below.*

The Future of Food

When we think of the future, most of us imagine hover boards and flying cars, exciting new technological advancements and developments, perhaps even scientific achievements and breakthroughs. What we spend little time contemplating, however, is what we will be eating. Nevertheless, food futurologists and organisations around the world have examined the prospects, and they might, at first glance at least, appear less than thrilling.

One thing that's for certain, according to food futurologist Morgaine Gaye, is that meat will once again become a luxury. "In the West," she proclaims, "many of us have grown up with cheap, abundant meat." Unfortunately though, rising prices are spelling the doom of this long–lasting trend. "As a result we are looking for new ways to fill the meat gap." Professor Sheenan Harpaz of the Volgani Centre in Beit Dagan, Israel, agrees: "As the price of raising livestock goes up, we'll eat less beef." So, what will we eat?

According to Harpaz as well as Yoram Kapulnik, the director of the Volcani Centre, the answer to that question lies with our reliance on genetic engineering. As overpopulation and resource depletion will inevitably lead to a struggle to feed the masses, they predict, the food industry will experience a shift in focus from "form" to "function". "Functional foods" will be genetically modified to provide additional value, and they will be targeted at each group of the population—with foods customised to meet the needs of men, women, the elderly, etc. "Once we have a complete picture of the human genome," explains Kapulnik, "we'll know how to create food that better meets our needs."

But food still has to come from somewhere and leading food futurologists and other scientists are firm on their belief that the foods of the future will come from insects. "They are nutritionally excellent," says Arnold Van Huis, lead author of *Edible Insects*, a 2013 report by the UN's Food and Agriculture Organisation. Not only that but, according to researchers at Wageningen University in the Netherlands, they are also full of protein, and on par with ordinary meat in terms of nutritional value.

Insects are already a part of people's diets in various cultures in Asia and Africa; however, one major hurdle that will need to be overcome with regards to Western countries is presentation. As Gaye suggests, "things like crickets and grasshoppers will [have to] be ground down and used as an ingredient in things like burgers". There is already such an initiative in Kenya and Cambodia (the quite successful WinFood project), and the Netherlands is already investing into research on insect–based diets and the development of insect farm legislation.

Another source of future food, according to Dr Craig Rose of the Seaweed Health Foundation, could be algae. Algae, like insects, are extremely nutritious and already popular in Asia, and could be the perfect solution for three very important reasons: first of all, they can grow both in fresh and salt water—a notable advantage, considering the shortage of land we are bound to experience in the future; secondly, they grow at an astounding pace the likes of which no other plant has ever been found to achieve before; and finally, with 10,000 different types of seaweed around the world, they can open up an exciting world of new flavours for us to discover. But that's not all: several scientists believe that the biofuel we would extract from algae could lead to a diminished need for fossil fuels, thereby improving our carbon footprint. Algae would, much like insects, need to be refashioned to appeal to Westerners, but research such as the one conducted by scientists at Sheffield Hallam University, who replaced salt in bread and processed foods with seaweed granules with efficacious results, suggests that this is unlikely to pose a problem.

The final option brought forth by scientists is lab–grown, artificial meat. In early 2012, a group of Dutch scientists managed to produce synthetic meat using stem cells originating from cows, and there are already a few companies, such as the San Francisco start–up *Impossible Foods* and the Manhattan Beach–based *Beyond Meat*, which are dedicated to manufacturing plant–made meat. The benefits of a worldwide move towards in–vitro meat would be tremendous for the environment, which would see a reduction in energy and water waste and greenhouse gas emissions, and would significantly reduce animal suffering. There is one hindrance to such plans at the moment, sadly, and that's the price: the first artificial burger, grown at Maastricht University in 2013, cost a whopping €250,000 (£190,545) to make.

Questions 29–33

Complete the summary.

*Choose **NO MORE THAN TWO WORDS** from the passage for each answer.*

Write your answers in boxes 29–33 on your answer sheet.

There are several not particularly **29** .... theories as to what food might look like in the future, according to several organisations and food futurologists around the world. Morgaine Gaye, a prominent food futurologist, believes that meat is set to all but disappear from our daily diets again due to **30** .... Professor Harpaz offers the same opinion, contending that **31** .... will continue to become costlier and costlier. To fill the gap left by meat, he says, we will have no choice but to turn to **32** .... , with "functional foods" that will be aimed at each demographic. The only step we'll need to take to get there is to manage to decode the **33** ....

Questions 34–40

Complete the table.

*Choose **NO MORE THAN THREE WORDS** from the passage for each answer.*

Write your answers in boxes 34–40 on your answer sheet.

Future Food	
Insects	<ul><li>**34** .... and full of protein</li><li>Similar to meat in terms of nutritional value</li><li>Regularly consumed in **35** ....</li><li>**36** .... will need to be adjusted for unaccustomed cultures</li></ul>
Algae	<ul><li>Easy and quick to **37** ....</li><li>Up to 10,000 different flavours</li><li>Might positively influence **(38)** .... by providing us with alternative fuels</li></ul>
Lab–grown meat	<ul><li>Made with bovine **39** .... and/or plants</li><li>Would lead to a drop in energy and water waste, as well as greenhouse gas emissions</li><li>Would also alleviate **40** ....</li><li>Too expensive at the moment</li></ul>

WRITING MODULE

Writing Task 1

You should spend about 20 minutes on this task.

The graphs below show the opening and closure and the types of magazines that opened in Southern Europe between 1995–2015.

Summarise the information by selecting and reporting the main features, and make comparisons where relevant.

Write at least 150 words.

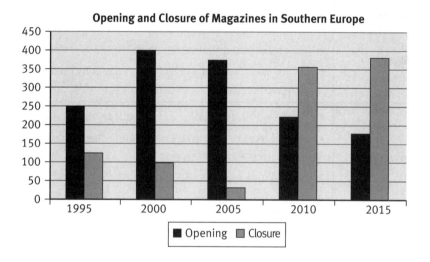

Opening and Closure of Magazines in Southern Europe

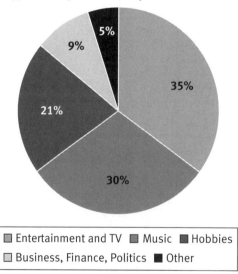

Types of Magazines that Opened 1995–2015

Writing Task 2

You should spend about 40 minutes on this task.

Some people believe that song lyrics which glorify violence and criminal lifestyles should be banned. Discuss the advantages and disadvantages of such a ban.

Write at least 250 words.

SPEAKING MODULE

Time: 11–14 minutes

Part 1: Introduction and interview (4–5 minutes)

[This part of the test begins with the examiner introducing himself or herself and checking the candidate's identification. It then continues as an interview.]

Let's talk about your country.

- *Are there any traditional dresses or clothes that people wear in your country?*
- *Are there any hand gestures that are unique to your country?*
- *What's your favourite cultural element of your country?*
- *What type of music is traditional in your country?*
- *How do your music tastes differ from those of people in your immediate family?*

Part 2: Individual long turn (3–4 minutes)

[Candidate Task Card]

Task Card

Please read the task below carefully. You will be asked to talk about it for one to two minutes. You will have one minute to think about what you are going to say. You can make some notes to help you if you wish.

Describe a song that reminds you of a person. You should say:

- *what the song is about, and where you first heard it*
- *who the person is, and what is their relation to you*
- *why the song reminds you of that person*

Also, explain how this song makes you feel when you listen to it.

Rounding off questions

- Does this person know this song reminds you of them?
- Do any other songs remind you of that person?

Part 3: Two-way discussion (4–5 minutes)

Let's talk about music for a moment.

- *Why is music such an important element of culture and society?*
- *How has the music industry changed in the past fifty years in your country?*
- *The Internet has changed the way musicians are discovered and promoted. Have the changes been positive or negative, in your opinion?*
- *How severe should punishments be for people who are caught pirating or illegally downloading music?*

Now let's talk about culture in general.

- *How would you define the word "culture"? What does "culture" constitute for you?*
- *Do you think our cultural background affects our personality?*
- *When moving or travelling to a new country, how important is it to adapt to that country's culture, in your opinion? Why?*
- *How does a country's culture affect the law making process in that country?*
- *Is it important for schools to teach children about their cultural background, in your opinion? Why (not)?*

LISTENING MODULE

 Practice Test 6, Track 1 (Track 36)

Section 1: Questions 1–10

Questions 1–5

*Choose the correct answer: **A**, **B** or **C**.*

Write your answers in boxes 1–5 on your answer sheet.

1 What is the caller's surname?

   A   Fleischer

   B   Fischer

   C   Bennett

2 The caller says the correct colour of his car is

   A   Sky blue

   B   Light green

   C   White

3 What time does the caller say he went to collect his car?

   A   9:30pm

   B   8pm

   C   8:30pm

4 Where does the caller usually store the front panel of his radio?

   A   In his pocket

   B   The hospital

   C   In the glove compartment

5 What does the advisor say she will send through the mail to the caller?

   A   A radio

   B   Some CDs

   C   Some forms

Questions 6–10

Complete the notes below.

*Write **NO MORE THAN TWO WORDS AND/OR A NUMBER** for each answer.*

Write your answers in boxes 6–10 on your answer sheet.

Insurance Claim Report
CUSTOMER FIRST NAME: Bennett
POLICY NUMBER: **6** ....
TYPE OF CLAIM: Stolen **7** ....
PLACE WHERE OFFENCE WAS REPORTED: York **8** .... Station
CUSTOMER AWARE OF THE DANGER: No
OTHER ITEMS STOLEN: Car radio, CDs and an old **9** ....
DOCUMENTS REQUESTED TO SUPPORT CLAIM: Police report and **10** ....

Practice Test 6, Track 2 (Track 37)

Section 2: Questions 11–20

Questions 11–13

Complete the sentences below.

*Write **ONE WORD ONLY** for each answer.*

Write your answers in boxes 11–13 on your answer sheet.

11   There are two entrances to the ....

12   The first section you enter when leaving the staffroom is the ....

13   The .... pass through the dungeons as a group.

Questions 14–18

Complete the labels on the map.

*Write **NO MORE THAN TWO WORDS** for each answer.*

Write your answers in boxes 14–18 on your answer sheet.

Stevensbridge Dungeons – Floor Plan

Staff entrance

Makeup

Prison cells

Lockers

Main dungeon

15 ....

Visitor toilet

Interactive display

14 ....

17 ....

Main entrance

Shower   16 ....   18 ....

Questions 19–20

*Choose **TWO** letters, A-E.*

Write your answers in boxes 19–20 on your answer sheet.

What are TWO things the speaker suggests the employees should do to help visitors?

   A   help to carry their bags

   B   guide them if they have gone the wrong way

   C   talk to them in a strange accent

   D   scare them so they have a more authentic experience

   E   answer any questions they might have

Practice Test 6, Track 3 (Track 38)

Section 3: Questions 21–30

Questions 21–24

*Which **FOUR** features below are mentioned by the woman as characteristic of pu-erh tea? Choose FOUR letters: A–H.*

Write your answers in boxes 21–24 on your answer sheet.

- **A**   Pu-erh is a dark tea
- **B**   The tea leaves are picked and sorted by machines
- **C**   It comes from a region of southern China called Yunnan
- **D**   It undergoes a period of aging in the open air
- **E**   It is a white tea
- **F**   Pu-erh tea is expensive
- **G**   The taste is very bitter
- **H**   The tea is sold in tea bags

Questions 25–26

Choose the correct answer: A, B or C.

Write your answers in boxes 25–26 on your answer sheet.

25   What is the likely job of the man?
- **A**   A journalist
- **B**   A tea farmer
- **C**   An artist

26   Why does the woman dislike teabags?
- **A**   She is allergic to them
- **B**   They smell strange
- **C**   Because the tea is trapped and cannot move freely

Questions 27–30

Complete the sentences below.

*Write **ONE WORD** for each answer.*

Write your answers in boxes 27–30 on your answer sheet.

27   Tea must be brewed in the .... way to fully experience it.

28   The effect of .... on the taste of pu-erh is similar to that of wine.

29   Pu-erh tea leaves are gathered into big piles by the ....

30   Tea meditation involves focussing on two things: .... and body.

Practice Test 6, Track 4 (Track 39)

Section 4: Questions 31–40

Questions 31–36

Complete the flow-chart below.

*Write **NO MORE THAN ONE WORD AND/OR A NUMBER** for each answer.*

Write your answers in boxes 31-36 on your answer sheet.

William the Conqueror defeated the **31** .... army in 1066.

The words beef, hour, fruit and **32** .... all entered the English language from French.

Gothic **33** .... architecture also arrived in England from France.

Construction of Wells Cathedral started in **34** ....

It was **35** .... in 1490.

Wells Cathedral is one of twenty-six cathedrals in England. This **36** .... is called the medieval cathedrals of England.

Questions 37–40

Complete the table below.

*Write **NO MORE THAN TWO WORDS AND/OR A NUMBER** for each answer.*

Write your answers in boxes 37–40 on your answer sheet.

Architectural information		Design Notes
Cathedral name	Wells	The cathedral's lancet windows have no tracery.
Style	**37**	
Construction began	1175	West front of the cathedral is celebrated for its life-sized **39** ....
Construction completed	1490	
Nave height	20 metres	In the past the sculptures and decorative carvings would have been **40** .... and gilded.
Length	**38**	

READING MODULE

Reading Passage 1

*You should spend about 20 minutes on **Questions 1–13**, which are based on Reading Passage 1 below.*

In 1979 the Chinese government introduced a policy that no other country had ever introduced before. Each couple was restricted by law to having to only one child. This one-child policy, although highly controversial, is believed to have helped prevent the rapidly growing Chinese population from becoming unsustainable.

In 2015 the one-child policy was finally relaxed, allowing couples to now have two children. According to the Communist Party of China, 400 million births have been prevented since the policy was introduced, and the Chinese population has become sustainable. Meanwhile other developing countries like India and Nigeria, where such a policy has never been nationally enforced, continue to struggle with population explosions.

On a statistical level it is easy to suggest that the one-child policy has been rather successful in China. It has lessened the negative environmental impact that rapid industrialisation and population growth have had on China since being implemented. However, there are plenty of grounds for criticism, especially from human rights activists, as well as advocates for freedom of choice. The main question raised by such a move is should a government be allowed to control family size, or is that too much control over individual liberty?

In the poorer rural areas of China, where life has changed very little for hundreds of years, farmers often used to rely on their children to help out on the farm. It was common for couples to have many children because infant mortality was high and the burden of work could not be handled by just a few people. It was generally considered that a girl was bad luck in this case because she would not be able to do as much manual labour. However backwards this way of thinking may seem to many people, the sad reality was that the instances of infanticide of female babies began to rise rapidly in the 1980s in China, as a result of the one-child policy.

Despite this raising other important concerns such as gender inequality in China, the growing problem of infanticide did lead to change; the government relaxed the one child policy so that a couple could have a second child, but only if their first child was a girl. On the other hand, the government has also faced heavy criticism of its methods of trying to enforce the one-child policy in the past. In rural areas it was very difficult for the government to enforce the policy, and so only really applied in urban areas of the country.

In extreme cases the government in China would force pregnant women who already had one child to have an abortion. However they were also forced to introduce laws in 2005 outlawing sex-selective abortions, which were increasingly common choices being made by couples who knew the sex of their baby to be female before birth.

Whilst true statistics are difficult to obtain from China, it is thought that there are now 60 million more men than women in China. This gender imbalance is almost certainly an indirect result of the one-child policy. Another theory suggests that there are unofficially millions more women in China who were never registered with local authorities by their parents through fear of being fined or losing their child.

The necessity of having children in some parts of China is something many in the West have trouble understanding. After all, increasing numbers of adults in the West now choose not to have children purely for environmental reasons.

Research by statisticians at Oregon State University in America found that because of the average American's huge carbon footprint, having a child in America increased a person's long-term carbon output by up to 20 times. To put this into greater context, the long-term pollution output of a child born in the U.S. can be up to 160 times higher than that of a child born in Bangladesh.

One of the reasons in China for changing the one-child policy to a two-child policy in 2015 was that the original policy was almost redundant anyway. The original legislation was only aimed at a single generation. Under the ruling, any couple in China who were both sole children to their respective parents were allowed to have two children. Therefore the two-child policy was already in effect for most couples already by 2015.

China has a rapidly developing economy, and with such development comes a higher average carbon output per person. This leads some authorities to worry that the already-strained environment in China will suffer even more in decades to come. Having said that, as China continues to experience such rapid economic development, Chinese people are enjoying increased personal wealth and financial stability. With that may also come the philosophy of choice, such as having the luxury to choose not to have children purely for environmental reasons, just like in the U.S.

Questions 1–7

Do the following statements agree with the information given in Reading Passage 1?

In boxes 1–7 on your answer sheet, write

TRUE	*if the statement agrees with the information*
FALSE	*if the statement contradicts the information*
NOT GIVEN	*if there is no information on this*

1   China's one child policy is believed to have kept population growth in the country at sustainable levels.

2   The negative environmental impact of population growth in China is less because of the one-child policy.

3   The number of cases of infanticide of female babies decreased in China during the 1980s.

4 In India effective population control is becoming an increasingly important concern for the government.

5 Estimates suggest that there are 60 million more men than women living in China.

6 Long-term pollution output of a child born in the U.S. is roughly the same as for a child born in Bangladesh.

7 The original one-child legislation in China was designed to apply to one generation only.

Questions 8–12

Choose the correct letter, A, B, C or D.

Write your answers in boxes 8–12 on your answer sheet.

8 According to the passage, there is criticism of the one-child policy, particularly from

    A other countries.

    B family planning organisations.

    C Chinese citizens.

    D human rights activists.

9 One other important concern raised by infanticide of female babies is

    A housing prices.

    B gender inequality.

    C the wellbeing of mothers.

    D the loneliness of children in China.

10 Laws passed in 2005 banned

    A parents having three children.

    B sex-selective abortions.

    C all abortion in China.

    D same sex marriage.

11 The author suggests that increasing numbers of westerners are choosing not to have children

    A before the age of 30.

    B before marriage.

    C   for environmental reasons.

    D   because it is too expensive.

12   The passage suggests that there is a link between a rapidly developing economy and a higher

    A   average carbon output per person.

    B   demand for electronic goods.

    C   desire for couples to have more children.

    D   level of crime in urban areas.

Question 13

Choose the correct letter: A, B, C, D or E.

Write your answer in box 13 on your answer sheet.

13   Which of the following is the most likely title for the passage?

    A   The Environmental Impact of Big Families

    B   China Reinstates the One-Child Policy

    C   A Brief History of Family Management

    D   The End of China's One-Child Policy

    E   The Story of the Chinese Power

Reading Passage 2

*You should spend about 20 minutes on **Questions 14–26**, which are based on Reading Passage 2 on the following pages.*

Questions 14–20

The reading passage below has eight paragraphs, A–H. Choose the correct heading for each paragraph from the list of headings below.

Write the correct number, I–xi, in boxes 14–20 on your answer sheet.

i	Atmospheric impacts
ii	Ideal forestry management example
iii	No trees, less people
iv	Good uses for wood
v	Looking after the forests
vi	Numbers of lost trees
vii	Wasted water
viii	Replanting forests
ix	Happy trees
x	Flood risks
xi	Poorer nations at higher risk

Example	Answer
Paragraph **A**	**vi**

14　Paragraph B

15　Paragraph C

16　Paragraph D

17　Paragraph E

18　Paragraph F

19　Paragraph G

20　Paragraph H

The Effects of Deforestation

A   Every year it is estimated that roughly 5.2 million hectares (52,000 km^2) of forest is lost worldwide. That is a net figure, meaning it represents the area of forest not replaced. To put this size in context, that is an area of land the size of Croatia lost every single year. There are a wide range of negative effects from deforestation that range from the smallest biological processes right up to the health of our planet as a whole. On a human level, millions of lives are affected every year by flooding and landslides that often result from deforestation.

B   There are 5 million people living in areas deemed at risk of flooding in England and Wales. Global warming, in part worsened by deforestation, is responsible for higher rainfalls in Britain in recent decades. Although it can be argued that demand for cheap housing has meant more houses are being built in at-risk areas, the extent of the flooding is increasing. The presence of forests and trees along streams and rivers acts like a net. The trees catch and store water, but also hold soil together, preventing erosion. By removing the trees, land is more easily eroded increasing the risk of landslides and also, after precipitation, less water is intercepted when trees are absent and so more enters rivers, increasing the risk of flooding.

C   It is well documented that forests are essential to the atmospheric balance of our planet, and therefore our own wellbeing too. Scientists agree unequivocally that global warming is a real and serious threat to our planet. Deforestation releases 15% of all greenhouse gas emissions. One third of the carbon dioxide emissions created by human activity come from deforestation around the globe.

D   In his book *Collapse*, about the disappearance of various ancient civilisations, writer Jared Diamond theorises about the decline of the natives of Easter Island. European missionaries first arrived on the island in 1722. Research suggested that the island, whose population was in the region of two to three thousand at the time, had once been much higher at fifteen thousand people. This small native population survived on the island despite there being no trees at all. Archaeological digs uncovered evidence of trees once flourishing on the island. The uncontrolled deforestation not only led to the eradication of all such natural resources from the island, but also greatly impacted the number of people the island could sustain. This underlines the importance of forest management, not only for useful building materials, but also food as well.

E   Forestry management is important to make sure that stocks are not depleted and that whatever is cut down is replaced. Without sustainable development of forests the levels of deforestation are only going to worsen as the global population continues to rise, creating higher demand for the products of forests. Just as important though is consumer awareness. Simple changes in consumer activity can make a huge difference. These changes in behaviour include, but are not limited to, recycling all recyclable material; buying recycled products and looking for the FSC sustainably sourced forest products logo on any wood or paper products.

F   Japan is often used as a model of exemplary forest management. During the Edo period between 1603 and 1868 drastic action was taken to reverse the country's serious exploitative deforestation problem. Whilst the solution was quite complex, one key aspect of its success was the encouragement of cooperation between villagers. This process of collaboration and re-education of the population saved Japan's forests. According to the World Bank 68.5% of Japanese land area is covered by forest, making it one of the best performing economically developed nations in this regard.

G   There is of course a negative impact of Japan's forest management. There is still a high demand for wood products in the country, and the majority of these resources are simply imported from other, poorer nations. Indonesia is a prime example of a country that has lost large swaths of its forest cover due to foreign demand from countries like Japan. This is in addition to other issues such as poor domestic forest management, weaker laws and local corruption. Located around the Equator, Indonesia has an ideal climate for rainforest. Sadly much of this natural resource is lost every year. Forest cover is now down to less than 51% from 65.4% in 1990. This alone is proof that more needs to be done globally to manage forests.

H   China is leading the way in recent years for replenishing their forests. The Chinese government began the Three-North Shelter Forest Program in 1978, with aims to complete the planting of a green wall, measuring 2,800 miles in length by its completion in 2050. Of course this program is in many ways forced by nature itself; the expansion of the Gobi Desert threatened to destroy thousands of square miles of grassland annually through desertification. This is a process often exacerbated by deforestation in the first place, and so represents an attempt to buck the trend. Forested land in China rose from 17% to 22% from 1990 to 2015 making China one of the few developing nations to reverse the negative trend.

Glossary

exemplary: serving as a perfect example

exacerbate: make worse

Questions 21–26

Complete the summary below.

*Choose **NO MORE THAN TWO WORDS AND/OR A NUMBER** from the passage for each answer.*

Write your answers in boxes 21–26 on your answer sheet.

The effects of deforestation are widespread and various. Some examples include flooding at a local scale to the wider effects of global warming on a worldwide scale. In Britain, for example **21** .... people live in areas at risk of flooding. This risk is increased by deforestation. Trees catch and **22** .... water lowering the chance of flooding. By removing trees land erosion is also higher, increasing the chance of **23** .... Deforestation also affects global warming by contributing 15% of the **24** .... of greenhouse gasses. To make sure that the cutting down of trees is done in a sustainable way, good forestry **25** .... is important. In most countries more trees are cut down every year than planted. One country that is reversing this trend is China, making it one of the few nations to **26** .... the more common negative trend.

Reading Passage 3

*You should spend about 20 minutes on **Questions 27–40**, which are based on Reading Passage 3 below.*

Film Noir

After the Second World War, a curious change came over the outlook of Hollywood films. Rather than the positive, happy-ending stories that dominated the silver screen before the war, a pessimism and negativity had entered American cinema. This post-war disillusionment was evident in Hollywood and the movement became known as film noir.

One would be mistaken to call film noir a genre. Unlike westerns or romantic comedies, film noir cannot be defined by conventional uses of setting or conflict in the way that is common to genre films. Film noir is more of a movement, pinned to one specific point in time in much the same way as Soviet Montage or German Expressionism was. Instead, the defining quality of film noir was linked to tone, lighting and an often a sombre mood.

True film noir refers to Hollywood films of the 1940s and early 1950s that dealt with dark themes such as crime and corruption. These films were essentially critiquing certain aspects of American society in a way film had never done before. Since that time there have occasionally been other great noir films made, such as *Chinatown*, but the mood and tone are often different to the original film noir movies. One possible reason for this is the time in which the films were made. A common perception of art is that it reflects the society and time in which it is made. That makes film noir of the Forties and Fifties quite inimitable because, luckily, the world has not had to endure a war of the scale and destruction of the Second World War again.

Paul Schrader, writer of films like *Taxi Driver* and *Raging Bull*, sees film noir as one of Hollywood's best and least known periods. In his essay *Notes on Film Noir* he admits that classifying film noir is almost impossible because many films considered as film noir vary greatly in style. He observed that there were four main traditions in film noir.

First were the films specifically about war and post-war disillusionment. Schrader believes these films were not only a reflection of the war, but also a delayed reaction to the great economic depression of the 1930s. The trend in Hollywood throughout this period and into the war was to produce films aimed at keeping people's spirits up, hence the positivity. As soon as the war ended, crime fiction started to become popular, which mirrored growing disillusionment in America. Films such as *The Blue Dahlia* and *Dead Reckoning* picked up on a trend started during the war with *The Maltese Falcon* in 1941, which is seen as the first example of film noir.

Another film noir tradition was post-war realism. This style of film was similar to some European films of the same era, such as Italy's neorealist films like Vittorio De Sica's *Bicycle Thieves* and Roberto Rossellini's *Open City*. Part of this style was created by filming in real locations and away from constructed sets. The honesty of this style of film suited the post-war mood in America and is demonstrated well in Jules Dassin's *Night and the City*, much of which was filmed in and around London.

The third tradition of film noir according to Paul Schrader involves what he characterises as 'The German Influence'. Especially during the 1920s German Expressionism was one of the most unique and creative forms of cinema. Many German, Austrian and Polish directors immigrated to America before or during the rise of Hitler and in part due to the increasing control and prevention of artistic freedom. Many of them, such as Fritz Lang and Billy Wilder, would find their way into the Hollywood system and to this day remain some of the most celebrated directors of all time.

It was the lighting developed in German Expressionism in particular that was most influential on film noir. The interplay of light and shadow created by chiaroscuro was highly suggestive of hidden darkness and was largely responsible for creating the mood and feeling of film noir. But it was the coupling of expressionist lighting with realistic settings that really gave film noir its authenticity. It is no surprise then that two of the most popular film noir feature films, *Sunset Boulevard* and *Ace in the Hole*, were both directed by Billy Wilder.

The final tradition of film noir noted by Schrader is what he dubs 'The Hard-Boiled Tradition'. He notes how American literature of the time was the driving force behind much of this style of film noir. Ernest Hemingway, Raymond Chandler and James M. Cain were tough, cynical and uncompromising and their work reflects this type of attitude. If German Expressionism influenced the visual aspect of film noir, it was this hard-boiled writing style that influenced the characters, stories and scripts depicted on screen. Raymond Chandler adapted the screenplay for film noir classic *Double Indemnity* from a James M. Cain story. This writing team, with Billy Wilder again directing, was the perfect combination for one of Hollywood's most celebrated films.

Questions 27–32

Do the following statements agree with the claims of the writer in Reading Passage 3?

In boxes 27–32 on your answer sheet, write

YES	*if the statement agrees with the claims of the writer*
NO	*if the statement contradicts the claims of the writer*
NOT GIVEN	*if it is impossible to say what the writer thinks about this*

27 The First World War had a big influence on the types of films being made in Hollywood.

28 Film noir is an official genre.

29 True film noir can be from any time and be about any kind of social issue.

30 Filmmaker Paul Schrader believes that film noir is almost impossible to classify.

31 Mixing light and shadow was mainly responsible for creating the unique mood and feeling of film noir.

32 During the 1950s film noir was the most successful type of film at the box office.

Questions 33–37

Complete the notes below.

Write **NO MORE THAN TWO WORDS AND/OR A NUMBER** *for each answer.*

Write your answers in boxes 33–37 on your answer sheet.

THE FOUR TRADITIONS OF FILM NOIR
War and post-war disillusionment: A delayed **33** .... to the great economic depression. The Hollywood trend during the depression and war was to produce films aimed at keeping people's spirits up.
Post-war realism: Part of the style was created by shooting the films in real locations instead of on sets. Similar to European film styles such as **34** .... in Italy.
The German Influence: Many directors from Germany, Austria and Poland **35** .... to America during the 1920s and 1930s. The use of lighting styles developed by German Expressionist films was very influential on film noir. Combining chiaroscuro lighting with filming in real locations gave film noir its **36** ....
The hard-boiled tradition: These films were heavily influenced by popular literature of the time by writers like Ernest Hemingway. The hard-boiled writing style influenced the depiction of **37** .... , stories and scripts in film noir.

Questions 38–40

Complete each sentence with the correct ending, A–F.

Write your answers in boxes 38–40 on your answer sheet.

38 After the war, instead of the positive films that existed in Hollywood before

39 The honesty of post-war realism in film noir

40 *Double Indemnity*, directed by Billy Wilder, is

A	suited the mood in America well.
B	one of Hollywood's most notable films.
C	there were a lot more romantic comedies released in America.
D	was something most people were not ready for.
E	a negativity had entered Hollywood films.
F	a film that very few people know about today.

WRITING MODULE

Writing Task 1

You should spend about 20 minutes on this task.

The graph below gives information about monthly electricity, water and gas use at a leisure centre in Manchester.

Summarise the information by selecting and reporting the main features, and make comparisons where relevant.

You should write at least 150 words.

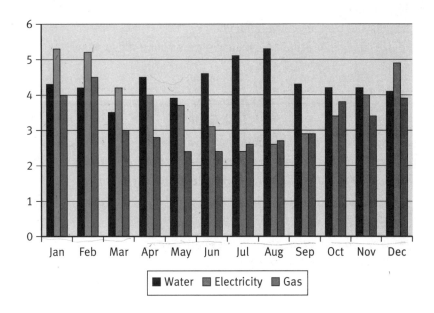

Writing Task 2

You should spend about 40 minutes on this task.

Some people believe that violent films are bad for you and encourage people to be violent. Others argue that violence and films are unrelated because violence existed before films.

Which of these opinions do you agree with, and to what extent do you agree? Give reasons for your answer and include any relevant examples from your own knowledge and experience.

Write at least 250 words.

SPEAKING MODULE

Time: 11–14 minutes

Part 1

Introduction to interview (4–5 minutes) [This part of the test begins with the examiner introducing himself or herself and checking the candidate's identification. It then continues as an interview.]

Let's talk about the place where you grew up

- Describe the town or city where you grew up.
- When did you move away?
- Do you live on your own or with your family?
- Has the place changed much since when you were young? [If so, how?]

Part 2

> ### Task Card
>
> Please read the topic below carefully. You will be asked to talk about it for one to two minutes. You will have one minute to think about what you are going to say. You can make some notes to help you if you wish.
>
> *Describe your idea of the perfect holiday destination. You should say:*
>
> - *Where it is*
> - *Why you prefer that place to anywhere else*
> - *Who you would take with you*
>
> *Also, explain what qualities you look for in a holiday destination.*

Individual long turn (3–4 minutes): *Candidate's Task Card*

The examiner may then ask you a couple of brief questions to wrap up this part of the test.

Rounding off questions:

- *What is your favourite city to visit? [Why?]*
- *Do you prefer to visit the city or the countryside? [Why?]*
- *What is your favourite thing about travelling?*

Part 3

Two-way discussion (4–5 minutes): *In Part 3, the examiner will ask you further questions related to the topic in Part 2.*

Let's talk about the benefits of travelling to a big city.

- *Among your friends and family, what seems to be the most popular city destination to travel to?*
- *What experiences have you had whilst visiting a big city that you could not experience in your hometown?*
- *What are some advantages of visiting a capital city over smaller towns or villages?*

Finally, let's talk about the disadvantages of travelling to big cities.

- *What do you consider to be the main disadvantage of travelling in a big city?*
- *Have you ever experienced any problems when visiting a big city? [If so, what?]*
- *Given the opportunity, which city that you have already visited would you most like to visit again? [Why?]*

PART SEVEN

Listening Scripts

CLASSROOM LISTENING SCRIPTS

Track 1

EMMA:	Hi, Will? It's Emma. We ought to come up with an idea for the <u>graduation</u> party. It's only a month away.
WILL:	Goodness, that soon! What do we need to do?
EMMA:	Umm, we have to decide on the type of party. We could have a meal. Everyone likes a proper dinner. Or we could have the party at someone's house. Or we could do an activity, like bowling.
WILL:	<u>I hate bowling. It's expensive</u>, and anyway, it's not connected with graduation or anything.
EMMA:	Right. So we won't go bowling.
WILL:	If we have a graduation dinner, would we cook it ourselves, or go to a restaurant?
EMMA:	Do you want to cook a dinner for <u>twelve</u> people?
WILL:	My kitchen isn't big enough! My table has only <u>six</u> chairs.
EMMA:	Okay, then. We can see about getting a booking at a restaurant, but a lot of students will be having their graduation parties in the next few weeks. It will be tough to get a booking.
WILL:	It will probably be expensive. <u>Last year, my brother paid thirty pounds per person</u>!
EMMA:	Well, why don't we look at having the party at someone else's house? I know some of our class have quite big houses that are not far from college. Let's think. Peter's house is huge, and he has a big garden – I'm sure he'd be able to host it.
WILL:	Hang on. What about Emily? Her family have got a huge terrace with a barbecue and a pool.
EMMA:	<u>Great! That's an excellent idea</u>. We can all bring some food and drink.
WILL:	Brilliant. Let's give her a call now. That's graduation sorted, then.

Track 2

RECEPTIONIST:	Hello, Woodland College. How may I help?
CALLER:	Yes, hello. I was calling about your evening art classes. Could you tell me about your painting class?
RECEPTIONIST:	Of course! <u>The painting class meets on Thursdays at six-thirty p.m.</u> There are a total of eight sessions, and the class costs seventy-five pounds.

CALLER:	Is that seventy-five pounds per class, or seventy-five pounds total?
RECEPTIONIST:	Oh, no. <u>Seventy-five pounds is the total charge</u>.
CALLER:	Hmm. It's less than ten pounds per class. That's quite a good deal.
RECEPTIONIST:	Indeed, it is. The painting class is very popular. (pause) In fact, the next painting class may already be full. Let me check for you.
CALLER:	Thanks. (pause) So when is the next painting class?
RECEPTIONIST:	<u>The next class starts on the eleventh of April</u>. And I'm happy to report, there are two places available.
CALLER:	The eleventh of April… OK… and the class is eight weeks, so it will continue into June?
RECEPTIONIST:	Umm, no, actually, <u>the final session is on the thirtieth of May</u>.
CALLER:	That's perfect. We're away on holiday in June, anyway. Can I sign up now?
RECEPTIONIST:	Sure. May I take your name?
CALLER:	It's Ruby Byrne.
RECEPTIONIST:	Is that <u>B-Y-R-N-E</u>?
CALLER:	Yes, that's right.
RECEPTIONIST:	And what's your address?
CALLER:	It's number four, King Street, right here in Greenwood.
RECEPTIONIST:	And the postcode?
CALLER:	<u>GR5 2MQ</u>.
RECEPTIONIST:	And your phone number?
CALLER:	Well, it's usually easiest to reach me on my mobile. That's <u>07989 457015</u>.
RECEPTIONIST:	Was that 07989 457015?
CALLER:	Yes, that's correct.

Track 3

IT WORKER:	You're through to Victoria University IT department. How may I help?
STUDENT:	Yes, <u>I've been locked out of my email account</u>. Can you help?
IT WORKER:	Are you a student or an employee?
STUDENT:	Both. I work at the University Union. In the café?
IT WORKER:	All right. Which email account is giving you trouble? Is it your personal account?

STUDENT:	Actually, it's for a society.
IT WORKER:	A society. Right. Which society is it, then?
STUDENT:	It's the Rugby Club. <u>I'm the vice-president</u>.
IT WORKER:	That's good, because I can only give information on the account to one of the officers of the society. Let me see. (pause) Could you confirm your name?
STUDENT:	Rakesh Singh.
IT WORKER:	How do you spell that?
STUDENT:	<u>R-A-K-E-S-H</u>…
IT WORKER:	I mean the last name? Is it just 'Sing,' as in 'Sing a song of sixpence'?
STUDENT:	No, it's sing with an H on the end.
IT WORKER:	Oh, right. That's what I thought. They have your name spelt incorrectly in the system.
STUDENT:	Oh, dear. Will that be a problem?
IT WORKER:	I can fix it. What exactly was the trouble you were having with the Rugby Club email account?
STUDENT:	Well, I was trying to log in just now, and it said I had the <u>wrong password</u>.
IT WORKER:	That's not good.

Track 4

IT WORKER:	What password were you using?
STUDENT:	Offside, with an exclamation mark at the end.
IT WORKER:	Offside, starting with an O?
STUDENT:	That's the password I was given. I was just elected to be an officer of the club.
IT WORKER:	Good for you! Unfortunately, that's not the password we have in the system. It's offside with an exclamation mark at the end, but it starts with a naught instead of an O.
STUDENT:	A naught?
IT WORKER:	A zero?
STUDENT:	Oh. Okay. Yeah, <u>I can see that it could be an O or a zero</u>.
IT WORKER:	Don't worry. It happens all the time. We can reset your password now.
STUDENT:	Great. Hmm. (pause) <u>Can we make it tackle</u>?
IT WORKER:	I see what you did there. Tackle is a great starting point, but you're forgetting the university policy on passwords. To be secure, a password must include at least one number, and at least one special symbol, such as a question mark or a dollar sign.

STUDENT:	Okay, okay. What if we make it tackle, but <u>with an asterisk instead of a K</u>, and a one instead of the L?
IT WORKER:	Umm, right. So the new password is T-A-C-asterisk-one-E?
STUDENT:	Will that do?
IT WORKER:	It's all changed in our system. You'll want to be sure to write it down.
STUDENT:	I'm making a note of it now… (pause) By the way, would you be the ones to help if we were having trouble with the club's website?
IT WORKER:	That's right. What's the issue with the website?
STUDENT:	Well, it's not a problem, exactly. We've got some photos from some of our matches, and a few clips that we've filmed… Is it possible to put these on the website?
IT WORKER:	Of course! That's a great way to show what the club has been up to. (pause) How long are these films?
STUDENT:	They're not films. Just some short videos from practice, and some key moments from our matches. <u>I think the longest video is maybe three minutes? A bit less than that</u>.
IT WORKER:	You'll want to compress the videos before posting, as there are size limits. <u>The university will not allow videos that are more than fifty MB on our websites</u>.
STUDENT:	Fifty MB? That's not very much.
IT WORKER:	It doesn't sound like a lot. But you shouldn't have a problem with a video that's three minutes or less. I'd say that you could probably even shoot the video in high definition, and once it's compressed, it should fit within the size limits. (pause) I suppose you follow international rugby?
STUDENT:	Doesn't everyone?
IT WORKER:	Who do you support?
STUDENT:	<u>Fiji</u>. I think we might have a chance in the next World Cup. How about you?
IT WORKER:	England, of course.

Track 5

I know many of you have travelled quite a long way to join us to continue your studies here in Shipsbury. So you'll want to get acquainted with our town, and find your way around, as Shipsbury will be your home for the next few months. Here in the <u>student centre</u>, we're just across London Road from the college's main campus, right on the corner of the High Street. If you haven't done so already, you'll need to register with the police – be sure to take your passports and your letter from the college with you, and present yourself at the <u>police station</u>, which is a block away from the college, at the corner of Park Lane and Sheep Street. Be sure to check out <u>Victoria Park</u>, which is half a block east of the police station. The park extends to the north, past London Road, and as far south as Church Lane.

You're likely to spend quite a bit of time in the <u>public library</u>, which is located on Park Lane, between the police station and the park. Just north of the public library is the <u>Park Hotel</u>. This is the finest hotel for miles around, and does a very tasty, very traditional English tea on Sunday afternoons. You'll need to book ahead, and it's well worth the price.

Track 6

<u>Straight across from the library, you'll find the town hall</u>. There's a lovely atrium there, and the café serves some very tasty soups and sandwiches. Well worth checking out. The town hall was rebuilt in the 1960s, in the same style as <u>the supermarket, which is just beside the police station in Park Lane</u>. That part of Shipsbury was hit by a bomb during the Second World War, so some rebuilding was necessary. You'll find, though, that the rest of the town centre retains its charming, historic character, including <u>the post office, which is opposite the Park Hotel</u>.

Coming down Sheep Street, you'll find St Mary's church at the corner of Church Lane. <u>The church is across the road from the primary school, which is between Sheep Street and the park</u>. On the last Sunday of the month, you can climb the church tower, which gives a lovely view of the river a block away.

On your way back to the student centre, <u>come along Church Lane. At the intersection with the High Street, you'll find Wok 'n' Roll</u> – our most popular Chinese takeaway, and with good reason. The food is delicious, and the prices are terribly affordable. Be sure to place your orders before 7pm on a Saturday night, or you'll be out of luck!

Track 7

Welcome to *In the Kitchen*! Today, we'll be continuing our weekly series on traditional foods from Eastern Europe, with a focus on Slovakia and the special homemade cheese called *cirak* [SEE-dik]. That's spelled C-I-R-A-K. This cheese is traditionally made in the days before Easter, and served as part of an Easter breakfast. From about 1880 to 1920, about half a million Slovaks emigrated to the United States, settling in large numbers in Pennsylvania and Ohio. They brought their tradition of making this special Easter cheese, which was a way of keeping the customs of the old country alive in the New World. This particular recipe for *cirak* was sent in by one of our listeners, Helen in Pittsburgh, Pennsylvania, who says that she has fond memories of helping her grandmother make the cheese and serve it to the family when they got home from church on Easter morning.

To make your *cirak*, you will need only a few ingredients: 4 cups of milk; 12 eggs; and a teaspoon of <u>salt</u>. Pour the milk into a large mixing bowl, then place the bowl atop a <u>saucepan</u> that is about half filled with water. Next, you'll want to heat the saucepan over a low to medium flame, so that the steam from the saucepan will <u>warm</u> the milk in the bowl. Now, be careful not to get the milk too hot – we don't want it to boil! Once the milk is warm, start cracking the eggs, one at a time, stirring them into the milk. Helen says that it's essential to keep <u>stirring</u> as you add the eggs, otherwise they will scorch. After adding all the eggs, continue stirring until what you have in the bowl looks like scrambled eggs.

The next step is to drain off the liquid. To do this, you need to pour the mixture into a cheesecloth bag, tie it off, and hang it over the sink for an hour or two. Now, I know what you're thinking: where can I get a cheesecloth bag? Helen reports that, when her grandmother couldn't get a cheesecloth bag, she would use a pair of pantyhose, and they worked just as well. For our British listeners, those are known as <u>tights</u>.

Anyway, once you've drained the cheese in your cheesecloth, or pantyhose, or tights, you need to compress it, to force out any remaining liquid. Put the cheese – still in the cheesecloth – under the flat side of a pan, such as a cast-iron skillet, just like you are putting the skillet on the stove – but instead, put it on the cheese. Put a cooling rack on top of the skillet, and place something <u>heavy</u> on top of the cooling rack. Helen recommends using several heavy cans on top of the cooling rack. This will distribute the weight onto the skillet, and the skillet will press the last of the liquid out of the cheese.

After two hours, you can remove the weight, the skillet and the cheesecloth. You will need to refrigerate the cheese <u>overnight</u> before it is ready to eat. You'll want to slice your Slovak cheese, and <u>serve</u> it with horseradish sauce for an authentic and very traditional Easter treat.

Track 8

Thanks, everyone, for coming out tonight, despite it being so bright and pleasant out. And thank you for offering to help with running our village fete! We're only three days away from this year's fete, and hopefully the weather on the big day <u>Saturday the nineteenth</u> will be just as good as today. Currently, the forecast is calling for twenty-two degrees and <u>plenty of sunshine</u> – let's hope that holds true!

This year's village fete is in aid of repairing the roof in the <u>village hall</u>. We need to raise a total of four thousand pounds to pay for the roof repairs. That's our overall target. Last year, we sold four hundred tickets for adults at £5 each, plus <u>300</u> discounted tickets – for children, students and pensioners – at £2.50 each. That comes to <u>a total of two thousand, seven hundred and fifty pounds from ticket sales alone</u>. Assuming similar figures this year, we'll need to bring in a minimum of one thousand, two hundred fifty pounds from the games and food sales to hit our overall target.

Once again, we'll hold the village fete in Riverside Park. You've all got a copy of the map of the park. Let's take a moment to explain the key locations for the fete. Entering from the car park, you'll take the path to the left, leading towards the Memorial Gardens. Before you reach the gardens, you'll come to the raffle. This will allow us to sell a lot of raffle tickets! Going on from the raffle, directly across from the Memorial Gardens is where we'll have the jam tasting. Our local jam makers have agreed to donate ten per cent of their sales at the fete, so that will help us reach our goal. Moving on from the jam tasting, as you come to the river, you'll find the face painting. We expect every child under the age of 10 to get their faces painted – but this activity is for children only!

On the other side of the park, past the pond, we'll set up the band stand right on the edge of the river. Several great local bands have agreed to perform for free, so we'll have great tunes throughout the day. Next to the band stand, heading back towards the car park, we'll have the drinks stand. This will be right next to the kids' games, so we'll be able to sell drinks to those enjoying the music, and any parents and little ones who work up a thirst at the games.

Again, all the kids' games are only for children… the exception is the egg and spoon race, which will be repeated at intervals throughout the day, so everyone can compete. The races will take place between the kids' games and the car park. Unfortunately, we've had to discontinue the three-legged race, for legal reasons – there were far too many injuries last year! That's why we're letting adults join in the egg and spoon race. It's two pounds per person, so we expect that will really help hit our goal.

In terms of the kids' games, there are quite a few… the balloon burst, the chocolate throw, and of course the always popular ladder game, where players throw beanbags in between the rungs of a ladder laid out on the ground. At last year's fete, the chocolate throw was the best liked and most played of the kids' games, and we expect it to be the same again this year. The kids throw a penny and it must land – and stay – on a chocolate bar. If it does, they win the chocolate. It's harder than it sounds. Last year, we charged 50p per throw, and we made 400 pounds from that game alone.

Track 9

TUTOR:	So, Sonia. I've had a chance to look through your report from your internship.
SONIA:	Thank you for reading it! What did you think?
TUTOR:	I found it all very fascinating. Why did you decide to do your internship there?
SONIA:	Well, I've always been curious about stained glass windows. You see them in churches and mosques, and I wanted to find out more about how to make things out of glass.

TUTOR: So you did your internship at a glass works.

SONIA: Yes. The glass works have two sides to their business: the industrial side, which makes glass for commercial customers, like offices and <u>factories</u>. And then there's the artisanal glass works. I worked on the artisanal side. We made artistic glass for homes, including stained glass <u>windows</u> and other glass products, like mosaics and tableware.

TUTOR: Tableware?

SONIA: Pitchers, cups, you know –

TUTOR: Right. What did you find most interesting about working with glass?

SONIA: Hmm. What was surprising to me was that we used a lot of found glass. We'd get it from charity shops, from anywhere, really. And then you would cut the glass into the shapes you'd need for your project. Of course, you could always melt it down, or you could make new glass. But working with found glass was really interesting.

TUTOR: What was the process for this?

SONIA: For <u>how to cut glass</u>? I'm an expert at cutting glass by now! The best approach is to <u>score</u> it. You draw a line on the glass, and then you break it along the line. The line is the 'score' – you have to score it so you're sure to break it just as you meant to.

TUTOR: Does it make a difference how big the glass is, before you break it? Like, if you have a sheet of glass, or smaller pieces?

B: Sure. <u>If you have a large sheet of glass, then the best option is a table break</u>. You score the glass, then you basically break it along the edge of a table. You have to be really careful, though!

TUTOR: What if it's a smaller piece?

SONIA: <u>For smaller pieces, the best thing is to use a knife, or some pliers</u>. It really depends on the size and shape of the piece you're starting with, and of course, what size and shape you want to end up with. You can get really specific, for instance, you could score the glass in the shape of a small crescent moon, and then use your knife to cut it out. Whatever you want, really.

TUTOR: That sounds like it could be difficult.

SONIA: <u>The most difficult approach is the third option. The tapping method</u>. What you do is you score the glass, then you knock gently all along the full length of the line. You can use the ball end of your glass knife, and you work down the line, tapping all the way. This causes tiny fractures inside the glass, without actually breaking it. Then, you fold along the line, holding both sides carefully. If you do it right, this will break the glass exactly as scored. <u>This method works best for curves</u>, particularly when you want to cut curves into a larger sheet of glass.

Track 10

A: Great, so let's get started. What should we do for the introduction?

B: Well, the tutor said we should start off by giving a <u>summary</u> of the problem. Then, the main part of our presentation will go through our proposals to address the problem.

A: The problem is the lack of tourists, obviously. We really need to get more people visiting the town!

B: That's right, and I'd say that the main cause of the decline in tourism is the <u>poor weather</u> we've had the last two summers. It wasn't very hot, and it rained a lot.

A: Nice one. We'll start with that. Now, what are we going to have in the main part of our presentation? We can't do much about the weather.

B: No, but we can make things more welcoming for tourists. There are a little things we can do – we can go through those, we'll need at least three or four <u>examples</u>.

A: Okay, we'll come to those in a minute. And then for the ending?

B: <u>The ending should be where we explain our strongest point</u> – our best example – the thing we can do that would have the biggest impact on increasing tourism.

A: Right. End on a high note. And how should we break up the presentation, on the day?

B: Probably works best if we <u>take turns</u> – if I do the intro, then you do the first example, I do the second example, and so on.

A: Hmm. Yep. Okay. Let's take turns then.

A: Shall we look at the things we want to improve? I thought we could start with the old pier. It's awfully popular, given that we are on the seafront, but it's terribly dark once the sun goes down. We could do with better lighting there.

B: We could do with *lighting* there, full stop. There's hardly any.

A: So <u>we want to put extra lights on the pier</u>. That's one down.

B: You know where else is a problem at night? Abbey Park. I know it's a big deal, as it's right by the abbey ruins, and everyone wants

A:	to take pictures of those. But it's not a place you'd want to go after dark – too many people smoking and drinking and carrying on.
A:	What's the solution there?
B:	Well, I was talking about it with my mum. She thinks <u>they should just shut the park gates at sunset</u>. That would make Abbey Park a daytime attraction, and it would be a lot cleaner during the day, too.
A:	That's great. You know what else could do with a proper clean-up? The beach. Seeing how were supposedly known for our fine beach, the state of it most mornings is appalling.
B:	We could say that <u>the beach should have the rubbish collected and littered cleared every night</u>.
A:	<u>And they should clear away the seaweed. Give it a total overnight cleaning</u>.
B:	That will make the beach much more attractive for families. (pause) You know what's also a problem for families? The shops in The Strand. They're always packed, but the toilets are not in great condition. They're terribly cramped, and when my sister was there with her little one, there was nowhere to change the nappies. She had to do it sitting on the toilet, with the baby and diaper bag both in her lap!
A:	So <u>we need to put some baby changing tables in the toilets at those shops</u>.
B:	Definitely! How many ideas is that so far?
A:	(pause) Four. That's enough, unless we really want to impress?
B:	I don't know about that. Mmm, although I will say, and I know it's obvious but worth mentioning. We get a lot of attention from the national press because of the Royal Art Gallery, and they have some really great exhibitions. But the ticket prices there are outrageous… it's 10 pounds to get in!
A:	Aren't most museums free? You'd expect it anyway. Okay, so let's say that <u>they should abolish the admission charge</u>.
B:	That's five. That's a lot of solutions. Want to start writing it up?

Track 11

MILLIE:	Hi, Robert. What are you up to this afternoon?
ROBERT:	Oh, hi, Millie. I'm just <u>working on my recycling report</u> for our ecology class.
MILLIE:	Oh, cool. I'm having a lot of fun with mine. Ecology is my favourite module!

ROBERT: I wish I could say the same. I mean, I care about the environment, and all, and climate change is really something we should all be concerned about. But the lecturer is so dull.

MILLIE: He can be a bit dry. What's the focus of your report?

ROBERT: I'm looking at the statistics for recycling collected by the local council for the last 3 years. It's so boring. But there are some interesting facts in there, I suppose.

MILLIE: Sounds interesting. I'm also looking at the local area. My report is all about what Greenwood Council are doing to increase the amount of rubbish that is recycled.

ROBERT: Right. Seems like we're always recycling more and more, but I guess it's never enough.

MILLIE: You're right. We can always do more. What's really interesting is how the council has got us recycling more. I've spoken to several councillors and local activists who have done a lot on this issue, and the politicians and activists agree: the biggest reason for the increase in recycling is the change in the size of our rubbish bins. You remember, last year, everyone was complaining when we got new rubbish bins, and they were almost half the size of the old ones?

ROBERT: And they reduced the rubbish collection to once a fortnight.

MILLIE: Yes, but the recycling bins were still the big, old size, and they kept collecting the recycling once a week. This made it easier to recycle, and, more important, it forced people to recycle more. There simply wasn't enough room in their bin for all that rubbish. Anything that could be recycled needs to go into the recycling bin now, so we're all recycling more.

ROBERT: That's one way to get a result.

MILLIE: So, tell me about your research. What have you found out about how much we're recycling here in Greenwood?

ROBERT: Well, Greenwood residents recycled thirty-one per cent of all our waste last year. Waste meaning rubbish plus recycling. That's up from twenty-seven per cent three years ago.

MILLIE: So, a rise of four per cent. That's brilliant!

ROBERT: It is, and it's even better, because the overall amount of waste increased as well, by ten per cent. So we recycled a greater share of a larger total. That means less rubbish going to landfill.

MILLIE: What did you learn about what people are recycling? Any big changes there?

ROBERT:	That was the surprising thing. People aren't recycling nearly as much paper and card as they used to – <u>the rate of paper and card recycling has dropped by six per cent</u>. I didn't expected that – you'd think that people are being a bit better about not putting packaging and old papers in the rubbish, but recycling it instead.
MILLIE:	Do you have any research about why the figure is down?
ROBERT:	Mmm, now, this is something. You know how we used to recycle all our old newspapers and magazines?
MILLIE:	I can't remember the last time I bought a newspaper, or a magazine!
ROBERT:	But you still read them, don't you?
MILLIE:	I guess… Well, actually, you're right. I *do* read newspapers and magazines. Only I read them online.
ROBERT:	That's just it. <u>People are reading their periodicals on computers and tablets</u>, instead of buying a physical copy. If you never buy a printed newspaper or magazine, you needn't recycle it.
MILLIE:	Wow, I wouldn't have thought of that.
ROBERT:	The other big change in the recycling figures is that we are recycling a fair bit more plastic than we did before. <u>In the last three years, the figure for plastic recycling has increased by a quarter</u>. They think that people here in Greenwood are recycling more plastic because of all the attention to recycling, rather than just binning, things like drinks containers and carrier bags. The local council did a big campaign around this last year, with lots of posters in supermarkets. They say it was a huge success.
MILLIE:	Who, exactly, is 'they'? Who did you talk to, as part of your research?
ROBERT:	You know I volunteered at the recycling centre last semester? So I dropped by there, talked to some of the guys, and they put me onto a lady from the council who gave me all the figures. She did go on a bit, but yeah, she was really helpful.

Track 12

EXTRACT 1: Most big cats are solitary animals. Tigers prefer to live alone, as do leopards and cougars. Lions break the trend. Unlike their big cat cousins, lions usually reside in same-sex groups, sharing responsibilities essential for survival. Female lions band together in prides. Prides normally range from between two to six adult female lions that collaboratively raise lion cubs. Lionesses of the same pride often synchronise breeding schedules, and if every member of the pride has cubs at roughly the same time, the group is then called a crèche. Male lions form their own groups called coalitions. Formed of two or more grown males, coalitions exert controlling interest over often multiple prides. This loose association with the pride involves fathering cubs, killing prey for the lionesses and their young, and protecting the group. This intense social organisation is truly unique in the cat kingdom, and zoologists have sought for decades to understand why lions are different.

EXTRACT 2: Despite medical advances, statistics show childhood allergies have increased in both developed and developing countries over the last 20 years. These include allergies to both food and non-food components. The most common foods to react to in childhood are peanuts, milk, egg, shellfish and wheat. Common environmental allergens are dust, mould, pollen and animal hair. The exact reason as to why there has been a rise is still uncertain, although there are several proposed theories, the most well known of which is known as the Hygiene Hypothesis. This hypothesis states that as result of a cleaner, more modern living environment, children born today are exposed to fewer particles whilst their immune systems are developing and therefore their immunity remains somewhat immature. Parents may also be more careful to introduce food substances at a later age. Subsequently, on first exposure to harmless particles such as dust and certain foods, their immune cells overreact and an allergy develops. Fortunately, most of the time children will grow out of the allergy. Certain allergies however, particularly to nuts, tend to persist into adulthood for unknown reasons.

EXTRACT 3: The sale and manufacturing of athletic footwear is a £12 billion industry, and avid runners frequently spend huge amounts on the latest shoe models. Recently, though, running scientists have questioned the impact footwear actually has on running performance. Evolutionary biologists at Harvard University have devoted years to studying the biomechanics of running and have recently speculated whether wearing footwear while running is actually necessary. Runners wear padded, thickly soled trainers for numerous reasons, including the support they provide under the heel and the foot's arch, and the protection they give against hard, painful surfaces. Early humans, however, ran long distances over varied terrain without any footwear, and scientists now wonder if this is how we are evolutionary designed to run.

Track 13

Good morning. We're going to start off with a look at a recent discovery that reveals quite a bit about the history of shipbuilding, along with the harsh realities of life in ancient England.

In 2011, a total of eight ancient boats were discovered in a quarry near the Flag Fen archaeological site, located immediately south-east of Peterborough in the Cambridgeshire fens. A fen, if you've never encountered one, is a type of wetland with peat, grass and a whole lot of water. In 2013, carbon-dating revealed that the boats were from 1600 BC, a full two centuries earlier than the original approximation. The boats, made from lime, oak or maple, were buried extremely deep underground, and were so well built that they were virtually intact and, if allowed onto water, would still be buoyant. This unusual, historical treasure trove led the archaeologists to take the exceptional (and costly) decision to transport the boats from the quarry to their facility at Flag Fen without first cutting the boats into chunks, which required a system of pulleys and special transport equipment reinforced with scaffolding poles to ensure that the boats were not damaged.

The boats had been deliberately submerged to the bottom of what was then a creek, in what is believed to be a Bronze Age ritual of some religious significance. The area of the fens where the boats were found had been crisscrossed with creeks and rivers during the Bronze Age, and the custom of the time was to sink offerings to the gods underwater. Many daggers and jewels were found near the boats, leading archaeologists to believe that the site may have been of religious as well as commercial importance over 3,000 years ago. Some of the boats were well used by fishermen and must have been brought some distance inland in order to be sunk in the creek, and others appear to have been built only for that purpose. We know that they deliberately sank the boats because the transoms – the pieces of wood that close off the rear of the boat – had been removed.

The craftsmanship of the boats is extraordinarily practical and versatile, even by today's standards. The shipwrights used tools made of bronze to carve the tree trunks and shape the boats, some of which were hewn until only as thick as a finger, but so resiliently buoyant that they were able to float when rain filled the archaeologists' trench. The boats are now on display in a chilled container within a barn on the Flag Fen site. The technician responsible for conserving the boats must spend eight hours a day spraying them with water and removing impurities; once this process is complete, then the boats will be injected with a special wax with preservative powers and then dried out, a process that will take two years to complete.

Why did they sink the boats? The likeliest explanation is that an extended period of climate change led to a worrying rise in sea levels, so that the terrain of the fens became increasingly waterlogged over a very small number of years. As a consequence, the mostly agrarian society was not able to grow crops, and was at risk of starvation. The ritual sinking of the boats was thus likely intended to be a profoundly desperate offering to appease the gods and stop the seas from rising.

Track 14

Let's consider the history of one of our tastiest and chilliest foods: ice cream. Now, when researching the history of ice cream, you have to be really careful to separate fact from fiction. There are more than a few legends, or origin stories, that have worked their way into the popular imagination over the years – we'll discount some of these here.

The first ice cream was made in China, dating to around 200 BC. The Chinese prepared a mixture of milk and rice, then packed the mixture in snow. Nearly a thousand years later, King Tang of Shang is reported to have employed more than 90 'ice men' to mix buffalo milk, flour and camphor with ice. As you might expect, these earliest examples would have resulted in a creamy frozen dessert, quite similar to our ice cream today, except without any of the fruit or chocolate flavourings that we love.

There are other early examples of flavoured frozen desserts, but these are quite unlike what we would consider to be ice cream. For example, some Roman emperors would have snow collected from the mountains, then flavoured with fruit juice – this would result in something more like a snow cone, or perhaps sorbet. There's also the supposed 'ice cream' recipe that Marco Polo took home to Europe after his travels in China. Marco Polo's ice cream was not really ice cream, but more like sherbet, consisting mainly of fruit and ice mixture, with a very small amount of milk fat, rather than milk. The earliest ice creams always included milk. This European version of the frozen dessert was developed over the years, eventually adding larger amounts of milk, so that in time, Europe came to have ice cream of its own.

By the 18th century, ice cream was very popular in Europe and North America. By then, the common recipe included milk, cream and eggs, just as it does today. In 1790, George Washington paid two hundred dollars – a huge sum at the time – for a supply of ice cream. So he wasn't only the first president – he was the first president to love ice cream! There is also a story that his wife Martha invented ice cream accidentally, by leaving a pot of cream out on her porch one night; the next morning, she is said to have opened the pot to find ice cream! Of course, this is pure legend; while it's true that Martha Washington frequently served ice cream in her time as First Lady, there is no record of her having made it.

By the mid 19th century, ice cream was being produced in large quantities in factories, allowing it to become available much more widely, and at much lower cost. For the first time, ice cream could be enjoyed by people of all classes and backgrounds. This might lead us to consider why was ice cream so unavailable, and so unknown to the masses, for so much of its history? There are two main reasons: first, remember that early ice cream always included snow or ice, as an ingredient as well as part of the process of making it. In those days, all the ice or snow would have to be brought in from mountains or the colder regions, which could only be done at great expense. Second, there is the challenge of keeping the ice cream cold, once it's made. Electric refrigerators didn't exist until the 20th century; before then, the only way to keep cold foods cold was to use an icebox, which was – as the name suggests – a box or cupboard that was packed with ice. Once again, there was the problem of where the ice would come from. It's no wonder that baked desserts were more popular in those days!

Track 15

Today, we're going to consider the results of a recent experiment into the behaviour of wild mice. Now, if you've ever kept a mouse, or a hamster or guinea pig, as a pet, you probably kept it in a cage with a water bottle, a food dish and an exercise wheel. Small pets like mice will spend a lot of time running inside the exercise wheel, making it spin round and round. And if you've ever seen a pet mouse running in an exercise wheel, you've no doubt seen them smiling and really going for it – you can't help getting the idea that mice enjoy running in exercise wheels.

But is this actually the case, and what can science tell us? Traditionally, there were two explanations for why mice in captivity – whether kept as pets, or for research – would run in exercise wheels. First, there's the possibility that the mice are running to relieve the <u>stress</u> of being confined. This means that there is a psychological benefit, or reward, from running in the exercise wheel. The other explanation is that running in the exercise wheel is a stereotyped behaviour – an activity that is repetitive, that is repeated in the same way countless times, without ever achieving any <u>goal</u>.

Until recently, the common view among scientists was that all this running in exercise wheels by mice in cages was a stereotyped behaviour. To understand the prevalence of this view, let's consider the three main criteria that define a stereotyped behaviour: the behaviour is observed only in animals in <u>cages</u>, not in the wild; second, the behaviour is repetitive, invariably the same, with no apparent purpose or benefit; and finally, the behaviour does not depend on external stimuli, such as a <u>reward</u>, or is only partially dependent on such stimuli.

The traditional understanding, then, is that captive mice run on exercise wheels even when there is no external stimulus because it's a stereotyped behaviour. This would be similar to when people are confined to a small room, or <u>prisoners</u> to a cell, and they will pace back and forth for no reason – that pacing is also a stereotyped behaviour. However, this understanding depends on the idea that the mice are running in the wheels because they are confined, and that they wouldn't run in the wheels in other circumstances.

A team of Dutch scientists set out to investigate whether this was actually the case, by setting up exercise wheels outside. They placed exercise wheels in small boxes – so that larger animals could not interfere – and the boxes were placed in two areas that were populated by wild mice and other small animals: an <u>urban</u> area – one of the professor's back gardens – and a rural area, a remote dune that could not be accessed by the public. Cameras recorded all visits to the exercise wheels over a period of three years. Most importantly, there was food in the box, but the animals could eat the food whether or not they chose to run in the exercise wheel.

In the course of the experiment, the running wheels were used more than <u>12,000</u> times, by animals including mice, frogs, slugs and birds. Mice, however, accounted for 88% of the wheel running. For the final months of the experiment, the researchers removed food from the boxes, leading to a drop in the frequency of visits to the boxes. Even so, visits where the wheel was used increased by <u>42%</u>. This suggests that mice visited the boxes solely to run on the exercise wheel. As a result, the scientists concluded that running in an exercise wheel is inherently <u>rewarding</u> to wild mice.

This research has proven that wheel running is not a stereotyped behaviour, as it was observed in wild mice. Effectively, this means that we are left with the first theory of why mice run in wheels – there is a fundamental benefit or goal to the activity, that is, the activity is psychologically rewarding. What's the reward to mice in running in a wheel? The answer is simple: they run because they <u>enjoy</u> it.

LISTENING SCRIPTS

Practice Test 1, Section 1 (Track 16)

RECEPTIONIST:	Good morning, Clevedon College, can I help you?
CALLER:	Yes, please. I'd like some information about evening courses this term.
RECEPTIONIST:	Okay. Which subjects are you interested in?
CALLER:	Two subjects, actually. Languages and Computer Skills.
RECEPTIONIST:	Okay. What languages are you interested in?
CALLER:	Actually, I'm not sure. I have to fulfil a language requirement for school, but I haven't really decided what language to study. Um… how many language courses do you run each week?
RECEPTIONIST:	We have two every night, from Monday to Friday.
CALLER:	I'm sorry, but would you mind going through the schedule for me?
RECEPTIONIST:	Not at all. Monday to Wednesday are Modern European Languages: French, Spanish, German, Dutch and Polish. Thursday night we offer ancient languages: Latin and <u>Ancient Greek</u>. And on Friday we finish off with the Asian languages of Hindi and Bengali.
CALLER:	Monday to Wednesday, Modern European; Thursday, Ancient Languages; and Friday, Asian… Can you spell Bengali please?
RECEPTIONIST:	Yes, it's <u>B-E-N-G-A-L-I</u>.
CALLER:	Great. And how much do the courses cost?
RECEPTIONIST:	Each course costs twenty-five pounds per person per term, but if you want to do two language courses, there's a ten per cent discount, but <u>only if you book for two terms</u>.
CALLER:	So the ten per cent discount is if I take two courses, for two terms, is that right?
RECEPTIONIST:	Right.

CALLER: Would it be possible for me to book my classes right now?

RECEPTIONIST: No, sorry, the computer's down. What I suggest you do is call extension 9694… no, sorry… 6994, after 6 p.m., and ask for Mrs Johnson.

CALLER: I'm sorry, I didn't get that. Did you say 6994… after 6 p.m.?

RECEPTIONIST: Yes, 6994… please ask for Mrs Johnson.

CALLER: Thanks. OK, can we now look at the Computer Skills courses?

RECEPTIONIST: Yes, of course. Computer classes always start in the first week of the month, and the way it works is we offer one computer class for the entire month. So you might spend one month on databases… another month on Excel, and so on. Classes meet once a week, on Tuesday afternoons. The next class starts February first.

CALLER: OK, so for the upcoming month… February?

RECEPTIONIST: February is going to be Databases. There are twenty-four places still free on that course, and it costs forty pounds per person.

CALLER: February… Databases… twenty-four openings… forty pounds… okay…

RECEPTIONIST: Excel starts in March, and that's nearly full – only four slots left. It's forty-five pounds.

CALLER: Okay, Excel… March… only four slots left. Got it.

RECEPTIONIST: April is Outlook. That is never as popular since it costs so much more, but you get a free CD. It is sixty pounds for the month, and there are nineteen places left.

CALLER: Okay, April… Outlook… sixty pounds. Is that it?

RECEPTIONIST: No, on the third of June, we start a Word course. We have sixteen vacancies for that at the moment. It's also expensive at fifty-five pounds.

CALLER: Third of June… Word… sixteen vacancies… fifty-five pounds. Now, do I call the same number to book a place on one of these classes?

RECEPTIONIST: No, you have to call Mary Jones, I think. Yes, Mary Jones… extension 9623.

CALLER: Sorry, could you repeat that number?

RECEPTIONIST: Yes… extension 9623. Please call her before 6 p.m.

CALLER: Okay. Many thanks for all your help.

Practice Test 1, Section 2 (Track 17)

Good afternoon, ladies and gentlemen. I'm Doctor Donovan, the principal of Donleavy University, and I would like to welcome you to the Dingle Wood Campus, which is one of the three campuses belonging to this university. This campus, Dingle Wood, is where I have my office, and it's also the location of the Languages and Science Campus, so some of you will be studying here. Dingle Wood is the most northerly campus. The Business Studies blocks are in the Churchdown Campus in the centre of town, and the southern or Trailway Campus, where History and Architecture are situated, is to the south of the town. Those of you who are enrolled in any of those courses will be taken to your respective buildings at the end of this meeting. Those of you studying on the Dingle Wood Campus… you will have a tour later, too.

This building we are assembled in is the office and administration block – block 39 – and is where the weekly meetings are held. You are welcome to attend these meetings, as are all the university staff. You may want to, as many university issues are discussed at these weekly meetings. The meetings take place at one-thirty every Tuesday, so please stop by. Two other important buildings are also located on this campus, the cafeteria and the on-site shop. You can purchase all the required books and any stationery you need for your courses at this shop. Please bear in mind that, even though you have shown your ID passes to enter this site, you still need to use them again to buy anything in the shop or cafeteria… This is for security reasons.

Now if I could draw your attention to the back page of your joining instructions booklet, you will see a small map of this campus – Dingle Wood. The block we are in now, the office and administration block, is located between the Languages Centre, block thirty-eight, and the Physics School, block thirty – that's three-oh. These are both on the right of the plan. The cafeteria, which is open from seven a.m. to nine-thirty p.m., is on the left of the plan. It is between the Chemistry block, number thirty-five, and the university shop, block thirty-three. At the university shop, you can get all you will need in terms of course materials.

The Biology block is block number 29, and you'll find the Biology block between the Chemistry block and the Languages Centre. Be careful with the numbers, as they are not always logical.

As you will see, there are gardens on the right-hand side of the gate. These are being extended over the next two months, and a memorial fountain is being installed in the middle of the campus. This means that the campus will be very noisy during normal working hours; however, the campus will look much nicer when it is all finished.

Right, so that's it for your initial campus orientation. At this point, could the language students all follow me, please, and the rest of you – please assemble under the banners which show your main topic of study, and you will be directed to the other campuses.

Practice Test 1, Section 3 (Track 18)

SARAH: Hi, Bill. How are you?

BILL: I'm okay now, Sarah, but I was so ill last week.

SARAH: Oh dear, what was the problem? Did you eat that dodgy fish in the canteen?

BILL: No. At first I thought it was a cold, but then <u>my head started hurting</u> and my eyes started to go blurry…

SARAH: I'm so sorry… that sounds serious.

BILL: It's okay, actually. I went to the doctor, and he diagnosed me with a migraine. He gave me some medicine, and I'm starting to feel much better.

SARAH: I'm glad to hear that. Well, I'm also glad you're in today because we have to work on a new project together.

BILL: Oh, are we in the same section?

SARAH: No, it's just us – no one else. Mr Donaldson put us down as B team because <u>we live near each other</u>.

BILL: That could be fun! What do we have to do?

SARAH: Well, the project is <u>partly internet research, then checking reference book for information to prepare a survey</u>, which we have to use with people we know.

BILL: Great, what's the topic?

SARAH: It's to do with shopping over the last ten years. We have to find out how customers have changed their behaviour.

BILL: Okay. So what's the first step?

SARAH: I think the first thing to do is to check the list of references he gave me. But my computer is in for repair, so…if I check in the reference library, <u>would you be willing to look up some references online?</u> Once we're done with the reference checks, we can write the questions together.

BILL: That's fine, I'll do the internet research. So… what sort of shopping are we looking at? Only food, or goods, or clothes shopping?

SARAH: We have to find people who are willing to tell us about <u>personal things like deodorants, cosmetics,</u> soap or vitamin creams. The other groups are doing food, electrical goods and clothes.

BILL: That won't be so easy, Sarah. <u>People might think those things are a bit private</u>.

SARAH: Yes, I thought about that. I'll ask the women and you can ask the men. That should work okay.

BILL:	Well, if you think so. Give me the list of references then.
SARAH:	Sorry, I left them in my other bag at Joseph's house. I'll get them for you tomorrow.
BILL:	Okay. Well, then, <u>this afternoon I think I'll catch up on the notes from last week</u>. Can you help me, or are you busy?
SARAH:	<u>I've made you a copy of the notes already, to save you time. Here you are!</u>
BILL:	Wow, thanks, Sarah. That's so thoughtful! Well, since there's nothing for us to do right now, shall we go for lunch?
SARAH:	Actually, I'll have to catch you later. I have to go to a meeting this afternoon. Can I phone you tonight to arrange when to meet?
BILL:	No, sorry, I have a date. Can we meet in the laboratory for the first class tomorrow?
SARAH:	I'm not sure because <u>I have to go to the library to collect some books</u>… What about meeting there at lunchtime?
BILL:	Do you mean in the lab?
SARAH:	Yes.
BILL:	Okay, <u>see you in the laboratory tomorrow</u> at noon, then. Sounds like we have a lot of work to do.

Practice Test 1, Section 4 (Track 19)

Good evening, everybody, and welcome to the first in this year's series of public lectures offered by the Art Gallery. <u>As chief curator of the gallery</u>, I was given the honour of presenting the first lecture – and, let me tell you, I had a difficult time deciding what to talk about tonight.

Being the curator, I naturally know just about everything that's in this gallery, but <u>I wanted to choose an artist who has a wide appeal</u> – that seems only fair, yes? But I didn't want to talk about someone so well known that anything I said would be familiar. I wanted someone modern – my personal preference is for modern art – but again, I wanted to choose someone who had the potential to appeal to all art lovers, whether they're attracted to traditional forms, Impressionism, surrealism, or what have you.

So, having spent the last five years as a visiting professor in Barcelona, it's not surprising that I finally chose to talk about one of the greatest Catalan artists – one whose work is likely to be familiar to many of you: Joan Miró.

Look at this… and this… and this. Ring any bells? Miró's most famous – and most widely reproduced – works tend to be like this. <u>Bright primary colours</u>, with lots of asymmetrical forms. He painted on <u>large canvases</u> – larger than himself, quite often – and his paintings depicted <u>birds, trees</u>, flowers and other features of the natural world.

But Miró produced a great variety of work, and it's about some of his lesser-known paintings that I would like to speak this evening.

Miró was born in Barcelona in 1893, the son of a goldsmith. He began to show talent very early, and in 1926, went to Paris where he was drawn to the surrealists of Montparnasse. He did not define himself as a surrealist, however; he preferred to stay free to experiment with other artistic styles as he wished. Miró had an intense dislike of much of the painting and many of the painters he knew. He wished to do something totally different, to express his contempt for bourgeois art – and yet, ironically, Miró's success has made his work much in demand among art collectors of the world.

But we can't really talk about the artist without looking at his art, and that's what I'd like to do now – to take a look at just a few of Miró's works and think about what it is that makes them special – special to me and to a great number of people who flock every day to the Miró Foundation in Barcelona.

Let's start with this, one of Miró's best-known and brightest works – _Woman and Bird_, a sculpture created in 1982. It is on display in a park in Barcelona, often known as the Joan Miró Park. A huge sculpture, towering up into the sky, it reflects Miró's eternal interest in these themes, as well as his more technical interest in materials; this sculpture is covered in mosaic, which gives it a naive and cheerful appearance. It is interesting that this sculpture was completed in 1982, just a year before Miró's death. I think it shows that, towards the end, he was feeling as playful as a young man, and I think he wanted to share this playfulness in a park – on such a big, very public scale.

And now, another representation of a woman, this time just called _Woman_. This was painted in 1976 – a late work for Miró – and is a work we often see reproduced, or on sale as postcards or posters in gallery shops around the world. So why is it so popular? I think the use of colour has something to do with it; people respond to these rounded shapes filled with primary colours, especially on a large canvas like this. Also the fact that, while it is rather surreal, it is still possible to recognise the form of a woman and to see it as a sympathetic representation. It's a bold, bright painting, and I think that it awakens a reaction in many of us.

And finally, something quite different – though still a woman. A harsh, even violent work that was completed in 1939, at a time when Miró was greatly influenced by the events of the civil war in Spain. It's titled _Seated Woman II,_ but it can be hard to find the woman here, as she's been transformed into rather a horrendous creature. So is that how Miró viewed women – as grotesque? Not at all. This picture can also be seen as strong, with a huge base and solid shoulders to support those who depend on her. In this painting, her arms and neck seem to grow as vegetation out of her shoulders – representing woman as fertile ground, perhaps. We also see here the fish and birds, the moon and stars so typical of Miró's work – making her a creature of nature and of the heavens as well.

And that's all we have time for this evening, I'm afraid. I hope that you've enjoyed this brief look at Miró's work and that you will enjoy the other lectures that follow this one. Thank you and good night.

Practice Test 2, Section 1 (Track 20)

MALE VOICE:	Hello Accommodation department, how can I help you?
MARIA:	er…do you look after accommodation for international students?
MALE VOICE:	Yes, we look after accommodation for all the students.
MARIA:	Good, I hope you can help me then, I've only just been accepted onto a post-graduate course and I want to know if there is any accommodation available from this September. I know it's very short notice.
MALE VOICE:	Mmmm, yes, it is rather late, but I'm sure we'll be able to find you something. First of all, can you give me your name and student number so that I can find you on the system
MARIA:	Sure, my name is Maria Teresa Gonzalez.
MALE VOICE:	Ma-ri-a……. Te…..re…..sa……Gonzalez…….How do you spell that?
MARIA:	<u>G-O-N-Z-A-L-E-Z.</u>
MALE VOICE:	Thank you……vil……a…….got it, and your student number please
MARIA:	<u>SHU300715PG</u>
MALE VOICE:	S-H-U-3-0-0-7-1-5-P-G…….ah! Here you are. Department of Modern <u>Languages</u>.
MARIA:	Yes, that's me.
MALE VOICE:	OK, now, there are several options for Post Graduate students. Firstly there is The Trigon. This is a new block near to the <u>station</u> and not far from the main campus. Accommodation is what we call 'cluster' accommodation.
MARIA:	What does that mean?
MALE VOICE:	There's a small group of rooms, usually 6, each with its own bathroom clustered around a lounge/kitchen area which is shared.

MARIA:	Oh, I see, that sounds good.
MALE VOICE:	They are very popular, the price for these is <u>£99 per week</u> and we do have some availability left. However for post graduate students there are other options.
MARIA:	And what are they?
MALE VOICE:	There is another apartment block called The Cube located near the <u>west</u> gate of the campus. Accommodation there is in 1 or 2 bedroom self-contained flats.
MARIA:	How does that work?
MALE VOICE:	Well, basically, they are just like ordinary apartments, each apartment has one or two <u>study bedrooms</u> with <u>ensuite bathroom</u>, a lounge and a <u>kitchen</u>.
MARIA:	And what is the price of those.
MALE VOICE:	For the one bedroom it is £180 per week and for the two-bedroom it is £110 per week for each person.
MARIA:	And can I choose who I share with?
MALE VOICE:	If you have a friend and you would like to share with then of course we can reserve a two bedroom apartment for you both. Otherwise you just have to share with whoever else is there. Obviously it will be another woman.
MARIA:	Mmmm, I will have to think about this, do I have to make a decision now?
MALE VOICE:	No, but we don't have much accommodation left so I can't guarantee that there will be still be availability if you leave it too long.
MARIA:	Yes, that's fair. I have a friend in the Management Department who might like to share. I will speak with her and get back to you this afternoon.
MALE VOICE:	OK, fine, do let us know as soon as you can.
MARIA:	I will do, thanks for all your help.
MALE VOICE:	My pleasure.
MARIA:	Bye
MALE VOICE:	Bye

Practice Test 2, Section 2 (Track 21)

First of all a warm welcome to Barkers' Country Safaris; we're delighted to have you all on board for this season. I know you've all been told a bit about the company when you had your job interview but I thought it would be worth telling you a bit more about ourselves.

Barkers was set up 10 years ago by myself, John and my then girlfriend and now wife, Nancy. We started it, initially, just has a hobby, we felt that there was a good opportunity to share our love of the countryside in this part of the world with the many visitors who come here. As you know, most people come for the beaches in the summer, but there is so much more to region and this is what we wanted to exploit.

Nancy and I were born near here and as teenagers we went climbing, kayaking, white-water rafting, pot-holing and just straight-forward walking. This district is in our blood and we love it!

While we were still at university we started taking small groups of visitors out into the National Park in Nancy's brother's old Land Rover. We'd drive them around the back lanes and into the forest. We'd also organise rock-climbing tours for friends of friends. Then, each year, without us having to advertise, people came back to us to ask for more excursions and trips.

So, 5 years ago we gave up our other jobs to focus full time on Barkers' Country Safaris. Two years after that we set up the activity tour part of the business and one year ago we expanded into organising activities for school groups during term time. Obviously, this was a massive challenge with all the health and safety requirements but it's proving a great success.

Anyway, we'll certainly not be dealing with school parties during the summer holidays. Our clients for the next 3 months are mostly family parties or groups of friends. And I'd like to talk a bit now about the tours we offer and what your responsibilities will be.

Our most popular excursion is the 'woodland tour and trail'. Often this is sold out and we have all of our 10 jeeps in convoy, with 8 people in each jeep, it's a lot of fun. These tours really offer a taster of what we can provide so as both driver and guide it is important that you do a good job here so they come back for the bigger tours. I will talk about the commission package later. As the summer days are so long we have 3 tours each day, but you will not be expected to work on more than two of them. Morning tours start at 8am and go to midday. Afternoon tours are from 2pm to 6pm and then evening ones, 7pm to 11pm. All the tours follow the same route and you should have made yourselves familiar with all the key information. This was provided to you in the information pack you were sent when you accepted the job offer. This is important so if you haven't had time yet, please do so now.

Our second most popular tour is the 'family exclusive'. This tour is for the whole day and for only one group. Usually it is just one jeep but sometimes there are two if the party is large. These tours go from 10am till 5pm and include lunch at The Brown Bear in Lower Middleton. We have a number of different routes for these tours as we don't want our premium clients being made to feel they are part of a large 'package' deal. You will be told which route to take with your weekly schedule.

Now, I'd like to move onto the speciality tour packages.....these are the ones that are keen to book people on once they have done the 'woodland tour and trail' trip...

Practice Test 2, Section 3 (Track 22)

MATTHEW:	Hey, Jess, glad you could make it, we've got a lot to discuss.
JESSICA:	Hi Matt, yes, sorry I'm a bit late, I did bring all my notes with me.
MATTHEW:	Yes, me too. Where shall we start?
JESSICA:	Well, I think it would be a good idea to <u>clarify our objectives just one more time</u>.
MATTHEW:	Yes, Good idea......OK, here we are....<u>we need to record, photograph and identify the plant species</u> in ten, one square meter plots.
JESSICA:	Does it say anything about where these plots should be and how they should be laid out?
MATTHEW:	ah.....here it is. It says that all the plots need to be <u>no more than 10 metres apart</u>......
JESSICA:	and how do we choose them?
MATTHEW:	Ah, this is the fun bit. I remember this......here we are "Make a one meter square frame, using bamboo sticks <u>available from the department stores</u>"....
JESSICA:	Yes,....we've already done that...
MATTHEW:	I know, I'm just reading the whole section.
JESSICA:	OK
MATTHEW:	...One person stands roughly in the middle of the chosen are and throws the frame. <u>The other person uses a tape to mark out the square where the frame landed</u> and returns frame to thrower. The thrower then turns a few degrees on the spot and throws again. The thrower must turn slightly after each throw and vary the force of the throw until after the 10th throw they are pointing in almost the same direction as the first."
JESSICA:	<u>That sounds a bit complicated.</u>
MATTHEW:	<u>That's only because it's all in writing</u>. It's just a simple throw, turn, throw, turn, throw turn until we have 10 squares.
JESSICA:	And I guess you want to do the throwing......
MATTHEW:	Well if you don't mind. I'm sure you'll be more accurate at marking the squares.
JESSICA:	Yes, I'm sure I am and <u>I'm sure you've got a stronger throwing arm</u>!
MATTHEW:	Ok, good, we've got that sorted, now we need to decide where to go.
JESSICA:	Yes, I've been thinking about that, and I've brought the map.

MATTHEW:	Oh well, done I forgot mine
JESSICA:	Now, I've identified three possible locations, but they've all got some disadvantages.
MATTHEW:	OK, fire away....
JESSICA:	Well, the area around this <u>lowland marsh</u> could be interesting, there'll be a lot of interesting water plants here.
MATTHEW:	Looks good, but what's the problem.
JESSICA:	Mainly that it's already a designated nature reserve and I think there's already been a lot of research done here.
MATTHEW:	Ahhh, I see, well, <u>I'd rather do something that's new and can be useful</u>.
JESSICA:	I agree, that's why I identified this area further west, see here......<u>behind the beach</u>.....
MATTHEW:	Oh yes, I see, that area there, where it's flat but quite high.
JESSICA:	Exactly. If you look a bit further inland you'll see that there are hills which will protect that area from the strong north winds.
MATTHEW:	I see. Excellent. But what's the problem?
JESSICA:	<u>Just that it may not be very interesting</u>. We know that the geology there is not conducive to a wide variety of plants.
MATTHEW:	Mmmmm, I agree. So what's your last idea?
JESSICA:	Well, I think this one is a bit of a winner, although I did want to show you the other two. Look here up on the north coast...
MATTHEW:	Where...?
JESSICA:	<u>See, this bay</u>? Well I know that there's been quite a lot of studies done here, <u>but a bit further to the east, behind this headland</u>, ...no one has ever looked at that. Well I certainly couldn't see any studies.
MATTHEW:	That is interesting.....and the plant life could be a bit different because of the shelter from the wind the headland provides.
JESSICA:	Exactly.
MATTHEW:	Brilliant, Jessica......That's a great idea. <u>We'll go there</u>.
JESSICA:	Thanks.....Now all we have to decide is when is a good time
MATTHEW:	Well.......

Practice Test 2, Section 4 (Track 23)

Now, I'd like to move on to talk about something called geo-tourism. Geo-tourism is, very basically leveraging the benefits of tourism for local communities. I would just like to give you a couple of statistics, which are very illustrative of the current situation with regard to young travellers and international tourism. Firstly, <u>tourism has an impact on more people worldwide than any other industry</u>. Indeed it has an impact on one in every two people, either directly or indirectly. The second statistic is that <u>in global tourism there is a 97% economic leakage</u>. This means that if you spend £100 on going on holiday, normally only £3 of that money will actually reach the people who are giving you the services, the accommodation etc in the destination. If you put these two figures together you can understand why <u>some of the regions of the world which have very high levels of tourism still have very high levels of poverty and huge developmental challenges</u>. These countries have this massive industry demanding a huge number of services but <u>they are not seeing a fair reward for these services. Geo-tourism is about changing this</u>.

Projects are now being developed with financial organisations such as the World Bank. One of these involves developing a technology platform which is bringing grass-root travel products – hotels, locally owned hotels, not global chains, very locally owned tour operators, to the international travel market will <u>avoiding the middle men</u>. These middle men often cut them out of the market completely or just make their business unsustainable.

Another way that geo-tourism can be promoted is through the niche travel market of volunteering. These days a significant number of older teenagers want to <u>spend a 'gap year'</u>, either between school and university or university and employment. Often these people want to spend some or all of their year volunteering but they either don't have the money or don't feel inclined to pay the main 'volunteering organisation businesses' the fees they require, which can be <u>as high as thirty-five hundred pounds</u>. What they are looking for is an organisation who can connect them with people "on the ground" who can suggest <u>worthwhile local projects</u>. So, this is a real win-win scenario. The organisers <u>charge a small flat fee</u>, which then goes to the local contact. Thus, the local contact gets <u>a very good commission just for one customer</u>. The customer is also saving a large amount of money and time both of which they can give to the projects they end up working on.

There is still quite a long way to go before poverty in the most popular of tourist areas is eradicated but a focus on this type of Geo-tourism could provide an answer…

Practice Test 3, Section 1 (Track 24)

EMPLOYEE:	GB Airlines, this is Kyle speaking. How can I help?
CUSTOMER:	Hi, my name is Matt Walsh. I'm calling on behalf of Mr <u>John Sparrow</u> to claim expenses for a delay in his flight last week.
EMPLOYEE:	Good morning, Mr Walsh. Thank you for calling. Could you please tell me the flight number and the date of departure?
CUSTOMER:	The date of departure was the <u>24th of January</u>, 2016. I'm afraid I don't have the flight number in front of me at the moment.

EMPLOYEE:	OK, that's all right. One moment. [typing] Could you tell me, where was Mr Sparrow departing from?
CUSTOMER:	He was departing from Athens.
EMPLOYEE:	Is that Athens, Greece or Athens, Georgia?
CUSTOMER:	<u>Athens, Greece</u>.
EMPLOYEE:	Right. And what was the destination?
CUSTOMER:	It was Heathrow, London.
EMPLOYEE:	Right. We've got two flights from Athens to London Heathrow on the 24th of January, 2016. Was it the 3:25 p.m. flight, or the 9:45 p.m.?
CUSTOMER:	It was the later one, <u>9:45</u>.
EMPLOYEE:	OK, so the flight number is GB1011.
CUSTOMER:	Right, OK.
EMPLOYEE:	OK, yes. I can see that Mr Sparrow's flight was cancelled, and he was booked on the next flight on the 25th of January, at 3:25 p.m. Is that correct?
CUSTOMER:	Yes, that is correct.
EMPLOYEE:	According to our system, one of my colleagues spoke with Mr Sparrow on the phone on the 24th to inform him of the cancellation, and offered to book a hotel for him for the night, but Mr Sparrow preferred to book one himself.
CUSTOMER:	Yes, because he didn't want to stay near the airport as the next flight was in the afternoon.
EMPLOYEE:	Yes, of course. Could you tell me which hotel he stayed at?
CUSTOMER:	Yes. He stayed at the <u>Hypnos</u> Hotel.
EMPLOYEE:	Could you spell that for me?
CUSTOMER:	Of course. That's H-Y-P-N-O-S.
EMPLOYEE:	Right, thank you for that. And could you please tell me how much the total cost was for the night?
CUSTOMER:	Sure, it was 73 euros.
EMPLOYEE:	Right. Do you have a copy of the receipt for that?
CUSTOMER:	Yes, of course. Would you like me to send it to you?
EMPLOYEE:	Yes, please.
CUSTOMER:	Can I email a picture of it to you?
EMPLOYEE:	Absolutely. The email address is refunds@gbairlines.co.uk.
CUSTOMER:	Great, thank you.

EMPLOYEE:	No problem. Were there any other expenses you wish to claim?
CUSTOMER:	Actually, yes. There was also the taxi ride to the airport, and the taxi ride back the next day.
EMPLOYEE:	Right, and what was the total cost?
CUSTOMER:	Uhm, the first taxi ride was 53 euros and the second one was 42, so… 63, 73, 83… Yeah, so the total was 95 euros. I'll send you the receipt for those as well.
EMPLOYEE:	Thank you. Are there any other expenses?
CUSTOMER:	No, I think that's it.
EMPLOYEE:	Excellent. So, if you could please send us the receipts for the hotel and the taxi rides, and after we receive them it should take about 48 hours for the funds to reach Mr Sparrow's account.
CUSTOMER:	Perfect, thank you very much.
EMPLOYEE:	My pleasure. Is there anything else I can help you with?
CUSTOMER:	Actually, yes, there's one more thing. Um, Mr Sparrow complained about the meal during the flight. He said that it was a bit…bland.
EMPLOYEE:	Right.
CUSTOMER:	So he asked me if it was possible to switch to a different meal option for his upcoming flight to Kiev next week.
EMPLOYEE:	Right, of course. Just give me a minute, please. [typing] Right, I see that Mr Sparrow had the light meal option for his flight to London, and you would like to change that. What would you like to change it to?
CUSTOMER:	What are the other options?
EMPLOYEE:	We've got twelve different meal options. Would you like me to list all of them for you?
CUSTOMER:	Well, Mr Sparrow has told me that he would prefer something without meat, so…how many of these do not contain meat?
EMPLOYEE:	We've got three meal options without meat: we've got the vegetarian option, the vegan option, and the Asian vegetarian.
CUSTOMER:	What's the difference?
EMPLOYEE:	There's a variety of different dishes served with each option. For example, next week the vegetarian option will be a small spinach and feta cheese pie, a bread roll, a salad, and tropical fruit.
CUSTOMER:	And the vegan option?

EMPLOYEE:	The vegan option doesn't include any <u>dairy products</u>, and it also doesn't include fowl, eggs, or honey. I'm afraid I don't have the specific menu for this week, but I can email it to you as soon as it becomes available.
CUSTOMER:	Oh, could you do that? That would be great.
EMPLOYEE:	Yes, of course. I can email you a detailed description of all the meal options, if you like.
CUSTOMER:	Yes, please.
EMPLOYEE:	No problem. Please do not forget to call us back to change the meal option. You need to do that 48 hours before the departure time for international flights, and 24 hours for domestic flights.
CUSTOMER:	So, 48 hours for this one, then?
EMPLOYEE:	Yes, exactly.
CUSTOMER:	Perfect.
EMPLOYEE:	No, I'm sorry. Um, *transatlantic* flights require 48 hours. All flights within Europe require 24 hours, so in this case you will need to call us <u>24 hours</u> in advance. I apologise for that.
CUSTOMER:	OK, great.
EMPLOYEE:	So, could I please have your email address so I can send you the menus?
CUSTOMER:	Certainly. It's matt.walsh@sparrowltd.com...

Practice Test 3, Section 2 (Track 25)

RADIO PRESENTER:	And here with us today we have Patricia Abaddon, author of the best-selling book *Beginners' Guide to Self-Publishing* and owner of the self-publishing company *Make A Book*.
PATRICIA:	Hello.
RADIO PRESENTER:	Hello, Patricia. Now, I know a lot of our listeners are interested in self-publishing their novels, but they don't know where to start. As a successful self-published author, what would you say are some of the pitfalls they'd need to avoid?
PATRICIA:	I'm glad you asked that, Mark. The thing is that with the e-book revolution that started in the early 2000s, we experienced a shift in the literary market

and suddenly aspiring writers didn't have to rely on agents and traditional publishers any more to get the opportunity to publish their books. But just because we *can* publish, does that mean we should? For me, there are four questions that each writer needs to ask themselves before they attempt to join the market.

The first question is, is my book ready? One of the *biggest* mistakes new writers do is that they get *so* excited with the prospect of publishing their book that they rush through the process and they don't bother with technicalities such as <u>thorough editing</u>. And they should, because editing is about 50% of the final product. It's not as glamorous as the process of actually creating the story, but it's just as important. <u>The final product needs to be immaculate</u>—not just in terms of grammar, but also in terms of plotting, characterisation…and even spelling.

Secondly: do I understand the market? Unless you're publishing just for your friends and family, you need to have <u>a sound marketing strategy</u>. The beauty of self–publishing is that anyone can do it, but that also means that you're fighting for attention against millions of other titles. Do you know what sets your book apart? Do you understand who your audience is, and how you're going to reach them? Do you have a solid presence in social media? In general, do you know how you're going to sell the book to people?

The third question, and I hope I don't sound too pragmatic, is: <u>have I worked out how much money I'm willing to spend</u>? This extends beyond the cost of self–publishing itself, obviously. There's the cost of advertising, the cost of proofreading and copyediting, the cost of giving away free copies to reviewers, and let's not forget the cost of a professionally done cover. The truth is that the more you see your book as an investment, the more of a return you're going to get—but either way, you need to know what your <u>available funds</u> are.

And the final thing! The final thing is something most writers overlook, but it's just as important as the other three: <u>have I started my next project yet</u>?

Remember, one book is never going to make you rich, and it's never going to make you famous. If you want to succeed, you need to keep writing and keep publishing as many books as you can. That's how you build an audience, and how you get your book to the top of the charts.

RADIO PRESENTER: Thank you, Patricia. So, tell us: how did *you* do it? You started publishing five years ago, and now you have your own publishing company. How did you get here so fast?

PATRICIA: To be honest with you, the first book I ever published was a <u>flop</u>, and it was because I didn't follow almost any of the rules I just told you. My novel was poorly edited, it had a cheap–looking self–made cover, and I had no idea how to get people to buy it. For about a year, <u>I checked its dismal sales every month and I wallowed in self–pity</u>. But then I decided it was time to change, and do something.

The first thing I did was get a subscription to all the writing magazines I could find out there. I read them all from cover to cover, and <u>followed the experts' advice as if it was gospel</u>. I wrote almost every single day, and I submitted short stories to every competition I could find out there. I also started a blog, and I set up my own page. Over time, I started building a name for myself, and a solid fan base.

I didn't want to be associated with my first book, so I decided to publish my next book under a <u>different name</u>. This time I sought professional help with editing, and I spent months working on it until it was ready. I also sought the advice of friends who worked in marketing and tech–savvy friends, who helped me come up with a marketing plan. Since I already had a platform—my website and my <u>social media</u> pages—, it was much easier to reach the people who would be interested in reading my book. And, of course, while all of this was happening, I was also in the middle of my next novel, which I planned to have <u>ready for editing</u> by the time the previous one was out. So, yeah, I published my second book about two

	years after my first, and it was a completely different experience. And now here I am.
RADIO PRESENTER:	Thank you very much, Patricia. I'm sure our listeners have been inspired by your…

Practice Test 3, Section 3 (Track 26)

GALE:	Hey, guys.
LINDSAY:	Oh, hey Gale! You made it.
GALE:	Yeah, sorry, I was stuck at the library paying late fees. Have you guys started going through the data yet?
KEVIN:	Yeah, we've already collated it, and we've started designing the graphs we're going to use in the presentation.
GALE:	Oh, really? That's fast!
LINDSAY:	Well, anyway, here's what we've got so far.
GALE:	OK, so… Wow, <u>38% said they'd thought about quitting school</u> in the first year? That's a huge number.
KEVIN:	Yeah, and only <u>10% said they were happy at school</u> from beginning to end. Amazing, isn't it?
GALE:	Yeah, I thought the majority would be happy here.
LINDSAY:	Well, just remember that about 30% of the school population are foreign students, and from the UK students, only 2% are actually from the area, so… I guess it makes sense that people would miss home.
GALE:	Yeah, but to want to actually quit school…
KEVIN:	Well, they didn't *want* to, exactly. They just thought about it.
GALE:	OK. So, how should we organise the presentation? What did you guys decide?
LINDSAY:	Well, Kevin and I were saying that we should start by explaining what the topic of our research was, and how we decided to collect the data. So <u>I'll start by saying that our topic was how first–year students felt a month after beginning school, and how their attitudes progressed and changed by the end of the academic year.</u>
KEVIN:	So, then we were thinking that <u>I should explain that the population we want to study was obviously first–year students,</u> but because we need their complete experience from the beginning to the end of their first year, we'd have to actually poll students in their second and third year. And then we said that you should explain how we accessed the population.

GALE:	So <u>I'll say that we got the permission from the school to go to different classes from different departments and hand out the surveys in paper form</u>. Right?
LINDSAY:	Right, and that it took us about three weeks to complete this part of our research.
KEVIN:	So, then we need to describe the <u>three different areas of focus of our survey, so Lindsay can do that</u>: say that the survey had three sections, the first one asking just some general questions about the age, gender, nationality, and field of study of each student—then the second one focused on how they felt in their first six months at school, and the third how they felt in the summer, after their first year was complete.
GALE:	That sounds good. OK, so let me see the breakdown. OK, so we've got an equal distribution of boys and girls, that's good.
LINDSAY:	<u>Almost equal</u>. 51% of the participants were boys, the rest were girls.
GALE:	Right, and 70% of the participants were British, while the other 30% were…
KEVIN:	10% were from America and Asia, 2% were from Africa, and 18% were European. We had a small number of Australians as well, 0.03%, so I guess Europeans were <u>17.97</u>% if you want to be precise.
LINDSAY:	Which we should. Anyway, and obviously the age was all 20 or 21, with a few 19–year–olds—only about 5%. No, wait. 4%. Right?
KEVIN:	No, it's <u>5%</u>, look.
GALE:	Right. OK, so Lindsay will describe the three sections, and then you Kevin, you'll describe the demographic and geographical breakdown, and I…
KEVIN:	You can start with the graph, and then we'll all explain the data together.
GALE:	Right, so we'll put this graph up on the board and explain that most students experienced some form of homesickness or <u>mild depression</u> in the beginning of their course.
LINDSAY:	But we need to point out that by the end of the year it was only 5% that still felt like quitting school.
GALE:	Yeah, but remember that we didn't actually have the opportunity to interview or poll any of the students who *left* school—so the information we have only relates to current students, and those numbers might be bigger in reality.
LINDSAY:	Yeah, I guess we need to mention that. But we did check the <u>drop–out rate</u> for the last two years and it was very low so, at the end of the day, the numbers can't be much bigger.

KEVIN: Yeah. Anyway, so after we explain the data and we show the three graphs with the background information and the responses for six months and one year, we should spend some time also talking about…

Practice Test 3, Section 4 (Track 27)

Those of you who were here last week will remember that we talked about the journey of the English language from its early Indo–European origins through to Old English, Middle English, and then to Early and Late Modern English before it reached the form that it has today. Today we will be continuing that theme by focusing on the future of the English language, and all the places it might go from here.

There are about 2.1 billion people around the world who can speak English. Out of these, only 400 million are native speakers—which means that 4 in 5 English speakers are non–natives. This is obviously quite an impressive number, considering that just two centuries ago, in 1801, there were only about 20 million speakers of English around the world, and languages like French and German were ahead of English in terms of how many people were using them. But what does it mean?

What it means is that the future of the English language doesn't really depend on its native speakers, but on that massive number of non–native speakers learning it around the world. Has anyone heard of the term "pidgin" before, or "creole"? A pidgin is a simplified version of a language which acts as a bridge between two people who don't have a common language, allowing them to communicate with each other, while a creole is a language that evolves from a pidgin—with the difference that it is fully formed, with clear grammatical rules and vocabulary. There are currently dozens of pidgin and creole languages based on English around the world, for example Nigerian Pidgin or Jamaican Patois. These languages are also known as "Englishes".

What's interesting about these "Englishes" is how different they sound to, for lack of a better term, "proper" English. Take the word "trousers", for instance: in Sheng, which is a Kenyan creole language, they're called "longi"—because they're long.

But even versions of English that are recognised as official variations or dialects still differ greatly from each other. Americans and Jamaicans would call the back of a car where you store your luggage the "trunk"; Britons, Australians, Canadians and other Commonwealth countries would call it the "boot". A subway in the UK is a tunnel under a road that allows pedestrians to cross safely; in the US, it's an underground train. You might think of these differences as minute, but when you take into account the dozens of different versions of English out there, a very intriguing parallel arises, with another language from the past: Latin.

Latin, too, used to be a lingua franca. Nowadays it's all but dead, spoken only by a few clerics and scholars. At some point in history it splintered into various different languages, which became known as Romance languages, for example Spanish, Italian, or French. There are some that theorise that the same thing might happen to English in the near or distant future; that all these "Englishes" we have today in different countries will continue to develop, so pidgins will turn into creole languages, and creole languages will turn into just languages, and English itself as we know it today will disappear, or become less and less important.

It's an interesting theory, if nothing else. It makes sense that as English grows in popularity, countries—especially those with a strong sense of identity and tradition—will develop their own versions of the language, marked by the idiosyncrasies of their culture. Just think of the contribution of dialects such as <u>Jamaican or South African English. In the past fifty years alone, they've added about 25,000 words to the English language, most of these related to a local context that wouldn't have existed in English before the spread of colonialism</u>. In terms of numbers, just those are enough for a brand new language.

There are some flaws to this theory too, however. While it's true that Latin and English have a lot of similarities in terms of how they developed, or have developed, throughout history, there is one big difference: we currently live in an era of globalisation. Today, you can be in India and stream an American film or TV series in seconds. You can be in Nigeria, and listen to British music. You can be in Brazil, and read a novel from an Australian author. Just a few centuries ago, this was unthinkable.

So what's the other way that English could go? According to some experts, there is the possibility that it could maintain its status as the world's global language, but with a few differences. Already today most conversations in English occur between non–native speakers. While many of these might be fluent, the majority probably have only an intermediate understanding of the language, devoid of the nuances, colloquialisms and complex collocations that native speakers employ in their interactions. <u>This means that, over time, English could turn into some sort of Worldspeak—the official lingua franca for the entire world, but in a simplified form</u>. Some scholars have even started trying to develop that version of English, by selecting the most useful words in the English vocabulary for non–native speakers to learn. Robert McCrum has compiled a comprehensive list of 1,500 words, for example—a version of English that he calls "Globish". And what about traditional, native–speaker English? It might continue to exist, but lose its popularity—as the previous theory suggests.

There are many more theories about the future of the English language, of course. I've only focused on the two main ones, because they clearly demonstrate our uncertainty when it comes to how this beautiful language will develop. <u>English is in a unique, unprecedented position; no other language has achieved the same levels of popularity in human history, especially in terms of non–native speakers</u>. So, as this is clearly uncharted territory, only time will be able to tell us what will happen.

Practice Test 4, Section 1 (Track 28)

EMPLOYEE:	Pet Protect UK, how can I help?
CUSTOMER:	Oh, hello, there. I'm calling to inquire about your pet insurance plans.
EMPLOYEE:	Of course, just give me a second, please.
CUSTOMER:	Sure.
EMPLOYEE:	So, have you checked our website already to see the options we offer?
CUSTOMER:	I've had a quick glance, and I think I'm interested in the Basic Plan.
EMPLOYEE:	Great. I just need to ask a few questions first, then. Is your pet a dog, a cat or a rabbit?
CUSTOMER:	It's a dog.
EMPLOYEE:	And is it a puppy, or…?
CUSTOMER:	No, he's three years old.
EMPLOYEE:	Right. May I ask, has your dog been insured before?
CUSTOMER:	I just adopted him from the rescue centre last week and I think he'd been there a while, so I doubt it.
EMPLOYEE:	OK. So you've had him for a week, then.
CUSTOMER:	That's correct.
EMPLOYEE:	Great. I apologise for asking this, but your dog… What's his name, by the way?
CUSTOMER:	Fenton.
EMPLOYEE:	Fenton. Is that spelled with an F?
CUSTOMER:	Yeah, F–E–N–T–O–N.
EMPLOYEE:	Great, thank you for that. So, according to the rescue centre, has Fenton ever attacked, bitten or been aggressive towards a person or another animal?
CUSTOMER:	No, not at all.
EMPLOYEE:	Excellent. And is he a guide dog, or…?
CUSTOMER:	No, just a house pet.
EMPLOYEE:	Great. And you said he's three years old. Do you know the exact date of birth?
CUSTOMER:	Oh, yes, it's on the adoption certificate. Just give me a sec. Um, it's May 19th, 2013.
EMPLOYEE:	And do you know, has Fenton been neutered?

CUSTOMER:	Yes, he's been castrated.
EMPLOYEE:	Excellent. And final question, what type of dog is Fenton? Is he a pedigree, a crossbreed or a mixed breed?
CUSTOMER:	A crossbreed, I think.
EMPLOYEE:	Right. Cross…breed…
CUSTOMER:	Wait, sorry. What's the difference between the three?
EMPLOYEE:	A pedigree is a dog whose parents are of the same breed. A crossbreed is from two different breeds, while a mixed breed is three or more.
CUSTOMER:	Then he's a mixed breed. Sorry about that.
EMPLOYEE:	Right, no worries. So, could I take your full name, please?
CUSTOMER:	My name is Peter Pischinger. That's P–I–S–C–H–I–N–G–E–R.
EMPLOYEE:	Right, thank you for that. And your address?
CUSTOMER:	That's 27 Cherry Drive, NW8 3HD.
EMPLOYEE:	3…H…D… And finally a telephone number, please?
CUSTOMER:	020 3634 7957.
EMPLOYEE:	Thank you. Now, you said you were interested in the Basic Plan, is that correct?
CUSTOMER:	Yes, that's correct.
EMPLOYEE:	May I ask, are you planning to switch insurance providers after the first year of your pet insurance, or is there a possibility you might renew with us?
CUSTOMER:	I haven't really thought about it. Why?
EMPLOYEE:	The reason I'm asking is because if you plan to renew with us, it might be worth considering our Premium or Ultimate Premium plan. With the basic plan you will have to pay the same fee of £8 per month regardless of how long you stay with us. If you choose one of our other two plans, though, you will receive a discount for the first six months—you'll only have to pay £12 for Premium and £15 for Ultimate—, and then depending on your circumstances you might be eligible for further discounts after your first year, depending on how many expenses you claim. If you claim less than £300, you'll have to pay the same as for the Basic plan, but receive the cover provided by the Premium plan.
CUSTOMER:	Huh.
EMPLOYEE:	Is that something you might be interested in?

CUSTOMER:	I'll have to think about it. Is it possible to switch to one of the other plans later on?
EMPLOYEE:	Yes, of course; you can always upgrade.
CUSTOMER:	Let's stick to the basic plan for now, then, and then I might call you back to switch.
EMPLOYEE:	No problem.
CUSTOMER:	So, what happens now?
EMPLOYEE:	Well, first we would need you to come over with little Fenton so we can have a look at his documents and medical history. We'd also need you to get him to the vet for a quick check–up, all of this is standard procedure before we can proceed with the insurance plan, and then when all that's done you can either set up a direct debit in person or you can call us back and do it over the phone.
CUSTOMER:	Right. And the basic plan will cover...
EMPLOYEE:	Well, the basic plan covers veterinary fees, obviously, plus a few more things such as boarding costs, loss by theft or straying, advertising and reward, death by accident or illness... You can find a comprehensive list on our website, or I could forward it to you via email if you prefer.
CUSTOMER:	Thanks, I'll check the website.
EMPLOYEE:	No problem. So, shall we book you an appointment so you can come over...

Practice Test 4, Section 2 (Track 29)

Good morning everyone, and welcome to Climb Summer School. Now, I know most of you have travelled a long way to get here and you're probably looking forward to settling into your rooms, so I promise I won't keep you long, but we've got to get through this very brief induction just to make your stay here as pleasurable as possible.

Now, as you can see, while we're located very close to the centre of London, we're actually quite cut off from the main road, and we've got plenty of space for our facilities and our students. This was part of our founder's vision, Jasmine Climb, who thought that the best environment for teenage students would be a place that combines the comforts of a big, cosmopolitan city with the beauty and serenity of a quiet, remote site. Now, back in 1983 when our school was founded, this all here was an abandoned warehouse, and classes were held in the main building that you can see over there. There were no trees, no conifers surrounding the property, there wasn't even a main gate! It took years and a great deal of effort to get our school to where it is today, and I'm sure that if you take a look at page 34 in your brochures, where you can find a picture of what the school used to look like back then, you'll agree that the changes we've made are more than impressive.

But it's not just the facilities that make Climb Summer School special, obviously, and I'm certain you already know this. Over the following <u>ten weeks</u>, you'll receive an assortment of classes on a variety of topics ranging from language, literature and poetry to creative writing, communication, and project management. All of these modules have been designed to improve your chances of getting a place in the universities of your choice while also giving you the opportunity to learn, excel, and of course also socialise with people from all over the world. I can tell you, just among the thirty of you, we've got about 21 different nationalities.

So, what happens now? First of all, I'll be handing out a map of the premises for you to have a look at, and explaining where everything is. Once we're done here, you'll all be taken to your rooms where you can unpack and relax for a couple of hours, and later on we'll be having our first activity of the day, a mix–and–match lunch in the main hall where you'll have the chance to meet your new classmates. Later on in the afternoon we'll be handing out your first project assignments and splitting you into teams, and tonight we'll be having our very first <u>film night</u>, starting with an early 20th century special.

So, let's get on with the map. You've already got a version of it in your brochures, so if you can open them to the last page so we can have a look…? Very well. As I showed you before, the actual school is right over there in the middle. That's where you'll be having most of your classes. Adjacent to it you'll find the <u>main hall</u>, which is where we'll be hosting most events, such as today's lunch.

On the left from the main building you'll find a smaller building, which is where the accommodation and welfare offices are located. This is labelled as the <u>Garden Office</u> at the front, and it's easy to spot because it has a green door.

Each of you is assigned to a different residence hall. We've got three residence halls in total, one on the left and two on the right. The one right next to the garden office is Ursula Hall, named after our founder's sister, while the other two are <u>Peter</u> Hall and William Hall.

Now as you can see there are three more buildings to the left of the semi–circle here, and one more building on the right–hand side next to William Hall. So that one, which is shaped a bit like a dome, is the <u>Pavilion</u>. This is where all of your letters will be delivered, and in the basement floor you'll also find a laundrette—please make sure you've got plenty of £1 coins, as you'll need one for the washing machine and another for the dryer.

And that row of buildings on the left, the one closest to us here at the gate is the <u>canteen</u>, where you'll be able to buy snacks, as well as breakfast, lunch and dinner on days when we don't have an event with food provided. The next one is the gym, which is open from 7 a.m. to 8 p.m. from Monday to Friday and until 10 p.m. at the weekend, and the last building, right over there, is the <u>study centre</u>, where you'll find plenty of computers and books, as well as a great selection of DVDs and magazines that you can borrow with only a small, refundable deposit of £5.

Now, please remember to keep your student card with you at all times, as you'll need it to access most of these facilities, and…

Practice Test 4, Section 3 (Track 30)

LECTURER:	James, Carol, thank you for coming in. Have a seat. So, I take it both of you have completed your interviews with the managers?
JAMES, CAROL:	Yeah.
LECTURER:	Right. Great. Remind me, who was supposed to do the interview with the manager from the <u>chain supermarket</u>?
JAMES:	That was me.
LECTURER:	Right, so that means you were going to do the interview with the <u>clothes shop</u>, Carol, right?
CAROL:	Yeah, but we decided to swap in the last minute so I did the supermarket instead.
LECTURER:	OK, so let's start with you first, Carol. If I remember correctly, you reported that your interviewee was difficult to get through to, is that right?
CAROL:	Yeah, he had a <u>very busy schedule</u> so it was hard for him to fit me in and show me around the store and everything. We had to reschedule about three times before I finally managed to do the interview with him.
LECTURER:	And how was it for you, James?
JAMES:	Oh, I had no issues at all. I just went in on a weekday and the shop was empty, so we did it right there and then.
LECTURER:	Great. So, Carol, how did you find the management scheme? Let's start with how they recruit their trainees.
CAROL:	So, according to the manager, the way it works is that graduates go through a <u>rigorous recruitment</u> process that includes an interview with a panel and a trial day. Then they have to go through a probationary period of three months, and if their performance is satisfactory during those three months, they're offered a place in the scheme.
LECTURER:	And yours, James?

CAROL:	Well, it's quite similar to Carol's actually, the only differences are that they're on probation for <u>six months</u>, and there are three individual interviews instead of a panel. Oh, and you don't need to be a graduate—sometimes they recruit people internally for the scheme, if their performance suggests they could be a good fit for it.
LECTURER:	OK. And how about the training offered? Carol?
CAROL:	It's all very <u>on–the–job</u>. Trainees start at the bottom as shelf stockers or delivery merchandisers, then they slowly move up the ranks by becoming cashiers, shift supervisors, assistant managers and, finally, managers. It's actually very similar to what any employee would have to go through if they wanted to become managers; the only difference is the time scale. The whole process would normally take more than five years, but in the scheme they cram it down to three.
LECTURER:	Right. James?
JAMES:	Well, again, very similar to Carol's. The only thing is that there's also plenty of external training involved; people on the management scheme are sent abroad for six months, usually to <u>Italy or France</u>, to witness first–hand the production of a new season's collection. So they spend some time with the designers, and they tour the factories where the clothes are produced. They also receive training on management skills through college courses paid for by the company.
LECTURER:	And how long would it normally take someone on the scheme to become managers?
JAMES:	It depends on their performance, but normally about two years. There's also the part–time option, though, which would take about four. […] No, sorry, <u>five</u> because their probation period is a year instead of six months.
LECTURER:	Great. So, what was your overall impression of the scheme from your interviews with the managers?
CAROL:	Well, the manager I spoke to was very friendly and incredibly knowledgeable. He'd been through the scheme himself and he attested to its efficiency and helpfulness. The only criticism I'd have is what James said—in their company there's almost no <u>external training</u> involved and I think it would be useful to send graduates to courses at further education colleges to improve their general knowledge and understanding of management skills. But overall, yes, very positive.

LECTURER:	Great. And you, James?
JAMES:	The same as Carol, the manager I spoke to was incredibly friendly and eager to promote her scheme. She hadn't actually gone through it herself, but she was very involved in the process, both in training and in recruitment. She's actually on of the three people who do the interviews for the new trainees. And I really like the structure with the classes at college, I think that's very useful and it improves the trainees' chances of getting another job eventually, should they decide to leave the company in the future. The only thing I have to say against it is that two years is <u>too short</u> in my opinion—it should really be closer to three years, as I imagine the trainees would get exhausted fairly quickly with all this information fired at them in such a short span of time.
LECTURER:	Thank you both. So now you know you need to compare your two interviews and decide which scheme would be most beneficial to someone from a disadvantaged background, especially those who...

Practice Test 4, Section 4 (Track 31)

Good evening. As I assume most of you are already aware, I have been asked to come here and talk to you, essentially give you a quick overview of the life of a foreign correspondent, along with a few tips on how to become a successful international reporter yourself, should this be a career choice you elect to pursue.

So, let me start by this: don't. Don't become a foreign correspondent. At least not due to the <u>romantic notions</u> that come attached to this job, or what you've seen in the movies. Being a foreign correspondent does not mean exotic adventures. It doesn't mean finding yourself at the heart of the action and putting yourself in danger to inform the world. Let me just tell you this: <u>80 journalists</u> are killed each year in the line of duty. Many more find themselves in prison, or are attacked. You need to think hard: is this the sort of career I want? Is this the kind of reporting I'm interested in? And only after you've carefully considered all the pros and cons should you decide.

But let's focus on those of you who believe that, yes, you've got what it takes to be a foreign correspondent, and this is definitely why you decided to study journalism here. You're all third–year students, which means I don't need to waste my time telling you the basics. Of course you need to <u>read a lot</u>—books, novels, newspapers, blogs—, and of course you need to be acceptably proficient in various media skills. But what is it that's going to separate you from normal journalists and reporters?

There are four things that'll make you different. The first thing is, your experience of the world. You can't call yourself an international reporter unless you've been around and seen different places and different cultures. Seize every opportunity to visit other countries, meet people from around the world. It doesn't matter if it's business or leisure, just hop onto a plane and go everywhere. This will expand your horizons and sharpen your mind—something that, as a foreign correspondent, will help you understand better the culture of the country you'll be covering.

And speaking of culture: this is a term you need to make sure you fully understand. What's culture? What makes a country's culture? Explore the culture of the country you're interested in, the music, the literature, the religion. Are there any cultural practices or conflicts you need to be aware of? Are there any tensions within the country? Why?

The most important element of culture, of course, is the language. Do yourselves a favour, whether you're planning to become foreign correspondents or not: learn a foreign language. So many of us are culpable for sticking to just English, and while English is a very important language in the world, and it would be foolish to think it's the only one. Pick a language whose sound you enjoy, a language you find interesting. Trust me: your future CV will thank you for it.

And, finally, history. Don't expect to be given a job as a foreign correspondent if you don't know anything about your target country's history. No piece of news is disconnected from the past; the whole world tells a story, and your coverage will suffer if you attempt to arrive in the middle, with no reference to or understanding of what came before. The hows and whys always lurk in the past; seek them.

Now, there's something else you need to understand. The world of international journalism is changing, like every other industry, due to the Internet. The arrival of globalisation brought with it a whole new set of rules, and you'll do well to comprehend what they mean for you. Unfortunately, gone are the days when a newspaper would hire you and deploy you to a country. Increasingly newspapers around the world are beginning to favour freelance journalism, offering opportunities to local reporters with the necessary chutzpah and an understanding of the zeitgeist in their region. What this means for you is that you won't just have to start at the bottom; if you want to sustain yourself as an international reporter, you'll also have to pursue many different avenues at once. You'll need to persevere and push and build contacts everywhere.

An old student of mine, a terrible student at university but an incredibly intelligent woman, she came to find me at a conference that was recently held in Yemen, where I delivered a speech on the future of journalism. She was working for three different newspapers as a freelance foreign correspondent, one of them *The Times*, and she told me that the one piece of advice I gave her that stayed with her and helped her with her career was this: don't be afraid to fail. It will happen, over and over again. It's how you deal with it that matters most. So keep this with you, this one piece of advice. Oh, and don't forget: your passports need to be kept current at all times. Thank you very much for listening.

Practice Test 5 Section 1 (Track 32)

EMPLOYEE:	This is George and Dragon, how may I help?
CUSTOMER:	Hi. I'm calling to inquire about your upstairs venue. I'm interested in booking it for a private event and I was wondering if I could ask a few questions?
EMPLOYEE:	Yes, of course. Just give me a second, please. […] So, before we start, could I please get a name and a phone number?
CUSTOMER:	Yes. My name is Clara Carleton.
EMPLOYEE:	Carlee… Umm, could you spell that for me please?
CUSTOMER:	Sure, it's <u>C–A–R–L–E–T–O–N</u>.
EMPLOYEE:	And the phone number?
CUSTOMER:	Well, I'm going to give you my work number as I'm booking the venue for a work event.
EMPLOYEE:	Right.
CUSTOMER:	So it's <u>020 8322 1479</u>.
EMPLOYEE:	Great. So, what would you like to know?
CUSTOMER:	Well, I saw on your website that the price can be from £20 per hour, so I would like to get an exact quote if possible.
EMPLOYEE:	Well, the price depends on the type of event, the date, the number of people and whether we will be providing food as well.
CUSTOMER:	Oh, it's for a retirement party for one of my colleagues.
EMPLOYEE:	OK, and for which date is that?
CUSTOMER:	Well, we were thinking next Tuesday, the 31st of May?
EMPLOYEE:	OK. […] Oh, I'm sorry, but the venue's already booked that day. We're free on Monday and Wednesday, if that would suit you?
CUSTOMER:	Well, Wednesday's no good 'cause the gentleman who's retiring will be gone by then, but <u>Monday works just as fine</u>.
EMPLOYEE:	Great. You'll get a cheaper rate for Monday, too.
CUSTOMER:	Excellent.
EMPLOYEE:	And how many people will there be?
CUSTOMER:	Well, at the moment it's supposed to be 16, but it might go up to 17; we're waiting for one of our co–workers to confirm whether they'll be available that night or not.

EMPLOYEE:	The boardroom in the venue only has space for <u>15 people, I'm afraid. We've got enough standing room for about 15 extra people</u>. Is that all right?
CUSTOMER:	Oh, I'm sure it'll be fine. We won't be sitting down much anyway. Would it be possible to provide two extra chairs just in case, though?
EMPLOYEE:	Yes, of course.
CUSTOMER:	Great.
EMPLOYEE:	And finally, will you be needing us to provide food as well?
CUSTOMER:	Well, we'll be bringing the cake, but I imagine that yes, we will be ordering some food as well. What are your options for nibblers?
EMPLOYEE:	Well, we've got quite a vast selection depending on which type of menu you're interested in. We've got meat—based tapas as well as some vegetarian and vegan options, and we've also got some sharers.
CUSTOMER:	Well, as far as I know, none of us are vegans, so I don't think we'll be needing that. Some meat–based and vegetarian options would be great, though.
EMPLOYEE:	Would you like me to talk you through them, or…?
CUSTOMER:	Well, you do have the menu online, right?
EMPLOYEE:	Yeah, you can find it on our website. The only thing is that a couple of options have been removed and replaced with new ones, and we haven't had the chance to update it online yet.
CUSTOMER:	OK. Let me just pull it up in my screen, just a second. […] All right.
EMPLOYEE:	So, in the meat–based food section, the dishes that have been discontinued are the mini fajitas and the pulled pork bruschetta.
CUSTOMER:	Ah, that's a shame. The pulled pork bruschetta looked really nice.
EMPLOYEE:	Yeah. But we've replaced them with two new really popular dishes: we've got a trio of sliders, which is three mini burgers made one each with chicken, beef, and pulled pork, and we've also got ham and cheese croquettes.
CUSTOMER:	Oh, that sounds nice. So I'll have 7 of the <u>mini burgers</u>, then. I see you've also got vegetarian croquettes, are they still in the menu?

EMPLOYEE:	Yeah, we've got the vegetable croquette and the potato croquette.
CUSTOMER:	And how many croquettes are there in each dish?
EMPLOYEE:	The vegetable one is five; the potato one is four.
CUSTOMER:	OK, so I'll have two of the vegetable croquettes. And…I'll also have two of the ham and cheese ones, please.
EMPLOYEE:	Great. Anything else?
CUSTOMER:	Well, I don't know. It all looks so nice! What would you recommend?
EMPLOYEE:	Hmm… Well, what I would recommend is the simmered squid—it's slow–cooked in wine and served with potatoes. I'd also recommend the hummus platters; our chef actually makes his own hummus, and it's one of our most popular sharers. And of course all of our salads, especially the Caesar salad—we're famous for them.
CUSTOMER:	Right. So I'll go for five hummus platters—or should I get six? No, you know what? Five is just fine. I… I won't be having any of the squid; it sounds lovely, but I'm just not sure how popular it'd be with my colleagues.
EMPLOYEE:	Yeah, fair enough.
CUSTOMER:	And finally, one Caesar salad, and one vegetarian—the goat's cheese one.
EMPLOYEE:	Great. And, just for the final question… For how many hours would you be booking the venue?
CUSTOMER:	Well, we'd be arriving straight after work, so somewhere around 7 p.m., and I'd expect we'd need it until at least 9 p.m., maybe even 10 p.m., so…
EMPLOYEE:	So, three hours?
CUSTOMER:	Well, probably, but let's make it four just in case.
EMPLOYEE:	Right. Great. So, just give me a minute and I'll get back to you with a quote, all right?
CUSTOMER:	Yes, of course. […]
EMPLOYEE:	Umm, hi. So, I spoke to my manager and the total with the food and a drink starter for 17 people would come up to £318.95.
CUSTOMER:	OK.
EMPLOYEE:	But he'd be happy to offer you a 5% discount, which would bring the total down to just £303—and that includes a pint of any beer, a glass of wine or a fizzy drink for each person.

| **CUSTOMER:** | OK, that sounds reasonable enough. Let's go for it. |
| **EMPLOYEE:** | Right, so I would just need a deposit of… |

Practice Test 5, Section 2 (Track 33)

Hello, everyone, and welcome to this year's award ceremony for the Antonia Watson Memorial Poetry Award. As with previous years, the competition has been particularly fierce and we have received numerous excellent entries, so it's an incredible achievement for our three finalists who are sitting here amongst you, and we should congratulate them all. However, as with every competition, there can unfortunately only be one winner, and we will be announcing them shortly. Before we do, though, a few words about the award itself.

As most of you know, the Antonia Watson Memorial Poetry Award has been presented annually since 2010, and was presented biannually for two more competitions prior, once in 2008 and once in <u>2006</u>. It is entirely funded by Antonia Watson's very generous parents, who offer £1,500 to the author of the best poem on a topic announced at each previous award ceremony, as well as <u>£500</u> to the first runner–up and £250 to the second, bringing the total up to £2,250.

Now, a few words on Antonia Watson herself, without whom none of us would be standing here today. I briefly knew Antonia while at university, where we were flatmates for a year, and I'm afraid that any speech I give will not be able to do her justice, as she was the kindest, sweetest person I've ever met. Thankfully, this part of my speech was written with the assistance of one of her <u>siblings</u>, Thomas Watson, who was not only her brother, but also her best friend.

Antonia was born in Sleaford, Lincolnshire, in December 1986. From a very young age, she displayed an inquisitive and creative nature, matched in volume only by the gentle kindness of her spirit. She wrote her first poem, named "Love Barks", about the death of her dog, at the age of ten. This was also her first poem to be published at her school's newspaper—just two months after another of her poems, <u>"Be Kind"</u>, won the 1996 Triad Children's Writing Competition and was published in the competition's anthology.

While her early forays into poetry were crowned with impressive success, Antonia unfortunately ceased to write for a few years following the death of her very dear grandfather, Peter William Watson in 1999. Despite her <u>writer's block,</u> however, her artistic nature didn't lie dormant during the next four years: she had an active role in various theatre plays, and she also ventured into painting. A few of the plays are available on the Internet, and you can also find several of her self–portraits on our website, and you can see for yourself how impressive they are. But <u>poetry, of course, remained her passion even then,</u> which is why in 2003 she resumed writing, and her next poem, "The War on Both Sides", was published in her college's journal.

At the age of 18, Antonia moved to Sheffield to study English Literature at the University of Sheffield. This is where she and I met, spending a whole year in adjacent rooms in a flat in central Sheffield. This is also where I met her good–natured, generous parents, Mr and Mrs Watson, who came to visit her regularly and always treated me like a daughter as well. <u>Antonia and I grew very close during that period and while we ran in different circles, we always found time for each other every week</u>.

<u>Antonia self–published one collection of poems in August, 2005</u>. It was named "Burning Stars", after the poem on page 16, which is also the date of her birthday. It was an immediate success amongst her peers at the University of Sheffield, and it was so cherished by her English Literature classmates specifically that it attracted the attention of one of her lecturers, who put her in touch with a literary agent. She had been due to begin working on her second collection right before <u>her tragic passing in a car accident just five days before her 19th birthday in December, 2005</u>.

Antonia was always interested in societal shifts and how they affect humanity as well as the environment, and this award was designed to reflect her faith that regardless of what we do, we are all <u>inherently good</u>. With this in mind, all of the topics this competition has dealt with have been about the potential and the positive side of humanity, such as this year's "young love" theme, or last year's "inner power" theme. We've had poems about personal strength, about immigration, about gender equality, and peaceful protest. And hopefully in twelve months, the poems we'll be awarding will be just as inspiring with the topic of "<u>poverty</u>". I know Antonia would be really proud of what her parents, and what all of you together have achieved.

So finally, let's get on with the actual award. As I said before, it's been a fierce competition this year and with more than 5,000 entries it was quite the task for our three judges to cut them down to just three, but our three finalists definitely deserve to be here, and without further ado I would like to…

Practice Test 5, Section 3 (Track 34)

MELANIE:	Hey, Chris. Thanks for coming. Are you ready to practise our presentation for tomorrow?
CHRIS:	Yeah, just give me a moment to switch on my laptop. […] There we go. What d' you think?
MELANIE:	Wow, that actually looks really nice. Well done! So…
CHRIS:	So I've put the title up here in the middle, "Reasons People Move Out of Their Parents' Homes". I thought we could start with the general graph outlining why people fly the nest at any age, and then we could break it down to age groups and social or ethnic backgrounds before we get into how our findings fit into what sociologists say about leaving your

	parents' house and what the effects of the timing and the circumstances of your decision can be.
MELANIE:	That sounds good to me. So we can start with the bar chart here… Do you think they'll be able to read the tiny letters here?
CHRIS:	No, which is why we'll have to read them out to them.
MELANIE:	OK, so we could take turns then. I'd start with Bar A, which says that the number one reason that young people leave home is to go to college or university.
CHRIS:	Exactly, and then I'd go on to the second bar, which gives <u>the number of people who said they felt smothered by their parents' control over their lives</u>, and decided to get their own house to avoid that.
MELANIE:	Right. Then in Bar C we've got people who found a job and decided that it was a good opportunity to move away because of their new income…
CHRIS:	Yep, and then those who didn't feel exactly… smothered by their parents per se, but more so <u>because of the lack of room in their parents' house, and the fact that their parents were around pretty much 90% of the time</u>.
MELANIE:	Maybe we should move this bar so that it can be next to Bar B? Since they seem to be quite similar to each other.
CHRIS:	Well, actually, that's why I kept them separate—but maybe you're right, they would lead smoothly into one another. So that means that jobs will now be Bar D, and Bar E…
MELANIE:	Bar E is about <u>those who moved because of their partner or spouse</u>.
CHRIS:	Right, and then at the end we've got those who were <u>pushed to leave by their parents</u>, and those who left because of a conflict at home.
MELANIE:	I guess at this point we should mention that, as expected, we had almost zero people reply that they left home because of emancipation or abuse, despite the fact that our study was conducted anonymously, probably because the participants didn't feel confident enough to share such private details with us, or maybe just because there was no one in our pool of participants with such experiences.
CHRIS:	Yeah, so… Then we can break it down to age groups, and show these four different graphs for our four age groups: under–18s, 18–20, 21–24 and 25 and above.

MELANIE:	Shall we take the graphs by age or should we start with the second group, what do you think? Because we haven't got that much data on under–18s, and starting with 25 and above would also feel a bit strange to me seeing as it was our second smallest group and most participants were between 18 and 24 when they moved out of their parents' home…
CHRIS:	Yeah, you're right. Perhaps we should start with our two biggest groups and then move on to the other two.
MELANIE:	So <u>you can present 18–20 and I can present 21–24</u>, and then we can maybe present the other two groups together?
CHRIS:	I think it's best if we present them separately, since the findings are so different.
MELANIE:	Yeah, I guess you're right. So I can present the under–18s and you can present the 25 and over.
CHRIS:	Perfect. […] Or, wait, <u>should we do it the other way around</u> so it flows more naturally?
MELANIE:	Yeah, sure. And then we can include a brief note at the end for <u>those who haven't moved out yet</u>.
CHRIS:	Yeah, great.
MELANIE:	Excellent. So, <u>then we can move on to the final chart before we get to the bibliography</u>, and explain what they said they found difficult when they moved out.
CHRIS:	Yeah, so <u>we can say the biggest issue for everyone was finding a place to live</u>, especially for those who didn't have a guarantor or didn't live in a student hall of residence.
MELANIE:	Yes, and that <u>30% of the participants also experienced some financial problems in the beginning</u>, with bills and rent and food and everything.
CHRIS:	Right. Then, <u>an even larger number reported that they didn't expect to miss their family that much, but ended up visiting their parents' home often just to see them and spend some time with them</u>…
MELANIE:	Although we should probably cut that number down a notch to exclude those who went back home just so their parents could cook and do their laundry for them… [laugh]
CHRIS:	[laugh] Yeah, sure. Anyway, then we should finish off with the final issue, which was flatmates.

MELANIE:	Oh, yeah. So we should say that a whopping 67% complained about the people they had to live with, and that they were often dirty and inconsiderate.
CHRIS:	Right. Great! So then we can move on to how our findings fit into…

Practice Test 5, Section 4 (Track 35)

Hello, everyone. I'm glad so many people have shown up here today to hear about these fascinating little creatures called the turbellaria. My name is Dr Baker, and I've spent twenty years researching thousands of different species of platyhelminths, what are commonly known as flatworms, both free–living and parasitic. So there are a lot of things I could tell you about these extremely interesting invertebrate, but I will try to keep it short.

Turbellaria are unique amongst flatworms in three ways. The first one is that, unlike 80% of all platyhelminths, turbellaria do not need to secure nourishment from a living source. This means that they do not generally parasitise a host, but are instead found living freely in the environment. So no need to worry about any of these little samples I've got here escaping and causing havoc! [Laughter]

The second way in which they're different is that they are…well, they're incredibly simple—and by simple I don't mean in terms of structure, as their structure is indeed quite complex and I'll get to that later; by simple, I mean that they're not the brightest bulbs in the box. Flatworms in general are not known for their cognitive abilities, especially when compared with other invertebrate such as cuttlefish or octopuses or even insects, but amongst flatworms turbellaria are by far the most primitive of the bunch.

Finally, and this is a direct result of the first thing I mentioned, turbellaria tend to have a much more complicated sensory system in their head region. This includes a set of eyes with receptors that can detect light, as well as chemical sensory organs that assist turbellaria in locating food. Obviously, as other flatworms receive nutrition directly from their host, they have no need for this.

Despite these three differences, however, turbellaria are quite similar to other flatworms in all sorts of other ways. First of all, as their name suggests, they're incredibly flat, which allows them to hide under stones. They're symmetrical on both sides, and they don't have a body cavity; they also don't have any specialised respiratory, skeletal, and circulatory systems. What they do have, however, and this is what I meant when I referenced their structure before, is three layers known as the endoderm, the mesoderm and the ectoderm, as well as a head region where their brain and sense organs are located, and a spongy connective tissue that fills all the space between their organs. Finally, like most species of flatworms, they're hermaphrodites. This means that a single flatworm has a set of each gender—but don't take this to mean they <u>reproduce alone</u>. Their preferred method of reproduction is called cross–fertilisation, which means that each flatworm fertilises the other.

I mentioned before that most flatworms need a host, but turbellaria feed from the environment. So what do they feed on? Most turbellaria can be found either in fresh or salt <u>water</u>, and they feed on small insects, microscopic matter, and crustaceans. They will pretty much eat anything they find—

they have no preference on whether their food is living or dead. Also, and this is the most remarkable part about their eating habits, if they ever find themselves in a situation where food is scarce, they might also feed on themselves! That's right, they'll start eating their own body, starting with the least essential muscles and organs and working their way up. They will shrink in size until they're able to find food again, at which point they'll begin to regenerate everything they've lost. One final thing about food, and apologies in advance if I disgust you: turbellaria don't possess an anus, which means that their <u>mouth</u>, which is a muscular opening on the underside of their body, has to serve as one.

Before I finish this presentation, one more thing you've probably heard before but weren't sure if it was a myth or not. I mentioned already that turbellaria can reproduce on their own—but there's a second method they can use, which is known as <u>fission</u>. Now, as a child you were probably told that if you cut a worm in half it will grow into two new worms. That's not entirely true, but flatworms are not worms exactly, and <u>they do have the ability to regenerate by splitting into two, perhaps even more smaller parts</u>, at which point each part regrows the missing organs and becomes a brand new turbellarian. Now this is extremely important for us, and this is how I'd like to close this presentation, because their ability to regenerate endlessly makes them virtually immortal, and <u>it might open pathways to regeneration in human cells, or slowing the human aging process—which is why scientists like myself have been studying these unique creatures</u>, hoping to get some answers. Thank you for listening, and please come along to see me and my samples if you have any further questions.

Practice Test 6, Section 1 (Track 36)

ADVISOR:	Good afternoon, Waddow Insurance, this is Janet speaking. How may I help you?
CALLER:	Yes, hello, I would like to make a claim on my car insurance please.
ADVISOR:	Certainly Sir. First of all I'd like to inform you that all of our calls are recorded for monitoring and training purposes. Is that okay?
CALLER:	That's okay.

ADVISOR:	Could you please tell me your full name?
CALLER:	Sure. It's Mr Bennett Fischer.
ADVISOR:	Okay. Sorry, how do you spell your surname?
CALLER:	It's spelled <u>F-I-S-C-H-E-R</u>.
ADVISOR:	Great, thank you. I see that you have taken out a third party fire and theft premium with us on a 2013 light blue Volkswagen Passat, is that correct?
CALLER:	Yes, well, almost. The colour is not light blue it's <u>light green</u>.
ADVISOR:	Okay, thank you for updating your information with us. What is the nature of your claim with us today?
CALLER:	Last weekend I had driven up to York on business and left my car in a monitored car park. However it was only monitored until 8pm, and I did not return to collect it until <u>9:30pm</u> after which no car park staff were present. When I arrived at the car park, my car wasn't there. It must have been stolen.
ADVISOR:	I see. Were there any valuable items left in your car, which could have been seen from outside?
CALLER:	Well, I had recently bought quite an expensive radio for my car, but the front panel is detachable, <u>and I always stow it in my glove compartment</u>. So no, there wouldn't have been anything valuable on display.
ADVISOR:	Okay Mr Fischer, thank you for that information. I'm going to send you <u>some forms</u> through the mail for you to fill in. Before I can do that, I need to ask you a couple more questions, is that okay?
CALLER:	Of course.
ADVISOR:	Thanks, Mr Fischer. First of all, could you let me know your policy number, please?
CALLER:	Of course, I have it right here. It's <u>G34C245</u>.
ADVISOR:	G34C245… thanks. And the type of claim? Shall we say <u>stolen car</u>?
CALLER:	Yes, the car was definitely stolen. I reported it to the police immediately, I actually have the report number here if that is of any use?
ADVISOR:	Not right now, but keep hold of that as we will need to see a copy of the police report eventually. Which police station did you report the offence at?

CALLER:	York <u>Police</u> Station.
ADVISOR:	Was it your first time in York?
CALLER:	No, but it was the first time I had driven there. I usually take the train.
ADVISOR:	Were you aware that the car park was only manned until 8pm?
CALLER:	No, I was not aware of that.
ADVISOR:	Were there any signs put up on the premises that informed car owners of the risks of leaving their cars after normal operating hours?
CALLER:	Yes, but they said the car park was going to be guarded until 10pm, at which point the entrance is barred so no cars can come in or out.
ADVISOR:	Was any reason given for that sudden change?
CALLER:	The police informed me that the staff on duty that night had left on an urgent call. I believe it was something about a family member being admitted to hospital.
ADVISOR:	Were there any personal items left in your car?
CALLER:	Yes, first of all, there was the car radio I mentioned before.
ADVISOR:	Ah yes, of course. Anything else?
CALLER:	Just some CDs and an old <u>jacket</u>.
ADVISOR:	Right. Thank you. Mr Fischer, I have everything I need for now, and will send these forms out to you shortly. When you get them please fill them with as much information as you can and, where possible, include copies of any relevant documents to support you claim, such as police reports and <u>registration details</u>. Once you have returned that to us we can then start to assess whether you will be eligible to receive compensation. Do you have any further questions for me today?
CALLER:	No, that is all. Thanks for your help.

Practice Test 6, Section 2 (Track 37)

Allow me to introduce myself. My name is Peter Myers and on behalf of everybody here at Stevensbridge Dungeons I would like to welcome you all to our entertainment team. This year the hiring process was especially competitive and it might interest you all to know that for every position there were almost 30 applicants, so you really are the best of the best. In a moment I will take you on a tour of the museum so you can get an idea of what the space is like. But first of all I would like to show you around the staffroom.

Our staffroom is located at the back of the building over here. You will notice that there are two entrances to the staffroom. One leads to the room we are in now, which is the main, and oldest, dungeon here at Stevensbridge, which we have turned into the museum. This is where you will greet the new visitors, and also where the tour throughout the dungeons will begin. I should mention now that we only ever send visitors through as part of a group, so even on the busy days you will still get roughly ten minutes of free time between each group, make sure you use that time wisely because you'll need to get straight back into character as soon as it's over.

Right, follow me and I'll show you the layout of the museum. From the museum, we can pass through this door near the Interactive display into the staffroom. From here, you can see the steps at the far side, in the opposite corner, that lead outside onto Berwick Street. When you arrive for a shift it will be much easier for you all to come in the Berwick Street entrance directly down the steps to the staffroom. If you come in through the main visitor entrance it will take you longer to get past security.

As you can all see, there are lockers on your right hand side. They should be big enough for you to put your bags and coats in. You will get given keys later that work with any of the lockers in here. Over on the other side, past the lockers is our most exciting area. This is where our wardrobe and makeup will take place. Every shift you will be transformed from normal people into grotesque medieval prisoners. If you're lucky you get to be the gaoler, but even they rarely bathed in those days.

Of course some of you might consider yourselves method actors, but please do try to shower before your shift. We don't want to give visitors an experience that is too authentic.

Now we do have a staff shower here if you really need it. It is located next to the staff toilets which are unisex. I hope nobody has too much of a problem with that. Unfortunately dungeons were not really designed with comfort in mind. You can find the bathroom at the other end of the room from the makeup area. There is also another toilet for the public concealed just to the right of the door into this room.

Let's move back into the museum. We have three main sections down here. The first one you pass into when you leave the staffroom is the museum. This is where all the useful information can be found such as dates, number of prisoners and the kinds of torture that were used. I know it is a lot of information to take in on your first day, but try to learn as much of it as you can. Even though you will mostly be in character, visitors might want to ask you some questions and it would be great if you could tell them more about the dungeons. I think it would be more interesting if visitors could learn directly from you rather than having to read about it.

As you can see, on the left we have an interactive display for children, and on the right we have a photo booth. This was the original dungeon, first built in 1435. Now let's pass through into the main dungeon that was added during the Tudor period in around 1570.

You might be able to feel that the air is a lot damper and cooler here. That is because we are now beneath the River Stevens. This is primarily the room in which most of you will be working. This is where many high profile religious figures were held, sometimes for years on end. Depending on the roles you will be playing, you can be either chained up, free to roam, or if you are a gaoler, wandering between prisoners to keep an eye on them.

Now we will pass into our third and final section: The prison cells. Over here you can see there are some wooden stocks and a fake gibbet. Don't worry, I can see a couple of you looking concerned, you don't need to re-enact any of the torture scenes for visitors. One person each shift will play the gaoler in here, where you will give a speech to the group about some of the more notable prisoners to stay here in the past. This is usually the end of the tour, but some visitors will certainly want to ask you more questions at this point, so please try your best to make yourselves available. Help them by answering any questions they have. Also feel free to guide the visitors through the museum if you see that they are going the wrong way.

This concludes our introduction to your new workplace. If you please follow me I will get you all issued with keys and some information about the dungeons that you can take home with you to study. I will also introduce you to our shift supervisor Alice Stiles, and you can ask her any questions you may have about your roles.

Practice Test 6, Section 3 (Track 38)

OLGA:	Hi Jacob, thank you so much for coming along today.
JACOB:	It's my pleasure. I am very intrigued about what a tea meditation entails exactly.
OLGA:	Well it's very simple really. I think the first thing you need to keep in mind is that it is mostly about leaving everything that you have been thinking or worrying about today to one side. Really focus on the present moment.
JACOB:	Sounds great, I certainly don't know very much about tea, and I'm keen to get started. But, before you go into more detail, can I ask you what your favourite kind of tea is?
OLGA:	Well I think the kind of tea we are going to have today is my favourite. It is a pu-erh tea from Yunnan province in southern China.
JACOB:	What makes this tea special?
OLGA:	Pu-erh is a dark tea. The regions of Yunnan, the north of Vietnam and Laos, have one of the best climates for growing tea in the world. Pu-erh is a post-fermented tea.
JACOB:	What is a post-fermented tea exactly?
OLGA:	It is a tea that has undergone a period of aging in the open air. They age the tea for days, even years. The exposure to humidity and oxygen helps to oxidise the tea leaves and encourage fermentation. This changes the smell of the tea and also removes a lot of the bitterness from the taste.

JACOB:	It sounds similar to the process of aging wine.
OLGA:	The process is different but the effect of aging on the taste is certainly similar.
JACOB:	Does this mean the tea can be quite expensive?
OLGA:	Absolutely. <u>It can be very expensive.</u> The tea is usually pressed into balls or 'cakes' and sold. At one time only tea enthusiasts cared about buying these cakes, but now many people have realised that they are an investment and so buy them like they would buy gold because the price goes up a lot over time. So now, I want you to focus on clearing your mind of anything other than this present moment. Let go of any concerns.
JACOB:	Okay, one slight problem, I will need to record our conversation. <u>And I will need to take notes for the article. I plan to write about this for my newspaper.</u> Is that is okay?
OLGA:	Oh yes, of course, whatever you need.
JACOB:	Thank you. I'll try to keep my notes to a minimum.
OLGA:	Good. So where was I? Oh yes, I think very few people really appreciate the complexity and variety of tea that exists in the world.
JACOB:	Right, most people are maybe like me and just use teabags.
OLGA:	Exactly, and with a teabag, <u>the tea is trapped inside and cannot move around freely.</u> You can really taste the difference drinking a brewed tea that was free to move around through all the water.
JACOB:	So do you ever use teabags?
OLGA:	Never. There are many kinds of tea: white, yellow, black, green, oolong, matcha, herbal and many others. Each one has its own unique properties. To fully experience what each tea has to offer you must first brew it in the <u>correct</u> way. I also believe in only drinking tea that is picked and sorted by hand, rather than using mechanical processes. Although it takes more time, the tea made by hand is so much better, that it leads to an increase in the tea's sales.
JACOB:	But in that case, surely if there is more interest in the tea, and with the time-intensive farming process, this means there could be shortages because the demand is higher than the ability to produce it.
OLGA:	There were shortages for a while, but then an artificial fermentation process was developed in the 1970s which helped to speed up the fermentation times. As I mentioned, this process has an <u>aging</u> effect on the taste of pu-erh tea that is very similar to the effect on the taste of wine that you get from that fermentation process, though for pu-erh tea today, we're talking about that artificial process.

JACOB:	How can they do this artificially?
OLGA:	The <u>farmers</u> gather the tea leaves into a big pile then cover it with a large sheet or tarp. They spray water on the tea every now and then and therefore fermentation happens faster. Usually the tea is left for 30, 45, 60 or even 90 days still. The farmer will check the tea every few days, and just by the feel of the tea he knows whether it is ready or if it needs more time.
JACOB:	Wow that sounds like a fascinating process. I never realised that there was such a science behind producing tea.
OLGA:	Well now you are ready for the best part, the tasting of it.
JACOB:	That sounds like a very good idea to me.
OLGA:	So what I will do now is boil the water and we can begin our meditation.
JACOB:	What does that entail?
OLGA:	We need to focus on only two things. The first is your <u>mind</u> and body. Forget everything that you have been worrying about today. Forget about what you have to do later on, or what somebody said to you earlier. Focus on your breathing and on how your body feels. If you have aches and pains, acknowledge them. Pinpoint where there is tension in your body and try to release it.
JACOB:	Oh yes, I can really feel tension in my shoulders.
OLGA:	Let it go. Close your eyes if that helps. Take deep breaths in and out. Soon we will drink the tea. When you drink it think about the taste and how it feels on your tongue. Is it easy to swallow the tea or do you need to gulp it?
JACOB:	Can you brew the tea leaves more than once?
OLGA:	Oh yes, you can brew some teas more than ten times. Now we will shift to noble silence, focusing only on ourselves and the tea. Enjoy.

Practice Test 6, Section 4 (Track 39)

During today's seminar we will be looking at English Gothic architecture and its origins with a specific case study of Wells Cathedral in England. The Gothic <u>style</u> was initially brought over to England from France. This was at a period of time in which England was ruled from France by the Normans, starting with William the Conqueror who first defeated the <u>English</u> army at the Battle of Hastings on October 14th, 1066.

After 1072 when some smaller rebellions in northern England had been defeated, the Normans gained complete control of the English monarchy, which they controlled until 1154. The peace that ensued in England had a large impact on many aspects of daily life. Thousands of French words entered the English language for the first time such as beef, fruit, <u>city</u> and hour. French ideas and styles, like Gothic, also began to flow across The Channel to England too, examples of which can still be seen in the architecture of many listed buildings. A listed building is one that is protected from alteration or demolition because of its historical or stylistic importance. One such building is Wells Cathedral.

Construction on Wells Cathedral began in <u>1175</u> at a time when Gothic architecture as a style was in its infancy. As a result it is one of the first entirely Gothic buildings ever constructed. From the first designs to the date it was <u>completed</u> in 1490, Gothic architecture flourished in England. Therefore later additions to the building were still influenced by this Gothic style, rather than by later architectural styles such as Tudor architecture.

Older cathedrals in England would have initially been influenced by Romanesque architecture, alternatively known as Norman architecture in England. As the former name suggests, Romanesque was a building style based on the skills passed on to various areas of Europe by the Romans. When the Western Roman Empire collapsed in the 5th Century, these methods were retained by Rome's former colonies and developed further. One such Roman gift to the Romanesque architects was the round arch, also known as the true arch. The Romans perfected this style by using wedge-shaped stones called *voussoirs,* which created pressure that held the structure together at the top.

Cathedrals in England such as the ones in Ely and Canterbury were started before the arrival of Gothic architecture. Even though parts of those two cathedrals which were constructed later are in the Gothic style, other sections predating the arrival of Gothic architecture are Romanesque. The result is known as eclectic because the building is constructed using more than one style.

All of these cathedrals belong to a <u>group</u> known as the medieval cathedrals of England. There are twenty-six different buildings that belong to this group in total; all of which were constructed or added to during a five hundred year period from 1040 to 1540.

The transition from Romanesque to Gothic began in 1144 at the Abbey Church of St-Denis on the edge of Paris. It was here that a Benedictine abbot by the name of Suger had just completed his plan to rebuild the Basilica of St-Denis in a new style through which he believed "the dull mind rises to truth through that which is material."

This refers to one architectural feature in particular: high, rib vault ceilings, which created much more space inside the cathedral and were designed to draw the attention of the people up towards heaven. This design feature also allowed whole walls of the cathedral to be transformed by colourful stained glass.

Work started on Wells Cathedral soon afterwards, greatly inspired by abbot Suger's work. Planned in the crucifix style with the head pointing east and foot pointing west, the cathedral is <u>126 metres</u> long and the nave is 20 metres high. This is quite low compared to some of the bigger cathedrals elsewhere.

Use of tracery, lancet windows and mullions are all characteristic of English Gothic architecture. Whilst examples of all three of these architectural elements can be found at Wells, the lancet <u>windows</u> have no tracery at all, which was more common in early English Gothic architecture before advances were made in the use of mullions and tracery with glass.

Lancet windows are tall, thin windows with a pointed arch at the top and are so named because they resemble the weapon often carried by a soldier called a lance. Examples of these lancet windows can be seen on the West front of the cathedral, which is the most celebrated for its life-sized <u>sculptures</u> and delicate floral carvings.

Inside the pinnacle-topped gable is a sculpture of 'Christ the Judge'. Immediately below him, sculptures of the 12 Apostles peer out over the small city of Wells. Below the Apostles are nine archangels, which are half-sized sculptures. At one time all of these, along with the decorative carvings, would have been <u>painted</u> and gilded. However today all the paint has worn away and the sculptures are the colour of the oolite sedimentary stone used to construct the cathedral.

It is remarkable to think that more than 800 years ago such magnificent buildings were created, without the use of large cranes and modern technology. It would have taken much longer, but it is possible to see the high level of craftsmanship and attention to detail that is less common in the modern day.

PART EIGHT

IELTS
Practice Test
Answer Keys

PRACTICE TEST 1

Listening Section 1

1 [ancient] Greek

2 Bengali

3 2

4 6994

5 Databases

6 4

7 £60

8 June

9 16

10 6 p.m.

Listening Section 2

11 University

12 3

13 office

14 meetings

15 required books

16 ID passes

17 Physics

18 shop

19 Biology

20 [memorial] fountain

Listening Section 3

21 C

22 A

23 A

24 C

25 A

26 B

27 A

28 B

29 C

30 C

Listening Section 4

31 C

32 B

33 B

34 E

35 G

36 bird

37 park

38 mosaic

39 1976

40 civil war

Academic Reading Passage 1

1 **NOT GIVEN**

2 **NOT GIVEN**

3 **TRUE**   Text: Conventional wisdom states that the father's sperm is the main determinant of a child's gender... (Paragraph 2)

4 **FALSE**   Text: ...she changed the blood sugar level of female mice... (Paragraph 3)

5 **FALSE**   Text: Elissa Cameron's research, conducted in 2007 at the University of Pretoria, South Africa... (Paragraph 3)

6 **TRUE**   Text: This decrease could be ascribed to the decline in the number of adults and adolescent girls eating breakfast on a regular basis. (Paragraph 6)

7 **NOT GIVEN**

8 **FALSE**   Text: Lower-calorie diets among Western women could be biologically echoing the effects of scarcity – hence, the decline in male births. (Paragraph 7)

9 **G**   Text: There are also health reasons for gender selection... (Paragraph 1)

10 **A**   Text: ...she changed the blood sugar level of female mice prior to conception by putting a chemical in the animals' water. Mice that received the additive saw their blood sugar levels fall... (Paragraph 3)

11	C	Text: Her study followed 740 pregnant women who kept detailed records of their diets before conception... (Paragraph 5)
12	K	Text: Among women eating cereals on a daily basis, 59% had boys, compared with 43% of women who ate less than one bowl of breakfast cereal per week. (Paragraph 5)
13	D	Text: The recent decline in male births...appears to make sense if one looks at it from an evolutionary standpoint. (Paragraph 7)
14	C	Text: If you would like to have a son, it might be a good idea to eat a breakfast that includes cereal. On the other hand, if you would prefer to give birth to a daughter, then cut out breakfast and continue a weight reduction diet, at least until after conception. (Paragraph 8)

Academic Reading Passage 2

15	B	Text: MS patients can have one of two main varieties of the disease...
16	I	Text: Sense of touch can be lost...
17	H	Text: First, tiny patches of inflammation occur in the brain or spinal cord. Second, the protective coating around the axons, or nerve fibres, in the body start to deteriorate. Third, the axons themselves become damaged or destroyed.
18	J	Text: ...no cure exists, although a number of medical treatments have been shown to reduce relapses and slow the progression of the disease.
19	G	Text: Where people live can be seen to have a clear effect...
20	Multiple sclerosis/MS	Text: Multiple sclerosis (MS) is a disease... (Paragraph 1)
21	Relapse form	Text: ...two main varieties of the disease: the relapsing form and the primary progressive form. (Paragraph 2)
22	10–15%	Text: This condition affects about 10–15% of sufferers at diagnosis. (Paragraph 3)
23	Where people live	Text: Where people live can be seen to have a clear effect... (Paragraph 7)

24	**Caucasian**	Text: It commonly affects Caucasian people... (Paragraph 7)
25	**colder**	Text: ...and the incidence of MS is generally much higher in northern countries with temperate climates... (Paragraph 7)
26	**twin**	Text: ...if one twin has the disease, then it is likely that the other twin will develop it. (Paragraph 6)
27	**spinal cord**	Text: First, tiny patches of inflammation occur in the brain or spinal cord. (Paragraph 8)

Academic Reading Passage 3

28	**A**	Text: This steady electrical supply is subject to minimal variations... (Paragraph 2)
29	**A**	Text: Most overcurrents are temporary and harmless... (Paragraph 3)
30	**D**	Text: ...the most basic requirement of protective equipment is that it is reliable... (Paragraph 5)
31	**A**	Text: ...each piece of equipment...must be protected by a grounding or earthing mechanism... (Paragraph 6)
32	**D**	Text: ...when the source of an overcurrent is far away, the overcurrent relays delay slightly before shutting down... (Paragraph 7)
33	**B**	Text: ...it is also advisable to purchase additional tripping devices for sensitive electrical devices... (Paragraph 8)
34	**FALSE**	Text: ... variations...are imperceptible to the consumer and do not normally harm electrical devices. (Paragraph 2)
35	**NOT GIVEN**	
36	**FALSE**	Text: Electrical storms and lightning are among the biggest causes of major distribution overcurrent worldwide. (Paragraph 4)
37	**FALSE**	Text: ...67 people are killed every year by these types of storms... (Paragraph 4)
38	**TRUE**	Text: ...it should shut down the minimum number of devices... (Paragraph 5)
39	**NOT GIVEN**	
40	**TRUE**	Text: ...the grounding mechanism allows the excess electricity to be discharged into the earth... (Paragraph 6)

Academic Writing Task 1: Model Answer

According to a recent survey in the UK, people attribute poor attendance in schools to a number of causes. The respondents were asked to choose from five causes: upbringing, both parents working, lack of school discipline, peer group pressure and bullying.

First, the way a child is brought up was considered by about 40 per cent of respondents to be a cause of poor attendance. Among the five causes suggested in the survey, this was the opinion most commonly held, whereas only 25 per cent of those asked thought having both parents working might lead to children missing school.

Second, about 15 per cent of people surveyed thought lack of school discipline might also be a contributing factor. The same number of people thought that peer group pressure was a cause of poor attendance.

Bullying was not widely seen to be an important cause, with only 5 per cent of respondents considering it a cause of poor school attendance.

According to the data shown, it appears that poor attendance in schools in the UK is not seen as being attributable to only one category of causes.

Academic Writing Task 2: Model Answer

Digital technology has changed the way people access information. Since their introduction in the 1980s, technologies such as mobile phones and the internet have become cheap and commonplace. Some people see this as a window of opportunity to deal effectively with such problems as unemployment. They argue that the government should make mobile phones and the internet available free of charge to anyone looking for a job. I disagree with this point of view for several reasons. In the first place, one of the most common reasons why jobless people cannot find employment is that the skills they have not needed are out of date. Instead of investing public funds in an expensive infrastructure or distributing mobile phones for free to those out of work, the government should organise training programmes that people who are out of work could sign up for in order to learn new skills.

Another argument against the idea is the way the use of the internet and mobile phones would be controlled. It would be technically very challenging to control how these technologies are used. Instead, public money could be used to provide subsidised public transport for the unemployed who, for example, need to travel for a job interview.

Moreover, it would be prohibitively expensive to maintain such a system and ensure that it worked properly. The government could instead invest public funds into training courses for the staff working in job centres to make them more efficient at helping the unemployed to find jobs.

To sum up, I am convinced that public money should not be wasted on expensive technology. It could be better used to deal with the problem of unemployment by giving the unemployed free and better-quality training.

GENERAL TRAINING READING MODULE

General Training Reading Passage 1

1	**132**	This is the cafeteria.
2	**212**	This is the waiting room for the Tropical Diseases Unit, where Dr. Kynaston works.
3	**101**	This is the reception room of the Emergency Services Department.
4	**221**	This is the reception room of the Heart Disease Unit.
5	**134**	This is the children's play room.
6	**122**	This is the reception room of the General Practice Unit; the text says to report to the reception area.
7	**Drink water**	Water is provided in coolers. The rules ask visitors not to eat or drink (except the water provided) and not to use their phones.
8	**D**	This is the best answer because **D** is looking for a female flatmate, and **8** only wants to share with one other person. Both are vegetarians.
9	**C**	This is the best answer because in the college, **9** will not have to cook or clean and will have the company of other students.
10	**E**	This is the best answer, as in the hostel, **10** will be meeting other students but not flat sharing, which she has no experience of and may find difficult.
11	**A**	This is the best answer because **11** needs accommodation where he can work hard; he can't afford the other two options where this would be possible (**G** and **H**).
12	**B**	This is the best answer because **12** will be living with a family which will help her, as she is missing her own, and because she does not know how to cook or clean.
13	**F**	This is the best answer because **13** has experienced flat sharing and is sociable (the only other possibility is **G**—but that is needed for question **14**).
14	**G**	This is the best answer because the only other flat which meets their requirements is too expensive.

General Training Reading Passage 2

15	**student centre**	The section of the text states that 'this service will also help you find a part-time job'.
16	**67**	The section entitled Shopping Information tells us that 'Gundini has a bookshop', and the section entitled Transport says to catch the 67 bus to Gundini.
17	**Saturday**	The section entitled Shopping Information states that 'on Saturday mornings there is a wonderful farmers' market in Gundini . . . '
18	**International Student Office**	This section of the text states that 'There is also a lawyer available to help with visa and immigration solutions'.
19	**town hospital/Casualty**	The section entitled Health Services states that University Health Services are available only on weekdays and Saturday mornings; 'At all other times, please use the town hospital'. This paragraph also states that 'during holiday periods you must go to Casualty in town', so this is another possible answer.
20	**library**	In the second paragraph of the section entitled Student Centre, the text states that 'additional computers are available in the library'.
21	**student centre**	In the last two sentences of this section of the text, the union is mentioned.
22	**or equivalent**	This is from the beginning of the section entitled 'Minimum education requirements, prerequisites'.
23	**subjects**	The information is contained in the section entitled 'Minimum education requirements, prerequisites' (the word itself is not used).
24	**eligible**	From the section entitled 'Visa requirements'.
25	**a minimum of**	From the section entitled 'Visa requirements'.
26	**before**	From the section entitled 'Closing date'.
27	**further information**	From the section entitled 'Enquiries'.

General Training Reading Passage 3

28	B	from Paragraph E, line 4
29	D	from Paragraph G, lines 2–3
30	A	from Paragraph C, lines 5–6
31	E	from Paragraph G, line 9
32	C	from Paragraph F, line 3
33	True	from Paragraph D, lines 2–3
34	Not Given	No information is given about the number of deaths each year. In Paragraph G, the text states that one fish 'has enough poison to kill 30 people' to describe the potential strength of the poison.
35	False	Paragraph E, lines 3 and 4, states that fugu has a delicate flavour.
36	False	Paragraph C, lines 1 and 2, states that the venom is 'mainly concentrated in the internal organs of the fish'.
37	supermarkets	from Paragraph D, line 6
38	Korea	from Paragraph H, line 2
39	6	This is the best answer for Paragraph E. While this paragraph also discusses different ways to eat *fugu*, the main topic is chefs and their training.
40	1	This is the best answer for Paragraph G. The main topic of the paragraph is Kazuo Nishimura, an innocent victim. Although her symptoms are discussed, this is only a minor part of the paragraph.

GENERAL TRAINING WRITING MODULE

General Training Writing Task 1: Model Answer

Dear Sir or Madam,

I would like to report lost property. It seems that I left my red cabin bag on one of your flights. Last Tuesday, January 13, I flew from New York to Paris on BA246 with my cabin bag. I put it in the overhead bin. Unfortunately, after the long flight, I must have forgotten it on the plane.

The bag has wheels and two outside pockets. It is locked with a small lock. I had all of my school work and books in it. I also had a new sweater in it. I had just received it as a gift from my cousin in New York.

As you can imagine, these items are very important to me. Please let me know if you have my cabin bag and how I can get it back. Write to me at my return address or email: justinem@newcom.net

I'm looking forward to your reply.

Many thanks,

Justine Manfield

(164 words)

General Training Writing Task 2: Model Answer

The world is online. Everyone is using computers for business and pleasure. There is growing concern about the effects this has on children. They spend many hours on the computer playing games, chatting and watching videos. Valuable childhood hours are spent sitting indoors opposite a computer screen instead of playing outdoors and running free.

Many people argue that the time children spend online is actually very good for them. They say that children have to prepare themselves for their higher education and working lives. Therefore, the time they spend is actually helping them gain the computer skills they need in order to become productive adults.

In my opinion, there are advantages and disadvantages to children spending a lot of time using computers. It is clear that children need computer skills to further their education. However, there is a difference between time spent playing computer games and chatting and time spent working on school projects or doing online research. It is important to recognize that the online world is huge and offers limitless opportunities that are both useful and harmful.

Parents play a very important role in supervising the online activities of their children. It is their job to check the sites they are visiting and the games they are playing. It is also their duty to limit the number of hours that children spend in front of the computer. There are so many wonderful activities for children that don't involve the computer. Parents have to make sure that their children have a variety of interests outside the computer world.

In conclusion, it is clear that children today must be computer literate in order to succeed in life. But we have to remember that children should also experience many other joys of life that make childhood so special. It's possible to balance this out and make sure that children gain important computer skills and still enjoy the pleasures of childhood.

(320 words)

PRACTICE TEST 2

Listening Section 1

1   GONZALEZ
2   SHU300715PG
3   languages
4   station
5   £99
6   west
7   2

8-10 C, D, E (in any order)

Listening Section 2

11   10
12   (straightforward) walking
13   rock climbing
14   gave up
15   2
16   school
17   8
18   2
19   exclusive
20   large

Listening Section 3

21 C

22 B

23 B

24 A

25 C

26 A

27 B

28 C

29 C

30 A

Listening Section 4

31 B

32 A

33 B

34 C

35 middle

36 gap

37 £3,500

38 worthwhile

39 fee

40 commission

Academic Reading Passage 1

1	B	Text: Do you seriously want to be happy? Of course you do! But what does it take to be happy? Many psychologists are now using scientific methods to try to understand the nature and origins of happiness. (Paragraph 1)
2	A	has enabled scientists to calculate that 50-60% of self-identified happiness - and what other sort is there?–is down to genes. (Paragraph 2)
3	D	increases in wealth do not automatically turn into relative increases in happiness. (Paragraph 3)
4	wealth/money	Text: winning the lottery may give a rush of joy and excitement but does not ensure long-term contentment (Paragraph 3)

5	relative	Text: The perception of wealth is a relative thing: we are discontented when those who we compare ourselves with are better off than ourselves (Paragraph 4)
6	other people	Text: The only type of shopping that might provide longer term happiness is when we buy things for other people. (Paragraph 5)
7	No	Text: We can and should take control of our life to make it rewarding and satisfying. (Paragraph 6)
8	Not Given	
9	Yes	Text: happiness emerges as a by-product of who we are and what we do. (Paragraph 10)
10	G	Text: Many psychologists are now using scientific methods to try to understand the nature and origins of happiness. (Paragraph 1)
11	D	Text: Now, many people believe that money makes us happy. However, there is no clear relationship between wealth and happiness. (Paragraph 3)
12	H	Text: And saying 'no' to other people if necessary. Of course, this doesn't mean we have to be selfish. (Paragraph 10)
13	C	Text: To a large extent, happiness emerges as a by-product of who we are and what we do. (Paragraph 11)

Academic Reading Passage 2

14–18		**B, C, F, G, I** (*in any order*)
	B	Text: Since then, there have been seven space tourists who have paid large sums of money for a space experience. Yet, collectively, their financial contribution is minute, and certainly would not appear to represent a feasible business. (Paragraph 2)
	C	Text: Richard Branson, billionaire and entrepreneur, has formed Virgin Galactic, a spaceship company with some very ambitious plans for space travel. (Paragraph 3)
	F	Text: It seems that people who want to take short zero gravity suborbital flights are fully aware of the dangers and are willing to take the risk. (Paragraph 4)
	G	Text: $20 billion is an interesting figure as it is about the same amount generated by the film industry in the

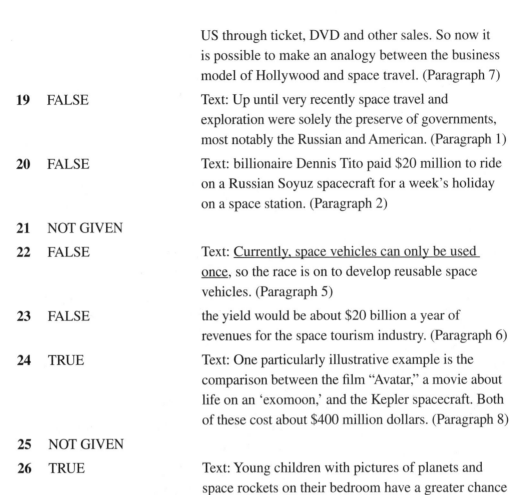

| 19 | FALSE | Text: Up until very recently space travel and exploration were solely the preserve of governments, most notably the Russian and American. (Paragraph 1) |

US through ticket, DVD and other sales. So now it is possible to make an analogy between the business model of Hollywood and space travel. (Paragraph 7)

20	FALSE	Text: billionaire Dennis Tito paid $20 million to ride on a Russian Soyuz spacecraft for a week's holiday on a space station. (Paragraph 2)
21	NOT GIVEN	
22	FALSE	Text: <u>Currently, space vehicles can only be used once</u>, so the race is on to develop reusable space vehicles. (Paragraph 5)
23	FALSE	the yield would be about $20 billion a year of revenues for the space tourism industry. (Paragraph 6)
24	TRUE	Text: One particularly illustrative example is the comparison between the film "Avatar," a movie about life on an 'exomoon,' and the Kepler spacecraft. Both of these cost about $400 million dollars. (Paragraph 8)
25	NOT GIVEN	
26	TRUE	Text: Young children with pictures of planets and space rockets on their bedroom have a greater chance than ever of actually going into space than ever before. (Paragraph 11)

Academic Reading Passage 3

27	vii	Text: cryptography is central to how our money is kept secure, even though we may not be aware of it. Our money is no longer in a tangible form, but in the form of information kept with our banks.
28	i	Text: Our credit cards have 16-digit numbers on the front and a 3-digit number on the back. They also contain a 'chip' that can do all sorts of mysterious operations with these numbers. Finally, we also have a Personal Identification Number which we all need to memorize.
29	x	Text: A very different approach was developed in the 1970s, based on a different way of using the keys.

30 ii Text: [RSA is] is based on a collection of several mathematical algorithms. The first is a process that allows the user, Amir, to calculate two numerical keys: private and public, based on two prime numbers. To complete the RSA system, two more algorithms are then needed: one for encrypting messages and one for decrypting them.

31 viii Text: The effectiveness of RSA depends on two things...

32 v Text: When the RSA system was first written about in the Scientific American journal, the strength of the system was shown by challenging the readers to find the prime factors – the two original numbers - of a certain number with 129 digits.

33 secure/safe Text: cryptography is central to how our money is kept secure, even though we may not be aware of it. (Paragraph **B**)

34 code makers Text: On a practical level, it is clear that the work of code-makers has been introduced into our daily financial lives. Our credit cards have 16-digit numbers on the front and a 3-digit number on the back. (Paragraph **C**)

35–36 public/private (key) Now the main idea is that the typical user, let us call him Amir, has (35 & 36) two keys; a 'public key' and a 'private key'. (Paragraph **D**)

37 NOT GIVEN

38 YES Text:

39 NO Text: only one key was needed by both the sender and the receiver to understand the message. (Paragraph **D**)

40 NOT GIVEN

Academic Writing Task 1: Model Answer

The table depicts the number of Trillion Watt Hours, or TWh, produced by five different renewable energy sources over three years from 2009 to 2012. The table shows that production from all five renewable energy sources has increased over the time period. Hydraulic energy has consistently produced the greatest number of TWh, indeed, Hydraulic energy produced more TWh than all of the other renewable energy sources combined. Geothermal energy showed the smallest increase in TWh produced, being overtaken in 2012 by solar energy, which generated the smallest number of TWh in the previous three years. The amount of wind energy produced in 2012 is almost double the amount produced in 2009, showing one of the greatest percentage increases. Although the amount of solar energy produced annually only increased by 83.5TWh from 2009 to 2012, we can see that the figure has more than quadrupled from 21KWh to 104.5KWh, showing that solar energy has shown the greatest Individual percentage increase.

(159 words)

Academic Writing Task 2: Model Answer

The number of children who are obese, or considerably overweight, has increased dramatically over past decades. The increase in childhood obesity causes a problem throughout the developed world because lifelong obesity has been associated with decreased life expectancy, and is thought to increase the likelihood of certain illnesses and diseases, such as high blood pressure and some forms of diabetes.

In an effort to combat obesity beginning in childhood, and therefore decrease the likelihood of children becoming obese as adults, some people have proposed that adverts for unhealthy foods high in sugar and fat such as sweets and fast food should be banned from schools and colleges. People argue that the benefit of banning such adverts is that children will be less likely to crave and then buy unhealthy foods if they are not surrounded with appetising images of unhealthy snacks which are known to increase the risk of obesity.

Although this could be true, and would certainly help students who were trying to be healthier to ignore unhealthy options, it is unlikely to get to the root of the problem. Children typically learn what to eat from their parents, and as such obese children often come from obese families. Even if children are not reminded of unhealthy food at school, if they are used to eating unhealthy food at home, they are likely to expect to eat unhealthy food at school as well, even if unhealthy food is not advertised. Rather than simply removing adverts for unhealthy food, schools and colleges should be encouraged to emphasise the benefits of healthy food to individuals, in order to introduce an alternative diet to overweight and obese children and lower their risk of obesity in later life.

(285 words)

General Training Reading Passage 1

1	B	Text: (Under dining options column) None (**B**)
2	D	Text: <u>Recently refurbished</u> to a high standard to return it to its original glory from 1856.
3	C	Text: Next door to Old Trafford Football stadium.
4	A	Text: Award winning restaurant specialising in seasonal dishes. <u>An extensive vegetarian selection.</u>
5	(at) reception	Text: Tours can be booked through reception. (**C**)
6	Scottish (beef)	Text: Steak and rib house with finest <u>Scottish beef</u>, grilled over a charcoal barbeque (**A**)
7	(buffet) breakfast	Text: Buffet breakfast included in the room rate. (**C**)
8	D	Text: Additionally laptops, tablets and smartphones can be covered as long as they are specifically listed when we take out the policy. (**Belongings**)
9	C	Text: We need insurance that will cover any non-refundable deposit and other costs we have paid for should we have to cancel for reasons 'outside our control'. (**Cancelation**)
10	B	Text: I think it's important to include the cost of a flight back to Hong Kong with accompanying medical staff if necessary. (**Medical**)
11	C	Text: I know we have all committed to this trip however there may be some unforeseen circumstances that mean that one, some or all of us have to cancel. We need insurance that will cover any non-refundable deposit and other costs we have paid for should we have to cancel for reasons 'outside our control'. (**Cancellation**)
12	A	Text: Although we are not going to be taking anything that is very valuable I think it is important we include insurance for our belongings. This would cover loss or theft of our everyday belongings. For example the current value of items stolen – although for this you would need to be able to provide receipts. (**Belongings**)
13	D	Text: we will not be able to get insurance cover for all pre-existing medical conditions. So we need to

make sure that we check with the company before about any long-term illness or disabilities that any of us have. (**Medical**)

14 A — Text: This would cover loss or theft of our everyday belongings. (**Belongings**)

General Training Reading Passage 2

15 bakery — Text: a local <u>family-owned bakery</u> in Lincoln. (Paragraph 1)

16 specialist advisors — Concerned about the impact this waste was having on company profits Lincoln Breads called in <u>specialist advisors</u> to find out how they could reduce production waste. (Paragraph 2)

17 inconsistent — Text: Work on tracking the waste had already been carried out, but the figures were <u>inconsistent</u> and showed no obvious trends to help explain the causes of the waste generated. (Paragraph 3)

18 phase — Text: Following initial discussions, it was decided that the project should be divided into <u>two phases</u>. (Paragraph 4)

19 (a) report — Text: This data was then used to understand the key drivers of waste. They then produced <u>a report</u> containing actions for waste improvement that would allow Lincoln Breads to focus their efforts on the key areas Text: to reduce their production waste. (Paragraph 5)

20 changes/engineering work — Text: Lincoln Breads have now implemented a number of <u>changes</u> based on the recommendations (Paragraph 6)

21 employee (and) company — Text: This is to ensure that the needs of both the employee and the company are being met. (Paragraph 1)

22 (a) proposal — Text: If you wish to have a FWA then you need to prepare a proposal to submit to your supervisor. (**Considering a Flexible Working Arrangement**)

23 (the) HR (department) — Text: You are encouraged to use the "Is FWA right for me?" worksheet available from the HR department. (**Requesting a FWA**)

24 (the) supervisor — Text: The supervisor will be responsible for communicating the decision to approve or deny such a proposal. (**Requesting a FWA**)

25	(the) HR (department)	Text: In the event that a request for a FWA is declined, the employee can appeal to HR. (**Requesting a FWA**)
26	improved	Text: Employees with flexible work arrangements are more inclined to practice self-management, work productively and experience improved morale. (**Participating in a Flexible Work Arrangement**)
27		communication (and) availability Text: . In order to achieve these results, special attention should be paid to the following… Communication… Availability (**Participating in a Flexible Work Arrangement**)

General Training Reading Passage 3

28	ix	Text: There is no vaccine for malaria and the conditions that encourage the spread of the disease, such as high population density and high mosquito density, are frequently found in the countries of sub-Saharan Africa.
29	xi	Text: However, <u>currently diagnosis</u> involves finger-prick blood tests that are then screened in a laboratory. <u>This is both time-consuming and very expensive</u> and health authorities have <u>real difficulties</u> identifying who is carrying the malaria parasite in communities where the disease is present at a low level.
30	ii	Text: Using dogs to identify malaria carriers has the advantage that it is not invasive, the 'testing' can be done anywhere and it doesn't require a laboratory.
31	vii	Text: Dogs have an incredible ability to detect minute odour traces created by diseases… Thus, they are potentially able to detect diseases, such as malaria, much earlier than is currently possible with traditional methods.
32	i	Text: To train the dogs, sweat samples will be collected from 400 Gambian children.
33	iii	Text: So far the project has already <u>received sufficient funds</u> from the Bill and Melinda Gates foundation to cover the costs of the initial training and studies.
34	TRUE	Text: The vast majority of these are children under 15. (**A**)

35	FALSE	Text: It <u>can</u> kill within 24 hours of infection and some children in Africa can be infected up to 13 times a year. (**A**)
36	FALSE	Text: Because these symptoms are so non-specific it is not always clear that the patient is a victim of malaria which can delay identification. (**B**)
37	NOT GIVEN	
38	TRUE	Text: However, currently diagnosis involves finger-prick blood tests that are then screened in a laboratory. This is both time-consuming and very expensive (**D**)
39	TRUE	Text: Dogs have an incredible ability to detect minute odour traces created by diseases. Because they are able to detect tiny odour concentrations, around one part per trillion. This is the equivalent of one teaspoon of sugar in two Olympic sized swimming pools. Thus, they are potentially able to detect diseases, such as malaria (**F**)
40	FALSE	Text: if it is successful – and there is good reason to suppose it will be – there is every likelihood that the foundation will continue its support. (**H**)

General Training Writing Task 1: Model Answer

Dear Sir or Madam

I'm writing to you about the mobile phone I bought from you last week. Unfortunately it has stopped working. I think it might be an issue with the battery as I can't turn the phone on and it won't charge up. The phone I bought was your newest smartphone, the blue one with 4G capability.

To give you some more details, I bought the phone last Wednesday, in the afternoon, and it stopped working on Friday. Since then, I've called your shop many times, but although the shop assistants I've spoken to said they would get back to me, no further action has been taken.

I'm writing to you because I believe this is unacceptable, if you had got back to me sooner I would have asked you to exchange my phone for another one, but because your customer service has been so poor I would prefer a refund, please.

Yours faithfully

--

(155 words)

General Training Writing Task 2: Model Answer

Many of the world's poorer countries depend on tourism to generate more money and improve their economy. When tourists visit such countries, the money they spend on food, drink, accommodation and souvenirs allows individual locals and the country as a whole to profit.

Alongside this, tourism often provides many new jobs for locals, such as tour guides, or hired drivers, and as such tourism helps to raise the number of employed individuals. New jobs may also be created by the tourism industry indirectly, for example in the construction of new hotels and restaurants. Tourism may also improve the living conditions in poorer countries, as improved transport and water and sanitation facilities are implemented to attract tourists. These benefits can also be used by the local people.

On the other hand, in order to make more money, leaders of poorer countries may invest so much into their tourism industries that they neglect to look after their local population. School funding and medical care may be side-lined in order to ensure that tourists have an abundance of 5 star hotels to choose from. New jobs in these hotels might even be given to trained foreign workers, decreasing the amount of jobs created by tourism.

Similarly, although many tourists visit different countries in order to respectfully experience exotic and unfamiliar new customs, locals may find some tourists offensive and even exploitative.

Tourism creates many new opportunities for poorer countries, and offers an essential source of income, but the money generated by tourism will only benefit these countries if some of it is invested into improving the living conditions and prospects of the people who live in these countries, rather than simply strengthening the tourism industry.

(282 words)

ACADEMIC PRACTICE TEST 3

Listening Section 1

1 John Sparrow

2 24th January

3 Athens, Greece

4 9.45

5 Hypnos

6 95 euros

7 light meal

8 Asian vegetarian

9 dairy products

10 24 hours

Listening Section 2

11 A

12 C

13 D

14 E

15 C

16 B

17 C

18 different name

19 social media

20 ready for editing

Listening Section 3

21 A

22 B

23 C

24 A

25 B

26 almost equal

27 17.97

28 5

29 mild depression

30 drop – out rate

Listening Section 4

31   2.1 billion

32   German

33   non-native speakers

34   Englishes

35   trousers

36   Latin

37   Romance (languages)

38   B

39   A

40   C

Reading Passage 1

1	D	Text: Very few drawbacks have been described, usually minimal … personality (imagine meeting a very interesting person named "Lee", when the letter E has a dull or hideous colour for you – or vice versa). (Paragraph 4)
2	F	Text: … teaching people to create grapheme – colour associations the same way as a synaesthete may have the possibility to improve cognitive function and memory. (Paragraph 6)
3	G	Text: Once we do, however, it might not be too long before we find out how to teach non – synaesthetes how to imitate its symptoms in a way that induces the same benefits 4.4% of the world's population currently enjoy. (Paragraph 7)
4	A	Text: Imagine a page with a square box in the middle. The box is lined with rows of the number 5, repeated over and over. All of the 5s … you are a grapheme – colour synaesthete… (Paragraph 1)
5	C	Text: Synaesthesia was first documented in the early 19th century by German physician Georg Sachs, who dedicated two pages of his dissertation on his own experience with the condition. It wasn't, however, until the mid – 1990s… (Paragraph 3)
6	B	Text: This might mean that words have a particular taste (for example, the word "door" might taste like

ANSWER KEY

		bacon), or that certain smells produce a particular colour. It might also mean that each letter and number has its own personality—the letter A might be perky, the letter B might be shy and self – conscious, etc. (Paragraph 2)
7	E	Text: In a 2013 study, Dr Witthoft and Dr Winawer discovered that grapheme – colour synaesthetes who had never met each other before experienced strikingly similar pairings between graphemes and colours – pairings which were later traced back to a popular set of Fischer – Price magnets that ten out of eleven participants distinctly remembered possessing as children. (Paragraph 5)
8	FALSE	Text: …even though synaesthesia is believed to affect less than 5% of the general population, at least 60 different combinations of senses have been reported. (Paragraph 2)
9	NOT GIVEN	Text: Synaesthesia was first documented in the early 19th century by German physician Georg Sachs, who dedicated two pages of his dissertation on his own experience with the condition. It wasn't, however, until the mid – 1990s that empirical research proved its existence… (Paragraph 3)
10	NOT GIVEN	Text: …it is often linked to intelligence and creativity, with celebrities such as Lady Gaga and Pharrell Williams claiming to have it. (Paragraph 4)
11	TRUE	Text: …synaesthesia is predominantly considered to be a hereditary condition… (Paragraph 5)
12	memory	Text: …grapheme – colour associations the same way as a synaesthete may have the possibility to improve cognitive function and memory. (Paragraph 6)
13	function	Text: …grapheme – colour associations the same way as a synaesthete may have the possibility to improve cognitive function and memory. (Paragraph 6)
14	teach	Text: …it might not be too long before we find out how to teach non – synaesthetes how to imitate its symptoms… (Paragraph 7)

Reading Passage 2

15	Henley Beach	Text: The only things found on his body were an unused 10:50 a.m. ticket from Adelaide Railway Station to Henley Beach... (Paragraph 2)
16	cause of death	Text: the autopsy revealed that his death had been unnatural, but determined no cause of death... (Paragraph 2)
17	(secret) code	Text: ...in the back of the book, police discovered five lines of letters that appeared to be some sort of secret code... (Paragraph 4)
18	(phone) number	Text: In the back cover, they also found a phone number which led them to a 27 – year – old woman known as "Jestyn"... (Paragraph 4)
19	Moseley Street	Text: ..."Jestyn", who lived on Moseley Street... (Paragraph 4)
20	guarded and non-committal	Text: Jestyn denied any knowledge of the man, and was generally guarded and non – committal throughout the police interview. (Paragraph 4)
21	F	Text: As for the code? Despite years of research by cryptology experts and students, no one has managed to crack it to this day. (Paragraph 4)
22	D	Text: The next piece of evidence came when a journalist named Frank Kennedy discovered that the piece of paper with the printed words had been ripped from the last page of The Rubáiyát of Omar Khayyám... (Paragraph 3)
23	C	Text: Interest in the case was rekindled in 2013, following an interview on the show 60 Minutes with Kate Thompson, the daughter of "Jestyn"—whose actual name was revealed to be Jo Thompson. (Paragraph 6)
24	A	Text: Kate Thompson claimed that her mother had lied to the police about not knowing the Somerton Man. ... The two women have backed a request to get the man's body exhumed in the interest of proving this claim, which they also believe to be correct. (Paragraph 6)
25	D	Text: To make matters more interesting, the autopsy revealed that his death had been unnatural, but

determined no cause of death: although he had clearly died of heart failure, his heart had been healthy and no signs of violence or poisoning were discovered in his system. (Paragraph 2)

26 B Text: …a local man brought in the correct copy, which he reported having found in the back seat of his car six months earlier, around the time the corpse had been discovered. (Paragraph 3)

27 C Text: …many believing that he was American due to the predominantly US way the stripes slanted on his tie… (Paragraph 5)

28 D Text: Also participating in the show were Roma and Rachel Egan, wife and daughter respectively of Kate Thompson's late brother Robin... (Paragraph 6)

Reading Passage 3

29 ix Text: Typically, a coin or banknote will feature the effigy of a notable politician, monarch, or other personality from the country of origin on one side, and a recognisable state symbol (e.g. a building or an animal) on the reverse. This pattern, which has been around for more than 21 centuries… (Paragraph 1)

30 iii Text: As sea trade grew in the Mediterranean, however, the once popular barter system became difficult to maintain for two reasons… (Paragraph 2)

31 i Text: …the history of ancient Greek coins can be divided into three distinct chronological periods: the Archaic (600–480 BC), the Classic (480–330 BC), and the Hellenistic Period (330–1st century BC). As ancient Greece was not a united country like today, but rather comprised of many independent city – states known as poleis, each state produced its own coins. The island of Aegina was the first… (Paragraph 3)

32 vii Text: It was around that time that an agreement akin to way the EU's euro currency functions also appeared… (Paragraph 4)

33 vi Text: Another new feature, which was heavily criticised by the Greeks, was the introduction of profiles of kings and other important living figures as stamps in lieu of the traditional symbols of animals

		and buildings. (Paragraph 5)
34	v	Text: They marked the beginning of a new era in business and introduced a model of trade in Europe that is still present nowadays; they greatly influenced the design of modern coinage… (Paragraph 6)
35	poleis	Text: …ancient Greece was not a united country like today, but rather comprised of many independent city – states known as poleis… (Paragraph 3)
36	(a) turtle	Text: …the Aegina coin—which featured a turtle on its surface… (Paragraph 3)
37	6/six obols	Text: As the average human hand could grasp about six obols, that number soon came to represent a 'drachma'… (Paragraph 4)
38	bronze bars	Text: …Romans abandoned the bronze bars they'd been using in favour of coins… (Paragraph 5)
39	B	Text: Athens, still a powerful city at the time, eschewed these designs and continued to produce its own tetradrachm coins, even introducing a new – style coin characterised by broad, thin flans… (Paragraph 5)
40	C	Text: …since they were hand – made to high technical standards representative of ancient Greek perfectionism, many are even remarkable in their own right, as tiny metal works of art. (Paragraph 6)

Writing Task 1: Model Answer

The table illustrates the performance of three different branches of a chain of bakeries in three different locations in London for the year 2015. It is evident that the best performer is the shop in Covent Garden, which with 642 transactions a day on average has at least 100 more transactions than Oxford Circus and more than double from St John's Wood. Covent Garden is also ahead in terms of average transaction value (ATV), with £7.58 per transaction compared to Oxford Circus's £4.51 and St John's Wood's £5.01.

On average, eat – in and take – away transactions are almost equal in each store, with take – away transactions edging slightly ahead in two of them. St John's Wood is the only exception, with eat – in transactions surpassing take – away by 31.

The table also gives us information about the most popular item in each branch, revealing that the shopping habits of customers in each area are widely varied: Covent Garden's best seller is the croissant, while Covent Garden customers favour lattes, and St John's Wood's customers prefer strawberry tarts.

Overall, it is clear that the Covent Garden branch is the company's most profitable store, with the highest number of transactions and ATV. St John's Wood, on the other hand, lags far behind, despite the fact that its ATV is slightly higher than Oxford Circus.

(222 words)

Writing Task 2: Model Answer

With environmental concerns growing continually in the last few decades, the question of what each country can do to protect the environment has become more and more prominent. Some people believe that all countries around the world are equally responsible when it comes to combating climate change. Others, however, think that developed countries have a greater responsibility than developing countries.

It is indubitable that climate change is a universal, global problem; therefore, any solution to it will need to be on a global scale, too. Furthermore, developing countries are more likely to suffer as a result of climate change, so they should be just as motivated as developed countries to help the environment.

On the other hand, developed countries are clearly more capable of taking the lead in combating climate change and improving their carbon footprint, as they have fewer pressing concerns than developing countries. Not only that, but they are also going to have a more marked effect if they reduce their emissions, since developed nations have always been far ahead in terms of pollution—and are in fact mostly to blame for it. Finally, developed countries have the responsibility to set the example for others, introducing changes to encourage the rest to do the same.

Therefore, I firmly believe that while every country should be accountable for their emissions and contribute to combating climate change, developed countries have a slightly bigger responsibility to take action than developing countries, as they have both the means and the reasons to do so—as well as the ability to create a formidable wave of change in attitudes towards the environment around the world.

(272 words)

ACADEMIC PRACTICE TEST 4

Listening Section 1

1   Fenton

2   19th May

3   Yes

4   Mixed breed

5   Pischinger

6   020 3634 7957

7   12

8   8

9   medical history

10   veterinary

Listening Section 2

11   beauty and serenity

12   main gate

13   ten weeks

14   film night

15   main hall

16   garden office

17   Peter

18   pavilion

19   canteen

20   study centre

Listening Section 3

21   chain supermarket

22   clothes shop

23   (very) busy schedule

24   rigorous (recruitment)

25   six/6 months

26   on the job

27   Italy or France

28   5 (years)

29   external training

30   too short

Listening Section 4

31   romantic notions

32   80/eighty journalists

33   read a lot

34   A

35   C

36   D

37   G

38   C

39   A

40   B

Reading Passage 1

1	vi	Text: Recent years have seen a barrage of dystopian Young Adult novels grow in popularity almost overnight—from *The Hunger Games* to *The Maze Runner*, *Divergent*, and *The Knife of Never Letting Go*. (Paragraph 1)
2	iv	Text: … Huxley's *Brave New World* (1932) and Orwell's *1984* (1949), commonly regarded as the first dystopian novels that fit firmly into the genre… (Paragraph 2)
3	vii	Text: … it is the similarities that can be drawn between dystopian settings and the daily lives of teenagers that make YA dystopian stories so captivating… (Paragraph 3)
4	ii	Text: Deconstructing a score of popular YA dystopian novels released between 2007–2011, Scholes and Ostenson argue that the topics explored by dystopian literature are appealing to teenagers because … (Paragraph 4)
5	ix	Text: Moral principles burgeon through these works of fiction, particularly for young people… (Paragraph 5)
6	i	Text: Adolescents, she says, are increasingly dragooned into rigid moulds through "increased standardised testing, increased homework levels, etc." (Paragraph 6)

7	v	Text: Perhaps the market for dystopian novels has stagnated—only time will tell. One thing is for certain, however: the changes the trend has effected on YA literature are here to stay. (Paragraph 7)
8	Brave New World	Text: … Huxley's *Brave New World* (1932) and Orwell's *1984* (1949), commonly regarded as the first dystopian novels that fit firmly into the genre… (Paragraph 2)
9	Lois Lowry	Text: Even the first YA dystopian novel is older than 20—Lois Lowry's *The Giver*, which came out in 1993. (Paragraph 2)
10	honest	Text: Dystopian novels, according to author and book critic Dave Astor, feel honest in that regard as they do not patronise their readers, nor do they attempt to sugar – coat reality. (Paragraph 4)
11	environmental catastrophe	Text: Bestselling author Naomi Klein, offers a different explanation: the dystopian trend, she says, is a "worrying sign" of times to come. What all these dystopian stories have in common is that they all assume that "environmental catastrophe" is not only imminent, but also completely inevitable. (Paragraph 5)
12	personal identity	Text: As author Claudia Gray notes, what has also changed in recent years is humanity's approach to personal identity and young people's roles in society. Adolescents, she says, are increasingly dragooned into rigid moulds through "increased standardised testing, increased homework levels, etc." (Paragraph 6)
13	D	Text: But what is it about dystopian stories that makes them so appealing to readers and audiences alike? (Paragraph 1)

Reading Passage 2

14	humans and animals	Text: We might not normally think of plants this way, but much like humans and animals, they too have to fight for survival on a daily basis. (Paragraph 2)
15	natural light	Text: Some plants and trees are at an architectural advantage: taller trees have greater access to natural light… (Paragraph 2)
16	allelopathy	Text: Others, though, manage to defend their territory through "allelopathy", or chemical warfare. (Paragraph 2)

17	energy	Text: As Dr Robin Andrews explains, plants convert the nutrients they absorb from the ground to energy... (Paragraph 3)
18	organic compound	Text: ... energy with the aid of a type of organic compound known as metabolites. These metabolites can be divided into two categories: primary and secondary. (Paragraph 3)
19	inhibit growth	Text: These two cyclic hydroxamic acids were at the forefront of a study conducted by Sascha Venturelli and colleagues in 2015, which found that once they are released into the soil by the plants that produce them, they degenerate into toxic substances that have the power to inhibit growth in nearby plants once they soak them up. (Paragraph 4)
20	molecular mechanism	Text: As Dr Claude Becker notes, "the phenomenon" itself "has been known for years", but we now finally understand the "molecular mechanism" behind it... (Paragraph 4)
21	small doses	Text: Qualitative defences can be lethal even in small doses... (Paragraph 5)
22	all herbivores	Text: Quantitative defences, in contrast, are only effective "in larger doses", but unlike qualitative defences, can protect the plant against all herbivores. (Paragraph 5)
23	immediately lethal	Text: Qualitative defences are also not as immediately lethal... (Paragraph 5)
24	hollowed – out structures	Text: As Angela White of the University of Sheffield explains, the acacia tree has "hollowed – out structures" which invite ant colonies to build a home in them... (Paragraph 6)
25	giraffes	Text: In return, ants protect them against herbivores—and this includes not just the small ones like bugs, but also the ones as big as giraffes. (Paragraph 6)
26	TRUE	Text: ... apparently, certain allelochemicals— the aforementioned chemical compounds that are responsible for stunting growth in plants... (Paragraph 7)
27	NOT GIVEN	Text: This means that comprehending the way plants defend themselves against the enemies in their

environment might not just be of interest to plant biologists alone, but to medical researchers as well. (Paragraph 7)

Reading Passage 3

28   C   Text: … treated, in effect, in the same manner as the languages of other peoples who were oppressed and colonised, e.g. the Maori in New Zealand, or the Aborigines in Australia. (Paragraph 3)

29   D   Text: …'deafness' is a medical term with negative connotations that needs to be replaced… (Paragraph 4)

30   A   Text: Is it a synonym for 'deafness'? Is it a slightly more politically correct term to express the very same concept you've grown accustomed to—a person who lacks the power of hearing, or a person whose hearing is impaired? (Paragraph 1)

31   G   Text: This is a task not just for hearing people, but for deaf people as well, who have for decades internalised society's unfavourable views of them. (Paragraph 7)

32   E   Text: True Deafhood is achieved when a deaf person feels comfortable with who they are and connected to the rest of the deaf community through use of their natural language… (Paragraph 5)

33   B   Text: The term 'Deafhood' was first coined in 1993 by Dr Paddy Ladd, a deaf scholar in the Deaf Studies Department at the University of Bristol in England. (Paragraph 2)

34   F   Text: … recent developments in science and society—such as cochlear implants or genetic engineering—mean that Deafhood is once again under threat, and needs to be protected. (Paragraph 6)

35   C   Text: …it attempts to remove the limitations imposed on SLPs through their colonisation from hearing people. (Paragraph 2)

36   A   Text: Oralism is a philosophy that first emerged in the late 19th century, and which suggests that a reduced use of sign language would be more beneficial to SLPs, as it would allow them to integrate better to the hearing world. In that respect, sign language is

37	C	Text: ... sign language is dismissively regarded as a mere obstacle to listening skills and acquisition of speech—treated, in effect, in the same manner as the languages of other peoples who were oppressed and colonised, e.g. the Maori in New Zealand, or the Aborigines in Australia. (Paragraph 3)
		dismissively regarded as a mere obstacle to listening skills and acquisition of speech... (Paragraph 3)
38	natural language	Text: True Deafhood is achieved when a deaf person feels comfortable with who they are and connected to the rest of the deaf community through use of their natural language... (Paragraph 5)
39	eugenicists	Text: Deaf people have previously been a target of eugenicists through the aforementioned ideologies of Audism and Oralism... (Paragraph 6)
40	official recognition	Text: We should also seek recognition of the deaf community's accomplishments, as well as official recognition of sign languages around the world by their respective governments. (Paragraph 7)

Writing Task 1: Model Answer

The two charts demonstrate the trends in six presently popular male and female names across the span of seventy – five years. Each chart is dedicated to a different gender, and offers the number of children per mille which were given each name.

Out of the boys' names, Daniel has been the most consistently popular name, starting with 4 per thousand in 1925, then briefly reaching 12 in 1975 before dropping to approximately 10 in 2000. Conversely, Alexander has been the least popular, staying below 2 until 1975, at which point it experienced a sharp increase, taking it to 10 in 2000. Oliver, finally, has had the most erratic journey, jumping up and down between 0 and 5 before climbing up to 11 in 2000.

In comparison, the girls' names have been far more stable and far less favoured: both Sophia and Isabella were virtually inexistent up until 1975 when they suddenly began to rise, finding themselves at 11 and 9 respectively in 2000. Emily, while not as unpopular, was also below 2 until 1975 when it grew to 3.5, then rapidly rose to 11 in 2000.

Overall, we can see that both girls' and boys' name only became popular after 1975, but the change was far more sudden for girls' names, while some of the boys' names enjoyed occasional success prior to 1975.

(223 words)

Writing Task 2: Model Answer

The joys and merits of reading are regularly propounded both at schools and in society. Nevertheless, recent years have seen a sharp decline in the numbers of children who read for pleasure. There are several reasons for this unfortunate development, and a few possible ways to combat it.

It is perhaps no coincidence that as schoolwork has increased considerably in the past few years, so has children's interest in reading dwindled. This is not only due to the fact that they are forced to study too much, which might make them associate books with dull school tasks; it is also because they are left with little free time. If we also consider how little reading is usually promoted at home by parents and family, it is no wonder that children are choosing alternative activities for fun. The biggest culprit, however, when it comes to the drop in children's reading habits is technology. As children are nowadays exposed to a host of gadgets and technological distractions such as phones, tablets, laptops, etc., they are far less likely to dedicate time to books, which require more concentration and imagination than visual entertainment.

What can we do to get children to read more, then? It's simple: we should remind them—or, in many cases, teach them—that reading is fun. Parents should spare fifteen minutes per day to read with their children; libraries and schools should organise children's book clubs, literacy events, reading competitions, etc. Technology should be switched off every now and then, both at school and at home, to remind children that there is a world beyond the screens—and a thousand worlds within the pages of myriads of books.

To sum up, it is not surprising that children are not reading as much as before, considering recent developments in technology as well as in educational systems around the world. It is, however, highly preventable, as long as we adjust children's environment and continue to promote reading for pleasure with honesty and enthusiasm.

(332 words)

ACADEMIC PRACTICE TEST 5

Listening Section 1

1. Carleton
2. 020 8322 1479
3. 30th May
4. 30
5. mini burgers
6. vegetable croquettes
7. five hummus/houmous
8. goat's cheese
9. 4
10. 303

Listening Section 2

11. 2006
12. 500
13. siblings
14. be kind
15. writer's block
16. C
17. C
18. B
19. inherently good
20. poverty

Listening Section 3

21. C
22. H
23. A
24. F
25. B
26. A
27. B
28. A
29. C
30. D

Listening Section 4

31–33 IN ANY ORDER	A, D, F
34	hide under stones
35	spongy connective tissue
36	reproduce alone
37	water
38	mouth
39	B
40	A

Reading Passage 1

1	FALSE	Text: It is used by more than 1.3 billion people per year... (Para. 1)
2	TRUE	Text: The idea of an intricate train network running underneath a vibrant and heavily populated city like London might not be such a novelty in contemporary society... (Para. 2)
3	TRUE	Text: ... a Royal Commission of 1846 meant that central London was out of bounds for railway companies, whose mainline railways all had to stop just outside the City and West End. (Para. 2)
4	FALSE	Text: ...Charles Pearson, the man who originally envisioned a Fleet Valley rail tunnel just fifteen years after the first steam passenger service was opened in 1830, couldn't have come up with his plan for what was to become London Underground at a better time. (Para. 2)
5	NOT GIVEN	Text: And so the story begins, in 1863, with the opening of the Metropolitan Railway, which ran between Paddington (called Bishop's Road at the time) and Farringdon, serving a total of eight stations. Five years later, in 1868, the first section of the Metropolitan District Railway (now incorporated into the District and Circle lines) followed, running from South Kensington to Westminster. (Para. 3)
6	NOT GIVEN	Text: Unfortunately for them, none would get the financial returns they had been promised. (Para. 3)

7	C	Text: Nevertheless, the line was a smashing success from the very beginning, with more than 11 million passengers in just the first year. (Para. 4)
8	B	Text: The first deep – level electric railway was opened in December 1890 by the City and South London Railway, connecting King William Street to Stockwell. (Para. 5)
9	D	Text: Surprisingly, it would take until 1968 for an entirely new line to open again: the Victoria Line (provisionally named the Viking Line)... (Para. 5)
10	A	Text: ...London Underground's first lines were built by private developers, meaning that each line was owned by different companies. This changed in 1933, when all of those companies were nationalised and merged to form the London Passenger Transport Board... (Para. 6)
11	busking	Text: ... in 2003, the famous Oyster card was introduced—a wireless travel card that can be charged up with money to be used for single fares or weekly, monthly, and yearly travel tickets. Busking was also legalised the same year. (Para. 7)
12	melting pot	Text: The underground system that every Londoner loves to hate, but without which London never would have become the sort of financial hub and melting pot it is today. (Para. 8)
13	shortcomings	Text: But it is also a remarkable achievement, for Londoners and non – Londoners alike, and it should be treasured regardless of its shortcomings. (Para. 8)

Reading Passage 2

14	D	Text: The late 1990s were an important time for the field of astrophysics, with the Hubble Space Telescope observations of distant supernovae having only in 1998 confirmed that the universe is expanding at an accelerating rate. Anderson et al's confirmation of the Pioneer Anomaly the same year seemed to offer a demonstration of the very same phenomenon of expansion within our own solar system... (Para. 4)
15	G	Text: Once all the data had been collected, the formidable task of going through the volumes of information began. It was neither quick nor easy, and it

required the assistance of a variety of people, including JPL engineers and retired TRW engineers who had worked on the Pioneer project, who had to consult with each other in order to interpret old blueprints and reconstruct the probes' 3D structure. (Para. 7)

16 B — Text: Their claim to fame, however, changed the moment they skirted past Jupiter and began their journey towards Saturn… (Para. 2)

17 F — Text: …a lucky find, as punch cards were still the preferred method of data storage back in the 1970s… (Para. 6)

18 E — Text: Since the two spacecraft had stopped communicating with earth (Pioneer 11 first in 1995, and Pioneer 10 less than a decade later in 2003), all he could depend on were old communications and data… (Para. 5)

19 A — Text: …thanks to a recent study published in the journal *Physical Review Letters*… (Para. 1)

20 C — Text: In fact, when the deceleration was first observed, it was so small that it was dismissed as an insignificant, temporary phenomenon, and attributed to the effect of dribbles of leftover propellant still in the fuel lines after controllers had cut off the propellant. (Para. 3)

21 E — Text: Since the two spacecraft had stopped communicating with earth (Pioneer 11 first in 1995, and Pioneer 10 less than a decade later in 2003)… (Para. 5)

22 A — Text: …with the monetary aid of the Planetary Society and its eager, dedicated members, he began to gather the data… (Para. 5)

23 H — Text: … the scientists involved in the project had anticipated most of the slowing down due to "the gravitational pull of the Sun and other massive objects in the solar system". (Para. 3)

24 B — Text: …with the Hubble Space Telescope observations of distant supernovae having only in 1998 confirmed that the universe is expanding at an accelerating rate. Anderson et al's confirmation of the Pioneer Anomaly the same year… (Para. 4)

25	G	Text: All in all, there were more than 43 gigabytes of data—an admirable result, considering that at the time the two Pioneer spacecraft were launched there had been no formal requirement that NASA archive any of the records collected... (Para. 6)
26	A	Text: ...it required the assistance of a variety of people, including JPL engineers and retired TRW engineers who had worked on the Pioneer project... (Para. 7)
27	D	Text: ...it was the electrical subsystems and the decay of plutonium in the Pioneer power sources that were to blame for the spacecraft's bizarre trajectory—more specifically the heat they emitted. (Para. 7)
28	F	Text: It was neither quick nor easy... (Para. 7)

Reading Passage 3

29	thrilling	Text: Nevertheless, food futurologists and organisations around the world have examined the prospects, and they might, at first glance at least, appear less than thrilling. (Para. 1)
30	rising prices	Text: Unfortunately though, rising prices are spelling the doom of this long – lasting trend. (Para. 2)
31	raising livestock	Text: As the price of raising livestock goes up, we'll eat less beef. (Para. 2)
32	genetic engineering	Text: According to Harpaz as well as Yoram Kapulnik, the director of the Volcani Centre, the answer to that question lies with our reliance on genetic engineering. (Para. 3)
33	human genome	Text: "Once we have a complete picture of the human genome," explains Kapulnik, "we'll know how to create food that better meets our needs." (Para. 3)
34	nutritionally excellent	Text: ... the foods of the future will come from insects. "They are nutritionally excellent," says Arnold Van Huis... (Para. 4)
35	Asia and Africa	Text: Insects are already a part of people's diets in various cultures in Asia and Africa... (Para. 5)
36	presentation	Text: ... however, one major hurdle that will need to be overcome with regards to Western countries is presentation. (Para. 5)

37	grow	Text: …first of all, they can grow both in fresh and salt water—a notable advantage, considering the shortage of land we are bound to experience in the future; secondly, they grow at an astounding pace… (Para. 6)
38	carbon footprint	Text: But that's not all: several scientists believe that the biofuel we would extract from algae could lead to a diminished need for fossil fuels, thereby improving our carbon footprint. (Para. 6)
39	stem cells	Text: In early 2012, a group of Dutch scientists managed to produce synthetic meat using stem cells originating from cows… (Para. 8)
40	animal suffering	Text: The benefits of a worldwide move towards in –vitro meat would be tremendous for the environment, which would see a reduction in energy and water waste and greenhouse gas emissions, and would significantly reduce animal suffering. (Para. 8)

Writing Task 1: Model Answer

The two charts illustrate the numbers as well as themes of magazines that launched and ceased publication in the 20 – year period between 1995 and 2015.

According to the first chart, there was a steady growth in the number of new magazines from 1995 until 2005 with about 250 magazines opening in 1995, followed by 400 in 2000 and a little under 400 in 2005. Very few magazines folded during that period, with the lowest number observed in 2005, at well under 50. The trend, however, reversed somewhere between 2005 and 2010, as more than 300 magazines closed in 2010 and the number of new publications dwindled all the way down to about 185 in 2015.

As the second chart demonstrates, the vast majority of magazines —more than one third— that were started between 1995 and 2015 fell under the category of "Entertainment and TV", with music – related magazines a close second at 30%. A little over one fifth of new magazines focused on various hobbies, while less than one tenth were about business, finance, and/or politics. Finally, all other types of magazines amounted only to 5%.

(187 words)

Writing Task 2: Model Answer

During the past few decades, people have argued at length about the usefulness and appropriateness of songs that condone violence and give celebrity status to criminals and their lifestyles. Some suggest that a ban on all such songs would be the only suitable measure; others, however, disagree. But what would be the advantages and disadvantages should the government decide to pass such a law?

One potential advantage of a ban on such song lyrics is immediately apparent: young people, whose personalities are particularly malleable, wouldn't be exposed to songs that might influence them to commit criminal or otherwise violent acts. Additionally, as such songs usually target minorities such as women and gay people (essentially committing the crime of hate speech), a ban would be a small step towards protecting those minorities, whose rights are so often neglected by the state.

There are, however, quite a few disadvantages as well. A blanket ban on songs with such content would contravene artists' right to freedom of speech, one of the most cherished rights in the world of entertainment and art. This would be especially troublesome as violent lyrics are usually found in rap and hip hop, two music styles that are directly linked to already disenfranchised communities, and a ban like this would most probably put a strain on the relationship between the government and these groups. Finally, as there is no scientifically proven link between being exposed to art that propagates crime and violence and actually committing crimes and violence, a ban might not even achieve its most basic goal of bringing crime numbers down.

To sum up, a ban on song lyrics that promote violence and criminal acts would protect the minorities that are often targeted by these songs, for instance women and gay people. However, it would also inflame feelings of anger in the groups commonly associated with such music and exacerbate their relationship with the government, as well as constitute an infringement on artists' right to freedom of speech.

(331 words)

ACADEMIC PRACTICE TEST 6

Listening Section 1

1	B
2	B
3	A
4	C
5	C
6	G34C245
7	car
8	police
9	jacket
10	registration details

Listening Section 2

11	staffroom
12	museum
13	visitors
14	staffroom
15	steps
16	staff toilets
17	museum
18	photo booth
19	B
20	E

Listening Section 3

21	A
22	C
23	D
24	F
25	A
26	C
27	correct
28	aging
29	farmers
30	mind

Listening Section 4

31	English
32	city
33	style
34	1175
35	completed
36	group
37	Gothic
38	126 metres
39	sculptures
40	painted

Reading Passage 1

1	TRUE	Text: This one-child policy...is believed to have helped prevent the...Chinese population from becoming unsustainable. (Paragraph 1)
2	TRUE	Text: It has lessened the negative environmental impact that rapid industrialisation and population growth have had on China...(Paragraph 3)
3	FALSE	Text: ...the sad reality was that the instances of infanticide of female babies began to rise rapidly in the 1980s in China...(Paragraph 4)
4	NOT GIVEN	
5	TRUE	Text: ...it is thought that there are now 60 million more men than women in China. (Paragraph 7)
6	FALSE	Text: ...the long-term pollution output of a child born in the U.S. can be up to 160 times higher than that of a child born in Bangladesh. (Paragraph 9)
7	TRUE	Text: The original legislation was only aimed at a single generation. (Paragraph 10)
8	D	Text: ...there are plenty of grounds for criticism, especially from human rights activists...(Paragraph 3)
9	B	Text: Despite this raising other important concerns such as gender inequality in China...(Paragraph 5)
10	B	Text: However they were also forced to introduce laws in 2005 outlawing sex-selective abortions...(Paragraph 6)

11 C — Text: After all, increasing numbers of adults in the West now choose not to have children purely for environmental reasons. (Paragraph 8)

12 A — Text: China has a rapidly developing economy, and with such development comes a higher average carbon output per person. (Paragraph 11)

13 D — Text: In 2015 the one-child policy was finally relaxed, allowing couples to now have two children ... (Paragraph 2)

Reading Passage 2

14 x

15 i

16 iii

17 v

18 ii

19 xi

20 viii

21 5 million — Text: There are 5 million people living in areas deemed at risk of flooding in England and Wales. (Paragraph B)

22 store — Text: The trees catch and store water, but also hold soil together, preventing erosion. (Paragraph B)

23 landslides — Text: By removing the trees land is more easily eroded increasing the risk of landslides… (Paragraph B)

24 emissions — Text: Deforestation releases 15% of all greenhouse gas emissions. (Paragraph C)

25 management — Text: Forestry management is important to make sure that stocks are not depleted and that whatever is cut down is replaced. (Paragraph E)

26 reverse — Text: …making China one of the few developing nations to reverse the negative trend. (Paragraph H)

Reading Passage 3

27 NOT GIVEN

28 NO — Text: One would be mistaken to call film noir a genre. Unlike westerns or romantic comedies, film noir cannot be defined by conventional uses of setting

		or conflict in the way that is common to genre films. (Paragraph 2)
29	NO	Text: True film noir refers to Hollywood films of the 1940s and early 1950s that dealt with dark themes such as crime and corruption. (Paragraph 3)
30	YES	Text: …he admits that classifying film noir is almost impossible because many films considered as film noir vary greatly in style. (Paragraph 4)
31	YES	Text: The interplay of light and shadow created by chiaroscuro was highly suggestive of hidden darkness and was largely responsible for creating the mood and feeling of film noir. (Paragraph 8)
32	NOT GIVEN	
33	reaction	Text: Schrader believes these films were not only a reflection of the war, but also a delayed reaction to the great economic depression of the 1930s. (Paragraph 5)
34	neorealism	Text: This style of film was similar to some European films of the same era, such as Italy's neorealist films like Vittorio De Sica's Bicycle Thieves… (Paragraph 6)
35	immigrated	Text: Many German, Austrian and Polish directors immigrated to America before or during with the rise of Hitler… (Paragraph 7)
36	authenticity	Text: But it was the coupling of expressionist lighting with realistic settings that really gave film noir its authenticity. (Paragraph 8)
37	characters	Text: …it was this hard-boiled writing style that influenced the characters, stories and scripts depicted on screen. (Paragraph 9)
38	E	Text: Rather than the positive happy-ending stories that dominated the silver screen before the war, a pessimism and negativity had entered American cinema. (Paragraph 1)
39	A	Text: The honesty of this style of film suited the post-war mood… (Paragraph 6)
40	B	Text: This writing team, with Billy Wilder again directing, was the perfect combination for one of Hollywood's most celebrated films. (Paragraph 9)

Writing Task 1: Model Answer

The bar graph shows that during the year the use of the utilities electricity, gas and water at the leisure centre change depending on the time of year. While gas and electricity seem to experience a similar trend, water use is the opposite. During the winter months gas and especially electricity use are much higher than in the warmer summer months.

Both gas and electricity use follow a rough `U' shaped distribution over the course of an average year, with electricity use highest in January and gas use highest in February. This could be because the shortest days of the year come at the end of December and January, so lights are on for longer. Meanwhile, the coldest days of the year are usually in February, meaning frequent use of central heating consumes more gas.

Conversely water use is highest in the summer and follows a rough `n' shaped distribution over the year. This could be due to a number of reasons such as more people taking showers, or people drinking more water. If the leisure centre uses air conditioning, this could also be a factor.

(186 words)

Writing Task 2: Model Answer

Violence in society existed long before films, or even theatre for that matter, were invented. This suggests that the correlation between violence and movies is a false one. If anything it could be argued that in the western world life is safer now than it has ever been. Better technology and education have helped to reduce the levels of crime.

Films usually have a strong moral theme to them. They frequently depict the struggle of good vs. evil, and good almost always wins. Aside from the fact that this is done by filmmakers to please audiences, there is also a strong message here that suggests it is better to follow positive morals and make good life choices over negative ones like crime and violence. So if anything, film could be responsible for the lower levels of violence we see in the modern day compared with one hundred years ago.

But it would also be naïve to suggest that violence in films has not had an adverse effect on certain individuals. Whilst it is highly unlikely that healthy adults would ever consider being violent because of something they had seen in a film, people with underlying psychological conditions may well be encouraged by the violence they see in films. While this is something that does exist, the instances of such correlations are so rare that it would be absurd to censor films because of a tiny minority. Instead the root causes of their predilection towards violence need to be addressed through educational institutions and research.

(254 words)